T0338467

INVESTIGATING EXPLANATION-BASED LEARNING

THE KLUWER INTERNATIONAL SERIES
IN ENGINEERING AND COMPUTER SCIENCE

KNOWLEDGE REPRESENTATION, LEARNING AND
EXPERT SYSTEMS

Consulting Editor

Tom Mitchell
Carnegie Mellon University

INVESTIGATING EXPLANATION-BASED LEARNING

Edited by

Gerald DeJong
Computer Science Department
University of Illinois

KLUWER ACADEMIC PUBLISHERS
Boston/Dordrecht/London

Distributors for North America:
Kluwer Academic Publishers
101 Philip Drive
Assinippi Park
Norwell, Massachusetts 02061 USA

Distributors for all other countries:
Kluwer Academic Publishers Group
Distribution Centre
Post Office Box 322
3300 AH Dordrecht, THE NETHERLANDS

Library of Congress Cataloging-in-Publication Data

Investigating explanation-based learning / edited by Gerald DeJong.
     p. cm. -- (Kluwer international series in engineering and computer science)
     Includes bibliographical references and index.
     ISBN 0-7923-9125-X (alk. paper)
     1. Machine learning. 2. Artificial intelligence. 3. Natural language processing (Computer science) 4. Cognition. I. DeJong, Gerald. II. Series.
Q325.5.I58 1991
006.3'1--dc20   90-48514
                                           CIP

Printed on acid-free paper.

Printed in the United States of America

CONTENTS

PREFACE

Over the last ten years, Explanation-Based Learning (EBL) has grown steadily in popularity and acceptance so that today it is acknowledged as one of the major approaches to machine learning. EBL began as a hazy intuition of a few researchers that automated learning can be based upon the justification or *explanation* of an example. Analysis of the explanation can yield underlying general principles which may be productively employed to improve performance on subsequent related examples. EBL research attempts to sharpen the intuition into a computational theory.

This book chronicles an on-going struggle to achieve two goals: constructing a formal implementable model of EBL while at the same time respecting its original intuitive promise. It is not intended to be a definitive collection of the most influential EBL papers. Perhaps one day such a collection will be produced, but today it would be an unsatisfying task. No researcher has yet satisfactorily united these two essential but disparate goals.

The intent of this book is to communicate our ineffable intuition of EBL. We hope to impart an appreciation not of where EBL has been nor where it currently is but rather what it may become. The research described is a means to that end. Through a progression of research projects and implemented systems we recount the evolution of EBL, each uncertain step motivated by computational and psychological plausibility concerns together with new intuitions and insights developed from analyzing our dissatisfaction with previous work. We exhort the reader to ponder the pattern that emerges from this collection of investigations. For these research projects are intimately related, and their progression points to the true message we have to offer. This book is not finished, the vision not yet realized. But we hope that the reader may feel some of the excitement that drives our own continued explorations in EBL.

I am deeply indebted to a sequence of gifted students. With the exception of chapters one and eight, the work is theirs. Just when I was most lost another graduate student would come along to show me the way. With each I have felt hopeful, weary, euphoric, exasperated, but ultimately humble and immeasurably proud. I am fortunate to have served as their advisor. Many other researchers have influenced our thinking and work. Special mention must be made of many rousing interactions with Tom Mitchell's research groups at Rutgers and CMU. I wish to thank Carl Harris for conceiving the idea for the book and Tom Stone for overseeing its development. The research could not have been completed but for the excellent facilities and administration of the Beckman Institute and the Coordinated Science Laboratory along with the supportive atmosphere of the

Computer Science Department and the Department of Electrical and Computer Engineering at the University of Illinois. ONR, through grant N00014-86-K-0309, and NSF, through grants NSF-IST-85-11542 and NSF-IRI-87-19766, largely funded the research described. Finally, I wish to thank Sharon Collins and Francie Bridges whose tolerance, good nature, and hard work made this book possible.

GDJ
Urbana

Foreword

The pursuit of methods to make machines learn is one of the most ambitious branches of computer science. Within this field of Machine Learning, a major new paradigm has appeared over the past decade: explanation-based learning. This book presents a broad range of research from one of the most active groups working in this new area.

To illustrate explanation-based learning, consider the problem of learning to play chess. In particular, suppose we wish to learn how to classify chess positions according to whether they belong to "the class of chess positions from which I will lose my queen within two moves". One could, of course, collect many training examples of chess positions that are positive and negative examples of the above class, then search for features common to the positive examples that discriminate them from the negative examples. The difficulty with this approach is that there are thousands of features that happen to be satisfied by any specific board position (e.g., there is a black bishop in the northeast quadrant of the board). Since only a very small number of these features is relevant to the class we are trying to learn, we will need a huge number of training examples to figure out which ones they are. Explanation-based learning is an approach to dramatically reducing the number of training examples needed, and to extending the complexity of knowledge that can be learned, by taking advantage of the prior knowledge and reasoning capabilities of the learner. In explanation-based learning, the learner first analyzes each training example in detail to construct an explanation of why it belongs to the target class. In the chess learning task this explanation might be as follows: "in this specific chess position my king and queen are simultaneously attacked by my opponent's knight, therefore I must move my king, therefore my opponent may capture my queen, therefore I will lose my queen within two moves". Once the learner constructs such an explanation, it can use it to distinguish board features that are relevant (e.g., the opponent's piece that attacks my king and queen) from the many that are not.

Explanation-based learning promises to play a significant role in future approaches to machine learning, for two reasons. First, it offers an avenue toward scaling up computer learning methods to more complex learning tasks -- much more complex than can be handled by purely inductive methods. Second, explanation-based learning offers a possible model of cognitive learning processes in humans (consider how many training experiences you needed before learning to avoid a knight fork!), and a better understanding of human learning methods could lead to design of better educational curricula.

This book presents some of the best recent research on explanation-based learning. DeJong and his research group at University of Illinois have made seminal contributions to defining the basic paradigm of explanation-based learning, exploring it as a model of human learning, extending it to accommodate imperfect initial knowledge, and applying it to a variety of learning tasks from a variety of domains. I am pleased that they have invested the effort to produce a single volume that presents the key ideas to emerge from their years of research. I have learned a great deal from reading their papers and from our many lively interactions over the past years. I am sure you will be challenged and illuminated by their ideas as I have been.

Tom M. Mitchell
Pittsburgh, PA

Chapter 1

A Perspective on Explanation–Based Learning

Gerald DeJong

1. Introduction

Explanation–based learning (EBL) can be generally viewed as substituting background knowledge for the large training set of exemplars needed by conventional or *empirical* machine learning systems [1–4]. The background knowledge is used automatically to construct an explanation of a few training exemplars. The learned concept is generalized directly from this explanation.

The roots of EBL can be traced back a long way — long, at least, by AI standards. An argument can be made that the *analytic* learning method of Waterman's poker player system [5] contains the seeds of EBL. Unfortunately, the analytic method was not very successful and probably cost more than it benefited the system.

The first truly explanation–based research was the MACROPS learning work done in the STRIPS system [6]. It worked in a simple robot world and stored generalized versions of successful plans. The resulting general problem–solving concept was stored in an interesting data structure called a triangle table. The triangle table specified all of the preconditions that needed to be tested in the current world state to ensure that an entire sequence of actions would succeed.

In a historical context, MACROPS was a very impressive system. It included a notion of *operationality* by transforming all the preconditions of a plan's component operators into a form directly testable in one of a set of possible initial states. It also introduced as a central concept the notion of *chunked knowledge structures*. This notion was to be reinvented several years later as *frames, scripts,* and *schemata* [7–9]. Automatic acquisition of chunked knowledge structures would not reemerge for even longer [10–12].

Gerald Sussman's HACKER [13], Eliot Soloway's baseball system [14], and Jack Mostow's early work on operationalization [15] all contributed to what would later emerge as explanation–based learning.

The first EBL systems of the modern era were Mitchell's LEX2 [3], Silver's LP [16], and DeJong's KIDNAP natural language system [11].

Two of these systems, Mitchell's and DeJong's, have led to extensive follow–up research in EBL. This book outlines the significant steps in EBL research of the Illinois group under DeJong.

1.1. An Intuitive Specification of EBL

To understand the Illinois approach to EBL it is important to develop an intuitive understanding of EBL. Researchers have relied on such an intuitive feeling heavily to inspire their research. This is not to say that the definition of EBL should always be intuitive and ad hoc, for a crisp formal account is the only ultimate assurance that scientific progress has been made. However, there is a danger in prematurely formalizing a new research area such as EBL. Because such formalization necessarily defines its boundaries precisely, if an area is formalized before it is fully understood, the boundaries may reflect properties of the formalization tools more than the properties of the phenomena of interest. As an example consider the approach, currently popular with EBL researchers, of using a first–order predicate calculus proof as the explanation that drives generalization. A monotonic logical entailment proof, if one can be constructed, makes a very appealing explanation. The generalization of such proofs is straightforward; the approach is easily formalized [12, 17, 18]. But defining EBL in such a way that limits explanations to be only logical proofs stultifies EBL, relegating it to toy micro–world problems. In the real world, logical proofs are singularly uncommon. The complexities of the real world preclude them in all but trivial cases. Real–world explanations transcend the simplicities of logical proofs and often rely on informal reasoning or plausible inference or analogy or past precedents. The real world is rife with such issues as uncertainty, temporal and spacial reasoning difficulties, multiple agents, and simultaneous and overlapping interacting operators for which standard logic makes no explicit allowance.

The ultimate goal is a formalized account of EBL, but this goal may be precluded by a premature commitment to artificial limitations of a particular formalization. It is important in the early stages of EBL development to allow free rein in developing research results. Only after EBL is well understood can one hope to unify all of the theoretical results under a common formalism.

Nonetheless, the chapters that follow require an understanding, at least informally, of the EBL phenomenon. What follows is an informal specification of EBL based on a somewhat whimsical example.

Figure 1-1 is a reproduction of a "Far Side" cartoon that shows an example of early explanation–based learning. The group on the left are Neanderthals who are familiar with fire but have not yet discovered the concept of a cooking skewer. Zog, the Cro–Magnon with glasses on the right, has invented the world's first skewer and is happily broiling his pterodactyl drumstick over his own fire. Zog is creative and intelligent, the Einstein of the late Pleistocene age. It would be nice to develop a computer model that captures Zog's creative problem–solving ability. Sadly, that task is far beyond current AI technology. There is, however, another interesting individual in the picture. The smartest of the three Neanderthals has noticed Zog's invention. He realizes that Zog is not scorching his hand in the traditional way, and yet Zog is just as success-fully cooking his food. Our Neanderthal friend has done much more than rote learning: He has appreciated something of the generality of Zog's cleverness. For example, he probably knows that the cooking technique would work for him as well as for Zog and that it is not specific to Zog's drumstick but would work equally for his friends' lizard or tomorrow's yet–uncaught wild rabbit. He perhaps realizes some of the parametric constraints on the concept. The skewer concept could be applied to his own fire, though since the fire is larger and hotter than Zog's, a slightly longer stick would be propitious. He probably also understands some of

THE FAR SIDE   By GARY LARSON

"Hey! Look what Zog do!"

Figure 1-1:   "Hey, look what Zog do." Early Explanation–Based Learning [The FAR SIDE cartoon by Gary Larson is reprinted by the permission of Chronicle Features, San Francisco, California.]

the limitations of the concept: It would not work well when applied to giant turtle eggs or a whole woolly mammoth; the turtle eggs would shatter and the woolly mammoth would not be liftable with the stick. Our Neanderthal has done much more than simply store away a single uninterpreted episode. He has, in fact, acquired a new general concept.

In spite of the fact that our Neanderthal is not as intelligent (or at least not as creative) as the Cro–Magnon Zog, he now has a skewer concept which is quite possibly as effective as Zog's own. Furthermore, he did not have to waste the time or effort that Zog spent — the sleepless nights agonizing over his creation, the endless and tedious trial-and-error experiments. How did our Neanderthal friend learn this useful new concept? There are three steps. First, he *noticed* Zog had a better way of doing things. Second, he *explained* to himself why Zog's method works, using his knowledge about the world — knowledge about fire, sharp sticks, flesh, food, and so on. Third, he *generalized* the explanation of the single observed instance into a useful, broadly applicable problem–solving concept.

The Neanderthal's acquisition of the skewer concept illustrates what we term *explanation–based learning* (EBL). Our ultimate goal is to formalize this process. It is a much more modest AI goal than to build an implementable model for Zog's creativity. Much of AI seeks to do the latter, to automatically construct clever original solutions to difficult real–world problems. AI planning systems do everything from scratch. The fourth time through "monkeys and bananas" is no easier than the first time. Planning from scratch is, in general, very difficult [19] and has not met with much success. Instead, we will be content to let our EBL system gracefully acquire new concepts by observing others more intelligent than the system. We will not insist that the system produce a maximally general concept, just a useful concept. If our Neanderthal friend falsely believes that a skewer can be used only to roast pterodactyl parts, the concept is still well worth knowing. He should, of course, always be open to the possibility of later concept refinement. We will insist, however, that the general concept be tractable to learn and efficient to access and use.

Is this too modest a goal? Are we oversimplifying to ensure success? Will we be left with anything worthwhile? Consider what the EBL approach does not cover. Since EBL requires a substantial amount of world knowledge both to construct and to generalize the explanations, acquisition of initial world knowledge is beyond its scope. Also, invention, Zog's process of creative concept formation, is out of its scope. EBL will not result in computer programs that can invent the phonograph or electric light as Thomas Edison did. Although such creative insights are essential for our culture's technological advancement, they are very rare. Indeed, the number of truly creative advances made by any individual over a lifetime probably averages to be less than one. There are a few Thomas Edisons who make perhaps three or four creative advances, but most of us are just plain folk who can appreciate and use inventions but do no significant inventing of our own. The task *is* modest, but its modesty is derived from not trying to surpass average human abilities. This seems to be an entirely reasonable sort of modesty.

Much of adult learning seems to have the sort of characteristics that make it susceptible to an explanation–based learning approach. Apprenticeship learning is ubiquitous in human training. After a modicum of classroom–style learning, doctors, plumbers, carpenters, graduate students, farmers, and so on finish their training under an extended period of close observation of an established master. This is clearly a very large, interesting, and useful class of learning. We are not claiming that humans *must* be employing EBL in these apprenticeship domains. However, Chapter 8 shows recent experimental evidence for the psychological plausibility of the approach.

Informally, then, EBL encompasses determining that an example is worthy of learning, constructing an *explanation* for the example (or examples), generalizing the explanation into a new concept, and refining the concept in a similar way.

It is important to realize that the determining feature of an EBL system is not the presence or absence of something called an *explanation*. Many systems construct "explanations" but are not EBL systems (e.g., [20–22]). Rather, it is how the explanation is used that qualifies a system as taking an EBL approach. Each EBL system uses the explanation to drive concept generalization or refinement. Very few examples are required to define the boundaries of a concept. The concept's definition is determined through a domain–theory–guided inspection of why an example succeeded, not by similarities and differences between examples or their explanations.

2. Types of Generalization

Before examining the types of generalization that we will expect from explanation–based learning systems, it is important to clarify what is meant by the term *generalization*. In EBL we will use the term in a slightly different fashion than used in similarity–based learning. The difference is subtle, but it has caused past communication problems. Being precise will help shed light on the issues of overgeneralization and learning at the knowledge level [23]. It is important to make the difference in terminology explicit.

Generalization in empirical systems is a purely syntactic notion. It is best viewed as a *candidate* specification for the concept. Michalski [24] provided a taxonomy of these syntactic generalizations. There is no guarantee that such a generalization will be useful or even semantically well formed when interpreted in the real world. Rather, desired properties such as expected utility and semantic well–formedness are dependent on features of the training set as a whole (e.g., how representative it is of the actual concept). Since generalizing a particular instance is performed without regard to semantic considerations, the resulting generalization may be an overgeneralization of the desired concept. By contrast, the generalization process in EBL has semantic as well as syntactic components. The correct concept boundary may be defined by goal regression [25, 26]. Its shape can be very complex, even encompassing several disjointed areas. Its determination is intractable in all but the simplest of domains. Instead, EBL relies on efficient generalization techniques that may undergeneralize but do not overgeneralize if the domain theory itself is correct. In most real–world applications, the system's domain theory is at best an approximation to the world's behavior; the domain knowledge is necessarily wrong. Furthermore, complete explanations (i.e., logical proofs) are intractable in real–world applications. Simplifications must necessarily be made in the explanation due to finite computational resources of the system. In such approximate knowledge conditions, overgeneralization can and often does occur in EBL systems. This raises some interesting and important theoretical issues which are discussed in Chapters 4–6.

Thus, in EBL, the generalization process itself tends to cover a (possibly improper) subset of the concept's true boundaries. It is less susceptible to rampant, unmotivated overgeneralization. Overgeneralization creeps in only to the extent that the domain theory itself is an unfaithful description of the world (Chapter 6) or the explanation includes unwarranted simplifications (Chapter 4). Empirical learning does not make this commitment in the generalization process, and overgeneralization is much more common, even desirable. However, empirical learning requires a large training set of examples to justify the semantic correctness of its final concept.

It might have been desirable to use the term *generalization* consistently, especially since it is so central to learning. But perhaps not. The meaning of the term has already evolved; Soloway used it in a rather different empirical fashion 10 years ago [14]. Most researchers in the empirical camp have not so much *excluded* a semantic facet of the term as simply never *included* one, and when discussing a concept's limits in transformed spaces (as in constructive induction [27]), "generalization" is used freely to refer to volumes in more abstract spaces.

In EBL circles, attributing a semantic facet to the term *generalization* was consummated by Mitchell and colleagues [12]. This should not be thought of as a redefinition but rather as a natural evolution in the term to reflect simultaneous changes in syntactic feature space *and* in the semantic functional space. In any case, we will use the term generalization in this sense. Readers who object should do an internal RPLACA throughout of "generalization" with "valid generalization" or "useful generalization."

2.1. Irrelevant Feature Elimination

The first type of generalization is termed *irrelevant feature elimination*. Suppose the system is learning the concept "CUP," which might be functionally defined as anything that can contain hot or cold liquids, be stable without being held, be drunk from, and be manipulated using only one hand. It is presented with a particular positive example; call it OBJ1. The object OBJ1 is defined by a (possibly very large) number of features and relations among those features. Suppose further that the system has a domain theory sufficient to explain why OBJ1 indeed satisfies the functional requirements of being a cup. The explanation, of course, specifies why the particular collection of features referred to as OBJ1 are sufficient to realize the functional requirements of a cup. Any features that are not used to support the conclusion of cupness for OBJ1 (e.g., "color," "owner") can be altered without compromising the veracity of the explanation. Removing these features results in a generalization of the specific training example. We will call this kind of generalization *irrelevant feature elimination*. In the cup domain, the amount of generalization provided to OBJ1 may be rather modest. In rich domains, this method is powerful and, in large part, solves the feature selection problem faced by empirical learning methods. Furthermore, in problem–solving domains, this method can eliminate unnecessary operators, which means that the learning system can itself perform a measure of optimization, as well as generalization, of the observed training example.

2.2. Identity Elimination

The second generalization type, *identity elimination*, removes unnecessary dependence on particular objects. OBJ1, our cup instance, has a handle; call it HAN31. If the existence of the handle is used to explain why the cup can be manipulated while containing hot liquids, then without a handle the explanation of OBJ1's cupness would not be valid. It is not important, however, that OBJ1 must have handle HAN31. Any particular handle would work as well; if OBJ1 had an identical handle, HAN32 instead, it would be just as much a cup. Thus, we can parameterize specific components occurring in the explanation. OBJ1 will become ?X, and HAN31 will become ?Y. But this goes too far. The relations among the example's components that appear in the explanation must be maintained. For example, **Handle(?Y)** and **Has–part(?X,?Y)** must be true. With our particular training instance, this relationship is enforced by reality. OBJ1 in fact does have handle HAN31 as a part. Indeed reality can be no other way; the handle HAN31 is part of the actual cup OBJ1. Once the particular objects are replaced with variables, the EBL system must ensure that only mutually consistent objects be allowed to bind to the variables. Relations that appear in the explanation must be asserted as constraint requirements among the variables. This kind of generalization is called identity elimination since it is not the identity of the particular real–world item HAN31 that is important for "cupness" but only HAN31's property by virtue of the fact that it is a handle and is attached to the object of interest.

Identity elimination works because of generalities already built into the domain theory. These preexisting generalities are exploited to the advantage of acquiring new concepts. Such preexisting generalities are essential for EBL. This is not a requirement about theoretical functionality or the adequacy with which our domain theory captures the world but rather about how the domain theory is written. A different domain theory might support all of the same conclusions as our original domain theory but result in a very different EBL–acquired concept. Ideally, the role that an object may play in the domain theory is entirely determined by its properties—never by its identity. Philosophically, this feature has some interesting ramifications, but it is uncontroversial, at least so far, in

AI. It may be termed the principle of no "function in form" [28] and is often implicitly followed by AI researchers. Adherence to this principle helps to improve the generative power of the domain theory as well as allows EBL; a domain theory designed with this principle can often support the same set of inferences but uses fewer rules. The principle is also very important for the next type of generalization, operationality pruning.

2.3. Operationality Pruning

The third component of generalization, based on explanations, is *operationality pruning*. It eliminates easily reconstructable subexplanations from the explanation. We will call any constituent of the explanation *operational* (after Mostow [29]) if its truth can be easily verified. Parenthetically, we should note that this definition is rather informal and that "operationality" is a very complex issue (see Chapter 6 and [30, 31]). For now we will pretend that it is straightforwardly defined. The leaves of a well-formed explanation must all be operational, but some internal constituents may be operational as well. The particular subexplanation supporting an operational internal constituent should be dropped from the concept definition. Such subexplanations can be filled in as it is needed. This can lead to greater generality because the particular subexplanation used in the training instance may be arbitrary; a number of satisfactory alternative subexplanations might also have been used. Once the specific constituent's support is pruned, the concept is no longer constrained to the specific subexplanation.

To illustrate this component, consider a slight modification of the "cup" example. Suppose it were the case that OBJ1 is shown to be manipulable by one hand in part because it is graspable. Further suppose that the predicate "graspable" is operational. This does not necessarily mean that graspable is a feature that can be immediately observed (like "color") but only that the truth value of "graspable" can be easily determined for most objects of interest. In the case of OBJ1, "graspable" is true because OBJ1 has a handle. Suppose there are a few (say half a dozen) very easy ways to achieve "graspable." Further, suppose that there are a relatively few and easy ways to demonstrate "not graspable." It might be that if an object does not satisfy one of the half dozen easy methods, it is almost certainly not graspable. Then the predicate "graspable" itself is operational. There is no reason to keep a trace of the particular explanation, graspable-via-a-handle, as part of the concept definition for "cup." To determine the "cupness" of something, it is almost as easy for the system to remanufacture the graspable–via–a–handle explanation as to verify an already–expanded version. Greater concept generality is achieved by eliminating the commitment to specializing "graspable" to "graspable–via–a–handle." Furthermore, the incremental cost is slight. Operationality pruning is the name for the elimination of such easily reconstructable subexplanations.

2.4. Structural Generalization

The fourth type generalization, *structural generalization*, alters the internal structure of the explanation itself. The most difficult and most interesting of the generalization types, this one merits a subtaxonomy and is discussed in Chapter 3. The previous three generalization types— irrelevant feature elimination, identity elimination, and operationality pruning—do not alter the structure of the explanation for the training example, except perhaps to remove nodes. Structural generalization includes rearranging, transforming, and adding components to the explanation. We will briefly discuss three important subtypes of structural generalization: disjunctive augmentation, temporal generalization, and number generalization.

2.4.1. Disjunctive Augmentation

Disjunctive augmentation involves adding alternative options to an explanation constituent. If, as part of the domain theory, the system knows a different but acceptable method of supporting a constituent, that alternative is specified along with the method used in the example. Consider again the "cup" domain theory with the additional concept of a "zarf," which is a chalicelike holder for small round–bottomed objects (see Figure 1–2).

The domain theory includes a different method for achieving stability. The example cup, OBJ1, is perhaps a conventional cup that achieves stability without being held because it has a flat bottom, but stability might have been achieved in another way. If the domain theory included the possibility of employing a zarf to achieve stability, then the generalized operational concept should include a disjunct at the stability constituent. Note that this theory is very different from operationality pruning. Stable(?X) itself may not be operational while allowing Isa(?X,FLATBOTTOM) and Isa(?X,ZARF) to be operational. This is the case if stability can be achieved in ways that are conceptually difficult to explain in addition to the two easy ways of zarf and flat bottom.

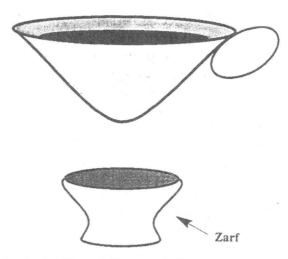

Figure 1–2: Zarf with Round–Bottomed Cup

Seemingly, disjunctive augmentation opens a rather nasty can of worms. It is possible, indeed likely, that in any interesting explanation augmentations are possible that are fraught with many subtle constraints and that result in only minor improvements in the concept's generality. Discovering and processing them is expensive, and their benefit is small. Indeed this is true of most forms of structural generalization. Does this call into question the validity or the desirability of performing such generalizations? Should we be dissatisfied with anything less than full generality? Not at all. An important point to remember for structural generalization, which applies to all of EBL, is that the resulting concept need not be fully general to be useful. *Any* generalization is better than none. There is a truism called the 80/20 rule: One gets 80% of the work done with 20% of the effort, and the remaining 20% of the work requires 80% of the effort. The rule is usually cited as a caution against extrapolating the performance characteristics of prototype systems. However, in EBL it works to our advantage. Getting 80% of the generalization with 20% of the work is a great bargain. We can afford to be content with less–than–totally–general concepts; there is nothing magical about generalizing any particular concept to its utmost limits. A problem–solving area not covered by one concept likely will be covered by another, and if not, the system's overall performance is still improved due to efficiency gains in the problem–solving areas that *are* covered.

2.4.2. Temporal Generalization

Temporal generalization applies particularly to planning. A plan is a sequence of operators that achieve a goal. The training example demonstrates how a goal is achieved by a particular sequence of operators. It is possible that a different sequence of the same operators would work as well. As long as preconditions are achieved before their operators, and provided the protection intervals are respected, any ordering will do. The example's explanation explicitly specifies required dependency orderings among states and operators. The timing of some operators may be arbitrary; other operator subsequences may require a particular ordering but allow other subsequences to be interleaved, and so on. The general problem–solving concept should allow for variations in operator orderings.

Chapter 3 includes a discussion of temporal generalization for STRIPS–type operators. This process can be quite involved and expensive. Things get much worse when considering a more general specification of operators. Noninstantaneous processes allow simultaneous and overlapping changes in the world (as is common in qualitative reasoning [32–34]). Full temporal generalization under such real–world conditions is not completely understood. One possibility might be to deny the apparently special status of "time." Time might be represented explicitly as one more aspect of the domain model (e.g., [35, 36]). Then temporal generalization might be adequately subsumed by the other EBL generalization types.

As with disjunctive augmentation, discovering all possible temporal orderings is not necessary. Any temporal variability aids in the generality of the concept.

2.4.3. Number Generalization

Number generalization refers to the recognition that a particular subexplanation can be replicated. For example, suppose we wish to teach a system how to build a tower of blocks given a domain theory about direct support of one block by another or by the table and stability. A training example is given in which three red blocks are stacked. With the generalization types described so far, the resulting concept will be limited to building three–block towers. The system will recognize that the particular blocks used in the example are not required (identity elimination), that the blocks need not be the same color (irrelevant feature elimination), and so on. The system will realize such requirements as the lower blocks be flat on top and that they be relatively incompressible, as dictated by the domain knowledge and explanation. However, the new concept will not apply to building towers with four blocks. Another training example of stacking four blocks will be required, and yet another for five blocks, and so on. Clearly, this method is inadequate. The system should itself realize that the particular techniques for building three–block towers also apply to stacking four and five blocks.

Number generalization is difficult because the parameter being generalized (in our example, the number of blocks) is not explicitly represented anywhere in the explanation. Rather the "threeness" of the tower is implicitly coded in the topology of the explanation itself. There are three subexplanations proving the resulting stability after each block is grasped and moved. The three subexplanations are not identical; the blocks are different, their initial and final locations are different, and so on. Number generalization crucially involves a representation transformation of the explanation into a form in which "sets" or "loops" are included in the theory's ontology. Several systems [37–39] have advanced directions to investigate number generalization. Chapter 3 gives more details on number generalization.

It is interesting to note that not all cases in which number generalization is theoretically supportable should result in number–generalized concepts. Consider rotating the tires on an automobile. Even though the procedure readily generalizes to automobiles with five, six, or seven tires (and such automobiles are logically possible), there is no particular advantage in complicating the ROTATE–TIRE problem–solving concept to include them.

3. Why Learn from Observation?

We believe that EBL systems are best used when the explanation is constructed by observing the behavior of an expert. However, some EBL researchers prefer systems that generalize their own successful problem-solving actions. Others are agnostic on the origins' explanations. But learning from observing experts has an advantage. More complex and interesting concepts can be acquired by relying on the intelligence and creative abilities of others, because the computational complexity of understanding is less than that of creative problem solving.

Suppose we have some initial state I that must be transformed into a goal state G. The system must select a planning schema (a chunked generalized planning concept acquired by EBL on prior experiences) that is capable of the desired transformation. If no single schema transforms I to G, then the system must combine a few schemata sequentially to do the job. However, the system must not be permitted to look for sequences of arbitrary length. Unconstrained search must be avoided because it reduces the schema system to a search problem solver with its concomitant inabilities to deal with rich domains.

Now assume that G can be achieved from I only through the application of many schemata in sequence; that is, no single schema nor any short sequence of schemata can transform I into G. In this case the problem is *intractable* for the system even though there is, in principle, a solution. In rich domains such intractable problems are, for all practical purposes, as insoluble as logically impossible problems. Without the appropriate schemata, search for a solution is a bit like the monkey recreating Shakespeare's *Hamlet* from random keystrokes on a typewriter.

All is not lost, however. True, the system cannot solve the problem of transforming I to G, but it can verify (and in some sense "understand") a solution presented to it. Furthermore, this process can be a very efficient one. The system has knowledge of all the operators necessary for the solution. It can, when given a solution, verify that all the preconditions for each operator are satisfied and that each operator application yields the desired effects. The time complexity of this verification is polynominal in n (linear in n with a reasonable simplifying assumption), where n is the number of operator steps in the solution transformation.

Verification of a proposed solution involves two parts. First, the sequence of operators must be viable; that is, at the time of application of each operator all of the preconditions for that operator must be satisfied. Second, the resulting state after application of the last operator of the sequence must be demonstrated to contain the goal state.

A state is made up of a collection of assertions. Each precondition can also be viewed as a required assertion (or proposition). It will be assumed that the cost of checking whether a particular precondition is satisfied in a state is proportional to the number of assertions in that state.

Let p_j be the number of preconditions for the jth operator.

a_j be the number of assertions added by the jth operator.

r_j be the number of assertions removed by the jth operator.

E be the number of assertions in the initial state.

The cost C of verifying the viability of the sequence is

$$C = K \sum_{j=1}^{n} p_j \left[E + \sum_{l=1}^{j-1} (a_l - r_l) \right] \tag{1}$$

where K is a constant of proportionality. If p is the largest p_j and a is the largest a_j, we have

$$C \leq K \sum_{j=1}^{n} p \left[E + \sum_{l=1}^{j-1} a \right] \tag{2}$$

Simplifying, the cost of demonstrating the viability of a solution is

$$C \leq KpEn + Kpa\frac{n(n-1)}{2} \tag{3}$$

Testing that the goal state is satisfied by the final state is at worst linear in n. The number of assertions in the final state is no greater than

$$E + \sum_{j=1}^{N} a \qquad \text{or} \qquad E + na. \tag{4}$$

Each constituent assertion of a goal must be checked against this state. However, since the number of assertions composing the goal state is independent of n, the cost is at most a constant multiplied by Expression (4).

If it is assumed that each operator deletes on the average about as many assertions from a state as it adds, then the inner summation in Expression (1) approaches zero and the cost becomes $O(n)$; the cost of testing the goal state against the final state becomes independent of n. $O(n)$ is also a trivial lower bound since one must at least consider each operator to verify the sequence.

Thus, understanding a solution is very efficient even if the original problem is intractable for the system. For this reason, we believe that explanation–based learning is best viewed as a kind of learning from observation [40, 41]. We also believe that it is advantageous to view EBL in the context of planning, or more precisely, learning about planning. As discussed in Chapter 4, EBL offers a unique and interesting solution to the McCarthy frame problem [42].

This volume describes theoretical research and computer systems that use a broad range of formalisms: schematas, production systems, qualitative reasoning models, nonmonotonic logic, situation calculus, and some home–grown ad hoc representations. This has been done consciously to avoid sacrificing the ultimate research significance to the expediency of any particular formalism. The ultimate goal, of course, is to adopt (or devise) the right formalism for EBL. However, only more experience with the EBL approach can dictate what that formalism will be.

References

1. R. S. Michalski, I. Mozetic, J. Hong and N. Lavrac, "The Multi–Purpose Incremental Learning System AQ15 and its Testing Application in Three Medical Domains," *Proceedings of the National Conference on Artificial Intelligence*, Philadelphia, PA, August 1986, pp. 1041–1047.

2. J. R. Quinlan, "Induction of Decision Trees," *Machine Learning 1*, 1 (1986), pp. 81–106.

3. T. M. Mitchell, P. E. Utgoff and R. Banerji, "Learning by Experimentation: Acquiring and Refining Problem–solving Heuristics," in *Machine Learning: An Artificial Intelligence Approach*, R. S. Michalski, J. G. Carbonell, T. M. Mitchell (ed.), Tioga Publishing Company, Palo Alto, CA, 1983, pp. 163–190.

4. P. H. Winston, "Learning Structural Descriptions from Examples," in *The Psychology of Computer Vision*, P. H. Winston (ed.), McGraw–Hill, New York, NY, 1975, pp. 157–210.

5. D. A. Waterman, "Generalization Learning Techniques for Automating the Learning of Heuristics," *Artificial Intelligence 1*, 2 (Spring, 1970), pp. 121–170.

6. R. E. Fikes, P. E. Hart and N. J. Nilsson, "Learning and Executing Generalized Robot Plans," *Artificial Intelligence 3*, 4 (1972), pp. 251–288.

7. W. Chafe, "Some Thoughts on Schemata," *Theoretical Issues in Natural Language Processing 1*, Cambridge, MA, June 1975, pp. 89–91.

8. M. L. Minsky, "A Framework for Representing Knowledge," in *The Psychology of Computer Vision*, P. H. Winston (ed.), McGraw–Hill,

New York, NY, 1975, pp. 211–277.

9. R. C. Schank and R. P. Abelson, *Scripts, Plans, Goals and Understanding: An Inquiry into Human Knowledge Structures*, Lawrence Erlbaum and Associates, Hillsdale, NJ, 1977.

10. J. E. Laird, P. S. Rosenbloom and A. Newell, *Universal Subgoaling and Chunking: The Automatic Generation and Learning of Goal Hierarchies*, Kluwer Academic Publishers, Norwell, MA, 1986.

11. G. F. DeJong, "Generalizations Based on Explanations," *Proceedings of the Seventh International Joint Conference on Artificial Intelligence*, Vancouver, B.C., Canada, August 1981, pp. 67–70.

12. T. M. Mitchell, R. Keller and S. Kedar–Cabelli, "Explanation–Based Generalization: A Unifying View," *Machine Learning 1*, 1 (January 1986), pp. 47–80.

13. G. J. Sussman, "A Computational Model of Skill Acquisition," Technical Report 297, MIT AI Lab, Cambridge, MA, 1973.

14. E. Soloway, "Learning = Interpretation + Generalization: A Case Study in Knowledge–Directed Learning," Ph. D. Thesis, University of Massachusetts, Amherst, MA, 1978. (Also appears as COINS Technical Report 78–13.)

15. J. Mostow, "Mechanical Transformation of Task Heuristics into Operational Procedures," Ph.D. Thesis, Department of Computer Science, CMU, Pittsburgh, PA, 1981.

16. B. Silver, "Using Meta–level Inference to Constrain Search and to Learn Strategies in Equation Solving," Ph.D. Thesis, Department of Artificial Intelligence, University of Edinburgh, 1984.

17. R. J. Mooney and S. W. Bennett, "A Domain Independent Explanation–Based Generalizer," *Proceedings of the National Conference on Artificial Intelligence*, Philadelphia, PA, August 1986, pp. 551–555.

18. S. T. Kedar–Cabelli and L. T. McCarty, "Explanation–Based Generalization as Resolution Theorem Proving," *Proceedings of the Fourth International Workshop on Machine Learning*, University of California, Irvine, June 1987, pp. 383–389.

19. D. Chapman, "Planning for Conjunctive Goals," *Artificial Intelligence 32*, 3 (1987), pp. 333–378.

20. E. Charniak, "MS. MALAPROP, A Language Comprehension System," *Proceedings of the Fifth International Joint Conference on Artificial Intelligence*, Cambridge, MA, August 1977.

21. R. W. Wilensky, "Understanding Goal–Based Stories," Technical Report 140, Ph.D. Thesis, Department of Computer Science, Yale University, New Haven, CT, September 1978.

22. R. C. Schank, *Explanation Patterns: Understanding Mechanically and Creatively*, Lawrence Erlbaum and Associates, Hillsdale, NJ, 1986.

23. T. G. Dietterich, "Learning at the Knowledge Level," *Machine Learning 1*, 3 (1986), pp. 287–316.

24. R. S. Michalski, "A Theory and Methodology of Inductive Learning," in *Machine Learning: An Artificial Intelligence Approach*, R. S. Michalski, J. G. Carbonell, T. M. Mitchell (ed.), Tioga Publishing Company, Palo Alto, CA, 1983, pp. 83–134.

25. R. Waldinger, "Achieving Several Goals Simultaneously," in *Machine Intelligenge 8*, E. Elcock and D. Michie (ed.), Ellis Horwood Limited, London, 1977.

26. N. J. Nilsson, *Principles of Artificial Intelligence*, Tioga Publishing Company, Palo Alto, CA, 1980.

27. L. Rendell, "Substantial Constructive Induction using Layered Information Compression: Tractable Feature Formation in Search," *Proceedings of the Ninth International Joint Conference on Artificial Intelligence*, Los Angeles, CA, August 1985, pp. 650–658.

28. J. R. Anderson and R. Thompson, "Use of Analogy in a Production System Architecture," in *Similarity and Analogical Reasoning*, S. Vosniadou and A. Ortony (ed.), Cambridge University Press, Cambridge, England, 1987.

29. D. J. Mostow, "Machine Transformation of Advice into a Heuristic Search Procedure," in *Machine Learning: An Artificial Intelligence Approach*, R. S. Michalski, J. G. Carbonell, T. M. Mitchell (ed.), Tioga Publishing Company, Palo Alto, CA, 1983, pp. 367–404.

30. R. M. Keller, "The Role of Explicit Contextual Knowledge in Learning Concepts to Improve Performance," Ph.D. Thesis, Department of Computer Science, Rutgers University, New Brunswick, NJ, January 1987.

31. A. Segre, "Operationality and Real–World Plans," *Proceedings of the AAAI Symposium on Explanation-Based Learning*, Stanford, CA, March 1988, pp. 158–163.

32. K. D. Forbus, "Qualitative Process Theory," *Artificial Intelligence 24*, (1984), pp. 85–168.

33. J. de Kleer, "Causal and Teleological Reasoning in Circuit Recognition," Technical Report 529, Ph.D. Thesis, MIT AI Lab, Cambridge, MA, September 1979.

34. B. Kuipers, "Commonsense Reasoning About Causality: Deriving Behavior from Structure," *Artificial Intelligence 24*, (1984), pp. 169–204.

35. J. F. Allen, "Maintaining Knowledge about Temporal Intervals," *Communications of the Association for Computing Machinery 26*, 11 (November 1983), pp. 832–843.

36. T. Dean, "Time Map Maintenance," Technical Report 289, Yale University, New Haven, CT, October 1983.

37. A. E. Prieditis, "Discovery of Algorithms from Weak Methods," *Proceedings of the International Meeting on Advances in Learning*, Les Arcs, Switzerland, 1986, pp. 37–52.

38. J. W. Shavlik, *Extending Explanation-Based Learning by Generalizing the Structure of Explanations*, Pitman, London, 1990.

39. W. W. Cohen, "A Technique for Generalizing Number in Explanation–Based Learning," ML–TR–19, Department of Computer Science, Rutgers University, New Brunswick, NJ, September 1987.

40. T. M. Mitchell, S. Mahadevan and L. I. Steinberg, "LEAP: A Learning Apprentice for VLSI Design," *Proceedings of the Ninth International Joint Conference on Artificial Intelligence*, Los Angeles, CA, August 1985, pp. 573–580.

41. G. F. DeJong and R. J. Mooney, "Explanation–Based Learning: An Alternative View," *Machine Learning 1*, 2 (1986), pp. 145–176.

42. J. McCarthy and P. J. Hayes, "Some Philosophical Problems from the Standpoint of Artificial Intelligence," in *Machine Intelligence 4*, B. Meltzer and D. Michie (ed.), Edinburgh University Press, Edinburgh, Scotland, 1969.

Chapter 2

Explanation Generalization in EGGS

Raymond J. Mooney

1. Introduction

Over the past few years, a number of similar explanation generalization techniques have been developed which constitute general domain-independent mechanisms for performing explanation–based learning [1–7]. Prior to the development of these techniques, a number of domain-dependent systems were built which used similar generalization techniques to learn concepts, heuristics, or plans from single examples by analyzing their underlying causal structure [8–17].

This chapter describes a particular domain–independent EBL system called EGGS which has been tested on a variety of examples from the literature on explanation–based learning. Many of these examples were originally used to demonstrate earlier, more domain–dependent systems such as STRIPS [8], LEX2 [9], CUPS [10], MA [11], and LEAP [16]. The examples from these systems come from a number of different domains including robot planning in a "blocks world," solving symbolic integration problems, learning artifact descriptions, proving theorems in logic, and designing logic circuits. Nevertheless, the same learning system can be used to generalize explanations for all of these examples. EGGS also includes performance systems which produce explanations for the learning system and in turn use the rules it generates to improve their ability to solve future problems. Currently, EGGS is capable of generalizing explanations composed of Horn clauses, term rewriting rules, and STRIPS operators.

EBG [2] is an alternative domain–independent technique for generalizing explanations which was independently developed at the same time EGGS was originally designed and implemented. The eventual implementation of EBG [4] has also been tested on several of the domains mentioned above. All of the original domain–dependent systems listed above used similar generalization techniques; however, until the development of EGGS and EBG, there was no general learning technique to generalize examples in all of these domains.

An outline of the learning process in EGGS is given in Figure 2–1, and an architectural diagram of the system is given in Figure 2–2. The tasks of constructing an explanation (step 1) and packaging a generalised explanation for future use (step 4) depend on the underlying representational formalism. Each representational formalism requires different modules for these tasks. For example, when using Horn clauses, a theorem prover is appropriate for constructing explanations, while when using STRIPS operators, a planner is appropriate. Unlike explanation construction and packaging, explanation generalization (step 3) can be

1. **Explain:**   Construct a complete explanation for a specific example by either proving that an example is a member of a concept, by independently solving a problem or constructing a plan, or by understanding and explaining the actions or operators executed by an external agent.

2. **Prune:**   Remove branches of the explanation that are more specific than needed for the operationality of the resulting plan or proof.

3. **Generalize:** Generalize the remaining explanation as far as possible without invalidating its underlying structure.

4. **Package:**   Create a macro–operator or macro–rule that summarizes the resulting generalized explanation, and index it so that it can be used to aid future task classification, problem solving, planning, or understanding.

Figure 2–1:   The Learning Process in EGGS

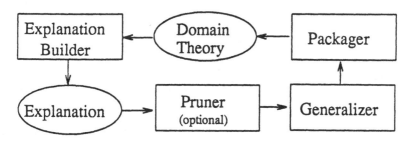

Figure 2–2:   EGGS Architecture

characterized in a very general way and is discussed in detail in this chapter. The process of pruning explanations for operationality (step 2) is also discussed in this chapter; however, determining exactly what should be pruned from a particular explanation prior to generalization is primarily a domain–dependent decision.

The chapter is organized as follows. Section 2 presents a specification of how explanations are represented in EGGS. In Section 3, a number of alternative explanation generalization algorithms are presented, including the EGGS algorithm, and in Section 4, the various generalization algorithms are compared. In Sections 5 and 6, the correctness and computational complexity of the explanation generalization process is analyzed. Section 7 discusses the process of pruning explanations for operationality, and Section 8 presents some problems with integrating the generalization process with explanation construction. In Section 9, the process of explanation generalization is compared with *chunking* and *composition* methods used to learn productions in SOAR [18] and ACT* [19], respectively. Finally, in Sections 10 and 11, some examples are presented of learning *macro–rules* by generalizing Horn clause proofs and term rewritings. Examples of learning *macro–operators* using STRIPS rules are presented in Chapter 3. Many other examples of EGGS' performance were presented by Mooney [20].

2. Explanations, Explanation Structures, and Generalized Explanations

In different domains, various types of explanations are appropriate. Mitchell and colleagues [2] defined an explanation as a logical proof that demonstrates how an example meets a set of sufficient conditions defining a particular concept. This type of explanation is appropriate for learning classical concept definitions, such as learning a structural specification of a cup, an example introduced in [10] and discussed in [2]. However, when learning general plans in a problem–solving domain (as in STRIPS [8] or GENESIS [14]), it is more appropriate to consider an explanation to be a set of causally connected actions that demonstrate how a goal state is achieved.

Consequently, this work takes a very broad definition of the term *explanation* and considers it to be a connected set of *units*, where a unit is set of related *expressions* in predicate calculus and an expression can be either a literal or a term. Horn clause proofs, where each Horn clause is a unit, and plans composed of STRIPS operators, where each operator is a unit, are special cases of this very general representation. Formally, a unit can be defined as follows:

> A unit is a connected directed acyclical graph (V,E) in which the vertices in V are expressions.

For example, a unit for a Horn clause rule has literals for its antecedents and its consequent, while a unit for a STRIPS operator has literals for its additions, deletions, and preconditions. An expression a in a unit is said to *support* another expression b in the unit if and only if there is a directed path from a to b. For example, in the unit for a Horn clause, each antecedent *supports* the consequent through a path containing a single edge.

A *domain theory*, **T**, is formally defined as a set of units. As defined by Nilsson [21], a *substitution* is a set of ordered pairs each specifying a term to be substituted for a particular variable. The form $p\theta$, where p is a expression and θ is a substitution, denotes the expression resulting from applying θ to p. The expression $\gamma\theta$, where both γ and θ are substitutions, denotes the substitution resulting from the *composition* of γ and θ, which is obtained by applying θ to the terms of γ and then adding any pairs of θ having variables not occurring among the variables of γ. An *instance* of a unit, α, is a unit obtained by applying a variable substitution to all of the expressions in α. Two expressions are said to be *identical* if and only if all of their corresponding predicates, functions, variables, and constants are exactly the same (i.e., their most general unifier is the null substitution). Before formally defining an explanation in this representation, a few additional definitions are needed:

> A unit–set is a pair (U, R), where U is a set of units: $\{(V_1, E_1),\ \ldots\ ,(V_n, E_n)\}$ and R is an equivalence relation defined on the set of expressions: $V_1 \cup V_2 \cup \ldots \cup V_n$. For each pair of expressions (a,b) in R, where $a \in V_i$ and $b \in V_j$, it must be the case that that $i \neq j$ (i.e., equivalent expressions must be from separate units).

Given a unit–set $S = (U\ R)$, where $U = \{(V_1, E_1),\ \ldots\ ,(V_n, E_n)\}$, let C_1, $C_2,\ \ldots\ ,C_m$ be the equivalence classes of expressions defined by R. Let G be the graph (V', E') where $V' = \{C_1, C_2,\ \ldots\ ,C_m\}$ and $(C_i, C_j) \in E'$ if and only if there are expressions $a \in C_i$ and $b \in C_j$ such that $(a, b) \in E_1 \cup E_2 \cup \ldots \cup E_n$. G is referred to as *the graph of S* and represents the directed graph obtained by "collapsing" all equivalent expressions into a single vertex. A formal definition of an explanation can now be stated as follows:

> An **explanation** is a unit–set, $S = (U, R)$, where the graph of S is connected and acyclic and where for each pair of expressions $(a, b) \in R$, a and b are identical. Furthermore, let the set $U' \subset U$ be the set of all units in U that are instances of units in the domain theory, **T**, and let R' be the equivalence relation such that $(a, b) \in R'$ if and only if both a and b are expressions from units in U' and $(a, b) \in R$. In order for S to be an explanation, U' must be nonempty and the graph of the unit–set $S' = (U', R')$ must also be connected and acyclic.

In other words, an explanation is a combination of units that forms an even larger connected acyclic graph by means of an equivalence relation defined on their vertices. Each pair of expressions that the relation defines as equivalent must be identical. Furthermore, if all units that are not instances of units in the domain theory are removed from an explanation, the remaining explanation also defines a connected directed acyclic graph. The *goal* is a distinguished expression in the explanation that is a sink of the graph of the explanation and represents the final conclusion in an inference chain or the desired state in a plan.

A Horn clause proof in this representation is an explanation whose units are Horn clauses and whose equivalence relation matches antecedents of some clauses to consequents of others. In this case, an explanation is analogous to the *data dependency* structure maintained by a *truth maintenance system* [22]. For example, consider the following domain theory for the problem of learning a structural definition of a cup, an example originally presented by Winston and colleagues [10]:

> Stable(?x) $\wedge$ Liftable(?x) $\wedge$ OpenVessel(?x) $\rightarrow$ Cup(?x)
> Bottom(?y) $\wedge$ PartOf(?y,?x) $\wedge$ Flat(?y) $\rightarrow$ Stable(?x)
> Graspable(?x) $\wedge$ Light(?x) $\rightarrow$ Liftable(?x) Handle(?y)
> $\wedge$ PartOf(?y,?x) $\rightarrow$ Graspable(?x) Concavity(?y) $\wedge$
> PartOf(?y,?x) $\wedge$ UpwardPointing(?y) $\rightarrow$ OpenVessel(?x)

Additional units needed for the problem are the following individual facts:

> Light(Obj1), Color(Obj1,Red), PartOf(Handle1,Obj1),
> Handle(Handle1), Bottom(B1), PartOf(B1,Obj1), Flat(B1),
> Concavity(C1), PartOf(C1,Obj1), UpwardPointing(C1)

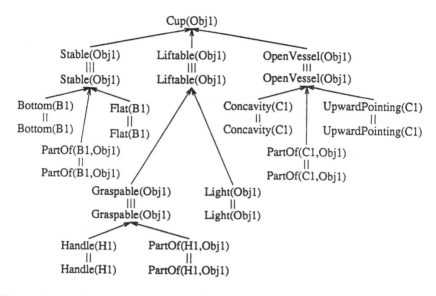

Figure 2-3:   Explanation for Cup(Obj1)

A proof tree for Cup(Obj1) is shown in Figure 2-3 as an explanation whose goal is Cup(Obj1). This proof explains why Obj1 is a cup by showing how its structural properties fulfill the functional purpose of a cup. Triple edges in the graphs indicate equivalences between expressions in two units that are instances of the domain theory, and double edges indicate equivalences to expressions in units that are not instances of units in the domain theory. Specifically, for explanations using Horn clauses as units, triple edges indicate connections between instantiations of rules from the domain theory, and double edges indicate connections to initial facts about the specific example. Examples of explanations where the units are rewrite rules and STRIPS operators are presented in Section 11 and Chapter 3, respectively.

An expression a is a *uniquized version* of an expression b if and only if a is obtained by substituting a uniquely named variable for each variable in b. In correspondence with the terminology in [2], an *explanation structure* is defined as an explanation with each instantiated unit from the domain theory replaced by a uniquized version of its general definition. Formally:

> An **explanation structure** of an explanation $E = (U, R)$ is a unit–set, $S = (U' \ R')$, where for each $u_i \in U$ where u_i is an instance of a unit $t_i \in T$, there is exactly one $u_i' \in U'$ such that u_i' is a uniquized version of t_i

and where $(u_i{}', u_j{}') \in R'$ if and only if $(u_i, u_j) \in R$.

The definition of an explanation ensures that an explanation structure defines a connected directed acyclic graph. For example, the explanation structure of the explanation for the cup example is shown in Figure 2–4.

The task of *explanation generalization* is to take an explanation containing instances of units from a domain theory and generate a *generalized explanation*, which is the most general instance of its explanation structure in which equivalent expressions are identical. The generalized explanation maintains matches between expressions from rules or facts in the domain theory but eliminates matches to expressions specifying facts of the particular specific example. This means that the most general substitution that results in all equivalent expressions being identical must be applied to the explanation structure. Formally:

> A **generalized explanation** of an explanation E with an explanation structure $S = (U, R)$ is an explanation $G = (U', R')$ such that there exists a substitution γ where for each $u_i \in U$ there is exactly one $u_i{}' \in U'$ such that $u_i{}' = u_i \gamma$ and where $(u_i{}', u_j{}') \in R'$ if and only if $(u_i, u_j) \in R$. Furthermore, if $(u_i{}', u_j{}') \in R'$, then $u_i{}'$ and $u_j{}'$ must be identical. Finally, for any other substitution, θ, satisfying these constraints, there must exist a substitution θ' such that $U\theta = U\gamma\theta'$ (this ensures that γ is the *most general* substitution that satisfies the constraints).

The generalized explanation of the cup example is shown in Figure 2–5. This generalized explanation can then be used to obtain the following *macro–rule* representing a general structural definition of a cup:

Bottom(?y1) $\wedge$ PartOf(?y1,?x1) $\wedge$ Flat(?y1) $\wedge$ Handle(?y2)
$\wedge$ PartOf(?y2,?x1) $\wedge$ Light(?x1) $\wedge$ Concavity(?y3) $\wedge$
PartOf(?y3,?x1) $\wedge$ UpwardPointing(?y3) $\rightarrow$ Cup(?x1)

For explanations that are logical proofs, a macro–rule like the one above is easily obtained by taking the leaves of the generalized explanation as the antecedents and the goal of the generalized explanation as the consequent. In planning domains, the generalized explanation represents a general plan schema or macro–operator [8] for achieving a particular class of goals. Creating a new action definition for the composed plan from the generalized explanation requires a few additional steps, which are discussed in Chapter 3.

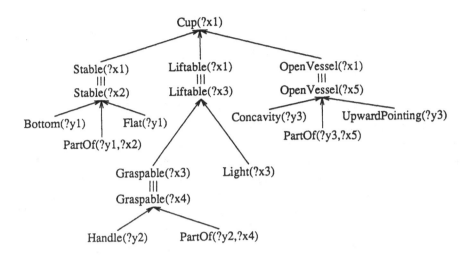

Figure 2–4:   Explanation Structure for the Cup Example

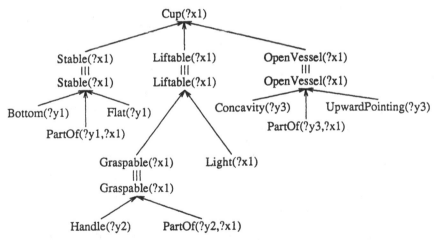

Figure 2–5:   Generalized Explanation for the Cup Example

3. Explanation Generalizing Algorithms

Several algorithms have been developed for generalizing various types of explanations. The STRIPS system [8] incorporated a method for generalizing blocks–world plans into macro–operators. The EBG method [2] uses a modified version of goal–regression [23] to generalize proofs of concept membership. The EGGS explanation generalization algorithm was developed for generalizing the broad class of explanations defined in the previous section. This algorithm was first published by DeJong and Mooney [1] along with a description of an error found in the specification of the EBG algorithm. Kedar–Cabelll and McCarty subsequently developed a PROLOG version of EBG [4] which corrected this problem with the original algorithm.

The general technique used by STRIPS, EBG, EGGS, and PROLOG–EBG can be abstracted to apply to the class of explanations defined in the previous section. The rest of this section is devoted to presenting and comparing algorithmic descriptions of all of these methods as applied to this class of explanations. All of the algorithms rely on unification pattern matching, and the abbreviation MGU is used to refer to the substitution that is the *most general unifier* of two expressions [21, 24]. All of the generalization algorithms presented have been implemented and tested within the context of the overall EGGS system.

3.1. STRIPS Macrop Learning

The first work on generalizing explanations was the learning of robot plans in STRIPS [8]. STRIPS worked in a "blocks–world" domain. After its problem–solving component generated a plan for achieving a particular state, it generalized the plan into a problem–solving schema (a MACROP or macro–operator) that could be used to efficiently solve similar problems in the future. Work on the STRIPS system was the first to point out that a correct generalization of a connected set of actions or inferences *cannot* be obtained by simply replacing each constant by an independent variable. This method happens to work on the Cup example given earlier. The proper generalized explanation can be obtained by replacing Obj1 by ?x1, B1 by ?y1, H1 by ?y2, and C1 by ?y3. However, in general, such a simplistic approach can result in a structure that is either more general or more specific than what is actually supported by the system's domain knowledge.

Fikes and colleagues [8] used the following examples to illustrate that simply replacing constants with variables can result in improper generalizations. These examples assume the initial state shown in Figure 2–6 and use the following operators:

> GoThru(?d,?r1,?r2): Go through door ?d from room ?r1
> to room ?r2.
> PushThru(?b,?d,?r1,?r2): Push box ?b through door ?d
> from room ?r1 to room ?r2.
> SpecialPush(?b): Specific operator for pushing box ?b from

Room2 to Room1.

Given the plan

GoThru(Door1,Room1,Room2)
SpecialPush(Box1)

simply replacing constants by variables results in the plan

GoThru(?d,?r1,?r2)
SpecialPush(?b)

This plan is too general since SpecialPush is only applicable when starting in Room2, so having a variable ?r2 as the destination of the GoThru is too general and ?r2 should be replaced by Room2. Given the plan

GoThru(Door1,Room1,Room2)
PushThru(Box1,Door1,Room2,Room1)

simply replacing constants by variables results in the plan

GoThru(?d,?r1,?r2)
PushThru(?b,?d,?r2,?r1)

This plan is too specific since the operators themselves do not demand that the room in which the robot begins (?r1) be the same room into which the box is pushed. The correct generalization is

GoThru(?d,?r1,?r2)
PushThru(?b,?d,?r2,?r3)

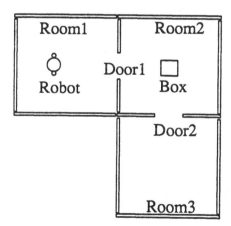

Figure 2-6:   Initial World State for STRIPS Examples

The exact process STRIPS uses to avoid these problems and correctly generalize an example is dependent on its particular representations (triangle tables) and inference techniques (resolution); however, the basic technique is easily captured using the representation discussed in Section 2. A description of the basic explanation generalizing algorithm used in STRIPS is shown in Figure 2–7. It should be noted that the generalization process in STRIPS was constructed specifically for generalizing robot plans. There was no attempt to present a general learning method based on generalizing explanations in any domain. However, the algorithm in Figure 2–7 is a straightforward generalization of the basic process used in STRIPS. The basic technique is to unify each pair of equivalent expressions in the explanation structure and apply each resulting substitution to all of the expressions in the explanation structure. After all of the unifications and substitutions have been made, the result is the generalized explanation since each expression has been replaced by the most general expression that allows all of the equality matches in the explanation to be satisfied.

3.2. EBG

Mitchell, Keller, and Kedar–Cabelli [2] described a technique called EBG (explanation–based generalization) for generalizing a logical proof that a particular example satisfies the definition of a concept. An example concept–membership proof showing how a particular object satisfies the functional definition of a cup was given in Figure 2–3. Unlike the STRIPS MACROP learning method, EBG was intended as a general method for learning by generalizing explanations of why an example is a member of a concept. In [2], detailed examples are presented illustrating how EBG can be applied to learning an operational definition for when it is safe to stack something on an endtable, to Winston's CUP example

for each equality between expressions x and y in the explanation structure
do
    let θ be the *MGU of x and y*
    for each expression z in the explanation structure **do**
        replace z with $z\theta$

Figure 2–7:   STRIPS Explanation Generalizing Algorithm

[10], and to an example from LEX2's domain of learning heuristics for symbolic integration [9]. A much more abstract description of how it might be used to learn a kidnapping plan like that learned by the original GENESIS system is presented in an appendix to [14].

The original EBG algorithm presented in [2] is based on *goal regression* [23] and involves back–propagating constraints from the goal through the explanation structure to the leaves. Figure 2–8 presents a formal specification of the original algorithm in terms of the explanation representation introduced earlier. The global variable R maintains the current set of regressed expressions and represents the most general set of antecedents necessary to prove the goal given the portion of the explanation structure already traversed. The explanation structure is traversed from the goal back to the leaves in a depth–first manner. Each time a unit (rule) is traversed, the set R is updated and the substitution resulting from the unit's unification to the structure already traversed is applied to all of the expressions in R. After the entire explanation structure has been traversed, R is the most general set of antecedents for the given

let g be the goal expression in the explanation structure
let R be the set of expressions supporting g
EBG(g)

procedure EBG(p)
    for each expression x supporting p **do**
        if x is equivalent to some expression e
            then
                let $R = R - \{x\}$
                for each expression y supporting e **do**
                    let $R = R \cup \{y\}$
                let θ be the MGU of e and x
                for y in R **do**
                    replace y with $y\theta$
                EBG(e)

Figure 2–8:   Original EBG Explanation Generalizing Algorithm

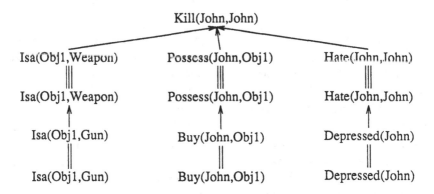

Figure 2–9:   Suicide Example — Specific Explanation

explanation structure.[1]

However, as DeJong and Mooney [1] initially pointed out, this algorithm is only guaranteed to determine the leaves of the generalized explanation and in certain situations fails to obtain the correct generalized goal. The "Suicide" example, originally introduced in [1], is an example for which the original EBG algorithm does not compute the correct generalized goal and as a result learns an incorrect macro–rule. This example involves inferring that an individual will commit suicide if he is depressed and buys a gun. The specific facts of the problem are

Depressed(John), Buy(John,Obj1), Isa(Obj1,Gun)

The domain rules are

Depressed(?x) $\rightarrow$ Hate(?x,?x)
Hate(?x,?y) $\wedge$ Possess(?x,?z) $\wedge$ Isa(?z,Weapon) $\rightarrow$ Kill(?x,?y)
Buy(?x,?y) $\rightarrow$ Possess(?x,?y),   Isa(?x,Gun) $\rightarrow$ Isa(?x,Weapon)

The proof that John will commit suicide is shown in Figure 2–9, its explanation structure is shown in Figure 2–10, and the correct general proof

---

[1]The algorithm presented in Figure 2–8 corrects problems with the BackPropagate function presented in [3]. As discussed in [3], the BackPropagate function (which was based on the informal description of this process given in [2]) does not properly propagate constraints across conjuncts and consequently in some situations does not compute the correct regressed expressions. The version in Figure 2–8 does not have this problem since each substitution is applied to all of the current regressed expressions in the set R.

that anyone who is depressed and buys a gun will commit suicide is shown in Figure 2–11. The general macro–rule learned from the generalized explanation is

$$\text{Depressed}(?y1) \wedge \text{Buy}(?y1,?c1) \wedge \text{Isa}(?c1,\text{Gun}) \rightarrow \text{Kill}(?y1,?y1)$$

Goal regression, as given in [2] and Figure 2–8, computes only the most general set of antecedents that would support a proof with the same explanation structure as the training example (i.e., the weakest preconditions [12, 25]). If only goal regression is performed, the proper description of the goal concept supported by the explanation is not always determined since the explanation itself may impose constraints on the goal concept. In terms of the Suicide example, the constraint that the killer be the same as the person killed is never imposed and, as demonstrated in [1], EBG constructs the following erroneous rule:

$$\text{Depressed}(?y) \wedge \text{Buy}(?y,?c) \wedge \text{Isa}(?c,\text{Gun}) \rightarrow \text{Kill}(?x,?y)$$

This rule states that everyone kills someone who is depressed and buys a gun, which is clearly not a conclusion warranted by the domain theory. Since the abstract STRIPS algorithm applies substitutions generated by each unification to the entire explanation structure, it computes the appropriately constrained goal concept and does not make this mistake.

As suggested in [1], the proper generalized goal and generalized explanation can be obtained by starting with the generalized antecedents obtained from regression and rederiving the general proof. Rederiving the proof propagates constraints from the regressed expressions to the goal, thereby appropriately constraining the goal concept. The resulting

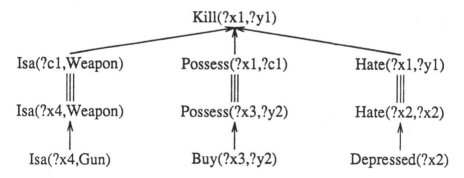

Figure 2–10: Suicide Example — Explanation Structure

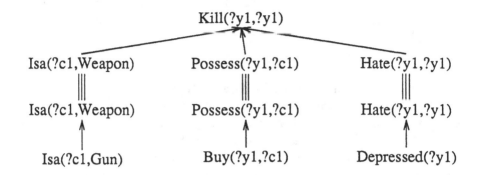

Figure 2–11: Suicide Example — Generalized Explanation

generalization algorithm is then a two–step process: goal regression (back–propagation) followed by proof reconstruction (forward–propagation). This approach was suggested based on a similar two–pass generalization process presented in [26]. A formal description of a version of EBG corrected in this manner is given in [3].[2] Kedar–Cabelli and McCarty [4] presented a PROLOG version of EBG which also corrects the problem and avoids making two separate passes through the explanation.[3] This version of EBG is considered in a subsequent section.

3.3. EGGS

The EGGS (explanation generalization using a global substitution) algorithm was developed for generalizing explanations of the abstract form defined and used in this chapter. The algorithm is quite similar to the abstract STRIPS algorithm and is shown in Figure 2–12. The difference between EGGS and the abstract STRIPS algorithm is that instead of applying the substitutions throughout the explanation at each

---

[2]Since, as mentioned in the previous footnote, the BackPropagate function presented in [3] does not properly propagate constraints across conjuncts, the corrected version of EBG presented in [3] required that ForwardPropagate be performed before BackPropagate. If the correct version of back–propagation presented in Figure 2–8 is used, it is not necessary to perform forward propagation first.

[3]Due to a typographical error, the EGGS algorithm presented in [3] did not include applying γ to x and y prior to computing their MGU. The original publication of the algorithm in [1] did not suffer from this mistake, and the longer technical report version of [3] included a corrected version of the EGGS algorithm.

let γ be the null substitution {}
for each equality between expressions x and y in the explanation structure
do
    let θ be the MGU of $x\gamma$ and $y\gamma$
    let γ be $\gamma\theta$
for each expression x in the explanation structure **do**
    replace x **with** $x\gamma$

Figure 2–12: EGGS Explanation Generalizing Algorithm

step, all the substitutions are composed into one substitution, γ. After all
the unifications have been performed, one sweep through the explanation
applying the accumulated substitution γ results in the generalized explanation. Table 2–1 demonstrates this technique as applied to the Cup
example. It shows how γ changes as it is composed with the substitutions
resulting from each unification. Applying the final substitution γ to the
explanation structure shown in Figure 2–4 results in the generalized
explanation shown in Figure 2–5. Table 2–2 shows how EGGS generalizes the Suicide example. Applying the final substitution to the explanation structure shown in Figure 2–10 results in the generalized explanation
shown in Figure 2–11. In the tables, equalities are processed in the order
produced by depth–first traversals of the explanation structures; however,
any order will result in equivalent generalized explanations up to a change
of variable names.

3.4. PROLOG–EBG

    Kedar–Cabelli and McCarty [4] presented a PROLOG version of
EBG which, unlike the original EBG, computed the proper goal concept.
PROLOG–EBG integrates the generalization process with the construction of explanations by PROLOG. A generalized proof is constructed in
parallel with the proof for the specific example. Any query results in both
a specific and and a generalized proof being returned.

    The algorithmic description presented in Figure 2–13 is an attempt
to specify the generalization algorithm underlying PROLOG–EBG as an
independent process (i.e., separated from the process of theorem proving).
Like EGGS, PROLOG–EBG constructs a global substitution, γ, which is
then applied to the complete explanation structure. However, unlike
EGGS, γ is constructed by traversing the explanation depth–first from
the goal in a manner analogous to trying to prove the general goal of the

Table 1: EGGS Applied To the Cup Example		
Equality	θ	γ
Stable(?x1) ≡ Stable(?x2)	{?x1/?x2}	{?x1/?x2}
Liftable(?x1) ≡ Liftable(?x3)	{?x1/?x3}	{?x1/?x2, ?x1/?x3}
Graspable(?x3) ≡ Graspable(?x4)	{?x1/?x4}	{?x1/?x2, ?x1/?x3, ?x1/?x4}
OpenVessel(?x1) ≡ OpenVessel(?x5)	{?x1/?x5}	{?x1/?x2, ?x1/?x3, ?x1/?x4, ?x1/?x5}

Table 2: EGGS Applied To the Suicide Example		
Equality	θ	γ
Isa(?c1,Weapon) ≡ Isa(?x4,Weapon)	{?c1/?x4}	{?c1/?x4}
Possess(?x1,?c1) ≡ Possess(?x3,?y2)	{?x1/?x3, ?c1/?y2}	{?c1/?x4, ?x1/?x3, ?c1/?y2}
Hate(?x1,?y1) ≡ Hate(?x2,?x2)	{?y1/?x2, ?y1/?x1}	{?c1/?x4, ?x1/?x3, ?c1/?y2, ?y1/?x2, ?y1/?x1}

explanation structure using backward–chaining. The substitution γ is constructed by finding a substitution that allows the goal to be proved from the set of operational expressions represented by the leaves of the explanation structure. The generalization algorithm is analogous to the algorithm for a backward–chaining deductive system (like PROLOG or the deductive retrieval system in [24]). In the algorithm in Figure 2–13, the function PROLOG–EBG returns two values: the current substitution (γ) and the subset of the expressions in the explanation structure that have already been traversed (E).[4] When the top–level call to PROLOG–EBG returns, E is the set of all expressions in the explanation structure and γ is the final global substitution.

It should be noted that Hirsh [5] simultaneously developed a version of EBG for logic programming (using the MRS logic programming system [27]) that uses a generalization algorithm equivalent in operation to PROLOG–EBG's. In addition to integrating theorem proving and generalization, MRS–EBG integrates both of these with operationality checking [2] or *pruning* [1, 3], a process discussed in Section 7.

---

[4]The notation "$(a, b) = F(x)$" and "return (a, b)" is used to denote the fact that the function F returns two values: a and b. All variables referenced by a procedure are assumed to be local to that procedure call.

let g be the goal expression in the explanation structure
let $(\gamma, E) = $ PROLOG–EBG(g, {})
for e in E do replace e with eγ

procedure PROLOG–EBG(x, θ)
   let S be the set of expressions supporting x
   for s in S do replace s with sθ
   let $(\gamma, E) = $ PROLOG–EBG–Supporters(S, {}, $\emptyset$)
   return $(\gamma\theta, E \cup \{x\})$

procedure PROLOG–EBG–Supporters(S, γ, E)
  if S $= \emptyset$
    then return (γ, E)
    else
      let f be the first element of S
      let R $= $ S $- \{f\}$
      if f is equivalent to some expression e
        then
            let ϕ be the MGU of f and e
            let $(\delta, P) = $ PROLOG–EBG(e, ϕ)
            for r in R do replace r with rδ
            PROLOG–EBG–Supporters(R, $\gamma\delta$, E $\cup$ P)
        else PROLOG–EBG–Supporters(R, γ, E $\cup \{f\}$)

Figure 2–13: PROLOG–EBG Explanation Generalizing Algorithm

4. Comparison of Explanation Generalizing Algorithms

It is reasonably clear that STRIPS, EGGS, and PROLOG–EBG all compute the same desired generalized explanation. They all perform a set of unifications and substitutions that constrain the explanation structure into one in which equivalent expressions are identical. The difference between them lies in the manner and order in which the unifications and substitutions are done. As described by O'Rorke [7], explanation generalization can be viewed as a process of posting and propagating the effects of equality or co–reference constraints. Neither the STRIPS nor EGGS algorithm imposes an ordering on the assimilation of the various equality constraints in the explanation structure. On the other hand, the various EBG algorithms order the assimilation of constraints by traversing the explanation structure in a depth–first manner. Although this ordering is not required by the generalization process, it is a natural consequence of integrating generalization with a backward–chaining theorem prover.

Actually, the task of producing a global substitution (γ) for an explanation structure can be easily shown to reduce to the task of finding a single most general unifier for two expressions. A single unification algorithm for explanation generalization is shown in Figure 2–14. The two unifying expressions for the reduction are constructed by having equivalent expressions in the explanation structure occupy corresponding argument positions in the two constructed expressions. For example, following are the two expressions constructed for the explanation structure of the Cup example (Figure 2–4).

P(Stable(?x2), Liftable(?x3), Graspable(?x4), OpenVessel(?x5))
P(Stable(?x1), Liftable(?x1), Graspable(?x3), OpenVessel(?x1))

An MGU for these two expressions is {?x1/?x2, ?x1/?x3, ?x1/?x4, ?x1/?x5}, which is the same as the global substitution EGGS constructed for this example (Table 2–1). The two expressions constructed for the Suicide example are:

P(Isa(?x4,Weapon), Possess(?x3,?y2), Hate(?x2,?x2))
P(Isa(?c1,Weapon), Possess(?x1,?c1), Hate(?x1,?y1))

An MGU for these two expressions is {?c1/?x4, ?x1/?x3, ?c1/?y2, ?y1/?x2, ?y1/?x1}, which is again the same as the global substitution constructed by EGGS (Table 2–2).

Consequently, in some sense the various explanation generalizing algorithms are just different ways of implementing unification. In fact, EGGS directly corresponds to the implementation of UNIFY in [24], which takes a pair of expressions and a current substitution and returns an updated substitution which includes variable bindings that unify the

let A and B be two expressions each containing one member
of each pair of equivalent expressions in the explanation
structure such that equivalent expressions occupy
corresponding positions in the two expressions.
let γ be the MGU of A and B
for each expression x in the explanation structure do
    replace x with $x\gamma$

Figure 2–14: Single Unification Explanation Generalizing Algorithm

two expressions in the context of the current substitution. In EGGS, this UNIFY is simply used to update the initially empty global substitution (γ) to include the variable bindings necessary to unify each pair of equivalent expressions in the explanation structure. In fact, showing that EGGS and the single unification algorithm are equivalent would simply require a proof of correctness for the unification algorithm given in [24]. The STRIPS generalizing algorithm, on the other hand, is more similar to the implementation of UNIFY presented in [21] in which the substitution unifying the first elements of two expressions is applied to the rest of the expressions before continuing. A unification algorithm that applied each substitution to the entire expression (thereby generating the resulting unified expression as well as a unifying substitution) would be equivalent to the STRIPS generalizing algorithm.

5. Correctness of Explanation Generalizing Algorithms

Intuitively, for an explanation generalizing algorithm to be "correct," its output should be logically entailed by the system's existing knowledge or domain theory, and it should be as general as possible given this constraint and the constraint that it retain the "structure" of the original explanation.

One approach to proving correctness of explanation generalization, discussed by O'Rorke [7], involves demonstrating that a generalization algorithm maintains all of the equality or co–reference constraints in the explanation structure in the most general way possible. This is an attempt to formally capture the intuitive notion that an explanation should be generalized as far as possible while still maintaining its underlying structure. As described by O'Rorke [7], explanation generalization can be performed by combining the individual co–reference constraints in order to compute the most general description of each expression in the explanation that satisfies all of these constraints. More details on this approach to verification and how it specifically applies to generalizers based on unification are given in [7].

The formal definition of a generalized explanation given in Section 2 captures O'Rorke's notion of correctness since it requires the global substitution γ to be the most general substitution that makes all equivalent expressions in the explanation structure identical. Based on known properties of unification, it is easy to prove the following theorem.

Theorem 1: Given an explanation and its corresponding explanation structure, the single unification algorithm produces a correct generalized explanation that is unique except for alphabetic variants.

Proof: Since unification produces the most general substitution that makes two expressions identical (as proved in [28]), the single unification algorithm is guaranteed to produce the most general substitution γ which makes all of the equivalent expressions in the explanation structure identical. Therefore, by definition, applying this substitution to the explanation results in a generalized explanation. Since a most general unifier is unique except for alphabetic variants, the generalized explanation is also unique except for alphabetic variants.

A proof that any of the individual algorithms given in Section 3 produce a generalized explanation could be constructed by proving that the algorithm is equivalent to the single unification algorithm. As previously mentioned, for the EGGS algorithm, this proof would involve proving the correctness of the unification algorithm in [24].

If it is assumed that explanations are logical proofs (as in [2]), one can also easily prove *soundness*, that is, that the learned macro–rule is logically entailed by the existing domain theory.

Theorem 2: A macro–rule extracted from a generalized explanation composed of Horn clauses is logically entailed by the Horn clauses in the domain theory.

Proof: By definition, all of the equivalent expressions in a generalized explanation must be identical. Since all of the Horn clauses in the generalized explanation are instantiations of clauses in the domain theory (i.e., they are the result of applying the global substitution to the explanation structure), the logically sound inference rule of *universal instantiation* guarantees that they are entailed by the domain theory. Finally, one needs to show that computing a macro–rule is simply performing logically sound deduction on the Horn clauses in the generalized explanation. If

$$k_1 \cdots k_{i-1} \wedge k_i \wedge k_{i+1} \cdots k_n \rightarrow c$$

and

$$l_1 \wedge \cdots \wedge l_n \rightarrow d$$

are two clauses in the generalized explanation, and d is equivalent to k_i, then d and k_i must be identical expressions. Assume the second clause is removed from the generalized explanation and the first clause is replaced by

$$k_1 \cdots k_{i-1} \wedge l_1 \wedge \cdots \wedge l_n \wedge k_{i+1} \cdots k_n \rightarrow c$$

Since d and k_i are identical expressions, the added clause is entailed by the domain theory because it is the resolvent of the two clauses and the resolution rule is sound [28]. Repeating this process for every set of equivalent expressions reduces the generalized explanation to the desired macro–rule. Since all of the clauses in the original generalized explanation are entailed by the domain theory, and since the clause added by each step in the reduction process is entailed by the existing clauses, by induction the completely reduced generalized explanation (i.e., the learned macro–rule) is entailed by the domain theory.

If it could be proven that a generalization algorithm such as EGGS or PROLOG–EBG computes the correct global substitution and is therefore equivalent to the single unification algorithm, then it would follow that the algorithm also produced a sound macro–rule. Once again, for EGGS, this would involve proving that the unification algorithm in [24] is correct.

Recently, a couple of additional approaches to proving the correctness of algorithms for generalizing logical proofs have been developed. In [29, 30], a definition and proof of correctness is based on showing that the generalization algorithm computes the set of *weakest preconditions* of a proof. In [31], a correctness proof for explanation–based generalization as resolution theorem proving is presented. The generalization algorithm proved correct in this chapter is similar to PROLOG–EBG, but it is a separate process for generalizing resolution proof trees and is not integrated with a theorem prover.

6. Computational Complexity of Explanation Generalization

The single unification generalization algorithm also demonstrates that the time complexity of producing a global substitution is linear in the size of the explanation since linear time algorithms exist for unification [32]. Since unification can be performed in linear time, obviously the size of the resulting MGU must also be linear in the size of the explanation since only a linear amount of output can be produced in linear time. Therefore, if $|E|$ represents the size of the explanation, we can let $c_1|E|$ be the time required to construct the global substitution and $c_2|E|$ be the length of the global substitution. Since the time complexity of applying a substitution to an expression is also linear in the length of its inputs,[5] let $c_3(c_2 |\, E\, | + |\, E\, |)$ be the time required to apply the global substitution to the explanation. Therefore, the time required for the complete process of constructing a generalized explanation is

$$c_3(c_2 |\, E\, | + |\, E\, |) + c_1 |\, E\, | = (c_1 + c_3(c_2 + 1)) |\, E\, |$$

which is clearly linear in size of the explanation.

Although this result does not reveal the time complexity of the individual algorithms in Section 3, it is a constructive proof of the existence of a linear–time explanation generalizing algorithm. Since linear–time unification algorithms have apparently found limited use in practice due to large overhead, it is unlikely that a generalizing algorithm based on one would be particularly useful in practice. Nevertheless, it is an interesting theoretical result which supports the important claim that a generalized explanation can be computed very efficiently.

In practice, the generalizing algorithms given in Section 3 are quite efficient using a standard (nonlinear time) unifier. For example, one of the largest explanations upon which EGGS has been tested had 25 equalities and took only 3.6 seconds of CPU time to generalize on a Xerox 1108.

7. Pruning Explanations for Operationality

Often, the explanation structure for a particular example is too specific to support a reasonably useful generalization. In these cases, the *operationality criterion* [2] is met by nodes higher in the explanation tree than the leaves, and it is advisable to *prune* units from the explanation structure that are more specific than required for operationality. The goal of pruning is to make an explanation (and resulting macro–rule) as general as possible while still keeping it *operational*, that is, useful and efficient for the purpose of classifying future examples or solving future problems. If this pruning is done prior to generalization as shown in Figure 2–1, it will result in a more abstract generalized explanation which is applicable to a broader range of examples. For example, if the rule for inferring Graspable is removed from the explanation structure shown in Figure 2–4, the following more general (but less operational) definition of Cup is acquired:

Bottom(?y1) $\wedge$ PartOf(?y1,?x1) $\wedge$ Flat(?y1) $\wedge$ Graspable(?x1) $\wedge$ Light(?x1)

---

[5]The literature on linear unification does not discuss linear time substitution application; however, a linear time algorithm for this procedure is presented in [20].

$\wedge$ Concavity(?y3) $\wedge$ PartOf(?y3,?x1) $\wedge$ UpwardPointing(?y3) $\rightarrow$ Cup(?x1)

Determining the appropriate operationality criterion has been the subject of much discussion in the EBL literature [1, 2, 33–36]. For most domains, there is generally a trade–off that must be resolved between operationality and generality. A more general explanation is useful in a larger set of future situations; however, it is normally also harder to apply in those situations. A more specific explanation, on the other hand, is generally easier to apply to future situations; however, it is less applicable. In the long run, it is probably best to retain explanations at several levels of generality as suggested in [37] and as done in the PHYSICS101 system [35]. This allows a more specific explanation to be used when it is applicable while still permitting a more general explanation to be used when a more operational one is not available.

A recent suggestion for determining operationality is the one used in ARMS, an EBL system for robotics [34]. It involves pruning all of the explanation below *shared substructure*. In terms of the representations used here, this approach would prune all nodes below the point where a subgraph of the explanation becomes a tree as opposed to a general directed acyclical graph. In other words, it keeps pruning leaves of the explanation until a node is found that supports more than one other node. Although this pruning algorithm may work well for the ARMS domain, it is not a general solution to the problem of determining operationality. Many explanations that support useful generalizations do not have any shared substructure. In fact, most of the examples of explanations on which EGGS has been tested are trees and consequently do not have shared substructure. The ARMS approach to pruning would remove the entire explanation in such cases and consequently miss the opportunity to learn useful new rules and operators.

Therefore, determining which predicates or operators are operational is now generally a domain–dependent decision. Consequently, the current EGGS system simply has a hook that allows an arbitrary pruning function to be called before an explanation is generalized. In Hirsh's MRS–EBG system [5], meta–level logical deduction is used to determine operationality. This approach has the advantage of allowing operationality proofs themselves to be generalized in an explanation–based manner in order to determine the most general operational explanation.

8. Integrating Explanation Construction, Pruning, and Generalization

Instead of performing the first three steps in Figure 2-1 sequentially, these steps can often be integrated and performed in an interleaved fashion. As discussed in [1, 3], the EGGS generalization algorithm is easily integrated with the explanation-building process by updating the global substitution each time a new rule is added to the evolving explanation. As mentioned earlier, PROLOG-EBG elegantly integrates generalization with the theorem-proving process, and MRS-EBG elegantly integrates both of these processes with pruning the explanation for operationality.

Although integrating these processes is aesthetically appealing, there is a price associated with it. For example, the integration of theorem proving and generalization in PROLOG-EBG and MRS-EBG involves unnecessarily generalizing dead-end branches of the search tree that are eventually abandoned and never become part of the final proof. If generalization were postponed until the final proof is available, this useless computation could be avoided. However, as noted in [5], integrating generalization and theorem proving can still be useful when there are multiple possible explanations for the specific example, only some of which are operational. In this case, integrated generalization, theorem proving, and operationality checking allows theorem proving to continue until an operational proof is eventually found.

Another problem with integration is that in many cases operationality cannot be determined until the complete explanation is available. When learning by observing the problem-solving behavior of an external agent, the eventual goal to be achieved is generally unknown until all of the agent's actions have been observed. However, the pruning algorithm often requires knowledge of the goal. Consequently, in these situations, pruning must be postponed until the complete explanation has been constructed. If generalization is performed before pruning, the resulting generalization may be too specific since it may incorporate constraints introduced by the pruned parts of the explanation. Therefore, when pruning must be performed after the explanation is complete, generalization and explanation cannot be easily integrated. As discussed in [1], if generalization and explanation are integrated, additional constraints introduced by pruned portions of the explanation can later be retracted; however, retracting equality constraints is very difficult and requires the capabilities of a truth maintenance system (TMS) [22]. The MA system [7] is an example of an EBL system that uses a TMS [38] to retract co-reference constraints; however, this system is very inefficient compared to simpler systems based on unification.

A final advantage of a separate and independent generalization process is that it does not constrain the process of explanation construction. Generalizers that are integrated with theorem provers, like PROLOG–EBG and MRS–EBG, require that explanations be constructed by the theorem prover. This process prevents the use of alternative methods of explanation construction such as building explanations by understanding the actions of an external agent.

Therefore, despite the aesthetic appeal of integration, it entails a number of important problems, but they are easily resolved by requiring a separate, independent generalization process. As a result, explanation construction, pruning, and generalization are performed sequentially in the EGGS system, as shown in Figure 2–1.

9. Explanation Generalization Versus Chunking and Production Composition

Explanation–based learning of macro–rules and macro–operators is closely related to production system learning mechanisms that compose production rules. The *chunking* process in SOAR [18, 39, 40] and the *knowledge compilation* process of *composition* in ACT* [19, 41] are two similar production system learning models. Both processes build macro–productions based on traces of productions produced by the problem solver when solving a particular problem.

Besides the fact that these systems, unlike STRIPS, EBG, and EGGS, do not rely on a logic–based representation, their primary difference lies in their less analytical generalization process. SOAR's generalization algorithm is described in detail in [42], where it is compared and contrasted to EBG. The generalization process is basically one of changing constants to independent variables. However, due to the difference in representation language, the problem of overgeneralization mentioned in Section 3.1 is avoided. Constants in SOAR come in two types: *identifiers*, which are symbols for particular objects, and more meaningful constants such as "5" and "blue." For example, representing the logical assertion $Color(\beta,blue)$ requires creating an extra identifier for the constant "blue" and using the two assertions $Color(\beta,\varsigma)$ and $Name(\varsigma, blue)$. The generalization process in SOAR changes only identifiers to variables, and since production rules cannot check for particular identifiers, the over–generalization problem is avoided. The cost incurred for avoiding the problem in this manner is an extra distinction in the representation language.

However, the problem of undergeneralization mentioned in Section 3.1 remains. For example, in the SOAR formulation of the Safe–To–Stack example (an example from [2]) presented by Rosenbloom and Laird [42], the rule learned is

$$\text{Volume}(x,v) \wedge \text{Density}(x,d) \wedge \text{Name}(y,\text{endtable}) \wedge \text{Product}(v,d,d)$$
$$\wedge \text{Less}(d,w) \wedge \text{Name}(w,5) \rightarrow \text{Safe–To–Stack}(x,y)$$

As noted in [42], this rule is an undergeneralization since it requires the density and the weight of the of object being stacked to be the same (i.e., d). Since the box in the example just happened to have the same weight and density, the simple variablization process requires them to be the same. For the same reason, the initial and final rooms would unnecessarily be required to be the same if this technique were applied to the STRIPS example. Retaining such spurious features of the example in the generalization is a basic violation of the explanation–based approach. EBL stipulates that only those constraints required to maintain the validity of the solution should be incorporated in the generalization.

In response to the problem of undergeneralization, Rosenbloom and Laird [42] stated, "If an example were run in which the density and the weight were different, then a rule would be learned to deal with future situations in which they were different" (p. 564). However, if the more general rule were learned from the original example, this new example could be solved more quickly by using the learned rule. Also, unless a check is made to remove subsumed rules (i.e., rules that are specializations of existing rules), this solution leaves useless rules lying around that decrease performance by increasing the number of rules the system must check for application. Rosenbloom and Laird also stated "The SOAR approach to goal regression is simpler, and focuses on the information in working memory rather than the possibly complex patterns specified by the rules" (p. 564). If the problems with a simple constant to variable generalization algorithm were offset by a marked increased in efficiency of generalization, then perhaps a case could be made for the simpler generalization process. However, as shown in Section 6, the computational complexity of a unification–based generalization algorithm is linear in the size of the explanation. Since simply tracing through the complete explanation to replace each constant with a variable is also a linear process, the gain in efficiency is at most a constant factor.

Of course, SOAR could probably be modified to include a generalizer that prevents undergeneralization. This process would require retaining copies of the general parameterized productions (with unique variables) in the production traces produced during problem solving. Generalization would then require constructing the most general set of variable bindings that allows all of the left–hand sides of general productions to match the right–hand sides of the general productions that they support in the production trace. A procedure analogous to unification for matching production conditions could be used to produce the required global substitution.

Finally, regarding composition in ACT*, discussions of the underlying generalization process in *production composition* [19, 41, 43, 44] fail to give explicit details of the generalization algorithm. However, the fact that no mention is made of the subtleties of generalization, the limits of simply changing constants to variables, or the use of a generalizer that analyzes variable bindings indicates that a more analytic generalizer is not used. Also, the examples given of composition involving telephone dialing [43], geometry problem solving [19, 44], and LISP programming [19, 41, 45] can all be accomplished by simply changing constants to variables.

10. Horn Clause Proof Explanations in EGGS

For dealing with explanations composed of Horn clauses, the complete EGGS system is equipped with general purpose subsystems for proving theorems, understanding incomplete proofs, and generating macro–rules. Figure 2–15 illustrates how these components combine with the generalizer to comprise a complete learning system. The theorem prover and proof verifier allow EGGS to construct explanations by either proving theorems itself or by filling in gaps in sketchy proofs provided by the user. These explanations can then be generalized using the EGGS generalization algorithm, resulting in macro–rules that can be used to construct and understand similar proofs more efficiently.

The Horn clause theorem prover in EGGS is a depth–first, backward–chaining system (like PROLOG) based on the deductive retriever given in [24]. The retriever can be given a depth bound, d, to prevent it from chaining more than d rules deep when attempting to retrieve a particular fact. When a macro–rule is learned, it is added to the front of the current list of rules so that the retriever attempts to use it before resorting to the initial domain theory.

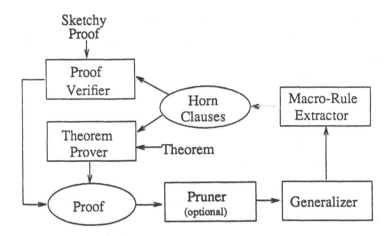

Figure 2–15: EGGS Architecture for Horn Clause Proof Explanations

The deductive retriever can also be used to fill in gaps in sketchy proofs given to the system. Sketchy proofs are ordered sequences of subgoals or lemmas to be proven before attempting to prove the ultimate goal. The system attempts to prove that each step in the proof follows deductively from the initial facts together with the facts deduced in previous steps. If it can safely be assumed that the sketchy proof will not be missing more than d inferences between steps, then the depth bound on the prover can be set to d during verification. This allows proof verification to be much more efficient than theorem proving.[6]

If the EGGS system is used solely as an independent theorem prover that learns macro–rules, it closely resembles a learning PROLOG interpreter, like that described by Prieditus and Mostow [46]. If, on the other hand, it is used to analyze sample proofs and learn macro–rules from them, it behaves more like a learning apprentice system [11, 16]. The important thing to note, however, is that the same generalization algorithm underlies both approaches to learning.

EGGS has been tested on a wide variety of examples that employ explanations based on Horn clauses, including robot planning in a "blocks world" [8], solving symbolic integration problems [9], learning artifact descriptions [10], designing logic circuits [16], and proving theorems in logic [11] and geometry [44]. The following subsection presents an

---

[6]See Mooney [20] for an analysis of the computational complexity of proof verification.

example from one of these domains.

10.1. MA Example

An explanation–based learning system in the domain of logic theorem proving is MA [7, 11], which learns proof schemata from sample natural deduction proofs. When the system cannot complete a proof for a particular theorem, a teacher steps in and completes the proof. MA then generalizes the teacher's proof in an explanation–based manner to generate a proof schema that can be used to solve future problems. Consider a variant of the example discussed in [11] of proving a particular case of the law of excluded middle: $NIL \Rightarrow (P \wedge Q) \vee \neg (P \wedge Q)$ (i.e., $(P \wedge Q) \vee \neg (P \wedge Q)$ can be deduced from the empty set of assumptions). The natural deduction proof the deductive retriever generates for this example is shown in Figure 2–16. The following rules of natural deduction [47] are employed in this proof:

Assumption Axiom: $(?x \; . \; ?y) \Rightarrow ?x$
Or Introduction: $?x \Rightarrow ?y \rightarrow ?x \Rightarrow ?y \vee ?z$
Or Introduction: $?x \Rightarrow ?y \rightarrow ?x \Rightarrow ?z \vee ?y$
Elimination Of Assumption: $(?x \; . \; ?y) \Rightarrow ?z \wedge (\neg ?x \; . \; ?y) \Rightarrow ?z \rightarrow ?y \Rightarrow ?z$

The expression $?x \Rightarrow ?y$ means that the wff $?y$ is deducible from the list of assumptions (wffs) $?x$. LISP *dot notation* is used to represent lists of assumptions. The generalized proof EGGS generates for this example is shown in Figure 2–17. From a specific instance of proving $(P \wedge Q) \vee \neg (P \wedge Q)$ from no assumptions, a general proof is learned for proving the disjunction of any wff and its negation from any set of assumptions. Notice again that simply changing the constants P and Q to variables would have resulted in an undergeneralization. The more general fact learned by EGGS allows it to solve the test problem: $NIL \Rightarrow P \vee \neg P$ in one step.

The same proof and generalization result from understanding the following sketchy proof:

$((P \wedge Q)) \Rightarrow (P \wedge Q) \vee \neg (P \wedge Q)$
$(\neg (P \wedge Q)) \Rightarrow (P \wedge Q) \vee \neg (P \wedge Q)$
$Q.E.D.: NIL \Rightarrow (P \wedge Q) \vee \neg (P \wedge Q)$

If the depth bound on the deductive retriever is set to two, explaining this proof takes only 4.5 CPU seconds compared to proving the theorem directly, which takes 9 CPU seconds with a depth bound of three, 18.5

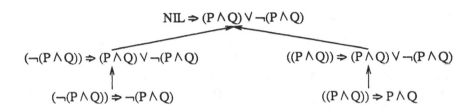

$$\text{NIL} \Rightarrow (P \wedge Q) \vee \neg(P \wedge Q)$$

$$(\neg(P \wedge Q)) \Rightarrow (P \wedge Q) \vee \neg(P \wedge Q) \qquad ((P \wedge Q)) \Rightarrow (P \wedge Q) \vee \neg(P \wedge Q)$$

$$(\neg(P \wedge Q)) \Rightarrow \neg(P \wedge Q) \qquad ((P \wedge Q)) \Rightarrow P \wedge Q$$

Figure 2–16: MA Example — Specific Explanation

$$?y17 \Rightarrow ?y16 \vee \neg ?y16$$

$$(?y16 \,.\, ?y17) \Rightarrow ?y16 \vee \neg ?y16 \qquad (\neg ?y16 \,.\, ?y17) \Rightarrow ?y16 \vee \neg ?y16$$

$$(?y16 \,.\, ?y17) \Rightarrow ?y16 \qquad (\neg ?y16 \,.\, ?y17) \Rightarrow \neg ?y16$$

Figure 2–17: MA Example — Generalized Explanation

CPU seconds with a depth bound of five, and 759 CPU seconds with a depth bound of ten! This simply demonstrates that, as expected, understanding a proof can be much more efficient than independently discovering one. After learning the macro–rule, the theorem can be proved in only 0.53 CPU second. Therefore, EGGS can be up to 1,432 times faster at proving a theorem after learning than before.

11. Rewrite Rule Explanations in EGGS

Compared to using logical deduction, many mathematical problems can be represented more concisely and solved more efficiently by using *rewrite rules* to perform term rewriting [48]. Like logical proofs, chains of rewrite rule applications can be represented as explanations. Each rewritten term is an expression in the explanation, and the chaining together of two rules is represented by a unification between the right–hand side (RHS) of the first rule and the left–hand side (LHS) of the second.

Figure 2–18 illustrates the components in EGGS that use and learn rewrite rules. The rewrite rule engine allows EGGS to construct rewrite rule explanations by solving problems itself. These explanations can then be generalized, resulting in macro–rules that can be used to solve similar problems more efficiently. EGGS has been tested on a number of examples which employ explanations based on rewrite rules. These include

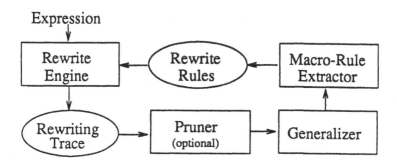

Figure 2–18: EGGS Architecture for Rewrite Rule Explanations

examples involving solving symbolic integration problems [9], designing logic circuits [16], and solving algebraic equations [13]. The following subsection presents an example from one of these domains.

11.1. LEAP Example

The LEAP system [16] is a learning apprentice in VLSI design which observes the behavior of a circuit designer. It attempts to learn in an explanation–based fashion by observing and analyzing specific examples of logic design. As an example of learning in this domain, consider the following example taken from [16]. Given the task of implementing a circuit that computes the logical function (a ∨ b) ∧ (c ∨ d), a circuit designer creates a circuit consisting of three NOR gates like that shown in Figure 2–19. The system attempts to verify that the given circuit actually computes the desired function. The explanation constructed by EGGS' rewrite engine showing that the circuit computes the desired function is shown in Figure 2–20. In this example, the domain knowledge available to the

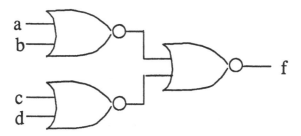

Figure 2–19: Circuit Design Learning Problem

system includes the following rewrite rules:

$$\neg\neg?x \to ?x$$
$$\neg(?x \vee ?y) \to \neg?x \wedge \neg?y$$

The explanation structure and generalized explanation for this example are shown in Figure 2–21 and Figure 2–22, respectively. Notice that if a rule rewrites only a subterm of an expression, "dummy variables" are added to the pattern in the explanation structure to fill out the expression so that it can be unified with the previous expression. LISP list notation is used in the illustration of the explanation structure since the technique used to add dummy variables relies on the underlying list representation. For example, after applying DeMorgan's law in the LEAP problem, the rule for eliminating a double negation is used to rewrite the first term in the resulting conjunction. In order to allow the LHS of this rule to unify with the RHS of the instance of DeMorgan's law in the explanation structure, this rule is padded with the dummy variables ?f1 and ?f2. During generalization, this unification results in the following substitution:

$$\{and/?f1,\ not(?x2)/?x1,\ (not(?y1))/?f2\}$$

Next, the rule for eliminating a double negation is used to rewrite the second term in the conjunction, and this instance of the rule is padded with the dummy variables ?f3, ?f4, and ?f5 in order to allow its LHS to unify with the previous instance. During generalization, this unification results in the following substitution:

$$\{and/?f3,\ ?f4/?x2,\ not(?x3)/?y1,\ NIL/?f5\}$$

Applying the composition of these two substitutions to the explanation structure results in the generalized explanation shown in Figure 2–22.

$$\neg(\neg(a \vee b) \vee \neg(c \vee d))$$
$$\downarrow$$
$$\neg(\neg(a \vee b)) \wedge \neg(\neg(c \vee d))$$
$$\downarrow$$
$$(a \vee b) \wedge \neg(\neg(c \vee d))$$
$$\downarrow$$
$$(a \vee b) \wedge (c \vee d)$$

Figure 2–20: LEAP Rewrite — Specific Explanation

The new rewrite rule macro–rule learned from the LEAP example is

$$\neg(\neg ?f4 \vee \neg ?x3) \rightarrow ?f4 \wedge ?x3$$

Once again, had generalization been performed by simply changing constants to variables, the result would have been overly specific. As a result of the explanation–based approach, the resulting generalization is not sensitive to the fact that the first stage of the circuit involved two NOR

(not (or ?x1 ?y1))
↓
(and (not ?x1) (not ?y1))
|||
(?f1 (not (not ?x2)) . ?f2)
↓
(?f1 ?x2 . ?f2)
|||
(?f3 ?f4 (not (not ?x3)) . ?f5)
↓
(?f3 ?f4 ?x3 . ?f5)

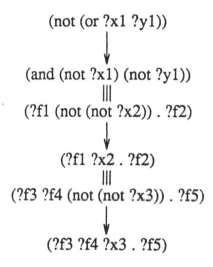

Figure 2–21: LEAP Rewrite — Explanation Structure

$\neg(\neg(?f4)\vee\neg(?x3))$
↓
$\neg(\neg(?f4))\wedge\neg(\neg(?x3))$
↓
$?f4\wedge\neg(\neg(?x3))$
↓
$?f4\wedge ?x3$

Figure 2–22: LEAP Rewrite — Generalized Explanation

gates.

12. Conclusions

This chapter has presented the EGGS system as a general domain–independent explanation–based learning system which has been tested on many examples in a variety of domains. Numerous other applications of EGGS as well as empirical data on the effect of learned macro–rules on future problem–solving performance are presented in Mooney [20].

The explanation generalization algorithm in EGGS was compared to generalization algorithms in other systems such as STRIPS, PROLOG–EBG, and SOAR. STRIPS, EGGS, and PROLOG–EBG were all informally shown to produce generalized explanations (as defined in Section 2); however, SOAR was shown to be susceptible to under-generalization. Unlike other generalizers that are tied to a particular representation of explanations, such as STRIPS plans (STRIPS) or Horn clause proofs (PROLOG–EBG), the EGGS system was shown to be capable of generalizing explanations composed of Horn clauses, STRIPS operators, *and* rewrite rules. Finally, several arguments were given for preferring an independent generalization process (as in EGGS) instead of integrating generalization with theorem proving (as in PROLOG–EBG). A primary advantage of an independent generalizer is that it allows learning from observed problem–solving behavior as well as internally generated problem solutions.

The chapter also analyzed the correctness and the computational complexity of explanation generalization, demonstrating the existence of a correct and sound generalization algorithm with linear time complexity. Although other research in explanation generalization has also addressed the issue of correctness [29, 31], the issue of computational complexity has not been addressed elsewhere.

The approach to explanation generalization taken in EGGS has served as a foundation for a number of explanation–based learning systems investigating advanced issues in EBL. The research presented in most of the remaining chapters of this book rely on the method of explanation generalization outlined in this chapter.

References

1.   G. F. DeJong and R. J. Mooney, "Explanation–Based Learning: An Alternative View," *Machine Learning 1*, 2 (1986), pp. 145–176.

2.   T. M. Mitchell, R. Keller and S. Kedar–Cabelli, "Explanation–Based Generalization: A Unifying View," *Machine Learning 1*, 1 (January

1986), pp. 47–80.

3. R. J. Mooney and S. W. Bennett, "A Domain Independent Explanation–Based Generalizer," *Proceedings of the National Conference on Artificial Intelligence*, Philadelphia, PA, August 1986, pp. 551–555.

4. S. T. Kedar–Cabelli and L. T. McCarty, "Explanation–Based Generalization as Resolution Theorem Proving," *Proceedings of the Fourth International Workshop on Machine Learning*, University of California, Irvine, June 1987, pp. 383–389.

5. H. Hirsh, "Explanation–Based Generalization in a Logic–Programming Environment," *Proceedings of the Tenth International Joint Conference on Artificial Intelligence*, Milan, Italy, August 1987, pp. 221–227.

6. S. Minton and J. G. Carbonell, "Strategies for Learning Search Control Rules: An Explanation–based Approach," *Proceedings of the Tenth International Joint Conference on Artificial Intelligence*, Milan, Italy, August 1987, pp. 228–235.

7. P. V. O'Rorke, "Explanation–Based Learning Via Constraint Posting and Propagation," Ph.D. Thesis, Department of Computer Science, University of Illinois, Urbana, IL, January 1987.

8. R. E. Fikes, P. E. Hart and N. J. Nilsson, "Learning and Executing Generalized Robot Plans," *Artificial Intelligence 3*, (1972), pp. 251–288.

9. T. M. Mitchell, "Learning and Problem Solving," *Proceedings of the Eighth International Joint Conference on Artificial Intelligence*, Karlsruhe, West Germany, August 1983, pp. 1139–1151.

10. P. H. Winston, T. O. Binford, B. Katz and M. Lowry, "Learning Physical Descriptions from Functional Definitions, Examples, and Precedents," *Proceedings of the National Conference on Artificial Intelligence*, Washington, D.C., August 1983, pp. 433–439.

11. P. V. O'Rorke, "Generalization for Explanation–based Schema Acquisition," *Proceedings of the National Conference on Artificial Intelligence*, Austin, TX, August 1984, pp. 260–263.

12. S. N. Minton, "Constraint–Based Generalization: Learning Game–Playing Plans from Single Examples," *Proceedings of the National Conference on Artificial Intelligence*, Austin, TX, August 1984, pp. 251–254.

13. B. Silver, "Learning Equation Solving Methods from Worked Examples," *Proceedings of the 1983 International Machine Learning Workshop*, Urbana, IL, June 1983, pp. 99–104.

14. R. J. Mooney and G. F. DeJong, "Learning Schemata for Natural Language Processing," *Proceedings of the Ninth International Joint Conference on Artificial Intelligence*, Los Angeles, CA, August 1985, pp. 681–687.

15. J. W. Shavlik, "Learning about Momentum Conservation," *Proceedings of the Ninth International Joint Conference on Artificial Intelligence*, Los Angeles, CA, August 1985, pp. 667–669.

16. T. M. Mitchell, S. Mahadevan and L. I. Steinberg, "LEAP: A Learning Apprentice for VLSI Design," *Proceedings of the Ninth International Joint Conference on Artificial Intelligence*, Los Angeles, CA, August 1985, pp. 573–580.

17. A. M. Segre and G. F. DeJong, "Explanation Based Manipulator Learning: Acquisition of Planning Ability Through Observation," *Proceedings of the IEEE International Conference on Robotics and Automation*, St. Louis, MO, March 1985, pp. 555–560. (Also appears as Working Paper 62, AI Research Group, Coordinated Science Laboratory, University of Illinois at Urbana–Champaign.)

18. J. E. Laird, P. S. Rosenbloom and A. Newell, *Universal Subgoaling and Chunking: The Automatic Generation and Learning of Goal Hierarchies*, Kluwer Academic Publishers, Norwell, MA, 1986.

19. J. R. Anderson, *The Architecture of Cognition*, Harvard University Press, Cambridge, MA, 1983.

20. R. J. Mooney, "A General Explanation–Based Learning Mechanism and its Application to Narrative Understanding," Ph.D. Thesis, Department of Computer Science, University of Illinois, Urbana, IL, January 1988.

21. N. J. Nilsson, *Principles of Artificial Intelligence*, Tioga Publishing Company, Palo Alto, CA, 1980.

22. J. Doyle, "A Truth Maintenance System," *Artificial Intelligence 12*, 3 (1979), pp. 231–272.

23. R. Waldinger, "Achieving Several Goals Simultaneously," in *Machine Intelligence 8*, E. Elcock and D. Michie (ed.), Ellis Horwood Limited, London, 1977.

24. E. Charniak, C. Riesbeck and D. McDermott, *Artificial Intelligence Programming*, Lawrence Erlbaum and Associates, Hillsdale, NJ, 1980.

25. E. W. Dijkstra, *A Discipline of Programming*, Prentice–Hall, 1976.

26. S. Mahadevan, "Verification–Based Learning: A Generalization Strategy for Inferring Problem–Reduction Methods," *Proceedings of the Ninth International Joint Conference on Artificial Intelligence*, Los Angeles, CA, August 1985, pp. 616–623.

27. S. Russell, "The Compleat Guide to MRS," Technical Report KSL 85–12, Computer Science Department, Stanford University, June 1985.

28. J. A. Robinson, "A Machine–Oriented Logic Based on the Resolution Principle," *Journal of the Association for Computing Machinery 12*, 1 (1965), pp. 23–41.

29. S. Minton, "EBL and Weakest Preconditions," *Proceedings of the AAAI Symposium on Explanation–Based Learning*, Stanford, CA, March 1988, pp. 210–214.

30. S. Minton, "Learning Effective Search Control Knowledge: An Explanation–based Approach," Ph.D. Thesis CMU–CS–88–133 , Department of Computer Science, Carnegie–Mellon University, Pittsburgh, PA, March 1988.

31. N. Bhatnagar, "A Correctness Proof of Explanation–Based Generalization as Resolution Theorem–Proving," *Proceedings of the AAAI Symposium on Explanation–Based Learning*, Stanford, CA, March 1988, pp. 220–225.

32. M. S. Paterson and M. N. Wegman, "Linear Unification," *Journal of Computer and System Sciences 16*, (1978), pp. 158–167.

33. R. M. Keller, "Defining Operationality for Explanation–Based Learning," *Proceedings of the National Conference on Artificial Intelligence*, Seattle, WA, July 1987, pp. 482–487.

34. A. M. Segre, "On the Operationality/Generality Trade–off in Explanation–Based Learning," *Proceedings of the Tenth International Joint Conference on Artificial Intelligence*, Milan, Italy, August 1987, pp. 242–248.

35. J. W. Shavlik, G. F. DeJong and B. H. Ross, "Acquiring Special Case Schemata in Explanation–Based Learning," *Proceedings of the Ninth Annual Conference of the Cognitive Science Society*, Seattle,

WA, July 1987, pp. 851–860.

36. R. Keller, "Operationality and Generality in Explanation–Based Learning: Separate Dimensions or Opposite Endpoints?," *Proceedings of the AAAI Symposium on Explanation–Based Learning*, Stanford, CA, March 1988, pp. 153–157.

37. R. J. Mooney, "Generalizing Explanations of Narratives into Schemata," M.S. Thesis, Department of Computer Science, University of Illinois, Urbana, IL, May 1985.

38. D. A. McAllester, "Reasoning Utility Package User's Manual, Version One," Memo 667, MIT AI Lab, Cambridge, MA, April 1982.

39. J. Laird, P. Rosenbloom and A. Newell, "Towards Chunking as a General Learning Mechanism," *Proceedings of the National Conference on Artificial Intelligence*, Austin, TX, August 1984, pp. 188–192.

40. J. Laird, P. Rosenbloom and A. Newell, "Chunking in Soar: The Anatomy of a General Learning Mechanism," *Machine Learning 1*, 1 (1986), pp. 11–46.

41. J. R. Anderson, "Knowledge Compilation: The General Learning Mechanism," in *Machine Learning: An Artificial Intelligence Approach, Vol. II*, R. S. Michalski, J. G. Carbonell and T. M. Mitchell (ed.), MORGAN, 1986, pp. 289–309.

42. P. Rosenbloom and J. Laird, "Mapping Explanation–Based Generalization into Soar," *Proceedings of the National Conference on Artificial Intelligence*, Philadelphia, PA, August 1986, pp. 561–567.

43. J. R. Anderson, "Acquisition of Cognitive Skill," *Psychological Review 89*, 4 (1982), pp. 369–406.

44. J. R. Anderson, "Acquisition of Proof Skills in Geometry," in *Machine Learning: An Artificial Intelligence Approach*, R. S. Michalski, J. G. Carbonell, T. M. Mitchell (ed.), Tioga Publishing Company, Palo Alto, CA, 1983, pp. 191–221.

45. J. R. Anderson and R. Thompson, "Use of Analogy in a Production System Architecture," in *Similarity and Analogical Reasoning*, S. Vosniadou and A. Ortony (ed.), Cambridge University Press, Cambridge, England, 1989.

46. A. E. Prieditis and J. Mostow, "PROLEARN: Towards a Prolog Interpreter that Learns," *Proceedings of the National Conference on*

Artificial Intelligence, Seattle, WA, July 1987, pp. 494–498.

47. Z. Manna, *Mathematical Theory of Computation*, McGraw–Hill, New York, NY, 1974.

48. A. Bundy, *The Computer Modelling of Mathematical Reasoning*, Academic Press, New York, NY, 1983.

Chapter 3

Generalizing Explanation Structures

Jude W. Shavlik and
Raymond J. Mooney

1. Introduction

The generalization algorithm given in Chapter 2 is not sufficient for all types of generalization. The EGGS algorithm and the similar EBG algorithm [1] are not capable of significantly altering the structure of the explanation. Nonetheless, such structural alteration is a distinguishing and crucial step in several noteworthy types of generalization. Of the three types of structural generalization discussed in Chapter 1 — disjunctive augmentation, temporal generalization, and number generalization — our research addresses aspects of the latter two. Disjunctive augmentation, while important, is judged not to be as crucial or as challenging as the other two. If the EBL approach cannot overcome the demands of temporal and number generalization, the system profits little from disjunctive augmentation.

With number generalization, an EBL system can represent in a single knowledge chunk what would otherwise require a large, possibly infinite, set of similar chunks. Thus number generalization has important implications for the knowledge representation and expressive power of EBL–acquired knowledge chunks. Temporal generalization is an important area in the AI realm of planning and problem solving. We believe it will be of increasing interest as EBL research matures.

Neither research effort should be seen as the last word on its topic; each discusses open and future problems. Although the solution to the number generalization problem is quite general, our temporal generalization research is limited to temporal ordering of actions represented as STRIPS operators with complete add and delete lists.

2. Temporal Generalization

A number of explanation–based learning systems have been constructed which learn *macro–operators* or *plan schemata*, that is, general compositions of actions which achieve a goal. The learning of macro-operators has been applied to a variety of domains including robot planning [2], puzzle solving [3, 4], and natural language text understanding

[5]. Recent explanation–based learning systems which operate in plan–based domains have addressed a variety of issues involving the learning of macro–operators. These issues include determining which macro–operators to learn [6], determining the appropriate level of generality for macro–operators [7], and learning iterative macro–operators (see Section 3). However, an issue which has not been addressed in other research is generalizing the temporal order of operators in a plan and thereby learning macro–operators which have partially ordered actions. Previous macro–operator learning systems maintained the ordering of operators present in a specific training example and consequently could acquire only plans represented as linear sequences of actions.

This section describes a procedure which generalizes the order of operators in plans composed of STRIPS operators [2] and thereby learns macro–operators with partially ordered actions. This procedure has been implemented as part of the EGGS domain–independent explanation–based learning system presented in Chapter 2. In addition to the normal process of explanation generalization, EGGS is capable of computing the most general partial ordering of the actions in the plan within the constraint that the *structure* of the original explanation be maintained. In a plan–based domain, the structure of an explanation refers to the manner in which the effects of actions fulfill preconditions of subsequent actions. Generalizing the order of actions frequently results in a more general macro–operator which can be used to solve a larger class of problems.

2.1. An Example

A simple illustration of the advantage of learning macro–operators with partially ordered actions involves assignment statements in a programming language. In the domain of programming for parallel machines, knowing the most general partial ordering of a set of operators which achieves a goal is very important. Operators without an ordering imposed on them can be executed in parallel; knowing the most general partial ordering allows one to obtain the maximum amount of parallelism.

Given the STRIPS operator for an assignment statement shown in Table 3-1, consider the problem of achieving the goal Value(A,2) $\land$ Value(C,4) given the initial state Value(A,1), Value(B,2), Value(C,3), and Value(D,4). Assume that the plan of sequentially executing the operators Setq(A,B) and Setq(C,D) is either observed or generated to solve this specific problem. Figure 3-1 shows the explanation for how this plan achieves the specified goal. Performing standard explanation

Table 1: Variable Assignment Actions		
Action	Preconditions	Effects
Setq(?a,?b)	Value(?a,?x) Value(?b,?y)	Value(?a,?y) ¬Value(?a,?x)

generalization which maintains unifications between effects and preconditions (see Chapter 2) results in the generalized explanation shown in Figure 3–2.

In most cases, the two assignment operators in the generalized plan (i.e., Setq(?a1,?b1) and Setq(?a2,?b2)) can be executed in parallel and should not have an ordering constraint imposed on them. For example, in the original problem, the two assignments Setq(A,B) and Setq(C,D) could be executed simultaneously. However, consider achieving the goal

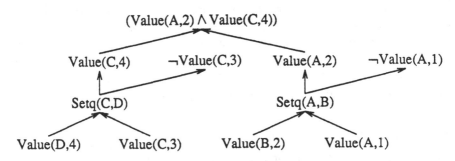

Figure 3–1:   Variable Assignment Example — Specific Explanation

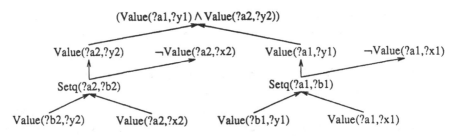

Figure 3–2:   Variable Assignment Example — Generalized Explanation

Value(A,3) $\wedge$ Value(C,4) given the same initial state. The operator sequence Setq(A,C), Setq(C,D) will achieve this goal; however, in this case, the sequential ordering of the operators is crucial. The operator Setq(C,D) must be executed after Setq(A,C) or else the value of C will be reset before it is referenced. In the planning literature, this problem is generally referred to as a *protection violation* since the state Value(C,3) must be protected until it is needed as a precondition for Setq(A,C). Whenever ?b1=?a2 or ?b2=?a1 in an instantiation of the "double Setq" macro–operator, an ordering constraint must be imposed on the two assignment statements in order to prevent a protection violation. As this example illustrates, determining the conditions under which protection violations will occur and imposing appropriate ordering constraints to prevent them is the crucial step in learning a partially ordered macro–operator.

2.2. Plan Explanations in EGGS

The representation of actions used in EGGS for plan–based explanations is a slight variation of STRIPS operators [2]. Actions have *preconditions*, facts that must be true in order to perform the action, and *effects*, facts that are true after the action is performed. Both *add* and *delete* items are included in the effects; delete items simply have an explicit negation. Existing facts that are not explicitly negated by the effects of an action continue to be true. Definitions of the actions used in the standard STRIPS example discussed in Chapter 2 are shown in Table 3-2. Departure from standard STRIPS operators which use separate add and delete lists allows a distinction between facts known to be false and facts simply not known to be true, because facts known to be false (i.e., deleted facts) are explicitly asserted as negations in the database. This in turn allows for negative preconditions that can check whether a fact is known to be false and allows positive effects to directly delete negative facts in the database.

Horn clause rules can be used to prove preconditions or goals from the facts which are true in the current state of the world. Individual actions and Horn clauses form the *units* of an explanation, and explanations are connected sets of actions and rules in which preconditions and antecedents are equated to effects and consequents. The specific explanation, explanation structure, and generalized explanation for the standard STRIPS example are shown in Figures 3–3, 3–4, and 3–5, respectively. In addition to action definitions given in Table 3-2, this example makes use of the following rule: Connects(?d,?r1,?r2) $\rightarrow$ Connects(?d,?r2,?r1), that

Table 2: STRIPS Actions		
Action	Preconditions	Effects
GoThru(?a,?d,?r1,?r2) Agent ?a goes thru door ?d from room ?r1 to room ?r2	InRoom(?a,?r1) Connects(?d,?r1,?r2)	InRoom(?a,?r2) ¬InRoom(?a,?r1)
PushThru(?a,?o,?d,?r1,?r2) Agent ?a pushes object ?o thru door ?d from room ?r1 to room ?r2	InRoom(?a,?r1) InRoom(?o,?r1) Connects(?d,?r1,?r2)	InRoom(?a,?r2) InRoom(?o,?r2) ¬InRoom(?a,?r1) ¬InRoom(?b,?r1)

is, a door connecting room ?r1 to room ?r2 also connects ?r2 to ?r1.

Figure 3–6 illustrates the components in EGGS that use and learn plans. The complete EGGS system is equipped with general–purpose subsystems for verifying or *understanding* plans and a technique for obtaining partially ordered macro–operator definitions from generalized explanations. The current system does not have a planner for independently generating its own plans; however, there are many well–known planning algorithms which could be used for this task [8–10].

Verifying a plan is the task of constructing a complete explanation given a chronologically ordered list of actions. An example of this task is generating the explanation shown in Figure 3–3 given only the following actions:

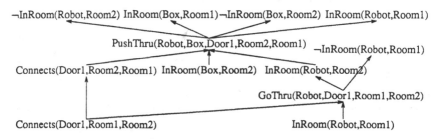

Figure 3–3:   STRIPS Example — Specific Explanation

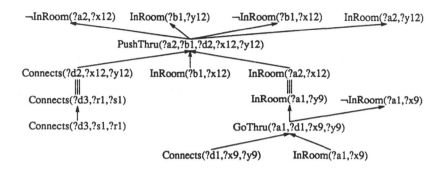

Figure 3-4: STRIPS Example — Explanation Structure

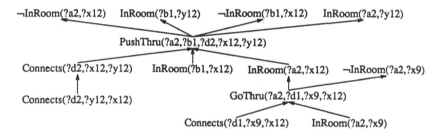

Figure 3-5: STRIPS Example — Generalized Explanation

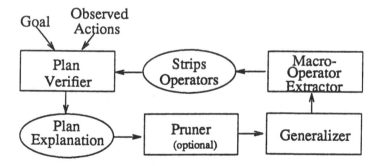

Figure 3-6: EGGS Architecture for Plan Explanations

GoThru(Robot,Door1,Room1,Room2),
PushThru(Robot,Box,Door1,Room2,Room1)

In addition to a set of actions performed, facts describing the initial state of the world and a fact describing the desired state of the world (the goal) may also be provided. The verification process attempts to causally connect these individual actions and states into an explanation that supports the goal (if provided). After an explanation has been constructed, it can be generalized and used to build a macro–operator.

The basic algorithm used in EGGS to explain simple robot plans is outlined in Figure 3–7. The function Retrieve(x) uses the EGGS deductive retriever (see Chapter 2) to try to derive the wff x from known facts. If successful, Retrieve asserts the retrieved fact in the database along with its dependencies and returns the retrieved fact. The function Assert adds a fact in the database, and the function Delete removes a fact from the database.

The explanation procedure is given a chronologically ordered list of facts representing states and actions. If an input is a state, such as InRoom(Box,Room1), and it cannot be inferred from what is already known, then it is simply asserted in the database. If an input is an

```
for x in the list of input wffs do
    if x is a state and ¬Retrieve(x)
        then Assert(x)
    if x is an action
        then
            Assert(x)
            for each precondition p of x do
                let s = Retrieve(p)
                if s
                    then equate p to s
                    else Assert(p)
            for each effect e of x do
                Assert(e)
                let d = Retrieve(¬e)
                if d then Delete(d)
    if goal is known and Retrieve(goal)
        then generalize explanation supporting goal
```

Figure 3–7:   Basic Plan Verification Algorithm

action, then the procedure first tries to infer that its preconditions are met. If a precondition cannot be inferred, then since the action is known to have taken place, it is assumed to be true and asserted in the database. Next, the effects of the input action are asserted and any existing facts that directly contradict them are deleted from the database. After every input, if a goal has been specified, then the system tries to infer that the goal has been met. When the goal has been achieved, the resulting explanation is generalized.

As an example of this process, consider the standard STRIPS example mentioned earlier. In addition to the two actions, assume the system is given the goal InRoom(Box, Room1). Given the input GoThru(Robot, Door1, Room1, Room2), the preconditions InRoom(Robot, Room1) and Connects(Door1, Room1, Room2) cannot be deduced but can be consistently assumed, so they are asserted to be true. The effects of the GoThru: InRoom(Robot, Room2) and ¬InRoom(Robot, Room1) are then asserted. The second effect causes InRoom(Robot, Room1) to be deleted. The system then tries to deduce that the goal, InRoom(Box, Room1), is satisfied, and fails. Next, the input PushThru(Robot, Box, Room2, Room1) is considered. The precondition InRoom(Robot, Room2) was already asserted as an effect of the GoThru, and the precondition Connects(Door1, Room2, Room1) can be deduced from Connects(Door1, Room1, Room2). The precondition InRoom(Box, Room2) is assumed as a necessary precondition for the action. The effects, InRoom(Robot, Room1), InRoom(Box, Room2), ¬InRoom(Robot, Room2), and ¬InRoom(Box, Room2) are asserted and the existing InRoom facts are deleted. The goal is then checked again and this time is successfully retrieved. The resulting explanation, shown in Figure 3–3, is then generalized to produce the generalization shown in Figure 3–5. The same procedure is used to construct the explanation for the Setq example shown in Figure 3–1 given the actions Setq(A,B) and Setq(C,D) and the goal Value(A,2) $\wedge$ Value (C,4).

2.3. Generating Partially Ordered Macro–Operators

The general problem of learning a partially ordered macro–operator as currently solved by the EGGS system can be specified as follows:

Given: Definitions for a set of STRIPS operators and a specific plan composed of instances of these operators that achieves a specific goal.

Determine: A macro–operator for the plan with the most general partial ordering of its operators such that all connections between preconditions and effects present in the original instance are maintained and such that the macro–operator achieves a generalization of the goal achieved by the original instance. Maintaining these two conditions is referred to as maintaining the *explanation structure* of the original plan.

It should be noted that a macro–operator in EGGS is not exactly like a MACROP in STRIPS. STRIPS used a triangle table to effectively store macro–operators for all subsequences of actions in the original plan. A macro–operator in EGGS specifies the complete set of initial preconditions needed to execute all of the actions in the plan and a complete set of effects specifying what is true in the world after all of the actions have been executed. A macro–operator also includes a set of ordering constraints that specify which actions must be executed before other actions.

A macro–operator is also different from a macro–rule learned from a proof in situation calculus which demonstrates that a fact is true in a particular state (see Section 3.1.1). A macro–rule in situation calculus specifies only one effect of a sequence of actions, whereas a macro–operator specifies *all* effects. In addition, terms representing states in situation calculus impose a total ordering on the actions in the plan and cannot represent partially ordered plans. Reordering actions in such a formulation requires completely altering the structure of the existing explanation. Consequently, generalizing the order of actions in such a formulation would be much more difficult.

The algorithm implemented in EGGS for determining a partially ordered macro–operator can be broken down into the following four steps:

(1)   Use the EGGS explanation generalization algorithm to produce a generalized explanation for the specific plan.

(2)   Determine the minimal set of ordering constraints on the operators in the generalized explanation such that the explanation structure is maintained.

(3)   Detect whether subsets of these ordering constraints are inconsistent, and add preconditions to the macro–operator to prevent such inconsistencies.

(4)   Determine the overall preconditions and effects of the final macro–operator.

The first step in this algorithm is standard explanation–based generalization as described in Chapter 2. The generalized explanation that EGGS produces for the Setq example is shown in Figure 3–2. The remaining steps are described in detail in the following subsections.

2.3.1. Determining a Minimal Set of Ordering Constraints

Most ordering constraints in a plan are imposed by one action achieving a precondition for another action. These ordering constraints are captured by the explanation structure of a plan: An action must precede another action if it eventually supports it. Any topologically sorted list of the actions in the generalized explanation graph will be an ordering that satisfies these constraints.[1] In the Setq example, the generalized explanation shown in Figure 3-2 does not impose an ordering on the operators and both permutations are topologically sorted. However, as in this example, some topologically sorted orderings may, in certain situations, result in protection violations in which an action deletes or *clobbers* the ultimate goal or a precondition for a later action.

Preventing protection violations involves determining which facts can be deleted in the general case and detecting deletions of protected facts. Figure 3-8 shows the algorithm implemented in EGGS which determines deletions for the generalized explanation and imposes additional ordering constraints to prevent protection violations. In the algorithm, Supports?(a, b) refers to a function that returns true if a eventually supports b in the generalized explanation, that is, if there is a directed path from a to b in the explanation graph. For each action, the algorithm determines the set of states in the explanation that could be true before the action is executed based only on the partial ordering of actions imposed by the explanation structure. These are called the *deletable* states since they are ones that the action could possibly delete. For each of these states, the condition (α) under which the action could delete the state in general is determined. For example, if an effect of an action is $\neg$Value(?x, ?y), then the state Value(?a, ?b) is deleted if ?x=?a and ?y=?b. If the deletable state is not supported by another action (i.e., it is a precondition of the macro-operator) or if it is an effect of an action that must precede the deleting action because it supports it, then the state must be true before the action is executed and it will be deleted when α is true. If the deletable state is also the goal or supports a proof of the goal, then $\neg\alpha$ is added to the preconditions to prevent the goal from being

---

[1] A *topological sort* of a directed acyclic graph is an ordering of the nodes in the graph such that a node u must occur before a node v in the ordering if there is a directed path from u to v.

for each action a in the generalized explanation do
   let deletable = $\emptyset$
   for each state s in the generalized explanation do
      if ¬Supports?(a, s) then let deletable = deletable $\cup$ {s}
   for each effect e of a do
      for each state d in deletable do
         if ¬d unifies with e
            then
               let α be the conditions under which ¬d and e unify
               let c be the action of which d is an effect (possibly NIL)
               if null(c) $\vee$ Supports?(c, a)
                  then
                     if d is the goal or supports a proof of the goal
                        then add ¬α to the preconditions for the macro–
                           operator
                        else d is deleted by e when α is true
                  else
                     if d is the goal or supports a proof of the goal
                        then a must precede c when α is true
                        else d is deleted by e when α is true and c precedes
              a PreventPreconditionClobbering(a, d, c, α)

procedure PreventPreconditionClobbering(a, d, c, α)
(* Add conditions to prevent action a from clobbering precondition d
  when α is true *)
   for each action b such that d is a precondition of b or supports a proof
  of a precondition of b do
      if Supports?(a, b)
         then
            if null(c) $\vee$ Supports?(c, a)
               then add ¬α to the preconditions for the macro–operator
               else a must precede c when α is true
         else
            if null(c) $\vee$ Supports?(c, a)
               then b must precede a when α is true
               else a must precede c or b must precede a when α is true

Figure 3–8:   Algorithm for Determining Deletions and Preventing Protec-
               tion Violations

clobbered. To maintain the explanation structure of the original example, the goal must not be deleted. Otherwise the deletable state is marked as being deleted when α is true. If the deletable state is not necessarily true before the action is executed, then it will be deleted when both α is true and the action supporting it precedes the deleting action. If the deletable state is the goal or supports a proof of the goal, then to prevent the goal from being clobbered, the deleting action must precede the action supporting the deleted state when α is true.

The procedure PreventPreconditionClobbering adds additional ordering constraints and preconditions to the macro–operator to prevent a precondition from being clobbered when action a deletes state d. Such a precondition deletion would violate the explanation structure. If an effect of action a deletes a precondition p of action b, then to avoid a protection violation, either b must precede a or a must precede action c where p is an effect of c [9, 11]. However, the existing partial ordering of the actions imposed by the explanation structure may rule out either or both of these possibilities. If both possibilities are ruled out, then $\neg\alpha$ is added to the list of preconditions for the macro–operator to prevent the plan from being used in such situations. Otherwise, the possible ordering constraints that will prevent the protection violation are recorded.

For the double variable assignment example, the ordering constraints imposed by this algorithm are shown below:

(1) Setq(?a1,?b1) should precede Setq(?a2,?b2) when (?a2=?b1 $\wedge$?x2=?y1) or else ¬Value(?a2,?x2) will clobber Value(?b1,?y1)

(2) Setq(?a1,?b1) should precede Setq(?a2,?b2) when (?a2=?a1 $\wedge$?x2=?x1) or else ¬Value(?a2,?x2) will clobber Value(?a1,?x1)

(3) Setq(?a2,?b2) should precede Setq(?a1,?b1) when (?a2=?a1 $\wedge$?x2=?y1) or else ¬Value(?a2,?x2) will clobber goal: Value(?a1,?y1)

(4) Setq(?a2,?b2) should precede Setq(?a1,?b1) when (?a1=?b2 $\wedge$?x1=?y2) or else ¬Value(?a1,?x1) will clobber Value(?b2,?y2)

(5) Setq(?a2,?b2) should precede Setq(?a1,?b1) when (?a1=?a2 $\wedge$?x1=?x2) or else ¬Value(?a1,?x1) will clobber Value(?a2,?x2)

(6) Setq(?a1,?b1) should precede Setq(?a2,?b2) when (?a1=?a2 $\wedge$?x1=?y2) or else ¬Value(?a1,?x1) will clobber goal: Value(?a2,?y2)

2.3.2. Time Complexity of Determining Ordering Constraints

The worst case time complexity of the algorithm in Figure 3–8 is relatively easy to determine. In the following discussion, loops will be referred to by their iterative variables (e.g., the a loop, the e loop, etc.).

Let the number of nodes in the generalized explanation graph be n. Since the function Supports? determines whether or not there is a directed path from one node to another in this graph, in the worst case it must traverse the entire graph. Since traversing a graph is $O(V + E)$ where V is the number of nodes and E is the number of edges and since $E \leq V^2$, the worst–case complexity of a call to Supports? is $O(n^2)$.

Since the number of actions must be less than n, the outermost loop (the a loop) is executed at most n times. Since the number of states is also less than n, the body of the loop for determining the set of deletable states (the s loop) is executed at most n times for each action for a maximum total of n^2 times. Since the body of this loop includes a call to Supports?, which is $O(n^2)$, the total maximum time needed for all executions of the s loop is $O(n^4)$. Since each deletable set is a subset of the set of states, its maximum cardinality is n.

Since the total number of effects of actions must be less than the number of states, the body of the e loop is executed at most a total of n times. Since n is the maximum size of a deletable set, the body of the d loop is executed at most n times for each effect for a maximum total of n^2 times. In addition to the call to PreventPreconditionClobbering, the operations in the body of the d loop that depend on the size of n include a call to Supports? and determining whether a state supports a proof of the goal. Since both of these operations involve finding a path between two nodes in the explanation graph, they take at most $O(n^2)$ time. Therefore, let the total maximum time needed for all executions of the e loop be

$$n^2(O(n^2) + P)$$

where P is the time complexity of a call to PreventPreconditionClobbering.

The body of the b loop in PreventPreconditionClobbering is executed less than n times since the *total* number of actions is less than n. Since executing the body of the loop requires two calls to Supports?, which takes $O(n^2)$ time, the maximum time required for a call to this function is $O(n^3)$. Therefore, the total maximum time needed for all executions of the e loop is

$$n^2(O(n^2) + O(n^3)) = O(n^5)$$

Since, the total maximum time needed for all executions of the s loop was calculated to be only $O(n^4)$, the worst–case time complexity of the complete process is also $O(n^5)$.

The fact that the $O(n^2)$ Supports? function is called within bodies of loops that are executed $O(n^2)$ and $O(n^3)$ times is a dominant factor in the complexity of the complete algorithm. If a call to this function could be reduced to constant time, a minor modification of the preceding analysis demonstrates that the complexity of the complete process would then be $O(n^3)$. The maximum time required for all executions of the s loop becomes $O(n^2)$. The total maximum time for all executions of the e loop becomes

$$n^2(c + P)$$

where c is a constant. The time complexity of a call to PreventPreconditionClobbering (P) becomes $O(n)$, and the overall worst–case complexity becomes

$$O(n^2) + n^2(c + O(n)) = O(n^3)$$

Since Supports?(a,b) simply determines whether or not there is a directed path from a to b, the value of this function for all pairs of the n nodes in the explanation graph can be precomputed by determining the graph's *transitive closure*.[2] Since there exist $O(V^3)$ algorithms for computing the transitive closure of a directed graph [12], all the values of Support? for a particular explanation can be precomputed in $O(n^3)$ time. Calls to this function will then take constant time, and the complete process of determining deletions and protection violations can be accomplished in $O(n^3)$ time.

In conclusion, although the algorithm implemented in EGGS is $O(n^5)$, computation of the transitive closure of the generalized explanation graph using one of the known $O(V^3)$ algorithms would result in an $O(n^3)$ algorithm for the problem of determining deletions and preventing

---

[2]The *transitive closure* of a directed graph $G=(V,E)$ is a directed graph $G'=(V,E')$ such that there is an edge $u \rightarrow v$ in E' if and only if there is a (nonempty) directed path from u to v in E.

protection violations. In any case, computing the minimal set of ordering constraints is a relatively efficient process that can be done in time which is polynomial in the size of the plan.

2.3.3. Detecting and Preventing Inconsistent Ordering Constraints

The ordering constraints posted to prevent protection violations may contradict each other in certain situations. For example, in the Setq example, when ?a2=?b1, ?x2=?y1, ?a1=?b2, and ?x1=?y2, constraints 1 and 4 listed earlier contradict each other since they each specify a different ordering of the two operators. With regard to assignment statements, this situation corresponds to swapping the values of two variables (e.g., Setq(A,B), Setq(B,A)), which cannot be done using only two variable assignments. To detect such situations, a resolution theorem prover is used to determine sets of ordering constraints that are inconsistent.[3] In addition to the posted ordering constraints, the theorem prover is given the following two axioms:

Before(?a,?b) $\land$ Before(?b,?c) $\rightarrow$ Before(?a,?c)
Before(?a,?b) $\rightarrow$ $\neg$Before(?b,?a)

When the resolution theorem prover finds a contradiction, it returns the set of axioms on which the proof depends. To prevent such a contradiction from arising during the subsequent use of the macro–operator, an additional precondition must be added. Assuming each of the n ordering constraints, c_i, in the contradictory set must be satisfied when condition α_i is true, the following precondition must be added to the macro–operator: $\neg(\alpha_1 \land \alpha_2 \, n \ldots \land \alpha_n)$. For the preceding variable swapping example, the added precondition would be

(P1) $\neg$((?a2=?b1 $\land$?x2=?y1) $\land$ (?a1=?b2 $\land$?x1=?y2))

A similar contradiction detected between constraints 2 and 5 results in the addition of the precondition

(P2) $\neg$((?a2=?a1 $\land$?x2=?x1) $\land$ (?a1=?a2 $\land$?x1=?x2))

This situation occurs when both assignment statements are attempting to set the same variable.

---

[3] Because of the possible presence of disjunctive ordering constraints such as Before(A,C) $\lor$ Before(B,A), a simple cycle–detecting algorithm cannot be used to find all sets of inconsistent constraints. In fact, disjunctive constraints seem to rule out a polynomial time solution to this problem.

Of course, using a resolution theorem prover to find all sets of contradictory axioms is a computationally intractable process which is not even guaranteed to halt. In EGGS, the theorem prover is given a time limit, after which it stops and returns proofs for all the contradictions it has found so far. Consequently, the system does not actually guarantee the prevention of ordering contradictions during later instantiation. Should such a contradiction arise, one could perform explanation–based learning from failure to modify the plan at that time in order to prevent similar problems in the future. Systems that use EBL to learn from failures due to unforeseen interactions are described in Chapter 4 and in Gupta [13].

2.3.4. Simplifying the Results

The final set of wffs describing the preconditions, effects, and ordering constraints for a macro–operator can be unnecessarily complex. Consequently, EGGS uses a system for simplifying logical expressions to clean up the final results. As described by Minton and colleagues [14], simplification or *compression* helps to decrease the matching cost needed to determine whether or not a macro–operator applies.

The simplifier currently used by EGGS first converts expressions to conjunctive normal form and eliminates tautological and subsumed clauses. Next, a set of axioms supplied by the user for each domain are used to further simplify the CNF formula. If a literal l in a clause together with the domain axioms and other clauses implies another literal in the clause, then the literal l is removed. The EGGS deductive retriever is used to prove the implication. This simplification is valid since

$$((P \wedge R) \rightarrow Q) \rightarrow ((R \wedge (P \vee Q)) \equiv (R \wedge Q))$$

Therefore, if $(P \wedge R) \rightarrow Q$ is true in the domain, then the reduced formula is equivalent to the original. Clauses that are implied by other clauses together with the domain axioms are also removed. Once again, the EGGS deductive retriever is used to prove the implication. This simplification is valid since

$$(P \rightarrow Q) \rightarrow ((P \wedge Q) \equiv P)$$

Therefore, if $P \rightarrow Q$ is true in the domain, then the reduced formula is equivalent to the original. Finally, DeMorgan's law is used to convert clauses that are more compactly represented as negated terms. That is, clauses of the form

$$\neg l_1 \vee \neg l_2 \ldots \vee \neg l_{n-1} \vee \neg l_n$$

are changed to

$$\neg(l_1 \wedge l_2 \cdots \wedge l_{n-1} \wedge l_n)$$

Of course, the EGGS simplifier is not guaranteed to produce optimal simplifications; however, general problems of minimizing logical expressions are known to be NP-Complete (see Minimum Axiom Set and Minimum Disjunctive Normal Form in [15]).

As an example of the simplification process, consider the preconditions added to prevent the inconsistent orderings in the Setq example. The system simplifies the first of these (P1) to $\neg(?a2=?b1 \wedge ?a1=?b2)$ using the following domain axiom: Value(?x,?a) $\wedge$ Value(?y,?b) $\wedge$?x=?y $\rightarrow$?a=?b. This axiom simply states that a variable has only one value at a time. The second added precondition (P2) is simplified to $\neg(?a1=?a2)$ using the same axiom.

2.3.5. Assembling the Partially Ordered Macro–Operator

Assembling the final macro–operator is a relatively simple task. The preconditions of the macro–operator include the leaves of the explanation as well as any additional constraints added during the prevention of protection violations or inconsistent ordering constraints. If an effect of an individual operator in the plan was never marked as deleted under any condition, then it is added to the list of effects of the macro–operator. If an effect was marked as being deleted under some set of conditions, then the overall effect is given by the following implication: If none of the deletion conditions are met, then the state is true [2]. Finally, the posted ordering constraints are added to the macro–operator with the exception that constraints whose condition contradicts a precondition of the macro–operator are eliminated. In the example, ordering constraints 2, 3, 5, and 6 can be eliminated since they require that ?a1=?a2, a condition which is now prevented by a precondition.

The final partially ordered macro–operator that EGGS learns from the "double Setq" example is shown in Table 3-3. In summary, the

Table 3: Macro–Operator Learned from the Variable Assignment Example		
SetqSetq(?a1,?b1,?x2,?y2,?x1,?y1,?a2,?b2)		
Preconditions	Effects	Orderings
Value(?a1,?x1)	Value(?a1,?y1)	?a1=?b2 $\rightarrow$ Before(Setq(?a2,?b2),Setq(?a1,?b1))
Value(?a2,?x2)	Value(?a2,?y2)	?a2=?b1 $\rightarrow$ Before(Setq(?a1,?b1),Setq(?a2,?b2))
Value(?b1,?y1)	$\neg$Value(?a1,?x1)	
Value(?b2,?y2)	$\neg$Value(?a2,?x2)	
?a2$\neq$?a1		
$\neg$(?a1=?b2 $\wedge$?a2=?b1)		

system notices that if the two variables being set are the same, then the goal of having them set to two different values cannot be achieved. Also, if either assignment references the variable set by the other, then the two cannot be executed in parallel. In these cases, the assignments must be properly ordered to prevent the referenced variable from being reset before it is used. Finally, if each assignment references the variable set by the other, then two assignments cannot solve the problem. This is the classic "variable swapping" problem which requires the use of a temporary variable.

2.4. Relation to Nonlinear Planning

Work in *nonlinear planning* [9] has addressed the issue of building plans with partially ordered actions by initially assuming there are no goal interactions and then detecting protection violations and imposing ordering constraints to prevent them. Although the task of building a specific partially ordered plan for achieving a specific goal is quite different from the task of generalizing a specific totally ordered plan into a general partially ordered macro–operator, some of the underlying processes are quite similar.

Nilsson [16] used the term DCOMP to refer to the procedure for detecting and preventing protection violations in nonlinear planning. The procedure in Figure 3–8 is in some ways more general and in some ways less general than DCOMP. It is more general because it must determine the conditions (α) under which a deletion will take place in the generalized plan. DCOMP works with a specific instance of a plan and therefore does not need to determine which instantiations of a plan result in a deletion. The procedure in Figure 3–8 is less general than DCOMP because it does not consider alternative ways of achieving the preconditions of an action. The explanation structure determines how preconditions were met in the particular example, and these constraints are retained in the generalization. Using Nilsson's terminology, the procedure presented here does not determine all of the possible *adders* of a precondition in the plan since each precondition is assumed to be added by the action that added it in the original specific instance. Of course, an even more general macro–operator could be produced by generalizing the explanation structure and considering alternative adders. However, this would complicate the procedure even further for generating a macro–operator.

The actual process of determining what Nilsson calls a *noninteractive* ordering for a particular instantiation of a plan must be done when the final macro–operator is used to solve a future problem. Assuming all inconsistent sets of ordering constraints were detected and prevented by adding additional preconditions to the macro–operator, for any situation that meets the preconditions, there is guaranteed to be a partial ordering of the actions that satisfies all of the ordering constraints. However, due to the possible presence of disjunctive ordering constraints, actually finding it may require an expensive search. However, this should not be surprising since the increased generality of a partially ordered macro–operator can clearly result in a corresponding decrease in operationality [7].

2.5. Another Example

An additional illustration of the importance of detecting protection violations when generalizing the order of operators in a macro–operator involves learning a schema for "arson for insurance." This is a concept learned by GENESIS, a text understanding system which uses EGGS to learn plan schemata by generalizing specific plans it observes in natural-language narratives (see Chapter 10). By understanding and generalizing the following story, GENESIS acquires a general schema for someone burning his own building in order to collect the insurance money:

> Stan owned a warehouse. He insured it against fire for
> 100000 dollars. Stan burned the warehouse. He called
> Prudential and told them it was burnt. Prudential
> paid him 100000 dollars.

The English paraphrase that the system generates for the schema it learns from this story follows:

> ?a3 is a person. ?o2 is an inanimate object. ?c3 is an
> insurance company. ?v3 is money. ?o2 is not burnt.
> ?a3 has ?o2. ?a3 insures ?o2 with ?c3 for ?v3 in case it
> is burnt. ?o2 is flammable. ?a3 burns ?o2. ?a3 con-
> tacts ?c3 and tells it that ?o2 is burnt. ?c3 indemnifies
> ?a3 ?v3 for the loss of ?o2.

The explanation for this plan is basically that both the burning and insuring actions achieve preconditions for the indemnify action which achieves a character's goal of possessing money. However, the structure of this explanation does not impose an ordering on the burning and insuring actions since neither of these actions enables the other in any way. However, the burning action clobbers a precondition of the insuring action since an object cannot be insured against fire if it is already burnt. The algorithm described above detects this potential protection violation and imposes the following mandatory ordering constraint on these two actions:

?a3 insures ?o2 with ?c3 for ?v3 in case it is burnt.
should proceed ?a3 burns ?o2. when T or else ?o2 is
burnt. will clobber ?o2 is not burnt.

In this example, the final schema is no more general than what
would be learned if order generalization were not performed. However,
since order generalization was attempted, the system has an explanation
for why the insuring action *must* precede the burning action. The ordering of the actions in the generalized schema is justified by the existing
theory of the domain, which it would not be if order generalization where
not attempted. Therefore the current approach more completely achieves
the goal of producing a justified generalization, which is one of the primary goals of explanation–based methods [1].

2.6. An Example Requiring Structural Generalization

As discussed earlier, the order–generalization process currently
incorporated in EGGS requires that preconditions be achieved as they
were in the original example. However, generalizing the order of operators in certain situations requires altering the explanation structure by
breaking some of the connections between preconditions and effects. For
example, consider the following plan for building two independent stacks
of blocks:

Pickup(A), Stack(A,B), Pickup(C), Stack(C,D)

Assuming the standard definitions for these blocks world actions [16], the
specific explanation for this plan is shown in Figure 3-9. Although the
process of building two separate stacks would seem to be two independent
operations, either of which could be performed first, the structure of this
explanation actually imposes a particular ordering on the two operations.
The reason is the precondition for building the second stack, that the
hand be empty, a precondition that was met by releasing the top block
after building the previous stack. Generalizing the order of these two
operations requires allowing the HandEmpty preconditions to be achieved
in a manner different from that observed in the original instance.

The current order–generalization routine in EGGS does not allow
altering the structure of the original explanation by breaking the connection between effects and preconditions. Unlike the double Setq example
discussed earlier, the explanation structure for this example imposes a
total ordering on the actions in the plan. Therefore the system cannot
generalize the order of these two block–stacking operations. More complex order–generalization techniques which consider the possibility of
altering the explanation structure are needed to perform generalizations

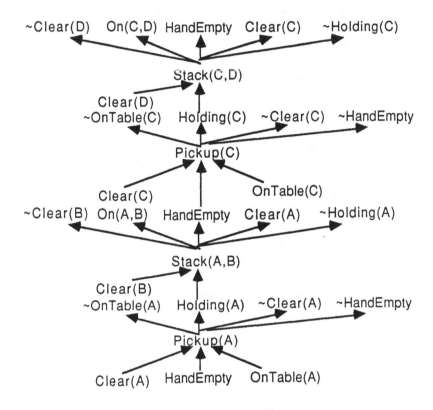

Figure 3–9:   Block Stacking Example — Specific Explanation

of this sort.

In the block–stacking example, although having the hand empty is a precondition for picking up block C, making the hand empty is not the "reason" for stacking A on B. On the other hand, the reason for picking up block A is to enable stacking it on B. Therefore, not all connections between effects and preconditions are created equal. Some seem to be more crucial to the overall explanation than others. One possible rule is to allow breaking the connection between an effect and a precondition only if another effect of the same action more directly supports the goal. This is the situation in the block–stacking example since the real reason for stacking A on B is not to enable Pickup(C) but rather to achieve

On(A,B).

2.7. Conclusions and Problems for Future Research on Temporal Generalization

Generalizing the temporal order of operators in a plan in order to produce partially ordered macro–operators can result in more general and as well as more justified concepts. As in the EGGS system, performing this task can be incorporated as part of a general explanation–based learning system. Empirical testing of this system on a number of examples from various domains such as programming, blocks–world planning, and narrative understanding has given promising results.

A theoretical analysis of the computational complexity of the order–generalization problem demonstrated that detecting potential protection violations in macro–operators and determining ordering constraints which prevent them can be performed in polynomial time. However, detecting inconsistencies in these constraints and adding preconditions to prevent them can be computationally expensive. Avoiding a complete search for inconsistencies could result in the omission of necessary preconditions and the resulting acquisition of macro–operators which are overly general. A promising area for future research involves developing failure–driven EBL techniques for detecting overlooked inconsistencies encountered during subsequent use of such macro–operators and refining the macro–operator to account for the detected interaction (see Chapter 4).

In addition, as discussed in the previous section, techniques are needed for allowing order generalizations which require altering the structure of the original explanation by breaking the connections between preconditions and effects. Finally, the current technique requires actions to be represented as STRIPS operators with complete delete lists. This requirement is frequently unrealistic, and techniques are needed for generalizing the order of weaker types of operators.

3. Number Generalization

Often a person will, in the course of solving a problem, repeatedly employ an action or collection of actions. It is an important, but difficult, problem, to correctly generalize this sequence once observed. Sometimes the number of repetitions itself should be the subject of generalization. Other times it is quite inappropriate to alter the number of repetitions. This section addresses the important issue in explanation–based learning of generalizing explanation structures, in particular, the task of *generalizing to N* [17–20]. This can involve generalizing such things as the number of entities involved in a concept or the number of times some action is performed. Generalizing explanation structures has been largely ignored in previous explanation-based learning research. Instead, other research has focused on changing constants into variables and determining the general constraints on those variables.

The central thesis of this section is:

> Explanation structures that suffice for understanding a specific example are not always satisfactory for generalizing the example. The explanation *structure* must often be *generalized* if a useful concept is to be produced.

Evidence for this claim and a technique for generalizing explanation structures are presented.

Although generalizing the structure of an explanation can involve more than generalizing the number of times a technique is employed — for example, the *order* techniques are applied or the actual techniques used can be generalized — this section largely focuses on the topic of *generalizing number*. Usually this involves generalizing a fixed number of applications of a technique into a possibly constrained but unbounded number of applications. The phrase *generalizing to N* is also used to indicate this process.

Generalizing number, like more traditional generalization in explanation-based learning, results in the acquisition of a new inference rule. The difference is that the sort of rule that results from generalizing number describes the situation after an indefinite number of world changes or other inferences have been made. Each such rule subsumes a potentially infinite class of rules acquired by standard explanation-based generalization techniques. Thus with such rules the storage efficiency can be dramatically improved, the expressive power of the system is increased, and, as shown in Chapter 11, the system's performance efficiency can also be higher than without these rules.

Consider the LEAP system [21]. The system is shown an example of using NOR gates to compute the boolean BAND of two ORs. It discovers that the technique generalizes to computing the boolean BAND of any two inverted boolean functions. However, LEAP cannot generalize this technique to allow constructing the AND of an arbitrary number of inverted boolean functions using a multi-input NOR gate. This is the case even if LEAP's initial background knowledge were to include the general version of DeMorgan's law and the concept of multi-input NOR gates.

Generalizing the number of functions requires alteration of the original example's explanation.

Ellman's system [22] also illustrates the need for generalizing number. From an example of a four–bit circular shift register, his system constructs a generalized design for an arbitrary four–bit permutation register. A design for an *N*–bit circular shift register cannot be produced. As Ellman pointed out, such generalization, though desirable, cannot be done using the technique of changing constants to variables.

Many important concepts, to be properly learned, require generalization of number. For example, physical laws such as momentum and energy conservation apply to arbitrary numbers of objects, constructing towers of blocks requires an arbitrary number of repeated stacking actions, and setting a table involves a range of possible numbers of guests. In addition, there is recent psychological evidence [23] that people can generalize number on the basis of one example.

Repetition of an action is not a sufficient condition for generalization to *N* to be appropriate. Compare two simple examples, where generalizing to *N* is necessary in one but inappropriate in the other:

- Observing a previously unknown method of moving an obstructed block.

- Seeing, for the first time, a toy wagon being built.

The initial states of the two problems appear in Figure 3–10. Suppose a learning system observes an expert achieving the desired states. In each case, consider what general concept should be acquired.

In the first example, the expert wishes to move, using a robot manipulator, a block on which four other blocks are stacked in tower form.

Figure 3–10: Initial States for Two Sample Problems

The manipulator can pick up only one block at a time. The expert's solution is to move all four of the blocks in turn to some other location. After the underlying block has been cleared, it is moved. In the second example, the expert wishes to construct a movable rectangular platform, one that is stable while supporting any load whose center of mass is over the platform. Given the platform and a bin containing two axles and four wheels, the expert's solution is to first attach each of the axles to the platform. Next, all four of the wheels are grabbed in turn and mounted on an axle protrusion.

This comparison illustrates an important problem in explanation-based learning. Generalizing the block–unstacking example should produce a plan for unstacking *any* number of obstructing blocks, not just four as observed. The wagon–building example, however, should not generalize the number 4. It makes no difference whether the system is given a bin of five, six, or one hundred wheels because only four wheels are needed to fulfill the functional requirements of a stable wagon.

Standard explanation–based learning algorithms [1, 2, 24–28] and similar algorithms for chunking [4] cannot treat these cases differently. These algorithms, possibly after pruning the explanation to eliminate irrelevant parts, replace constants with constrained variables. They cannot significantly augment the explanation during generalization. Thus the building-a-wagon type of concept will be correctly acquired but the unstacking-to-move concept will be undergeneralized. The acquired schema will have generalized the identity of the blocks so that the target block need not be occluded by the same four blocks as in the example. Any four obstructing blocks can be unstacked. However, there must be exactly four blocks.[4] Unstacking five or more blocks is beyond the scope of the acquired concept.

Figure 3–11 schematically compares the operation of standard EBL algorithms and a structure–generalizing EBL algorithm. Both algorithms assume that, in the course of solving a problem, a collection of pieces of general knowledge (e.g., inference rules, rewrite rules, or plan schemata) are interconnected, using unification to ensure compatibility. In both approaches the unifications necessary to connect the pieces together in the

---

[4] The SOAR system [4] would seem to acquire a number of concepts which together are slightly more general. As well as a new operator for moving four blocks, the system would acquire new operators for moving three blocks, two blocks, and one block, but not for five or more.

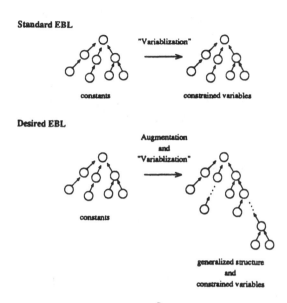

Figure 3–11: Generalizing the Structure of Explanations

general case are determined (see Chapter 2). Importantly, however, when generalizing an explanation structure, the explanation structure is also reformulated so that additional pieces of knowledge are incorporated. Unlike the result of standard explanation–based learning, the generalized structure in the lower right corner represents a *class* of potential explanation structures and not a single fixed structure.

Note that EBL systems do not work correctly on the building–a–wagon kind of problems either — they just get lucky. They do nothing to augment explanation structures during generalization. It just happens that to acquire a schema to build a wagon, *not* generalizing the explanation structure is the appropriate thing to do.

One can, of course, simply define the scope of EBL–type systems to exclude the unstacking–to–move concept and those like it. This is a mistake. First, the problem of augmenting the explanation during generalization, once seen, is ubiquitous. It is manifested in one form or another in most real–world domains. Second, if one simply defines the problem away, the resulting system could never guarantee that any of its concepts were as general as they should be. Even when such a system correctly constructed a concept like the building–a–wagon schema, it could not know that it had generalized properly. The system could not itself tell which concepts fall within its scope and which do not.

Observations of repeated application of a rule or operator may indicate that generalizing the number of rules in the explanation may be appropriate. However, alone this is insufficient. To be conducive to number generalization, there must be a certain recursive structural pattern. That is, each application must achieve preconditions for the next. For example, consider stacking blocks. The same sort of repositioning of blocks occurs repeatedly, each building on the last. In this chapter, the vocabulary of predicate calculus is adopted to investigate this notion of structural recursion. The desired form of structural recursion is manifested as repeated application of an inference rule in such a manner that a portion of each consequent is used to satisfy some of the antecedents of the next application.

The next section introduces an implemented system designed to generalize the structure of explanations. Subsequent sections describe the algorithm used and illustrate it with a detailed example. After that, there are a discussion of related work and descriptions of several open research problems.

3.1. The BAGGER System

The BAGGER system (building augmented generalizations by generating extended recurrences) analyzes predicate calculus proofs and attempts to construct concepts that involve generalizing to N. Most of the examples under study use situation calculus [29] to reason about actions, in the style of Green [30]. (Green's formulation is also discussed in [16].)

3.1.1. Situation Calculus

In situation calculus, predicates and functions whose values may change over time are given an extra argument which indicates the situation in which they are being evaluated. For example, rather than using the predicate $On(x,y)$, indicating that x is on y, the predicate $On(x,y,s)$ is used, indicating that in situation s, x is on y. In this formulation, operators are represented as functions that map from one situation to another.

Problem solving with BAGGER's situational calculus rules can be viewed as transforming and expanding situations until one is found to achieve the goal. The AGGER system has two types of inference rules: *intersituational* rules, which specify attributes that a new situation will have after application of a particular operator, and *intrasituational* rules, which can embellish BAGGER's knowledge of a situation by specifying additional conclusions that can be drawn within that situation.

Each intersituational inference rule specifies knowledge about one particular operator. However, operators are not represented by exactly one inference rule. A major inference rule specifies most of the relevant problem–solving information about an operator. But it is augmented by many lesser inference rules which capture the operator's frame axioms and other facts about a new situation. This paradigm contrasts with the standard STRIPS [8] formalism.[5] The inference rules of a STRIPS–like system are in a one–to–one correspondence with the system's operators. Each inference rule fully specifies an operator's add and delete lists. These lists provide all of the changes needed to transform the current situation into the new situation. Any state not mentioned in an add or delete list is assumed to persist across the operator's application. Thus the new situation is completely determined by the inference rule. In the BAGGER system this is not the case. Many separate inference rules are used to fully characterize the effect of an operator.

The advantage of the STRIPS approach is that the system can always be assured that it has represented all that there is to know about a new situation. However, this can also be a disadvantage. A STRIPS–like system must always muddle through all there is to know about a situation, no matter how irrelevant many facts may be to the current problem. Conversely, the advantages of BAGGER's approach are that the inference rules are far less complex and therefore more manageable, the system's attention focusing is easier because it does not bog down in situations made overly complex by many irrelevant facts, and a programmer can more easily write and update knowledge about operators. Furthermore, STRIPS–style operators do not allow disjunctive or conditional effects in their add or delete lists.

A potential disadvantage of BAGGER's approach is that to completely represent the effects of applying an operator in a particular situation, the system must retrieve all of the relevant inference rules. However, this is not a task that arises in BAGGER's problem solving. Indeed, there has been no attempt to guarantee the completeness of the system's inferential abilities. This means that there may be characteristics of a

---

[5] Fahlman [31] and Fikes [32] augmented the standard STRIPS model by allowing a distinction between primary and secondary relationships. Primary relationships are asserted directly by operators, and secondary relationships are deduced from the primary ones as needed. Although this serves the same purpose as BAGGER's intrasituational rules, multiple intersituational rules for an operator are not allowed [33].

situation which BAGGER can represent but cannot itself infer.

8.1.2. Some Sample Problems

One problem solution analyzed by BAGGER appears in Figure 3–12. The goal is to place a properly supported block so that its center is above the dotted line and within the horizontal confines of the line. BAGGER is provided low–level domain knowledge about blocks, including how to transfer a single block from one location to another and how to calculate its new horizontal and vertical position. Briefly, to move a block, it must have nothing on it and there must be free space at which to place it. The system produces a situation calculus proof validating the

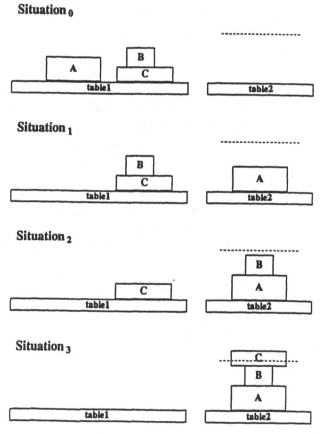

Figure 3–12: Constructing a Three–Block Tower

actions shown in Figure 3–12, in which three blocks must be moved to build the tower.

If a standard explanation–based generalization algorithm is applied to the resulting proof, a plan for moving *three* blocks will result. They need not be these same three blocks; any three distinct ones will suffice. Nor is it is necessary that the first block moved be placed on a table; any flat, clear surface is acceptable. Finally, the height of the tower need not be the same as that in the specific example. Given appropriately sized blocks, towers of any height can be constructed. Many characteristics of the problem are generalized. However, the fact that exactly three blocks are moved would remain.

If one considers the universe of all possible towers, as shown in Figure 3–13, only a small fraction of them would be captured by the acquired rule. Separate rules would need to be learned for towers containing two blocks, five blocks, and so on. What is desired is the acquisition of a rule that describes how towers containing any number of blocks can be constructed.

By analyzing the proof of the construction of the three–block tower, BAGGER acquires a general plan for building towers by stacking *arbitrary* numbers of blocks, as illustrated in Figure 3–14. This new plan incorporates an indefinite number of applications of the previously known plan for moving a single block. More details on this plan are provided later.

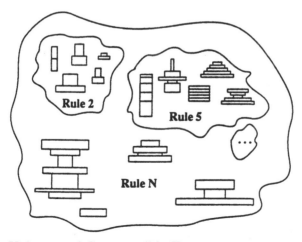

Figure 3–13: Universes of Constructible Towers

In another example, the system observes three blocks being removed from a stack in order to satisfy the goal of having a specific block be clear. Extending the explanation of these actions produces a plan for unstacking any number of blocks in order to clear a block within the stack. Figure 3–15 illustrates this general plan. The plan includes the system's realization that the last unstacked block is currently clear and thus makes a suitable destination to place the next block to be moved. This knowledge is incorporated into the plan, and no problem solving need be performed finding destinations once the first free location is found.

Unlike many other block–manipulation examples, in these examples it is *not* assumed that blocks can support only one other block. This means that moving a block does not necessarily clear its supporting block. Another concept learned by BAGGER, by observing two blocks being moved from the top of another, is a general plan for clearing an object directly supporting any number of clear blocks. This plan is illustrated in Figure 3–16.

The domain of digital circuit design has also been investigated. By observing the repeated application of DeMorgan's law to implement two cascaded AND gates using OR and NOT gates, BAGGER produces a general

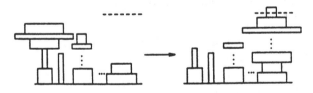

Figure 3–14: A General Plan for Constructing Towers

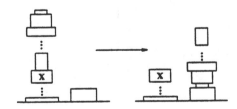

Figure 3–15: A General Plan for Unstacking Towers

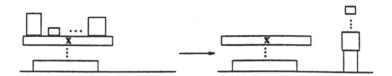

Figure 3–16: A General Plan for Clearing Objects

version of DeMorgan's law, which can be used to implement N cascaded AND gates with N OR and one NOT gate. This example, which does not use situation calculus, appears in Figure 3–17.

The next section presents the BAGGER generalization algorithm. Following that, there is a detailed presentation of the tower–building example, including the full proof tree and the acquired rule. The inference rules used in this example are described. Complete details on the other examples, including the complete set of initial inference rules, the situation calculus proofs, and the acquired inference rules, can be found in [20].

3.2. Generalization in BAGGER

This section describes how BAGGER generalizes explanation structures. Before the BAGGER's generalization algorithm is described, the type of rule the system acquires is discussed.

3.2.1. Sequential Rules

Like its standard inference rules, number–generalized rules in the BAGGER system are usually represented in situational calculus. The previous section discussed two types of BAGGER inference rules: intrasituational rules and intersituational rules. To define number–generalized

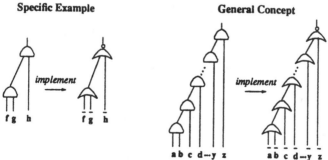

Figure 3–17: A Circuit Design Example

rules, the intersituational rules are further divided into two categories: simple intersituational rules and sequential intersituational rules (or simply *sequential rules*). Sequential rules apply a variable number of operators. Thus, within each application of a sequential rule, many intermediate situations may be generated. The actual number of intermediate situations depends on the complexity of the problem to be solved. The rule for building towers is an example of a sequential rule, one able to construct towers of any number of blocks in order to achieve a specified goal height. The rule itself decides how many blocks are to be used and selects which blocks to use from among those present in the current situation.

Sequential rules, like their simple intersituational counterparts, have an antecedent and a consequent. Also, like the simple versions, if the antecedent is satisfied, the consequent specifies properties of the resulting situation. Unlike the simple rules, the resulting situation can be separated from the initial situation by many operator applications and intermediate situations. For example, to build a tower, many block–moving operations must be performed. It is an important feature of sequential rules that no planning need be done in applying the intermediate operators. That is, if the antecedent of a sequential rule is satisfied, its entire sequence of operators can be applied without the need for individually testing or planning for the preconditions. The preconditions of each operator are guaranteed to be true by the construction of the sequential rule itself. Thus the consequent of a sequential rule can immediately assert properties which must be true in the final situation. A sequential rule behaves much as a STRIPSR–like macro–operator. It is termed a *sequential rule* and not a *macro–operator* because it is, in fact, a situational calculus rule and not an operator. It has a situation variable, does not specify ADD and DELETE lists and so forth.

Sequential rules can be much more efficient than simply chaining together simple constituents. This improved efficiency is derived from three sources: (1) collecting together antecedents so that redundant and subsumed operator preconditions are eliminated, (2) heuristically ordering the antecedents, and, especially, (3) eliminating antecedents that test operator preconditions which, due to the structure of the rule, are known to be satisfied.

3.2.2. Representing Sequential Knowledge

A representational shift is crucial to this chapter's solution to the generalization to N problem. Objects in the world are represented within simple inference rules directly as predicate calculus variables, but this is not possible for BAGGER's sequential rules. A standard operator interacts with a known number of objects. Usually, this number is small. The rule representing the operator that moves blocks, for example, might take as arguments the block to be moved and the new location where it is to be placed. A simple intersituational rule for this operator might specify that in the resulting situation, the block represented by the first argument is at the location specified by the second. This rule represents exactly one application of the move operator. There are always two arguments. They can be conveniently represented by predicate calculus variables. That is, each of the world objects with which a simple operator interacts can be uniquely named with a predicate calculus variable. Sequential rules cannot uniquely name each of the important world objects. A rule for building towers must be capable of including an arbitrary number of blocks. The uninstantiated rule cannot know whether it is to be applied next to build a tower of five blocks, seven blocks, or 24 blocks. Since the individual blocks can no longer be named by unique variables within the rule, a shift is necessary to a scheme that can represent aggregations of world objects. Such a representational shift, similar to that in Weld [34], makes explicit attributes that are only implicitly present in the example. Thus, it shares many characteristics of constructive induction [35, 36].

A new object called an RIS (for rule instantiation sequence) is introduced to represent arbitrarily large aggregations of world objects. A sequential rule works directly with one of these generalized structures so that it need not individually name every world object with which it interacts. A sequential rule's RIS is constructed in the course of satisfying its antecedent. Once this is done, the RIS embodies all of the constraints required for the successive application of the sequence of operators that make up the plan.

3.2.3. The BAGGER Algorithm

Figure 3–18 schematically presents how BAGGER generalizes the structure of explanations. On the left is the explanation of a solution to a specific problem. In it, some inference rule is repeatedly applied a fixed number of times. In the generalized explanation, the number of applications of the rule is unconstrained. In addition, the properties that must hold to satisfy each application's preconditions, and to meet the antecedents in the goal, are expressed in terms of the initial situation. This means that portions of the explanation not directly involved in the chain of rule applications must also be expressed in terms othe initial state. When the initial situation has the necessary properties, the results

of the new rule can be immediately determined, without reasoning about
any of the intermediate situations.

The generalization algorithm appears in Figure 3–19. This algorithm is expressed in a pseudo–code, and the actual implementation is
written in LISP. The remainder of this section elaborates the pseudo–
code. In the algorithm, back arrows ($\leftarrow$) indicate value assignment. The
construct

for each element in set do statement

means that <i>element</i> is successively bound to each member of <i>set</i>, following
which <i>statement</i> is evaluated. The functions <i>AddDisjunct</i> and
AddConjunct alter their first argument. If either of AddConjunct's argu-
ments is <i>fail</i>, its answer is <i>fail</i>. <i>AddRule</i> places the new rule in the database of acquired rules.

The algorithm begins its analysis of a specific solution at the goal
node. It then traces backward, looking for repeated rule applications. To
be a candidate, some consequent of one instantiation of a rule must support the satisfaction of an antecedent of another instantiation. These
repeated applications need not directly connect — there can be intervening inference rules. Once a candidate is found, all the interconnected
instantiations of the underlying general rule are collected.

The general rule repeatedly applied is called a <i>focus rule</i>. After a
focus rule is found, BAGGER ascertains how an <i>arbitrary</i> number of

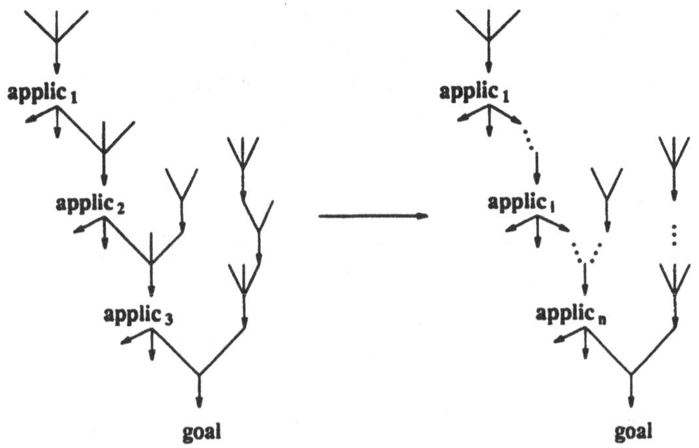

Figure 3–18: Generalizing the Structure of an Explanation

instantiations of this rule and any intervening rules can be concatenated. This indefinite–length collection of rules is conceptually merged into the explanation, replacing the specific–length collection, and a new rule is produced from the augmented explanation.

A specific solution contains several instantiations of the general rule chosen as the focus rule. Each of these applications of the rule addresses the need of satisfying the rule's antecedents, possibly in different ways. For example, when clearing an object, the blocks moved can be placed in several qualitatively different locations. The moved block can be placed on a table (assuming the domain model specifies that tables always have room), it can be placed on a block moved in a previous step, or it can be placed on a block that was originally clear.

BAGGER analyzes all applications of the general focus rule that appear in the specific example. When several instantiations of the focus rule provide sufficient information for different generalizations, BAGGER collects the preconditions for satisfying the antecedents of each in a disjunction of conjunctions (one conjunct for each acceptable instantiation). Common terms are factored out of the disjunction. If none of the instantiations of the focus rule provide sufficient information for generalizing the structure of the explanation, no new rule is learned by BAGGER.

Three classes of terms must be collected to construct the antecedents of a new rule. First, the antecedents of the initial rule application in the arbitrary length sequence of rule applications must be satisfied. To do this, the antecedents of the focus rule are used. Second, the preconditions imposed by chaining together an arbitrary number of rule applications must be collected. These are derived by analyzing each interconnected instantiation of the focus rule in the sample proof. Those applications that provide enough information to be viewed as the arbitrary ith application produce this second class of preconditions. Third, the preconditions from the rest of the explanation must be collected. This determines the constraints on the final applications of the focus rule.

To package a sequence of rule applications into a single sequential rule, the preconditions that must be satisfied at each of the N rule applications must be collected and combined. The preconditions for applying the resulting extended rule must be specifiable in terms of the initial state, *not* in terms of intermediate states. This ensures, given that the necessary conditions are satisfied in the initial state, a plan represented in a sequential rule will run to completion without further problem solving, regardless of the number of intervening states necessary. For example, there is no possibility that a plan will lead to moving N–2 blocks and

procedure BuildNewBAGGERrule (goalNode)

  focusNodes ← CollectFocusRuleApplications(goalNode)

  antecedentsInitial ← BuildInitialAntecedents(Earliest(focusNodes))

  antecedentsIntermediate ← φ

  for each focusNode **in** focusNodes **do**

    answer ← ViewAsArbitraryApplic(focusNode, focusNodes)

    if answer ≠ *fail* **then** AddDisjunct(antecedentsIntermediate, answer)

  antecedentsFinal ← ViewAsArbitraryApplic(goalNode, focusNodes)

  consequents ← CollectGoalTerms(goalNode)

  if antecedentsIntermediate ≠ φ ∧ antecedentsFinal ≠ *fail*

    then AddRule(antecedentsInitial, antecedentsIntermediate, antecedentsFinal, consequents)

procedure ViewAsArbitraryApplic (node, focusNodes)

  result ← φ

  for each antecedent **in** Antecedents(node) **do**

    if Axiom?(antecedent) **then** *true*

    else if SupportedByEarlierNode?(antecedent, focusNodes) **then**

      AddConjunct(result, CollectNecessaryEqualities(antecedent, Supporter(antecedent)))

    else if SituationIndependent?(antecedent) **then** AddConjunct(result, antecedent)

    else if SupportedByPartiallyUnwindableRule?(antecedent) **then**

      AddConjunct(result, CollectResultsOfPartiallyUnwinding(antecedent))

      AddConjunct(result, ViewAsArbitraryApplic(PartiallyUnwind(antecedent), focusNodes))

    else if SupportedByUnwindableRule?(antecedent) **then**

      AddConjunct(result, CollectResultsOfUnwinding(antecedent))

    else if SupportedByRuleConsequent?(antecedent) **then**

      AddConjunct(result, CollectNecessaryEqualities(antecedent, Supporter(antecedent)))

      AddConjunct(result, ViewAsArbitraryApplic(SupportingRule(antecedent), focusNodes))

    else return *fail*

  return result

Figure 3–19: The BAGGER Generalization Algorithm

then get stuck. If the preconditions for the ith rule application were expressed in terms of the result of the $(i{-}1)$th application, each of the N

rule applications would have to be considered in turn to determine whether the preconditions of the next are satisfied. This is not acceptable. In the approach taken, extra work during generalization and a possible loss of generality are traded off for a rule whose preconditions are easier to check.

When a focus rule is concatenated an arbitrary number of times, variables need to be chosen for each rule application. The RIS, a sequence of p–dimensional *vectors*, is used to represent this information. The general form of the RIS is

$$<v_{1,1}, \ldots, v_{1,p}>, <v_{2,1}, \ldots, v_{2,p}>, \ldots, <v_{n,1}, \ldots, v_{n,p}> \qquad (1)$$

In the tower–building example of Figure 3–11, initially $p = 3$: the current situation, the object to be moved, and the object upon which the moved object will be placed.

Depending on the rule used, the choice of elements for this sequence may be constrained. For example, certain elements may have to possess various properties, specific relations may have to hold among various elements, some elements may be constrained to be equal to or unequal to other elements, and some elements may be functions of other elements. Often, choosing the values of the components of one vector determines the values of components of subsequent vectors. For instance, when building a tower, choosing the block to be moved in step i also determines the location to place the block to be moved in step $i + 1$.

To determine the preconditions in terms of the initial state, each of the focus rule instantiations appearing in the specific proof is viewed as an arbitrary (or ith application of the underlying rule. The antecedents of this rule are analyzed as to what must be true of the initial state in order to guarantee that the ith collection of antecedents are satisfied when needed. This involves analyzing the proof tree, considering how each antecedent is proved. An augmented version of a standard explanation-based generalization algorithm [27] is used to determine which variables in this portion of the proof tree are constrained in terms of other variables.

Once this is done, the variables are expressed as components of the p–dimensional vectors described earlier, and the system ascertains what must be true of this sequence of vectors so that each antecedent is satisfied when necessary. All antecedents of the chosen instantiation of the focus rule must be one of the following types for generalizing to N to be possible:

(1)   The antecedent may be an *axiom*. Since an axiom always holds, it need not appear as a precondition in the final rule.

(2)   The antecedent may be supported by a consequent of an earlier application of the focus rule. Terms of this type place inter-vector constraints on the sequence of p–dimensional vectors. These constraints are computed by unifying the general versions of the two terms.

(3)   The antecedent may be *situation–independent*. Terms of this type are unaffected by actions.

(4)   The antecedent may be supported by an "unwindable" or partially "unwindable" rule. When this happens, the antecedent is unwound to an arbitrary earlier state and all of the preconditions necessary to ensure that the antecedent holds when needed are collected. A *partially unwindable* rule goes back an indefinite number of situations, from which the algorithm continues recursively. If no other inference rules are in the support of the unwindable rule, then it is unwound all the way to the initial state. The process of unwinding is further elaborated later. It, too, may place inter-vector constraints on the sequence of p–dimensional vectors.

(5)   The antecedent is supported by other terms that are satisfied in one of the above ways. When traversing backward across a supported antecedent, the system collects any intervector constraints produced by unifying the general version of the antecedent with the general version of the consequent that supports it.

Notice that antecedents are considered satisfied when they can be expressed in terms of the initial state, *not* when a leaf of the proof tree is reached. Conceivably, to satisfy these antecedents in the initial state could require a large number of inference rules. If that is the case, it may be better to trace backward through these rules until more *operational* terms are encountered. The relationship between *operationality* and *generality* [1, 24, 37–40] is a major issue in explanation–based learning but will not be discussed further here. Usually the cost of increased operationality is more limited applicability. An empirical analysis of the effect of this trade–off in the BAGGER system appears in Chapter 7.

A second point to notice is that not all proof subtrees will terminate in one of the preceding ways. If this is the case, this application of the focus rule cannot be viewed as an arbitrary ith application.[6]

The possibility that a specific solution does not provide enough information to generalize to N is an important point in explanation-based approaches to generalizing number. A concept involving an arbitrary number of substructures may involve an arbitrary number of substantially different problems. Any specific solution will have addressed only a finite number of these subproblems. Due to fortuitous circumstances in the example, some of the potential problems may not have arisen. To generalize to N, a system must recognize all the problems that exist in the *general* concept and, by analyzing the specific solution, surmount them. Inference rules of a certain form (described later) elegantly support this task in the BAGGER system. They allow the system to reason backward through an arbitrary number of actions.

Figure 3-20 illustrates how consequents of an earlier application of a focus rule can satisfy some antecedents of a later instantiation. This figure contains a portion of the proof for the tower-building example. (The full proof tree is presented and discussed later.) Portions of two consecutive transfers are shown. All variables are universally quantified. Arrows run from the antecedents of a rule to its consequents; double-headed arrows represent terms that are equated in the specific explanation. The generalization algorithm enforces the unification of these paired terms, leading to the collection of equality constraints.

There are four antecedents of a transfer. To define a transfer, the block moved (x), the object on which it is placed (y), and the current state (s) must be specified, and the constraints among these variables must be satisfied. One antecedent, the one requiring a block not be placed on top of itself, is type 3 — it is *situation-independent*. The next two antecedents are type 2. Two of the consequents of the $(i-1)$th transfer are used to satisfy these antecedents of the ith transfer. During transfer$_{i-1}$, in state s_{i-1} object x_{i-1} is moved on to object y_{i-1}. The consequents of this transfer are that a new state is produced, the object

---

[6] An alternative approach to this method would be to have the system search through its collection of unwindable rules and incorporate a relevant one into the proof structure. To study the limits of this chapter's approach to generalizing to N, it is required that *all* necessary information be present in the explanation; no problem-solving search is performed during generalization. Another approach would be to assume the problem solver could overcome this problem at rule application time. This second technique, however, would eliminate the property that a learned plan will always run to completion whenever its preconditions are satisfied in the initial state.

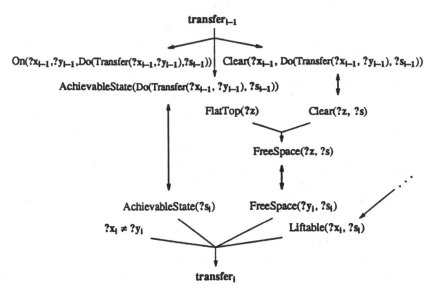

Figure 3-20: Satisfying Antecedents by Previous Consequents

moved is clear in the new state, and x_{i-1} is on y_{i-1} in the resulting state.

The state that results from $transfer_{i-1}$ satisfies the second antecedent of $transfer_i$. Unifying these terms defines s_i in terms of the previous variables in the RIS.

Another antecedent requires that, in state s_i, there be space on object y_i to put block x_i. This antecedent is type 5; hence the algorithm traverses backward through the rule that supports it. An inference rule specifies that a clear object with a flat top has free space. The clearness of x_{i-1} after $transfer_{i-1}$ is used. Unifying this collection of terms leads, in addition to the redundant definition of s_i, to the equating of y_i with z and x_{i-1}. This means that the previously moved block always provides a clear spot to place the current block, which leads to the construction of a tower.

The fourth antecedent, that x_i be liftable, is also type 5. A rule (not shown) states that an object is liftable if it is a clear block. Block x_i is determined to be clear because it is clear in the initial state and nothing has been placed on it. Tracing backward from the liftable term leads to several situation-independent terms and the term $Supports(?x_i, \phi, ?s_i)$. Although this term contains a situation variable, it is satisfied by an "unwindable rule" and is type 4.

Equation 2 presents the form required for a rule to be unwindable. The consequent must match one of the antecedents of the rule. Hence, the rule can be applied recursively. This feature is used to "unwind" the term from the ith state to an earlier state, often the initial state. Occasionally there can be several unwindable rules in a support path. For example, a block might support another block during some number of transfers, be cleared, remain clear during another sequence of transfers, and finally be added to a tower. The variables in the rule are divided into three groups. First, there are the x variables. These appear unchanged in both the consequent's term P and the antecedent's term P. Second, there are the y variables, which differ in the two P's, and the z variables, which only appear in the antecedents. Finally, there is the state variable (s). There can be additional requirements of the x, y, and z variables (via predicate Q); however, these requirements cannot depend on a state variable.

$$P(x_{i,1}, \ldots, x_{i,\mu}, y_{i-1,1}, \ldots, y_{i-1,v}, s_{i-1})$$
$$\text{and}$$
$$Q(x_{i,1}, \ldots, x_{i,\mu}, y_{i-1,1}, \ldots, y_{i-1,v}, y_{i,1}, \ldots, y_{i,v}, \ldots, z_{i,1}, \ldots, z_{i,\omega})$$
$$\text{and}$$
$$s_i = Do(x_{i,1}, \ldots, x_{i,\mu}, y_{i-1,1}, \ldots, y_{i-1,v}, \ldots, z_{i,1}, \ldots, z_{i,\omega}, s_{i-1})$$
$$\rightarrow$$
$$P(x_{i,1}, \ldots, x_{i,\mu}, y_{i,1}, \ldots, y_{i,v}, s_i) \tag{2}$$

Applying Equation 2 recursively produces Equation 3. This rule determines the requirements on the earlier state so that the desired term can be guaranteed in state i. Except for the definition of the next state, none of the antecedents depend on the intermediate states. Notice that a collection of y and z variables must be specified. Any of these variables not already contained in the RIS are added to it. Hence, the RIS is also used to store the results of intermediate computations. Since the predicate Q does not depend on the situation, it can be evaluated in the initial state.

$$P(x_{i,1}, \ldots, x_{i,\mu}, y_{j,1}, \ldots, y_{j,v}, s_1) \text{ and } 0 < j < i$$
$$\text{and}$$
$$\forall k \in j+1, \ldots, i$$
$$Q(x_{i,1}, \ldots, x_{i,\mu}, y_{k-j,1}, \ldots, y_{k-j,v}, y_{k,1}, \ldots, y_{k,v}, \ldots, z_{k,1}, \ldots, z_{k,\omega})$$
$$\text{and}$$
$$s_k = Do(x_{i,1}, \ldots, x_{i,\mu}, y_{k-j,1}, \ldots, y_{k-j,v}, \ldots, z_{k-j,1}, \ldots, z_{k-j,\omega}, s_{k-1})$$
$$\rightarrow$$
$$P(x_{i,1}, \ldots, x_{i,\mu}, y_{i,1}, \ldots, y_{i,v}, s_i) \tag{3}$$

The requirements on the predicate Q are actually somewhat less restrictive. Rather than requiring this predicate to be situation-independent, all that is necessary is that any term containing a situation argument be supported (possibly indirectly) by an application of a focus rule. The important characteristic is that the satisfaction of the predicate Q can be specified in terms of the initial situation only. Separately unwinding a predicate Q while unwinding a predicate P is not possible with the current algorithm, and how this can be accomplished is an open research issue.

Frame axioms often satisfy the form of Equation 2. Figure 3–21 shows one way to satisfy the need to have a clear object at the ith step. Assume the left–hand side of Figure 3–21 is a portion of some proof. This explanation says block x_i is clear in state s_i because it is clear in state s_{i-1} and the block moved in $transfer_{i-1}$ is not placed on x_i. Unwinding this rule leads to the result that block x_i will be clear in state s_i if it is clear in state s_1 and x_i is never used as the new support block in any of the intervening transfers.

To classify an instantiation of a rule as being unwindable, the rule must be applied successively at least *twice*. This heuristic prevents generalizations that are likely to be spurious. Just like when looking for multiple applications of the focus rule, multiple applications are required for unwindable rules. The intent of this is to increase the likelihood that a generalization is being made that will be prove useful in the future. For example, imagine some rule represents withdrawing some money from a bank and also imagine this rule is of the form of Equation 2. Assume that in state 5, John withdraws \$500 to buy a television, while in states 1–4, the amount of money he has in the bank is unaffected.

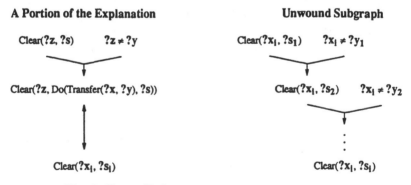

Figure 3–21: Unwinding a Rule

Although it is correct to generalize this plan to include any number of trips to the bank to get sufficient money for a purchase, it does not seem proper to do so. Rather, the generalization should be to a single trip to the bank at *any* time. Frame axioms are exceptions to this constraint — they need to be applied only once to be considered unwindable. Since frame axioms only specify what remains unchanged, there is no risk in assuming an arbitrary number of successive applications.

Once the repeated rule portion of the extended rule is determined, the rest of the explanation is incorporated into the final result. This is accomplished in the same manner in which antecedents are satisfied in the repeated rule portion, except that the focus rule is now viewed as the Nth rule application. As before, antecedents must be one of the five specified types. If all the terms in the goal cannot be satisfied in the arbitrary Nth state, no rule is learned.

The consequents of the final rule are constructed by collecting those generalized final consequents of the explanation that directly support the goal.

Even though all the antecedents of a sequential BAGGER rule are evaluated in the initial state, substantial time can be spent finding satisfactory bindings for the variables in the rule. Simplifying the antecedents of a rule acquired using EBL can increase the efficiency of the rule [14] [41]. After a rule is constructed by the BAGGER generalization algorithm, duplicate antecedents are removed and the remainder are rearranged by the system in an attempt to speed up the process of satisfying the rule. This involves several processes. Heuristics are used to estimate whether it is better to construct sequences from the first vector forward or from the last vector backward. Terms not affected by the intermediate antecedent are moved so that they are tested as soon as possible. Terms involving arithmetic are placed so that all their arguments are bound when they are evaluated. Finally, within each grouping, antecedents are arranged so that terms involving the same variable are near each other.

3.3. Details of the Stacking Example

This section presents the details of one of BAGGER's sequential rules. The proof that explains the tower–building actions of Figure 3–10 appears in Figure 3–22. This graph is produced by the system, but nodes have been rearranged by hand for the sake of readability. Since the situation arguments are quite lengthy, they are abbreviated and defined in the key. Arrows run from the antecedent of a rule to its consequent. When a rule has multiple antecedents or consequents, an ampersand (&) is used.

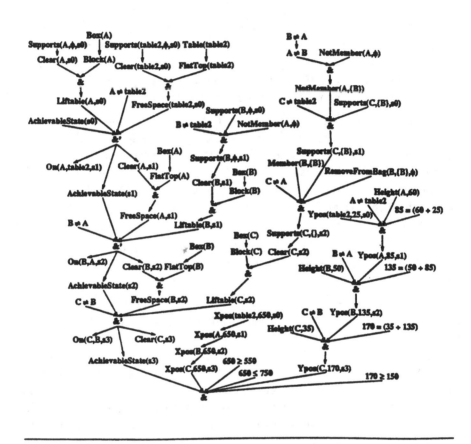

Abbreviation Key

s0 *the initial state*	s2 Do(Transfer(B,A),Do(Transfer(A,table2),s0))
s1 Do(Transfer(A,table2),s0)	s3 Do(Transfer(C,B),Do(Transfer(B,A),Do(Transfer(A,table2),s0)))

Figure 3–22: Situation Calculus Plan for Stacking Three Blocks

The primed ampersands are the instantiations of the focus rule, and the lowest ampersand is the goal node.

The goal provided to the backward–chaining theorem prover that produced this graph is

$$\exists \quad \text{AchievableState(?state)} \; \wedge$$
$$\text{Xpos(?object, ?px, ?state)} \; \wedge \; \text{?px} \geq 550 \; \wedge \; \text{?px} \leq 750 \; \wedge$$
$$\text{Ypos(?object, ?py, ?state)} \; \wedge \; \text{?py} \geq 150.$$

This says that the goal is to prove the existence of an achievable state, such that in that state the horizontal position of some object is between 550 and 750 and the vertical position of that same objects is at least 150.

The sequential rule produced by analyzing this explanation structure appears in Table 3–4. The remainder of this section describes how each term in this table is produced. Line numbers have been included for purposes of reference. For readability, the new rule is broken down into components, as shown in Equation 4. While BAGGER's reordering of a new rule's antecedents means the presented rule is somewhat harder to read, Table 3–4 accurately reflects the rule acquired and used by the system.

$$Antecedents_{initial} \land Antecedent_{intermediate} \land Antecedents_{rest} \rightarrow Consequents \quad (4)$$

3.3.1. Producing the Initial Antecedents

The initial antecedents in the first line of the rule establish a sequence of vectors, the initial state, and the first vector contained in the sequence. Subscripts are used to indicate components of vectors, as a shorthand for functions that perform this task. For example, $?v_{1,3}$ is shorthand for ThirdComponent($?v_1$). Lines 2 and 3 contain the antecedents of the first application in the chain of applications. These are the same terms that appear in the focus rule (the first rule in Table 3–8), except that the components of v_1 are used. The system has knowledge of which arguments are situation variables, and the initial state constant $s0$ is placed in these positions. The other terms in this grouping are produced by the unwinding process (Height, Xpos, Ypos, and the addition term) or are moved ($\geq$ and $\leq$) from the final antecedents to the initial antecedents because their variables are not influenced by the intermediate antecedents. The terms produced by unwinding are described further in what follows.

3.3.2. Analyzing the Applications of the Focus Rule

Lines 5–11 in Table 3–4 contain the preconditions derived by analyzing the three instantiations of the focus rule. In this implication, v_i — an arbitrary vector in the sequence (other than the first) — is used, as these constraints must be satisfied for each of the applications that follow the first. Vector v_{i-1} is the vector immediately preceding v_i. It is needed because some of the antecedents of the ith application are satisfied

---

Table 4: The Components of the Learned Rule

Antecedents initial

(1) $Sequence(?seq) \wedge InitialVector(?v_1,?seq) \wedge State(s0) \wedge ?v_{1,1} = s0 \wedge$

(2) $FreeSpace(?v_{1,3}, s0) \wedge Liftable(?v_{1,2}, s0) \wedge Height(?v_{1,2}, ?v_{1,4}) \wedge$

(3) $Xpos(?v_{1,3}, ?px, s0) \wedge Ypos(?v_{1,3}, ?new, s0) \wedge ?v_{1,2} \neq ?v_{1,3} \wedge$

(4) $?v_{1,5} = (?v_{1,4} + ?new) \wedge ?px \geq ?xmin \wedge ?px \leq ?xmax \wedge$

Antecedent intermediate

(5) $[Member(?v_i,?seq) \wedge ?v_i \neq ?v_1 \wedge Member(?v_{i-1},?seq) \wedge Predecessor(?v_{i-1},?v_i,?seq) \wedge$
      $\rightarrow$

(6) $?v_{i,3} = ?v_{i-1,2} \wedge ?v_{i,1} = Do(Transfer(?v_{i-1,2}, ?v_{i-1,3}), ?v_{i-1,1}) \wedge FlatTop(?v_{i,3}) \wedge$

(7) $Block(?v_{i,2}) \wedge Height(?v_{i,2}, ?v_{i,4}) \wedge ?v_{i,2} \neq ?v_{i,3} \wedge ?v_{i,5} = (?v_{i,4} + ?v_{i-1,5}) \wedge$

(8) $[[[Member(?v_j,?seq) \wedge Earlier(?v_j,?v_i,?seq) \rightarrow ?v_{i,2} \neq ?v_{j,3}] \wedge Supports(?v_{i,2},\phi,s0)]$

(9) $\vee [[Member(?v_j, ?seq) \wedge Earlier(?v_j, ?v_{i-1}, ?seq) \rightarrow NotMember(?v_{j,2}, \{?v_{i-1,2}\})]] \wedge$

(10) $[Member(?v_j, ?seq) \wedge Earlier(?v_j, ?v_{i-1},?seq) \rightarrow ?v_{i,2} \neq ?v_{j,3}] \wedge$

(11) $Supports(?v_{i,2}, \{?v_{i-1,2}\}, s0) \wedge ?v_{i,2} \neq ?v_{i,3}]]] \wedge$

Antecedents final

(12) $FinalVector(?v_n,?seq) \wedge ?py = ?v_{n,5} \wedge ?state = Do(Transfer(?v_{n,2}, ?v_{n,3}), ?v_{n,1}) \wedge$

(13) $?object = ?v_{n,2} \wedge ?py \geq ?ymin$

Consequents

(14) $State(?state) \wedge Xpos(?object, ?px, ?state) \wedge ?px \leq ?xmax \wedge ?px \geq ?xmin \wedge$

(15) $Ypos(?object, ?py, ?state) \wedge ?py \geq ?ymin$

This rule extends sequences $1 \rightarrow N$.

---

by the $(i-1)$th application. Although some preconditions in the new rule involve v_i and v_{i-1}, these preconditions all refer to conditions in the initial state. They do *not* refer to results in intermediate states.

The final two of the three instantiations of the focus rule produce sufficient information to determine how the antecedents of the rule can be satisfied in the ith application. In the first application (upper left of Figure 3–22), neither the support for Liftable nor the support for FreeSpace provides enough information to determine the constraints on the initial state so that these terms can be satisfied in an arbitrary step. In both cases, the proof had to address clearness only in the current state. No information is provided within the proof as to how clearness can be guaranteed to hold in some later state.

The two other instantiations of the focus rule provide sufficient information for generalization. Two different ways of satisfying the antecedents are discovered, and hence a disjunction is learned. The common terms in these two disjuncts appear in lines 6 and 7, and the remaining terms for the first disjunction are in line 8 and for the second in lines 9–11.

The third term in line 7 is the vector form of the inequality that is one of the antecedents of the focus rule. This, being situation-independent, is a type 3 antecedent. In vector form, it becomes $v_{i,2} \neq v_{i,3}$. It constrains possible collections of vectors to those that have different second and third members. This constraint stems from the requirement that a block cannot be stacked on itself.

Both of the successful applications of the focus rule have their AchievableState term satisfied by a consequent of a previous application. These terms are type 2 and require collection of the equalities produced by unifying the general versions of the matching consequents and antecedents. (See Figure 3–20 for the details of these matchings.) The equality that results from these unifications is the second term of line 6. Thus, the next state is always completely determined by the previous one. No searching is necessary to choose the next state. (Actually, no terms are ever evaluated in these intermediate states. The only reason they are recorded is so the final state can be determined for use in setting the situation variable in the consequents.)

Both successful applications have their FreeSpace term satisfied in the same manner. Traversing backward across one rule leads to a situation–independent term (FlatTop — line 6) and the consequent of an earlier application (Clear). Unifying the two clear terms (again, see Figure 3–20) produces the first two equalities in line 6. This first equality means that the block to be moved in the ith step can always be placed on top of the block to be moved in the $(i\text{–}1)$th step. No problem solving need be done to determine the location at which to continue building the tower.

The Block term in line 7 is produced during the process of analyzing the way the Liftable term is satisfied. The remaining portion of the analysis of Liftable produces the terms in the disjunctions. As in the initial antecedents, the Height and addition terms in line 7 are produced during the analysis of the terms in the goal, which is described later.

In the second application of the focus rule, which produces the first disjunct, a clear block to move is acquired by finding a block that is clear because it supports nothing in the initial state and nothing is placed on it later. The frame axiom supporting this is an unwindable rule. Unwinding it to the initial state produces line 8. The Supports term must hold in the initial state and the block to be moved in step i can never be used as the place to locate a block to be moved in an earlier step. The general version of the term NotMember(A, ϕ) does not appear in the learned rule because it is an axiom that nothing is a member of the empty set. (An earlier unification, from the rule involving Clear, requires that the second variable in the general version of NotMember term be ϕ.)

Notice that this unwinding restricts the applicability of the acquired rule. The first disjunct requires that if an initially clear block is to be added to the tower, nothing can ever be placed on it, even temporarily. A more general plan would be learned, however, if in the specific example a block is temporarily covered. In that case, in the proof there would be several groupings of unwindable rules; for a while the block would remain clear, something would then be placed on it and it would remain covered for several steps, and finally it would be cleared and remain that way until moved. Although this clearing and unclearing can occur repeatedly, the current BAGGER algorithm is unable to generalize number within unwindable subproofs.

The second disjunct (lines 9-11) results from the different way a liftable block is found in the third application of the focus rule. Here a liftable block is found by using a block that initially supported one other block, which is moved in the previous step, and where nothing else is moved to the lower block during an earlier rule application. Unwinding the subgraph for this application leads to the requirements that initially one block is on the block to be moved in step i, that block be moved in step $(i-1)$, and nothing else is scheduled to be moved to the lower block during an earlier rule applications. Again, some terms do not appear in the learned rule (Member and RemoveFromBag) because, given the necessary unifications, they are axioms. This time NotMember is not an axiom and hence appears. If the specific example were more complicated, the acquired rule would reflect the fact that the block on top can be removed in some *earlier* step, rather than necessarily in the *previous* step.

3.3.3. Analyzing the Rest of the Explanation

Once all of the instantiations of the focus rule are analyzed, the goal node is visited. This produces lines 12 and 13, plus some of the earlier terms.

The AchievableState term of the goal is satisfied by the final application of the focus rule, leading to the third term in line 12.

The final X position is calculated using an unwindable rule. Tracing backward from the Xpos in the goal to the consequent of the unwindable rule produces the first term in line 13, as well as the third term in line 12. When this rule is unwound, it produces the first term of line 3 and the second term of line 6. Also, matching the Xpos term in the antecedents with the one in the consequents, so that Equation 2 applies, again produces the first term in line 6. Since there are no "Q" terms (Equation 2), no other preconditions are added to the intermediate antecedent.

The inequalities involving the tower's horizontal position are state-independent; their general forms are moved to the initial antecedents because their arguments are not affected by satisfying the intermediate antecedent. These terms in the initial antecedents involving ?px ensure that the tower is started underneath the goal.

Unwindable rules also determine the final Y position. Here "Q" terms are present. The connection of two instantiations of the underlying general rule appears in Figure 3–23. This general rule is unwound to the initial state, which creates the second term of line 3 and the second term

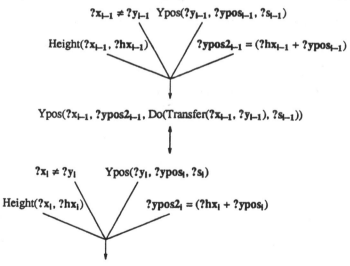

Figure 3–23. Calculating the Vertical Position of the ith Stacked Block

of line 6. The last three terms of line 7 are also produced, as the "Q" terms must hold for each application of the unwound rule. This process adds two components to the vectors in the RIS. The first $(?v_{1,4})$ comes from the ?hx variable, which records the height of the block being added to the tower. The other $(?v_{i,5})$ comes from the variable ?yPos2. It records the vertical position of the block added and hence represents the height of the tower. The ?ypos variable does not lead to the creation of another RIS entry because it matches the ?yPos2 variable of the previous application. All that is needed is a ?ypos variable for the first application. Similarly, matching the Ypos term in the antecedents with the one in the consequents produces the first term in line 6.

The last conjunct in the goal produces the second term on line 13. This precondition ensures that the final tower is tall enough.

Finally, the general version of the goal description is used to construct the consequents of the new rule (lines 14 and 15).

3.3.4 The Rule Learned by EGGS

Table 5: The Standard EBL Version of the Tower Rule

Antecedents

(16)   AchievableState(s0) ∧ Liftable(?x2, s0) ∧ FlatTop(?x2) ∧ Height(?x2, ?hx) ∧

(17)   Block(?x) ∧ Height(?x, ?hx2) ∧ ?x2 ≠ ?x ∧ FreeSpace(?y, s0) ∧ Xpos(?y, ?xpos, s0) ∧

(18)   Ypos(?y, ?pyy, s0) ∧ ?x ≠ ?y ∧ ?x2 ≠ ?y ∧ Supports(?x, {?x1}, s0) ∧

(19)   NotMember(?x2, {?x1}) ∧ Supports(?x1, φ, s0) ∧ Block(?x1) ∧ FlatTop(?x1) ∧

(20)   Height(?x1, ?hx1) ∧ ?x1 ≠ ?y ∧ ?x2 ≠ ?x1 ∧ ?x ≠ ?x1 ∧ ?xpos ≤ ?xmax ∧

(21)   ?xpos ≥ ?xmin ∧ ?pyx = (?hx + ?pyy) ∧ ?pyx1 = (?hx1 + ?pyx) ∧

(22)   ?pyx2 = (?hx2 + ?pyx1) ∧ ?pyx2 ≥ ?ymin

Consequents

(23)   AchievableState(Do(Transfer(?x,?x1),Do(Transfer(?x1,?x2),Do(Transfer(?x2,?y),s0)))) ∧

(24)   Xpos(?x,?xpos,Do(Transfer(?x,?x1),Do(Transfer(?x1,?x2),Do(Transfer(?x2,?y),s0)))) ∧

(25)   ?xpos ≤ ?xmax ∧ ?xpos ≥ ?xmin ∧

(26)   Ypos(?x,?pyx2,Do(Transfer(?x,?x1),Do(Transfer(?x1,?x2),Do(Transfer(?x2,?y),s0)))) ∧

(27)   ?pyx2 ≥ ?ymin

Table 6: Rules for Collections of Objects	
Rule	**Description**
Member(?x,?bag) → Member(?x,{?y | ?bag})	If an object is a member of a collection of objects, it is also a member of a superset of that collection.
Member(?x,{?x | ?bag})	See if an object is in a collection of objects.
?x ≠ ?y ∧ NotMember(?x,?bag) → NotMember(?x,{?y | ?bag})	If two objects are distinct, and the first is not in a collection of objects, then the first is not a member of the collection that results from adding the second object to the original collection.
NotMember(?x,φ)	Nothing is a member of the empty set.
RemoveFromBag(?x,?bag1,?bag2) → RemoveFromBag(?x,{?y | ?bag1},{?y | ?bag2})	If two collections of objects are related by the removal of one object, then this same relation holds if a second object is added to each collection.
RemoveFromBag(?x,{?x | ?bag},?bag)	Remove this object from a collection of objects, producing a new collection of objects.
AddToBag(?x,?bag1,?bag2) → AddToBag(?x,{?y | ?bag1},{?y | ?bag2})	If two collections of objects are related by the addition of one object, then this same relation holds if a second object is added to each collection.
AddToBag(?x,?bag,{?x | ?bag})	Add this object to a collection of objects, producing a new collection of objects.
Size(?bag,?m) ∧ ?n = (?m + 1) → Size({?x | ?bag},?n)	The size of a collection of objects is increased by one if another object is added to the collection.
Size(φ,0)	The empty set has size zero.
?x ≠ ?y → ?y ≠ ?x	Inequality is reflexive.

Table 3–5 contains the results **EGGS** produces from Figure 3–22's explanation. Note that several aspects of the problem are generalized. For example, any three blocks of any height can be stacked. However, the number of blocks is *not* generalized. Towers of various heights can be constructed using this rule, but they all will involve stacking *exactly* three blocks.

3.3.5. Initial Inference Rules

The inference rules and axioms used in the tower–building example are presented in this section. In these rules, all variables contain a leading "?" and are universally quantified. The construct {?a ¦ ?b} matches a list with head ?a and tail ?b. For example, if matched with {x,y,z}, variable ?a is bound to x and ?b to {y,z}.

Table 7: Blocks World Intra-Situation Rules	
Rule	**Description**
Clear(?x,?s) ∧ FlatTop(?x) → FreeSpace(?x,?s)	If an object is clear and has a flat top, space is available.
Table(?x) → FreeSpace(?x,?s)	There always is room on a table.
Clear(?x,?s) ∧ Block(?x) → Liftable(?x,?s)	A block is liftable if it is clear.
Box(?x) → FlatTop(?x)	Boxes have flat tops.
Table(?x) → FlatTop(?x)	Tables have flat tops.
Box(?x) → Block(?x)	Boxes are a type of block.
Pyramid(?x) → Block(?x)	Pyramids are a type of block.
Supports(?x,φ,?s) → Clear(?x,?s)	An object is clear if it is supporting nothing.

Table 3–6 contains those rules that describe properties of collections of objects. Included are rules for membership, rules for specifying how to add and remove elements, a rule about inequality, and rules about cardinality (size). These rules are used in the blocks world examples and in the example involving the setting of a table.

Table 3–7 contains *intra*situation rules for the blocks–world examples. For example, in the blocks world, there are tables and blocks. There are two types of blocks: boxes, which have flat tops, and pyramids. Rules for inferring that free space is present, a block is liftable, and an object is clear are included.

Tables 3–8 and 3–9 describe *inter*situation inferences for the blocks world. The first rule in Table 3–7 is the definition of the transfer action used in the examples. The other accessory rules describe how the location of blocks changes after a transfer. Table 3–8 contains rules for reasoning about support relationships following a transfer.

3.4. Related Work

The need to generalize number in EBL was first pointed out in [17], where the knowledge that momentum is conserved for any N objects is learned from an example involving the collision of a fixed number of balls. Besides BAGGER, several other explanation–based approaches to generalizing number have been recently proposed.

Prieditis [42] has developed a system which learns macro–operators representing sequences of repeated STRIPS–like operators. Although

Table 8: Some Blocks World Inter-Situation Rules	
Rule	Description
AchievableState(?s) ∧ Liftable(?x,?s) ∧ FreeSpace(?y,?s) ∧ ?x ≠ ?y → AchievableState(Do(Transfer(?x,?y),?s)) ∧ Clear(?x,Do(Transfer(?x,?y),?s)) ∧ On(?x,?y,Do(Transfer(?x,?y),?s))	If the top of an object is clear in some achievable state and there is free space on another object, then the first object can be moved from its present location to the new location. However, an object cannot be moved onto itself. Moving creates a new state in which the moved object is still clear but (possibly) at a new location.
AchievableState(S0)	The initial state is always achievable.
Xpos(?y,?xpos,?s) → Xpos(?x,?xpos,Do(Transfer(?x,?y),?s))	After a transfer, the object moved is centered (in the X-direction) on the object upon which it is placed.
?x ≠ ?y ∧ Height(?x,?hx) ∧ Ypos(?y,?ypos,?s) ∧ ?ypos2 = (?hx + ?ypos) → Ypos(?x,?ypos2,Do(Transfer(?x,?y),?s))	After a transfer, the Y-position of the object moved is determined by adding its height to the Y-position of the object upon which it is placed.
?a ≠ ?x ∧ Xpos(?a,?xpos,?s) → Xpos(?a,?xpos,Do(Transfer(?x,?y),?s))	All blocks, other than the one moved, remain in the same X-position after a transfer.
?a ≠ ?x ∧ Ypos(?a,?xpos,?s) → Ypos(?a,?xpos,Do(Transfer(?x,?y),?s))	All blocks, other than the one moved, remain in the same Y-position after a transfer.

BAGGER is very much in the spirit of Prieditis's work, STRIPS–like operators impose unwarranted restrictions. For instance, BAGGER's use of predicate calculus allows generalization of repeated structure and repeated actions in a uniform manner. In addition, the BAGGER approach accommodates the use of additional inference rules to reason about what is true in a state. Everything does not have to appear explicitly in the focus rule. For example, in the stacking problem, other rules are used to determine the height of a tower and that an object is clear when the only object it supports is transferred. Also, instantiations of the focus rule do not have to directly connect — intervening inference rules can be involved when determining that the results of one instantiation partially support the preconditions of another. Prieditis's approach only analyzes the constraints imposed by the connections of the precondition, add, and delete lists of the operators of interest. There is nothing that corresponds to BAGGER's unwinding operation nor are disjunctive rules learned.

Table 9: Inter-Situation Rules about Block Support	
Rule	Description
?a ≠ ?x ∧ On(?a,b,?s) → On(?a,?b,Do(Transfer(?x,?y),?s))	If an object is not moved, it remains on the same object.
?u ≠ ?y ∧ Supports(?u,?items,?s) ∧ NotMember(?x,?items) → Supports(?u,?items,Do(Transfer(?x,?y),?s))	If an object neither supports the moved object before the transfer, nor is the new supporter, then the collection of objects it supports remains unchanged.
?u ≠ ?y ∧ Supports(?u,?items,?s) ∧ Member(?x,?items) ∧ RemoveFromBag(?x,?items,?new) → Supports(?u,?new,Do(Transfer(?x,?y),?s))	If an object is not the new support of the moved object, but supported it before the transfer, then the moved object must be removed from the collection of objects being supported.
Supports(?y,?items,?s) ∧ NotMember(?x,?items) ∧ AddToBag(?x,?items,?new) → Supports(?y,?new,Do(Transfer(?x,?y),?s))	After the transfer, another item is supported if the new supporter did not previously support the moved object.
Supports(?y,?items,?s) ∧ Member(?x,?items) → Supports(?y,?items,Do(Transfer(?x,?y),?s))	If the moved object is transferred to the object that previously supported it, the new supporter still supports the same objects.

In the FERMI system [43], cyclic patterns are recognized using empirical methods and the detected repeated pattern is generalized using explanation–based learning techniques. A major strength of the FERMI system is the incorporation of conditionals within the learned macro–operator. However, unlike the techniques implemented in BAGGER, the rules acquired by FERMI are not fully based on an explanation–based analysis of an example and so are not guaranteed to always work. For example, FERMI learns a strategy for solving a set of linear algebraic equations. None of the preconditions of the strategy check that the equations are linearly independent. The learned strategy will appear applicable to the problem of determining x and y from the equations $3x + y = 5$ and $6x + 2y = 10$. After a significant amount of work, the strategy will terminate unsuccessfully.

Cohen has recently developed and formalized another approach to the problem of generalizing number [44]. His system generalizes number by constructing a finite–state control mechanism that deterministically directs the construction of proofs similar to the one used to justify the specific example. One significant property of his method is that it can generate proof procedures involving tree traversals and nested loops. A major difference between Cohen's method and other explanation–based algorithms is that in his approach no "internal nodes" of the explanation are eliminated during generalization. In other explanation–based algorithms, only the leaves of the operationalized explanation appear in the acquired rule. The generalization process guarantees that all of the inference rules within the explanation apply in the general case, and the final result can be viewed as a compilation of the effect of combining these rules as generally as possible. Hence, to apply the new rule, only the general versions of these leave nodes need be satisfied. In Cohen's approach, every inference rule used in the original explanation is explicitly incorporated into the final result. Each rule may again be applied when satisfying the acquired rule. Hence, there is nothing in this approach corresponding to unwinding a rule from an arbitrary state back to the initial state, and the efficiency gains obtained by doing this are not achieved. Finally, because the final automaton is deterministic, it incorporates disjunctions only in a limited way. For example, if at some point two choices are equally general, the ordering in the final rule will be the same as that seen in the specific example.

A fourth system, PHYSICS 101 [17, 18, 45], differs from the preceding approaches in that the need for generalizing number is motivated by an analytic justification of an example's solution and general domain knowledge. This system learns such concepts as the general law of conservation of momentum (which is applicable to an arbitrary collection of objects) by observing and analyzing the solution to a specific three–body collision. In the momentum problem, information about number, localized in a single physics formula, leads to a global restructuring of a specific solution's explanation. However, PHYSICS 101 is designed to reason about the use of mathematical formulae. Its generalization algorithm takes great advantage of the properties of algebraic cancellation (e.g., $x - x = 0$). To be a broad solution of the generalization to N problem, nonmathematically based domains must also be handled.

BAGGER 2 [46] is a successor to the original BAGGER. This system extends the original by being capable of learning more complicated forms of recursion, producing multiple generalizations to N from one example, and integrating the results of multiple examples.

Another aspect of generalizing the structure of explanations involves generalizing the *organization* of the nodes in the explanation, rather than generalizing the *number* of nodes. An approach of this form was presented in Section 2 of this chapter.

The problem of generalizing to *N* has also been addressed within the paradigms of similarity–based learning [35, 47–52] and automatic programming [53–56]. Michalski [35] advanced a general specification of number generalization. He proposed a set of generalization rules including a *closing interval rule* and several *counting arguments rules* which can generate number–generalized structures. The difference between such similarity–based approaches and BAGGER's explanation–based approach is that the newly formed similarity–based concepts typically require verification from corroborating examples, whereas the explanation–based concepts are immediately supported by the domain theory.

3.5. Some Open Research Issues

The BAGGER system has taken important steps toward the solution to the "generalization to *N*" problem, but the research is still incomplete. From the vantage point of the current results, several avenues of future research are apparent.

One issue in generalizing the structure of explanations is that of deciding when there is enough information in the specific explanation to usefully generalize its structure. Due to the finiteness of a specific problem, fortuitous circumstances in the specific situation may have allowed shortcuts in the solution. Complications inherent in the general case may not have been faced. Hence the specific example provides no guidance as to how they should be addressed. In BAGGER, the requirement that, for an application of a focus rule to be generalized, it be viewable as the arbitrary *i*th application addresses the problem of recognizing fortuitous circumstances. If there is not enough information to view it as the *i*th application, it is likely that some important issue is not addressed in this focus rule application. However, more powerful techniques for recognizing fortuitous circumstances need to be developed.

Related to this issue, BAGGER's method of choosing a focus rule needs improvement. Currently, the first detected instance of interconnected applications of a rule is used as the focus rule, but there could be several occurrences that satisfy these requirements. Techniques for comparing alternative focus rules are needed. Inductive inference approaches to detecting repeated structures [34, 47–52] may be applicable to the generation of candidate focus rules, from which the explanation–based capabilities of BAGGER can build.

A second research topic is performing multiple generalizations to *N* in a single problem. Especially interesting is *interleaved generalization to N*. Here, in the final result, each application in a sequence of arbitrary length would be supported by another sequence of arbitrary length. In other words, a portion of the intermediate antecedent of a BAGGER rule would be the antecedents of another BAGGER rule. Learning an interleaved sequential rule from one example may be too ambitious. A more reasonable approach may be first to learn a simple sequential rule and then use it in the explanation of a later problem. Managing the interactions between the two RIS's is a major issue. Approaches to the problem of interleaved generalization to N appear in [44, 46].

A third area of future research is to investigate how BAGGER and other such systems might acquire accessory intersituational rules, such as frame axioms, to complement their composite rules. Currently, each of BAGGER's new sequential inference rules specifies how to achieve a goal involving some arbitrary aggregation of objects by applying some number of operators. These rules are useful in directly achieving goals that match the consequent but do not effectively improve BAGGER's back-chaining problem-solving ability. This is because currently BAGGER does not construct new frame axioms for the rules it learns. (This problem is not specific to generalizing to N. Standard EBL algorithms must also face it when dealing with situation calculus.)

There are several methods of acquiring accessory rules. They can be constructed directly by combining the accessory rules of operators that make up the sequential rule. This process may be intractable, as the number of accessory rules for initial operators may be large and may increase combinatorially in sequential rules. Another, potentially more attractive, approach is to treat the domain theory, augmented by sequential rules, as intractable. Since the accessory rules for learned rules are derivable from existing knowledge of initial operators, the approach in Chapter 4 might be used to acquire the unstated but derivable accessory rules when they are needed.

Investigating the generalization of operator application orderings within learned rules is a fourth opportunity for future research. Currently, in the rules learned by the BAGGER algorithm, the order interdependence among rule applications is specified in terms of sequences of vectors. However, this is unnecessarily constraining. When valid, these constraints should be specified in terms of *sets* or *bags*[7] of vectors.

---

[7] A bag (or multiset) is an *unordered* collection of elements in which an element can appear more than once.

This could be accomplished by reasoning about the semantics of the system's predicate calculus functions and predicates. Properties such as symmetry, transitivity, and reflexivity may help determine constraints on order independence. An algorithm for generalizing the order of a fixed number of actions in a plan expressed in the STRIPS formalism appeared earlier in this chapter.

If a set satisfies a learned rule's antecedents, then *any* sequence derived from that set suffices. Conversely, if the vectors in a set fail to satisfy a rule's antecedents, there is no need to test each permutation of the elements. Unfortunately, testing all permutations occurs if the antecedents are unnecessarily expressed in terms of sequences. For example, assume the task at hand is to find enough heavy rocks in a storehouse to serve as ballast for a ship. A sequential rule may first add the weights in some order, find that the sum weight of all the rocks in the room is insufficient, and then try another ordering for adding the weights. A rule specified in terms of sets would terminate after adding the weights once.

A fifth area of future research involves investigating the most efficient ordering of conjunctive goals. Consider an acquired sequential rule which builds towers of a desired height, subject to the constraint that no block can be placed on a narrower block. The goal of building such towers is conjunctive: The correct height must be achieved, and the width of the stacked blocks must be monotonically nonincreasing. The optimal ordering is to select the blocks subject only to the height requirement and then sort them by size to determine their position in the tower. The reason this works is that a nonincreasing ordering of widths on any set of blocks is guaranteed so that no additional block–selection constraints are imposed by this conjunct. The system should ultimately detect and exploit this kind of decomposability to improve the efficiency of the new rules.

Satisfying global constraints poses a sixth research problem. The sequential rules investigated in this chapter are all *incremental* in that successive operator applications converge toward the goal achievement. This is not necessarily the case for all sequential rules. Consider a sequential rule for unstacking complex block structures subject to the global constraint that the partially dismantled structure always be stable. Removing one block can drastically alter the significance of another block with respect to the structure's stability. For some structures, only the subterfuge of adding a temporary support block or a counterbalance will allow unstacking to proceed. A block may be safe to remove at one point but be essential to the overall structural stability at the next, even though the block actually removed was physically distant from it. Such *nonincremental* effects are difficult to capture in sequential rules without permitting intermediate problem solving within the rule execution.

The RIS, besides recording the focus rule's variable bindings, is used to store intermediate calculations, such as the height of the tower currently planned. Satisfying global constraints may require that the information in an RIS vector increase as the sequence lengthens. For example, assume that each block to be added to a tower can only support some block–dependent weight. The RIS may have to record the projected weight on each block while BAGGER plans the construction of a tower. Hence, as the sequence lengthens, each successive vector in the RIS will have to record information for one additional block. Figuratively speaking, the RIS will be getting longer and wider. The current BAGGER algorithm does not support this.

Often, a repeated process has a closed–form solution. For example, summing the first N integers produces $(N(N+1))/2$. There is no need to compute the intermediate partial summations. A *recurrence relation* is a recursive method for computing a sequence of numbers. Recognizing and solving recurrence relations during generalization is a seventh area for additional research.

Many recurrences can be solved to produce efficient ways to determine the nth result in a sequence. It is this property that motivates the requirement that BAGGER's preconditions be expressed solely in terms of the initial state. However, the rule instantiation sequence still holds intermediate results. Although often this information is needed (if, for instance, the resulting sequence of actions is to be executed in the external world), BAGGER would be more efficient if it could produce, whenever possible, number–generalized rules that do not require the construction of an RIS. If BAGGER observes the summation of, say, four numbers, it will not produce the efficient result mentioned above. Instead it will produce a rule that stores the intermediate summations in the RIS. One extension that could be attempted is to create a library of templates for soluble recurrences, matching them against explanations. A more direct approach would be more appealing. Weld's technique of *aggregation* may be a fruitful approach [34]. Aggregation is an abstraction technique for creating a continuous description from a series of discrete events.

The issue of termination is an eighth research area. One important aspect of generalizing number is that the acquired rules may produce data structures whose size can grow without bound (for example, the rule instantiation sequence in BAGGER) or the algorithms that satisfy these rules may fall into infinite loops [57]. Although the *halting problem* is undecidable in general, in restricted circumstances termination can be proved [58]. Techniques for proving termination need to be incorporated into systems that generalize number. A practical, but less appealing, solution is to place resource bounds on the algorithms that apply number–generalized rules [57], potentially excluding successful applications.

Finally, it is important to investigate the generalization to N problem in the context of imperfect and intractable domain models [1, 59]. In any real–world domain, a computer system's model can only approximate reality. Furthermore, the complexity of problem solving prohibits any semblance of completeness. Thus far, BAGGER's sequential rules have relied on a correct domain model, and it has not addressed issues of intractability, other than the use of an outside expert to provide sample solutions when the construction of solutions from first principles is intractable.

3.6. Conclusions About Number Generalization

Most research in explanation–based learning involves relaxing constraints on the variables in an explanation, rather than generalizing the number of inference rules used. This section presented an approach to the task of generalizing the structure of explanations. The approach relies on a shift in representation which accommodates indefinite numbers of rule applications. As demonstrated in Chapter 11, compared to the results of standard explanation–based algorithms, more general rules are acquired, and since less rules need to be learned, better problem–solving performance gains are achieved.

To illustrate the approach, a situation calculus example from the blocks world was analyzed. This leads to a plan in which the number of blocks to be placed in a tower is generalized to N. In this example, the system observes three blocks being stacked on one another to satisfy the goal of having a block located at a specified height. Initially, the system has rules specifying how to transfer a single block from one location to another and how the horizontal and vertical position of a block can be determined after it is moved. By analyzing the explanation of how moving three blocks satisfies the desired goal, BAGGER learns a new rule that represents how an unconstrained number of block transfers can be performed to satisfy future related goals.

The fully implemented BAGGER system analyzes explanation structures (in this case, predicate calculus proofs) and detects repeated, interdependent applications of rules. Once a rule on which to focus attention is found, the system determines how an *arbitrary* number of instantiations of this rule can be concatenated. This indefinite–length collection of rules is conceptually merged into the explanation, replacing the specific–length collection of rules, and an extension of a standard explanation–based algorithm produces a new rule from the augmented explanation.

Rules produced by BAGGER have the important property that their preconditions are expressed in terms of the initial state: They do not depend on the situations produced by intermediate applications of the focus rule. This means that the results of multiple applications of the rule are determined by reasoning only about the current situation. There is no need to apply the rule successively, each time checking whether the preconditions for the next application are satisfied.

The specific example guides the extension of the focus rule into a structure representing an arbitrary number of repeated applications. Information not contained in the focus rule, but appearing in the example, is often incorporated into the extended rule. In particular, *unwindable* rules provide the guidance as to how preconditions of the *i*th application can be specified in terms of the current state.

A concept involving an arbitrary number of substructures may involve any number of substantially different problems. However, a specific solution will have necessarily addressed only a finite number of them. To generalize to N, a system must recognize all the problems that exist in the general concept and, by analyzing the specific solution, surmount them. If the specific solution does not provide enough information to circumvent all problems, generalization to N cannot occur because BAGGER is designed not to perform any problem–solving search during generalization. When a specific solution surmounts, in an extendable fashion, a subproblem in different ways during different instantiations of the focus rule, disjunctions appear in the acquired rule.

Generalizing to N is an important property currently lacking in most explanation–based systems. This research contributes to the theory and practice of explanation–based learning by developing and testing methods for extending the structure of explanations during generalization. It brings this field of machine learning closer to its goal of acquiring the full concept inherent in the solution to a specific problem.

References

1. T. M. Mitchell, R. Keller and S. Kedar-Cabelli, "Explanation-Based Generalization: A Unifying View," *Machine Learning 1*, 1 (January 1986), pp. 47–80.

2. R. E. Fikes, P. E. Hart and N. J. Nilsson, "Learning and Executing Generalized Robot Plans," *Artificial Intelligence 3*, (1972), pp. 251–288.

3. R. E. Korf, "Macro–Operators: A Weak Method for Learning," *Artificial Intelligence 26*, (1985), pp. 35–77.

4. J. E. Laird, P. S. Rosenbloom and A. Newell, *Universal Subgoaling and Chunking: The Automatic Generation and Learning of Goal Hierarchies*, Kluwer Academic Publishers, Norwell, MA, 1986.

5. R. J. Mooney and G. F. DeJong, "Learning Schemata for Natural Language Processing," *Proceedings of the Ninth International Joint Conference on Artificial Intelligence*, Los Angeles, CA, August 1985, pp. 681–687.

6. S. Minton, "Selectively Generalizing Plans for Problem–Solving," *Proceedings of the Ninth International Joint Conference on Artificial Intelligence*, Los Angeles, August 1985, pp. 596–599.

7. A. M. Segre, "On the Operationality/Generality Trade-off in Explanation-Based Learning," *Proceedings of the Tenth International Joint Conference on Artificial Intelligence*, Milan, Italy, August 1987, pp. 242–248.

8. R. E. Fikes and N. J. Nilsson, "STRIPS: A New Approach to the Application of Theorem Proving to Problem Solving," *Artificial Intelligence 2*, 3/4 (1971), pp. 189–208.

9. E. Sacerdoti, *A Structure for Plans and Behavior*, American Elsevier, New York, 1977.

10. D. Chapman, "Planning for Conjunctive Goals," *Artificial Intelligence 32*, 3 (1987), pp. 333–378.

11. G. J. Sussman, "A Computational Model of Skill Acquisition," Technical Report 297, MIT AI Lab, Cambridge, MA, 1973.

12. E. M. Reingold, J. Nievergelt and N. Deo, *Combinatorial Algorithms: Theory and Practice*, Prentice–Hall, Englewood Cliffs, NJ, 1977.

13. A. Gupta, "Explanation–Based Failure Recovery," *Proceedings of the National Conference on Artificial Intelligence*, Seattle, WA, July 1987, pp. 606–610.

14. S. Minton, J. G. Carbonell, O. Etzioni, C. A. Knoblock and D. R. Kuokka, "Acquiring Effective Search Control Rules: Explanation–Based Learning in the PRODIGY System," *Proceedings of the Fourth International Workshop on Machine Learning*, University of California, Irvine, June 1987, pp. 122–133.

15. M. R. Garey and D. S. Johnson, *Computers and Intractability: A Guide to the Theory of NP-Completeness*, W. H. Freeman, New York, 1979.

16. N. J. Nilsson, *Principles of Artificial Intelligence*, Tioga Publishing Company, Palo Alto, CA, 1980.

17. J. W. Shavlik and G. F. DeJong, "Building a Computer Model of Learning Classical Mechanics," *Proceedings of the Seventh Annual Conference of the Cognitive Science Society*, Irvine, CA, August 1985, pp. 351–355.

18. J. W. Shavlik and G. F. DeJong, "Analyzing Variable Cancellations to Generalize Symbolic Mathematical Calculations," *Proceedings of the Third IEEE Conference on Artificial Intelligence Applications*, Orlando, FL, February 1987.

19. J. W. Shavlik and G. F. DeJong, "BAGGER: An EBL System that Extends and Generalizes Explanations," *Proceedings of the National Conference on Artificial Intelligence*, Seattle, WA, July 1987, pp. 516–520.

20. J. W. Shavlik, *Extending Explanation–Based Learning by Generalizing the Structure of Explanations*, Pitman, London, 1990.

21. T. M. Mitchell, S. Mahadevan and L. I. Steinberg, "LEAP: A Learning Apprentice for VLSI Design," *Proceedings of the Ninth International Joint Conference on Artificial Intelligence*, Los Angeles, CA, August 1985, pp. 573–580.

22. T. Ellman, "Generalizing Logic Circuit Designs by Analyzing Proofs of Correctness," *Proceedings of the Ninth International Joint Conference on Artificial Intelligence*, Los Angeles, CA, August 1985, pp. 643–646.

23. W. Ahn, R. J. Mooney, W. F. Brewer and G. F. DeJong, "Schema Acquisition from One Example: Psychological Evidence for Explanation–Based Learning," *Proceedings of the Ninth Annual*

Conference of the Cognitive Science Society, Seattle, WA, July 1987.

24. G. F. DeJong and R. J. Mooney, "Explanation–Based Learning: An Alternative View," *Machine Learning 1*, 2 (1986), pp. 145–176.

25. H. Hirsh, "Explanation–Based Generalization in a Logic–Programming Environment," *Proceedings of the Tenth International Joint Conference on Artificial Intelligence*, Milan, Italy, August 1987, pp. 221–227.

26. S. T. Kedar–Cabelli and L. T. McCarty, "Explanation–Based Generalization as Resolution Theorem Proving," *Proceedings of the Fourth International Workshop on Machine Learning*, University of California, Irvine, June 1987, pp. 383–389.

27. R. J. Mooney and S. W. Bennett, "A Domain Independent Explanation–Based Generalizer," *Proceedings of the National Conference on Artificial Intelligence*, Philadelphia, PA, August 1986, pp. 551–555.

28. P. V. O'Rorke, "Explanation–Based Learning Via Constraint Posting and Propagation," Ph.D. Thesis, Department of Computer Science, University of Illinois, Urbana, IL, January 1987.

29. J. McCarthy, "Situations, Actions, and Causal Laws," memorandum, Stanford University, Stanford, CA, 1963. (Reprinted in *Semantic Information Processing*, M. Minsky (ed.), MIT Press, Cambridge, MA, 1968, pp. 410–417.)

30. C. C. Green, "Application of Theorem Proving to Problem Solving," *Proceedings of the First International Joint Conference on Artificial Intelligence*, Washington, D.C., August 1969, pp. 219–239.

31. S. Fahlman, "A Planning System for Robot Construction Tasks," *Artificial Intelligence 5*, 1 (1974), pp. 1–49.

32. R. Fikes, "Deductive Retrieval Mechanisms for State Description Models," *Proceedings of the Fourth International Joint Conference on Artificial Intelligence*, Tiblisi, Georgia, U.S.S.R., August 1975, pp. 99–106.

33. R. Waldinger, "Achieving Several Goals Simultaneously," in *Machine Intelligenge 8*, E. Elcock and D. Michie (ed.), Ellis Horwood Limited, London, 1977.

34. D. S. Weld, "The Use of Aggregation in Casual Simulation," *Artificial Intelligence 30*, 1 (1986), pp. 1–34.

35. R. S. Michalski, "A Theory and Methodology of Inductive Learning," in *Machine Learning: An Artificial Intelligence Approach*, R. S. Michalski, J. G. Carbonell, T. M. Mitchell (ed.), Tioga Publishing Company, Palo Alto, CA, 1983, pp. 83–134.

36. L. Rendell, "Substantial Constructive Induction Using Layered Information Compression: Tractable Feature Formation in Search (revised)," Technical Report UIUCDCS–R–85–1198, Department of Computer Science, University of Illinois, Urbana, IL, May 1985.

37. R. M. Keller, "The Role of Explicit Contextual Knowledge in Learning Concepts to Improve Performance," Ph.D. Thesis, Department of Computer Science, Rutgers University, New Brunswick, NJ, January 1987.

38. R. Keller, "Operationality and Generality in Explanation–Based Learning: Separate Dimensions or Opposite Endpoints?," *Proceedings of the AAAI Symposium on Explanation–Based Learning*, Stanford, CA, March 1988, pp. 153–157.

39. A. Segre, "Operationality and Real–World Plans," *Proceedings of the AAAI Symposium on Explanation–Based Learning*, Stanford, CA, March 1988, pp. 158–163.

40. J. W. Shavlik, G. F. DeJong and B. H. Ross, "Acquiring Special Case Schemata in Explanation–Based Learning," *Proceedings of the Ninth Annual Conference of the Cognitive Science Society*, Seattle, WA, July 1987, pp. 851–860.

41. A. E. Prieditis and J. Mostow, "PROLEARN: Towards a Prolog Interpreter that Learns," *Proceedings of the National Conference on Artificial Intelligence*, Seattle, WA, July 1987, pp. 494–498.

42. A. E. Prieditis, "Discovery of Algorithms from Weak Methods," *Proceedings of the International Meeting on Advances in Learning*, Les Arcs, Switzerland, 1986, pp. 37–52.

43. P. Cheng and J. G. Carbonell, "The FERMI System: Inducing Iterative Macro–operators from Experience," *Proceedings of the National Conference on Artificial Intelligence*, Philadelphia, PA, August 1986, pp. 490–495.

44. W. W. Cohen, "Generalizing Number and Learning from Multiple Examples in Explanation Based Learning," *Proceedings of the 1988 International Machine Learning Conference*, Ann Arbor, June 1988, pp. 256–269.

45. J. W. Shavlik, "Generalizing the Structure of Explanations in Explanation–Based Learning ," Ph.D. Thesis, Department of Computer Science, University of Illinois, Urbana, IL, January 1988.

46. J. W. Shavlik, "Acquiring Recursive and Iterative Concepts with Explanation–Based Learngin," *Machine Learning*, 1990.

47. P. M. Andreae, "Justified Generalization: Acquiring Procedures from Examples," Ph. D. Thesis, Department of Electrical Engineering and Computer Science, MIT, Cambridge, MA, January 1984. (Also appears as Technical Report 834, MIT AI Laboratory.)

48. T. G. Dietterich and R. S. Michalski, "A Comparative Review of Selected Methods for Learning from Examples," in *Machine Learning: An Artificial Intelligence Approach*, R. S. Michalski, J. G. Carbonell and T. M. Mitchell (ed.), Tioga Publishing Company, Palo Alto, CA, 1983, pp. 41–81.

49. B. Dufay and J. Latombe, "An Approach to Automatic Robot Programming Based on Inductive Learning," in *Robotics Research: The First International Symposium*, MIT Press, Cambridge, MA, 1984, pp. 97–115.

50. L. B. Holder, "Discovering Substructure in Examples," M.S. Thesis, Department of Computer Science, University of Illinois, Urbana, IL, 1988.

51. B. L. Whitehall, "Substructure Discovery in Executed Action Sequences," M.S. Thesis, Department of Computer Science, University of Illinois, Urbana, IL, 1987. (Also appears as Technical Report UILU–ENG–87–2256)

52. J. G. Wolff, "Language Acquisition, Data Compression and Generalization," *Language and Communication 2*, 1 (1982), pp. 57–89.

53. A. W. Biermann, "The Inference of Regular LISP Programs from Examples," *IEEE Transactions on Systems, Man and Cybernetics 8*, 8 (1978), pp. 585–600.

54. Y. Kodratoff, "A Class of Functions Synthesized from a Finite Number of Examples and a LISP Program Scheme," *International Journal of Computer and Information Sciences 8*, 6 (1979), pp. 489–521.

55. P. D. Summers, "A Methodology for LISP Program Construction from Examples," *Journal of the Association for Computing Machinery 24*, (1977), pp. 161–175.

56. L. Siklossy and D. A. Sykes, "Automatic Program Synthesis from Example Problems," *Proceedings of the Fourth International Joint Conference on Artificial Intelligence*, Tiblisi, Georgia, U.S.S.R., August 1975, pp. 268–273.

57. W. W. Cohen, "A Technique for Generalizing Number in Explanation–Based Learning," ML–TR–19, Department of Computer Science, Rutgers University, New Brunswick, NJ, September 1987.

58. Z. Manna, *Mathematical Theory of Computation*, McGraw–Hill, New York, NY, 1974.

59. S. Rajamoney and G. DeJong, "The Classification, Detection and Handling of Imperfect Theory Problems," *Proceedings of the Tenth International Joint Conference on Artificial Intelligence*, Milan, Italy, August 1987, pp. 205–207.

Chapter 4

Recoverable Simplifications and the Intractable Domain Theory Problem

Steve Chien

1. Introduction

People perform robustly in complex domains; current AI systems cannot. The underlying problem is that in any complex domain, the amount of potentially relevant data is enormous. Even in game domains such as chess, the contrast between human and computer approaches is glaringly apparent. Computer chess programs assess potential moves by evaluating millions of possible board positions. Human chess experts evaluate potential moves by analyzing a few key potential avenues of play.

Yet how do experts rule out irrelevant data? We believe that the intelligent use of simplifications is critical to reasoning in real–world, complex domains. People frequently deal with complexity by using assumptions and abstractions. Consider planning to drive to work by a usual route. It is not difficult to concoct plausible sets of circumstances in which any stated plan would not succeed. For example, there might be construction on the route usually taken, there might be an accident, or there might be bad weather. Any of these occurrences would cause a slowdown in traffic, resulting in a late arrival at the office.

Without simplifications, designing even simple plans becomes intractable. Consider attempting to exhaustively prove that one of your plans would succeed or explicitly reasoning about every minute action needed to get you to your office if you drove. Worse yet, imagine trying to prove that all other agents would not interfere (knowingly or unknowingly) with your plan. If humans operated in this fashion, they would spend unacceptably large amounts of time planning even the simplest of actions.

Nevertheless, most AI problem solvers have operated in exactly this fashion. Traditional AI planning systems [1] produce plans by anticipating every possible interaction. Within this framework, problem solving becomes a computationally demanding task for even simple problems (see [2] for an analysis of the computational complexity of planning).

A key aspect of effective use of simplifications in reasoning is the ability to recover from failures caused by inappropriate usage of simplifications. If one day major road construction causes your drive-to-work plan to result in a late arrival at work, you would likely try a different route the next day because the failure would be likely to recur that day. However, if a construction crew was merely painting lane stripes, they would probably finish before the next day, allowing the original plan to be used at that time. Any AI system that uses simplifications in reasoning must have the ability to (1) detect situations in which simplifications are incorrect and (2) recover appropriately in these cases.

This chapter describes an approach to dealing with complexity in problem solving and learning. In this approach, problem solving and learning are integrated through the selective use of simplifications. When initially learning plans, the system uses simplifying assumptions. During later usages of these plans, plan execution is monitored to detect situations in which original assumptions are incorrect. When such a situation is detected, the system explains and corrects the faulty assumption. This capability allows the system to effectively use simplifications to deal with complexity in problem solving and learning.

2. Using Simplifications in Problem Solving and Learning

This section outlines the approach to problem solving and learning that has been developed. First, a brief overview of the schema–based problem–solving and explanation–based learning paradigms are given. Second, an approach to the use of simplifications in problem solving and learning is discussed.

2.1. Schema–Based Problem Solving

Problem solving is a difficult task. Given an initial state, it involves finding and executing a sequence of actions to achieve a desired world state. Most AI planning systems have concentrated on building plans from base–level operators to achieve goals on demand [1, 3]. In a large plan space, as in real–world domains, however, the search involved in constructing plans from base–level operators makes this approach expensive.

A different approach to problem solving involves reasoning from higher–level knowledge structures [4]. In this approach, a system solves problems by relying on a library of high–level knowledge structures called schemata [5]. Schemata have preconditions, a goal, and an operator sequence. When the system is confronted with a problem–solving situation, it finds schemata which achieve the desired goal. These schemata are then tested to see whether their preconditions are met. Any schemata which has its preconditions met can be used to achieve the goal by executing its operator sequence.

However, the schema–based problem–solving paradigm requires a large number of these problem–solving schemata to achieve a high level of performance. This requirement presents a problem because it is often expensive or impossible for a programmmer to anticipate and hand–encode the large number of problem–solving schemata necessary for acceptable performance.

2.2. Explanation–Based Learning

One approach to acquiring problem–solving schemata is *explanation–based learning* (EBL) [6–8]. This approach has been applied to a wide range of domains including mathematical equation solving [9], learning concepts in classical physics [10], robotics [11], mathematical theorem proving [12], integration problems [13], learning functionality of artifacts [14], circuit design [15], and narrative processing [16]. EBL differs from similarity–based methods e.g., [17–19] in that it involves learning new concepts through a knowledge–intensive analysis of causal dependencies in a training example.

Explanation–based learning techniques are particularly well adapted for use with schema–based problem–solving systems. In this approach, a system is given an initial domain knowledge consisting of lower–level knowledge structures such as operators and rules. The system then increases its performance by learning higher–level structures such as macro–operators by explaining and generalizing observations of its own or an external agent's problem–solving behavior.

By endowing a system with this capability, the cost or difficulty associated with hand–encoding a large number of schemata is reduced to encoding the base–level rules and operators needed to learn schemata. Because there are typically a large number of useful combinations of operators, the task of encoding base–level operators is more reasonable.

However, EBL suffers from the same difficulties as other knowledge–intensive AI techniques. Mitchell and colleagues discussed [8], three classes of domain theory problems. First, *the incomplete domain theory problem* exists when the domain theory used by the learning system may not possess all of the information needed to properly explain observed events. With *the intractable domain theory problem,* a domain theory exists, but use of the theory to construct exhaustive proofs is computationally intractable. Last, the *incorrect theory problem* exists when the domain theory can derive false conclusions.

Because current EBL systems assume their domain theories are correct, any concepts they learn are also correct. This feature eliminates the need for refinement. Because these systems also assume tractable domains, they can use their domain theories exhaustively to learn complete concepts from a single input example.

2.3. Process Overview

This chapter describes a simplification–based approach to dealing with the intractable domain theory problem in explanation–based learning. In this approach, a system uses potentially incorrect simplifications in order to make the initial explanation process tractable. The system then relies on refinement to detect and deal with cases in which these simplifications are incorrect.

This approach has two requirements. For the first requirement, that a complete and sound domain theory exists, we presume that this domain theory exists at the level of rules and operators. This means that in theory the system can generate sound explanations given unbounded time and computational resources. Second, a set of simplifications must exist that can be used in portions of the proof to make the process tractable.[1] This model of problem solving and learning consists of five steps: initial learning, failure detection, failure explanation, failure generalization and packaging, and knowledge modification.

Initial learning. The system generates an approximate concept by first constructing an explanation of goal concept, using the base (intractable) domain theory and simplifications when necessary. This explanation is a causal description of how the operators comprising the plan combine to achieve the goal. One important point is that the system must be able to later recognize and analyze the usage of simplifications in this explanation.

---

[1] Development of methods for learning simplifications or a general theory of simplifications is an area for future research. An initial taxonomy of simplifications was described by Chien [20].

In complex domains, one of the major difficulties in reasoning is the so–called frame problem [21]. This difficulty requires a system to update the facts that have persisted. In our approach, the system uses assumptions to reason about changes in the world efficiently.

The simplifications used in the explanation process (in the default notation of [22]) are defeasible inferences of the sort shown in Figure 4–1. IN(P,s) means that the proposition P is believed by the system to be true in situation s. A proposition P contradicts a proposition Q if P is $\sim$ Q or if P specifies that object x has value y for attribute z in a situation s and Q specifies that object x has value w for attribute z in situation s, where y and w are ground values (not variables) and not equal. Precedes(a,b) means that situation a temporally precedes situation b. Thus the inference in Figure 4–1 says that a proposition may be believed in a situation if it is believed in a previous situation and not contradicted in any intervening situation.

One of the major concerns when making default inferences is conflicting defaults. Because the system uses default inferences in explanation, as opposed to prediction, powerful methods used to choose between conflicting defaults (such as minimality [23] or strength–based models [24, 25]) are not critical. However, the approach does presume at least a weak method of dealing with conflicting defaults (such as preferring the simplest explanation).

The initial concept explanation is then generalized using the EGGS technique [26] and packaged for problem solving in a manner that allows the simplifications used to be analyzed later if necessary. For the explanation to be used in problem–solving situations, three portions of the explanation must be determined. First, the *plan preconditions* are the base–level supports of the explanation and are facts given to the system as being true in the initial situation. These facts represent the conditions

∀ P,si,sj,sk   IN(P,si)   ∧ ¬∃ Q [contradicts(Q,P)   ∧   IN(Q,sj)   ∧   precedes(si,sj)   ∧   precedes(sj,sk)]

-> IN(P,sk)

Figure 4–1:   Defeasible Inference

under which the plan can be executed to achieve the goal. Second, the *operator sequence* is the sequence of operators executed to achieve the goal. These are the operators executed to use the plan. Finally, the *goal* is the desired world state achieved by execution of the plan.

Failure detection. The use of simplifications in the initial learning process introduces the possibility of learning flawed plans. Consequently, the system needs a method of detecting and recovering from these cases. In our approach, the system relies on goal failures to indicate situations in which learned concepts are incorrect. After execution of a plan, the system checks to see whether the goal is achieved. If there is a failure to achieve a goal, then the plan used must be flawed and must be refined to prevent repetition of the failure.

Failure explanation. After a goal failure is detected, the underlying causes for the failure are explained in two steps. First, the facts within the current situation that support the goal achievement are queried in the real world. These supports represent an easily verifiable level of failure backtracing. Any of these values which are not as expected are candidates for portions of the plan that require refinement. Second, the system now attempts to explain the manner in which each of these values occurred. Because the domain theory is sound, any failure must be due to an invalid simplification. Each of the failed supports that can be explained will result in a new constraint on the plan. Each of these explanations will be a specific proof of a fact Q that violates a simplification as described in Figure 4–1.

Failure generalization and packaging. In this step, each explanation for a failed simplification is generalized using the EGGS technique [26]. Each failure explanation has a set of *failure preconditions*, that is, the conditions beyond the preconditions for the plan which are the base–level supports for the failure. Failure preconditions represent the general conditions under which the designated failure will cause the plan to fail. This is a set of conditions under which the system previously believed that the plan would achieve the goal but now realizes otherwise.

Knowledge modification. Once the explanation and constraints for the failure have been computed, they are added to the preconditions of the original plan. The resultant plan is constrained by being applicable only when no set of failure preconditions are applicable, because each set of failure preconditions represents a case in which a simplification that the plan depends on is invalid. The revised set of plan preconditions requires that the previous plan preconditions be met but that none of the plan's failure precondition sets (including the newly created set) be met.

The revised plan preconditions cause a situation in which the system incorrectly believed that the plan was applicable to become a situation in which the system correctly believes that a plan is not applicable. That is, an overly general plan has been specialized to become closer to the correct applicability description.

Additionally, by packaging failures in a manner independent from the plan with which they are learned, they may be used by other plans. This can occur in two ways. First, the failure explanation may also cause a failure in the other plan. If this can be detected before plan execution, it can allow avoidance of the failure for the other plan. The second manner in which the failure structure can be used is to understand preventive measures. Given access to applicable failures, a plan can be checked to determine whether any of its actions prevents these failures. If so, these actions can be understood as preventing the appropriate failures.

2.4. Architectural Organization

The architecture of a learning system using our approach is shown in Figure 4-2. The system is initially given knowledge in the form of a complete and sound but intractable domain theory and simplifications. When the system is initially learning a plan, it receives as its input an initial state, operator sequence, and goal. Using the existing knowledge base of rules, facts, and operators, plus simplifications to make the understanding process tractable, the understander maintains the causal model which is the system's description of world events. The generalizer extracts the explanation for goal achievement from the causal model and generalizes the explanations to form a plan. This plan is then analyzed with respect to previously learned failures to check for preventive measures. The resultant structure is packaged into a plan and added to the plan library.

When the system is problem solving, it receives a goal as its input. The planner selects an applicable plan from the plan library to achieve the goal. The executive then executes the plan, updating the causal model to reflect the changes in the world caused by plan execution. After the plan has been completed, the goal verifier verifies the achievement of the goal. If the plan fails to achieve the goal, the goal verifier backtraces to find the set of violated supports responsible for the failure. Because the domain theory is sound, these violations must be due to violated simplifications. The understander explains the reasons for these violated simplifications. The resulting explanations are then generalized and used to modify the original plan preconditions. If the plan achieves the goal,

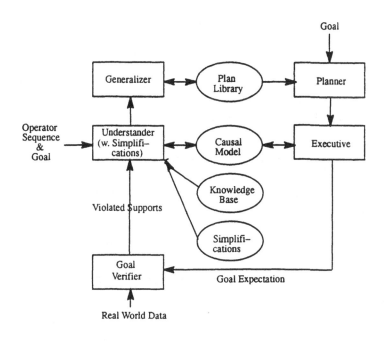

Figure 4-2:   System Architecture

no refinement of plan preconditions is necessary.

3. Knowledge Representation

This section outlines the knowledge representation used by our approach. First, the representation should be amenable to varying the amount of effort devoted to reasoning with a corresponding change in accuracy. Second, the representation should be sufficiently powerful so that the complexities of complete reasoning arise. Third, the representation (particularly for assumptions) should be explicit and clean enough to allow a system to analyze previously learned knowledge structures during refinement.

We use a representation roughly based on situational calculus. In a given situation, a fact may be true, false, or unknown. Facts may refer to objects in the world and to values, which are specifications of attributes for objects. There are two types of facts: definitional facts and situational facts. Definitional facts are true in all situations and specify properties or relations of values (e.g., the fact that 2 is greater than 1). Situational facts might be true only in a restricted set of situations and specify properties or relations among objects that may change over time.

A history consists of a sequence of situations connected by operators. In this representation, the assumption is made that all changes between temporally consecutive situations are instantaneous and brought about by the execution of a single operator. This means that within each situation the world is at a steady state.

Operators map from partial situations to partial situations. Operators are specified by an execution form, preconditions, effects, and a create list. The execution form is the list of parameters that must be specified in order to execute the operator. The preconditions are a set of facts that must be true in the situation in which the operator is executed. Effects are facts that are true in the situation resulting from the execution of the operator. Note that because preconditions and effects can contain negations, they can also require the falsity of facts before or after execution of the operator. The create list is a set of objects created by the execution of the operator.

There are three types of rules in the system: intersituational rules, intrasituational rules, and persistence assumptions. *Intersituational rules* map from partial situations to partial situations and consist of a consequent and an antecedent. The antecedent is a set of facts that must be true in a given situation for the rule to be applicable. The consequent is a fact that must be true in the state resulting from the execution of a certain operator in the antecedent state. These rules allow representation of operators whose effects depend on the state of the world in which the operator is executed (i.e., conditional effects). In *intrasituational rules*, the antecedent and consequent parts refer to facts in the same situation. Intrasituational rules allow the system to reason about properties such as transitivity, commutativity, and so forth.

A *persistence assumption* is an potentially unsound inference that a fact persists from a previous situation. These are inferences of the form:[2]

$$\forall \ P,si,sj,sk \quad IN(P,si) \ \wedge \ \neg \exists \ Q \ [contradicts(Q,P) \ \wedge \ IN(Q,sj) \ \wedge \ precedes(si,sj) \ \wedge \ precedes(sj,sk)]$$

$$\rightarrow IN(P,sk)$$

---

[2] Currently, these inferences are performed by specialized LISP code. Using a single general inference engine for both defeasible and standard inferences and a declarative representation for defeasible inferences are areas for future work.

Formally, IN(P,s) means that the fact P is believed by the system in situation s. A fact P is said to contradict a fact Q if P is Q or if P specifies that object x has value y for attribute z in a situation s and Q specifies that object x has value w for attribute z in situation s, where y and w are ground values (not variables) and not equal. Precedes(a,b) means that situation a temporally precedes situation b. Intuitively, this rule states that a fact P can be assumed to persist to a later situation provided it is not explicitly contradicted by a belief in an intervening situation.

Definitional facts, operators, and rules are the initial knowledge given to the system. Plans represent goal–directed problem–solving knowledge learned by the system. Censors represent corrections to plans produced by analysing observed failures and are similar to the censors described by Winston [27]. By processing examples consisting of a complete initial situation specification, goal, and operator sequence, the system is able to construct the higher–level knowledge structures of plans and censors.

An explanation for a fact is an instantiation of a set of applicable rules and assumptions which support the given fact. A rule in an explanation is a valid support for a fact if the instantiation of the consequent is the fact and for each fact in the rule antecedent there is a fact in the causal model that directly supports it or there is an applicable supporting rule or assumption. An assumption in an explanation supports a fact if the most recent value for the fact is the same as the assumed value.

Due to this recursive definition, every explanation support must be grounded in an initial state fact or the effect of an operator. This operator in turn will eventually be grounded in an initial state fact.

A plan is a representation for the manner in which a constrained sequence of operators achieves a desired world state. A plan consists of a goal state, plan preconditions, an operator sequence, a causal explanation, and a set of censors. A *goal state* is a partial situation that the system believes will be true after the execution of the plan. *Plan preconditions* are a partial world specification that is required for the proper execution of the plan. The *operator sequence* is a list of the operators which cause the goal state to be true, ordered as in the input example. The *causal explanation* is a description of how the plan preconditions allow the operator sequence to achieve the goal state.

A *censor* is a subsequent correction to a flawed plan. A censor consists of an explanation, an expected value, an observed value, and a set of failure preconditions. An *explanation* is a causal structure describing a case in which a plan is incorrect. In this case, the plan explanation states that a certain fact has a designated value, but due to a faulty persistence assumption, there is a different value in the real world. Three portions of this explanation are important. First, the *expected value* is the fact value which is supported by the plan explanation. Second, the *observed value* is the value which is supported by the censor explanation. Finally, the *failure preconditions* are a set of facts which must be true in order for the censor explanation to be applicable.

4. Explanation Construction and Generalization

This section discusses the initial learning phase of the simplification–based learning process. First, the causal model maintained by a system is described. Next the support network generalization is discussed. Finally, the packaging of plans is described.

4.1. The Causal Model

The causal model is a history representing the system's perception of the state of the world at various points in time and a causal description of how the execution of operators alters the world state. This causal model maintains support links for the system's belief of facts in the manner of truth–maintenance systems [28]. The system learns general plans from specific initial state descriptions and operator sequences through analysis of the dependencies maintained by the causal model. The initial state, operator sequence, and goal used to construct the causal model might be given explicitly to the system as training examples or could be derived from observation of a domain expert solving problems.

Understanding facts means that the system knows why the state represented by the fact is true. This can be done in two ways: as an initial condition or as an effect of an action (possibly via inference rules). When the system receives an input fact, it attempts to explain why the fact is true in the world. If the system succeeds in explaining the occurrence of the fact, the fact and supporting explanation for the occurrence of the fact are added to the causal model. If no explanation can be found, the fact is added to the causal model and marked as being an input fact.

For operators, understanding means knowing why each of the preconditions is true and knowing the effects of the operator. As operators are input to the system, they are added to the causal model by first incorporating the preconditions and then adding the effects. The preconditions are incorporated into the causal model in a manner identical to processing of input facts. The effects of the operator are added to the causal model by being asserted true in the situation representing the world state resulting from and caused by the execution of the operator.

After the initial state description and operator sequence, the system is given the goal that is achieved by the example plan. The system then attempts to construct an explanation for how the plan steps achieve the goal (as with any other input fact). If the system can construct an explanation, it learns a plan from the observed operator sequence.

4.2. An Example

To clarify the explanation construction and generalization process, a small plan for rolling a bar will now be presented. In the example are the following initial state, goal, and observed operator sequence:

Initial State (s0):
- (1) (at bar21 bench4)
- (2) (composition bar21 metal)
- (3) (state bar21 solid)
- (4) (at sheet22 bench1)
- (5) (shape sheet22 sheet)

Goal State:
(diameter bar21 10.0cm)

Operator Sequence:
- (1) (move bar21 heating–station)
         move the bar to the heating–station
- (2) (heat bar21)
         heat the bar
- (3) (move bar21 rolling–station)
         move the bar to the rolling–station
- (4) (move bar21 10.0cm)
         roll the bar to a diameter of 10.0cm[3]

---

[3] Because the domain model does not represent that rolling an object does not change its volume, the explanation does not reflect that the bar must initially have had a diameter of 10 cm or that the length of the bar will change.

Upon receiving the first input action, preconditions of the move operator are verified by noting that the previous location of the bar was bench4 and that the consistency of the bar was solid in the start state. Then the effect of the move is computed and the fact (at bar21 heating-station) is asserted in s1, the state caused by executing the first operator in s0. Next the second operator is processed. The one precondition of the heat operator is that the object to be heated be at the heating station. Since this fact was achieved by operator 1, it is easily confirmed. The effect of the heating operation — that the temperature of bar21 is hot — is asserted in situation 2. Then the third operator is processed. The fact that the state of bar21 is solid is verified by assuming that this fact persists from situation 0 to situation 2. The effect of the move — that the bar is at the rolling–station in situation 3 — is then added. Next the fourth operator — the roll operation — is processed. The roll operator has two preconditions. The first, that the object being rolled is at the rolling–station, is confirmed easily, as it was asserted by the move operator 3. The second precondition, that the object have malleable consistency, is verified by a rule which says that if an object is hot and metal, it is malleable. To apply this rule, the assumption is made that the hot temperature of the bar persists from state 2 and that the metal composition of the bar persists from state 0. Having verified the preconditions of the operator, the two effects of the roll are now asserted: (1) the bar now has a cylindrical shape and (2) the diameter of the bar is now 10.0 cm. The causal model constructed for this example is shown in Figure 4–3.

In the example, the goal is that the diameter of the bar be 10.0 cm. Because the goal is already supported by the causal model, no additional explanation is necessary. If the goal fact were not supported, it would be necessary to construct an explanation (which would be grounded in the causal model) for why the goal specification was achieved before proceeding with the generalization phase.

4.3. Explanation Generalization

After explaining goal achievement, a plan can be learned from the training example. The generalization and packaging phase consists of three steps. First, the bindings for the general plan are computed, using an adaptation of the EGGS technique [26]. Next, the plan is analyzed with respect to previous plans (discussed in Section 5.2). Finally, the new plan is packaged and indexed to enable usage in problem–solving situations.

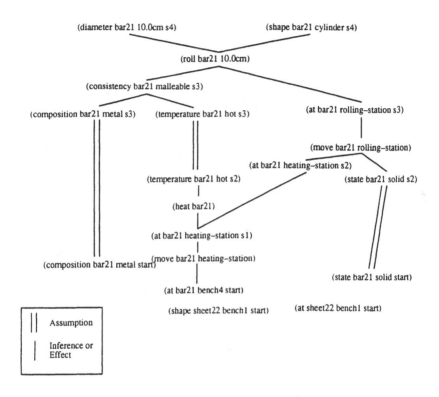

(diameter bar21 10.0cm s4)   (shape bar21 cylinder s4)

(roll bar21 10.0cm)

(consistency bar21 malleable s3)

(composition bar21 metal s3)   (temperature bar21 hot s3)   (at bar21 rolling-station s3)

(move bar21 rolling-station)

(at bar21 heating-station s2)

(temperature bar21 hot s2)   (state bar21 solid s2)

(heat bar21)

(at bar21 heating-station s1)

(composition bar21 metal start)   (move bar21 heating-station)

(state bar21 solid start)

(at bar21 bench4 start)

(shape sheet22 bench1 start)   (at sheet22 bench1 start)

| | Assumption

| Inference or
Effect

Figure 4-3:   Specific Causal Model

The first step in the plan learning process is the computation of general bindings. This is done by stepping through the causal network, tracing the actions and inferences supporting the goal. At each support, the assertion that is supported must match the assertion caused by the support. For example, the fact that an action supports must be equal to the appropriate effect of the action. This constraint is enforced by the bindings given by unifying these two forms. Persistence assumption supports are handled by unifying the assertions but not the time tags. This is because an assertion can be supported by a previously believed assertion through a persistence assumption. The generalized causal structure produced by this process represents the most general case in which this explanation will be valid. The general explanation for the rolling-bar example is shown in Figure 4-4.

The final step in learning a plan is packaging. This section describes the procedure necessary to learn a plan in isolation. The process

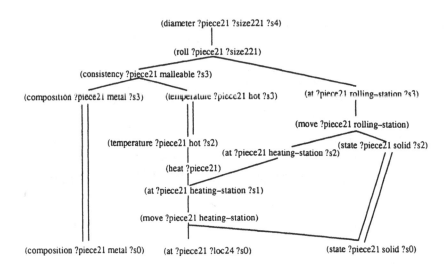

Figure 4–4:   Generalized Explanation

of analyzing related plans will be discussed in Section 5.2. Three parts of the general causal explanation are needed to use the plan in a problem-solving manner: the goal, operator sequence, and plan precondition. The *goal* is the general form supported by the causal explanation. This describes the partial world situation that is achieved by the plan. When this world state is desired, the plan may be useful. The *operator sequence* is the general list of operators in the observed operator sequence that appear in the general causal explanation. The operator sequence represents the operators that must be executed to achieve the plan. The *preconditions* are the initial state facts grounding the general causal explanation. These facts represent the partial world situation in which the plan can be executed to achieve the goal.

Figure 4–5 shows the goal, operator sequence, and plan preconditions for the rolling–bar plan. Note that many extraneous details of the training example have been removed, such as the desired diameter of the piece can be any value, there need not be a sheet shaped object at bench4,

GOAL: (diameter ?piece21 ?size221)

OPERATOR   (move ?piece21 heating–station)
SEQUENCE: (heat ?piece21)
                               (move ?piece21 rolling–station)
                               (roll ?piece21 ?size221)

PLAN   (composition ?piece21 metal)
PRECONDITIONS: (at ?piece21 ?loc24)
                               (state ?piece21 solid)

Figure 4–5:   Plan Goal, Operator Sequence, and Plan Preconditions

and the bar used need not be bar21.

5. Refinement

This section describes the refinement processes in the incremental learning approach and consists of two main parts. The first section describes the manner in which preconditions are refined to recover from incorrect usage of simplifications in the initial learning process. The second section describes the manner in which measures that prevent previously observed failures are learned.

5.1. Recovering from Incorrect Simplifications in Plans

The usage of simplifications in initial learning introduces the possibility of learning flawed plans. To deal with this contingency, the system must have a method of detecting and correcting such flaws. In our approach, the system relies on goal failures to indicate situations in which plans require refinement. In this case, the system incorrectly believes that a plan will succeed in a given situation, but due to a faulty simplification the plan fails. Subsequently, the system explains and generalizes the case in which the plan will fail and restricts the original plan preconditions so as to prohibit selection of the plan in these situations. The resultant refinement specializes an overly general plan by making a case in which the system that incorrectly believed the plan would apply becomes one that correctly believes the plan will not apply.

This section begins with an overview of the problem–solving and failure–detection processes used by the system. Next, the plan precondition refinement process is described. Finally, an example is shown to illustrate this process.

5.1.1. Problem Solving

In problem–solving mode, the system uses previously learned plans to solve problems. The problem–solving component of the system receives a goal as its input. Its task is to select and execute a plan to achieve this goal. An applicable plan must satisfy two constraints. First, the plan must achieve the desired goal. This constraint is satisfied by retrieving the set of plans which are indexed as achieving the goal state. Second, it must be possible to execute the plan, and execution of the plan should achieve the desired world state. The plan preconditions are the set of initial facts that support the explanation for goal achievement (from the initial learning process) plus the conditions necessary to avoid previously observed failures (from censors). The plan preconditions must be met for a plan to be applicable in a problem–solving situation.

If no applicable plan is found, the system cannot achieve the goal. The system does not modify plans to achieve goals similar to indexed goals. The system also does not actively plan to achieve unsatisfied plan preconditions or prevent anticipated failures, because attempting to modify plans is computationally expensive and requires the system to have significant problem–solving capability. Instead, the system waits until observing an applicable solution and then learns the desired plan.

Once the system has chosen an applicable plan, it executes the plan. In this process, the system outputs the instantiated operators to the world simulator. Concurrently, the causal model is updated to reflect the effects of the operators.

After completing the plan, goal achievement is verified. Currently this is done by an ad hoc module outside of the system. If the goal is achieved, the plan is successful and no refinement is necessary. However, if the goal is not achieved, the system has failed and must refine the plan to block repetition of the failure.

5.1.2. Refining Flawed Plan Preconditions

After a goal failure has indicated a flawed plan, the original plan preconditions are modified in a three–step process:

(1) *Verification of current state supports.* The supports for the goal in the current situation are checked. These are the set of facts which should be true in the current world state supporting the goal

achievement. However, some of these facts are not true — thus causing the failure.

(2)   *Explanation of support violation.* A causal explanation for why the support states are violated is formulated.

(3)   *Censor packaging.* This information is packaged into a censor. This censor is a knowledge structure to be added to the plan to prevent future inappropriate selection of the plan.

After a failure has been detected, goal support explanation is back-traced to find the lowest–level supports for goal achievement in the current situation. This is done by tracing backward in the causal network until any type of support other than an intrasituation rule is found. Then the world simulator is queried to verify these values (we assume either direct verifiability for these values or the existence of an outside module to indirectly verify these values). This process yields the set of violated supports. Note that because we do not allow defeasible inferences within the same situation, if the goal is not achieved in the current situation, one of the current situation supports must be invalid.

Given the set of violated assertions, the next step is to find the real–world value of each assertion and construct an explanation for how this value occurred. This is done in a backward–chaining manner using intersituation rules, intrasituation rules, and persistence assumptions. The resultant explanations are then generalized using the EGGS algorithm.

Each generalized explanation is then packaged into a censor. First, the conditions leading to each failed assumption are computed by tracing the appropriate explanation back to the leaves. These leaf justifications may be effects of actions in the plan, or they may be initial situation facts. Facts supported by action effects are met whenever the plan is executed and hence are not stored. However, the correspondences between objects and values in the plan and censor are computed by unifying these forms and become the bindings field of the censor. Initial situation facts are collected and become the failure preconditions field of the censor. These are the conditions under which the plan was previously thought to be applicable but has proven otherwise by an analysis of the failure. Next, the general unexpected value that the censor explanation supports becomes the censor observed value and the violated expected value of the plan becomes the expected value. The resultant censor represents a case in which a persistence assumption in the original plan can be violated by circumstances possibly in conjunction with actions executed in the plan.

5.1.3. An Example

To clarify the precondition refinement process, an example is described. In this example, the system has learned a general widget plan and begins with a metal rod, a plastic gear, and a sheet. It first heats and rolls the rod. Next, it drills holes into the gear and sheet. It then inserts the rod into the gear for a tight friction fit and through the sheet with a loose fit that allows the rod to spin. The goal, operator sequence, and preconditions for this plan are shown in Figure 4–6.

The system attempts to use this plan in the initial situation shown in Figure 4–7. The system attempts to build a widget and fails. As a result, the system backtraces the current situation supports for the widget plan used. The current situation portion of the widget plan is shown in

GOAL: (widget ?x32546 ?obj4571 ?obj7608 ?hole5572 ?loc44547 ?s124752)

OPERATOR   (move ?obj7608 oven ?situation440)
SEQUENCE: (heat ?obj7608 ?situation441)
            (move ?obj7608 rolling–station ?situation453)
            (roll ?obj7608 ?size6535 ?situation464)
            (move ?obj7608 ?loc44547 ?situation506)
            (move ?x43546 drilling–station ?situation519)
            (drill ?x43546 ?hole5534 ?size6535 ?situation520)
            (move ?x43546 ?loc44547 ?situation544)
            (move ?obj4571 drilling–station ?situation557)
            (drill ?obj4571 ?hole5572 ?size6573 ?situation558)
            (move ?obj4571 ?loc44547 ?situation582)
            (insert ?obj7608 ?x43546 ?hole5534 ?situation606)
            (insert ?obj7608 ?x4571 ?hole5572 ?situation633)

PLAN   (at ?x43546 ?old–loc45524 ?gen–sit782)
PRECONDITIONS: (slightly> ?size6573 ?size6535)
            (composition ?obj7608 metal ?gen–sit781)
            (at ?obj7608 ?old–loc45444 ?situation440)
            (state ?obj7608 solid ?situation440)
            (shape ?obj4571 sheet ?gen–sit780)
            (shape ?x43546 gear ?gen–sit779)
            (at ?obj4571 ?old–loc45561 ?gen–sit778)
            (state ?obj4571 solid ?gen–sit777)

Figure 4–6:   Plan Goal, Operator Sequence, and Plan Preconditions

(at r1 bench2)
(at g1 bench3)
(at base bench4)
(composition r1 metal)
(state r1 solid)
(shape g1 gear)
(shape base sheet)
(composition g1 plastic)
(state g1 solid)
(state base solid)

Figure 4–7:   Example Initial State

Figure 4–8. It then determines that all of the current situation supports are met except that g1 is not gear–shaped. It determines that in the real world the shape of the g1 is deformed in situation s13.

Next, an explanation of why the gear is deformed in s13 in the current example is constructed. This explanation is shown in Figure 4–9. The deformed shape of the gear is explained as follows. The gear g1 is plastic and became hot in situation s13 and thus the shape of g1 was

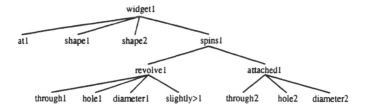

widget1	(widget g1 base r1 hole3 bench3 s13)
shape1	(shape g1 gear s13)
at1	(at base bench3 s13)
shape2	(shape base sheet s13)
spins1	(spins g1 base r1 hole788 s13)
revolve1	(revolve r1 base hole788 s13)
attached1	(attached r1 g1 s13)
through1	(through r1 base hole3 s13)
hole1	(hole hole788 base 15.1cm s13)
diameter1	(diameter r1 15.0cm s13)
slightly>1	(slightly> 15.1cm 15.0cm)
through2	(through r1 g1 hole787 s13)
hole2	(hole hole787 g1 15.0cm s13)
diameter2	(diameter r1 15.0cm s13)

Figure 4–8:   Goal Supports within Current Situation

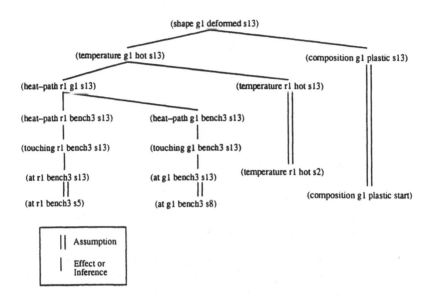

Figure 4–9:   Specific Failure Explanation

deformed. G1 is plastic in s13 because it was plastic in the start situation, and this property persisted through situation s13. G1 became hot
because there was a heat–path from the metal rod r1 to g1 in s13 and the
r1 was hot in s13. R1 was hot in s13 because it was hot in s2 as an effect
from the heating action, and this state persisted through situation s13.
There was a heat–path from g1 to r1 in s13 because there was a heat–
path from r1 to bench3 in s13 and also a heat–path from g1 to bench3 in
s13. There was a heat–path from r1 to bench3 in s13 because r1 was
touching bench3 in s13. R1 was touching bench3 because r1 was at
bench3 in s13, which persisted from s5. Likewise, there was a heat–path
from g1 to bench3 in s13 due to g1 touching bench3 in s13, which was
supported by g1 being at bench3 in s13, which persisted from g1 being at
bench3 at s8.

The resulting failure explanation is then generalized using the
EGGS algorithm. This is done in exactly the same manner as plan generalization except that no actions appear within the failure explanation.
The general form of the explanation is shown in Figure 4–10. This general explanation of the failure will form the explanation of the resulting
censor.

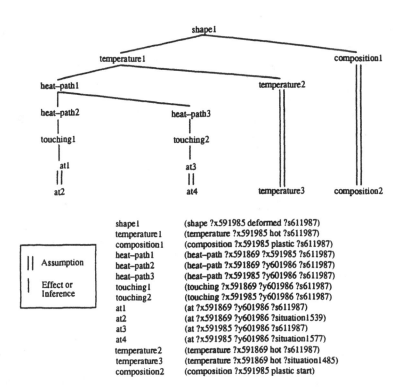

Figure 4-10: General Failure Explanation

Next, the failure preconditions are found by examining the leaf nodes of the general failure explanation. Of the leaves in the failure explanation, all but the fact that the gear is plastic are effects of actions in the plan and hence will be true in any plan execution. The fact that the rod is at the same location as the gear is a result of the rod being moved to location ?y601986 (the fifth action in the plan) and the gear being moved to location ?y601986 (the eighth action in the plan). The fact that the rod is hot is an effect of the heating step (the second action in the plan). Because the fact that the gear is plastic is a start condition, it becomes the failure preconditions of the censor.

After the failure preconditions are found, the correspondences between the failure and plan are computed. This involves unifying the leaves of the failure explanation which are supported by action effects with the general effects of the actual actions in the plan. These correspondences (a set of variable bindings) become the binding field of the new censor.

In the melted gear failure, the action supports are shown in Figure 4–11. Of these, the gear being moved to the assembly location is a direct support. Hence the correspondences from this support are given by unifying the location effect with the location node in the failure explanation. The other two supports are assumption supports. The correspondences for these supports are computed by unifying all but the situation portion of the facts. The resulting correspondences are also shown in Figure 4–11.

Next, the observed value for the censor is determined by finding the general form that the failure explanation supports. The expected value is retrieved by examining the general form in the assumption from the original plan that the censor blocks. A censor name is then created from the attribute name for the observed value. Finally, the censor is created with the computed values and added to the relevant plan. The failure preconditions, expected value, and observed value of the censor are shown in Figure 4–12.

The censor affects plan applicability as follows. In problem–solving situations in which the censor applies, the plan will not be selected due to the expectation of plan failure represented by the censor. In this manner,

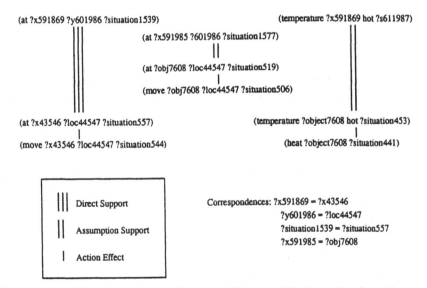

Figure 4–11: Correspondences Between Plan and Failure Explanation

Censor Values

Failure Preconditions: ((composition ?x591985 plastic start))

Expected Value: (shape ?x591985 gear ?s1241784)

Observed Value: (shape ?x591985 deformed ?s611987)

Figure 4–12: Failure Preconditions, Expected Value, and Observed Value
of Censor

the original plan has been modified to reflect the knowledge learned by
analyzing the failure.

5.2. Analyzing Plans with Respect to Previous Failures

Consider planning a surprise party for Bill while not allowing Bill
to find out about the party. Or getting to your office without your boss
seeing you. Or carrying four glasses over to the table without spilling the
water in them. All of these tasks involve prevention. More specifically,
prevention is executing actions to achieve a partial world specification
while not allowing another partial world specification to become true.

This section describes the process by which previously observed
failures can be understood to relate to new plans. In our approach, the
system understands preventive measures by analyzing examples in which
an observed plan succeeds in a case where the system expects the plan to
fail. While it would be desirable to understand preventive measures
before having observed the circumstances which they prevent, postulating
and checking potential failures is a combinatorially explosive process and
would require exhaustive reasoning. In order to avoid this difficulty, the
system waits until it has a known instance of a plan which prevents the
failure. The system is then faced with a contradiction. The censor
predicts that the plan will fail and yet the system has observed the plan
succeeding. Given this situation, the system can then focus upon the portions of the specific failure explanation that can be defeated and examine
the plan for operators that successfully prevent these conditions.

After a plan is generalized and packaged as discussed in section 4,
the system compares the newly learned plan to known censors. If the system determines that the current plan could fail in the manner described
by a censor, it analyzes the current plan to see if it contains operators to
prevent the failure. If so, these operators are marked as preventing the

failure. If the failure is not prevented, the system modifies the plan
preconditions of the new plan to prohibit its usage in situations where the
failure will occur.

5.2.1. Understanding Relevant Failures

This analysis of relevant failures consists of three steps:

(1)   *Determine Relevant Censor.* The set of censor whose action sup-
      ports are supported by actions in the current plan is determined.

(2)   *Check for Prevent Operators.* The current plan is analyzed to
      determine if it contains operators that prevent the designated
      failure.

(3)   *Modify the New Plan.* If the failure is prevented, mark the
      appropriate operators are doing so. If the failure is not prevented,
      modify the plan preconditions as to not allow the plan to be used
      in cases where the failure is applicable.

The first step in understanding failures relevant to a new plan is to
find potentially relevant censors. This is done by finding the set of all
censors that are supported by actions which occur in the current plan
which is computed by matching (unifying) the action supports of censors
of previously learned plans to actions in the plan currently being learned.
If it is possible to match, in order, all of the actions that occur in the censor to actions in the observed plan, then the system checks if the censor
observed value will violate an assumption in the current plan. If this is
the case, then the censor is relevant to the current plan.

The second step involves checking for preventive actions in the
current plan. If a censor has its conditions apply in the current example,
yet the plan did not fail, it is desirable to understand how the failure was
avoided. The failure explanation consists of sound inference rules and
defeasible persistence assumptions. If the failure conditions and actions
are met, and the failure does not occur, one of the persistence assumptions in the failure explanation must be invalid. The system examines the
actions in the operator sequence to determine which persistence assumption is defeated. This blocking of the failure is then explained and the
new plan is marked as avoiding the failure in the manner detailed by the
blocking explanation. The explanation for the blocking of the failure is
now part of the plan, and these additional constraints become part of the
plan.

The third step involves modifying the plan with respect to the applicable censors. If the failure represented by the censor is not prevented by the plan, the censor is added to the censors for the newly learned plan. This censor will prevent the plan from being used in cases where the censor applies. This possibility is shown in Figure 4–13. In this circumstance, the plan contains an assumption that a fact will persist over some interval. However, under some set of circumstances, an explanation holds (the failure explanation in Figure 4–13) that details how this fact does not persist. As a result, the plan will fail in these circumstances.

However, the failure may have been prevented by operators in the plan. In this case, the failure contains an assumption which is blocked by an action in the plan. This possibility is shown in Figure 4–14. In this case, there is an assumption in the failure explanation that a fact persisted over some interval, but an effect of an operator in the plan (possible through inferences) blocks the persistence of this fact. Hence the failure explanation is invalid.

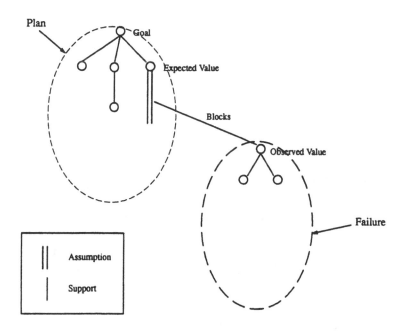

Figure 4–13: Failure Blocks Assumption in Plan

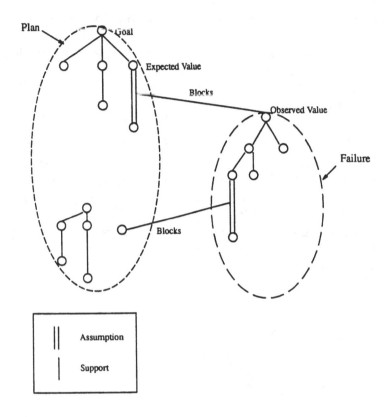

Figure 4–14: Plan Blocks Assumption in Failure

5.2.2. An Example

To clarify the process of incorporating previously observed failures, the example from Section 5.1.3 is extended. In this example, the system has learned a plan to assemble several pieces into a widget. One of the pieces, a metal bar, is heated and rolled to fit into a hole drilled into a gear. This plan, as detailed in Section 5.1.3, contains a censor representing a failure in which the gear is plastic and is deformed by being placed at the same location as the heated rod.

The system is now shown an initial state and operator sequence in which the metal rod is cooled after being rolled to the correct size. This initial state and operator sequence is shown in Figure 4–15. When the cool metal rod is inserted into a plastic gear, no deformation occurs. An analysis reveals that the deformed gear failure from the previous plan

Initial State: (at r21 bench2)   Operator Sequence:
               (at r2 bwnch1)

```
Initial State:     (at r21 bench2)          Operator Sequence:
                   (at r2 bwnch1)
                   (at g312 bench3)                (move r21 oven)
                   (at g2 bench1)                  (heat r21)
                   (at p1 bench1)                  (move r21 rolling-station)
                   (composition r21 metal)         (roll r21 10.0cm)
                   (state r21 solid)               (cool r21)
                   (state base16 solid)            (move r21 bench1)
                   (composition g312 plastic)      (move g312 drilling-station)
                   (shape g312 gear)               (drill g312 hole1 10.0cm)
                   (at base16 bench1)              (move g312 bench1)
                   (shape base16 sheet)            (move base16 drilling-station)
                                                   (drill base16 hole2 10.1cm)
                                                   (move base16 bench1)
                                                   (insert r21 g312 hole1)
                                                   (insert r21 base16 hole2)
```

Figure 4–15: Initial State and Operator Sequences for the Cooling Plan Example

applies to the current plan and that the system deduces the failure conditions were met. Hence, a persistence assumption in the failure must have been blocked by the new plan. The system notes that the cooling step blocks the persistence assumption about the heat of the rod, thus preventing the deformed gear failure. This circumstance is shown in Figure 4–16.

Because the cooling step did not appear in the general explanation for goal achievement, it was previously thought by the system to be an unimportant action. Although in theory the system had the base–level knowledge necessary to understand this prevention upon initially learning the plan, this would have required the system to postulate the possibility of the melted gear failure, which is a computationally expensive process. However, after the system has observed the failure and learned the corresponding censor, the censor predicts that the plan will fail and observed data that the plan has succeeded. This contradiction serves to focus the system's attention on portions of the failure that can be blocked, allowing tractable understanding of the preventive measure.

The next step is to find the appropriate constraints on the plan required to prevent the failure. This is done by propagating the constraints between the expected and observed values in the failure explanation (yielding the correspondences between the objects and values in the failure and the objects and values in the plan), computing the constraint that the effect of the cool action must block the persistence assumption in the failure explanation, and adding the supporting causal explanation for

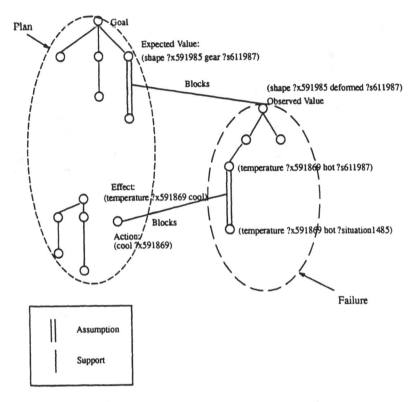

Figure 4-16: Cooling Action in Plan Blocking Failure

the cooling step to the plan (i.e., the the supporting causal model for the preconditions of the cooling step).

6. Comparisons to Other Work

There are several similar approaches to problem solving and learning. A number of incremental knowledge-based learning systems have been constructed. In addition to the ARIES system (the predecessor of the current approach), there has been work on incremental knowledge-based learning approaches by Bennett, Hammond, Doyle, and Gupta.

The approach described in this chapter evolved from the ARIES system [29, 30]. The ARIES (for Automated Refinement and Indexing of Explanatory Schemata) system is an incremental EBL system designed to extend the GENESIS system, which understands narratives. The ARIES system refines schemata for understanding narratives describing criminal plans. Because of the computational intractability of exhaustively proving that other agents do not interfere with the planning agent's plans, the ARIES system assumes that other agents do not not perform actions to interfere with the original agent's plans (i.e., counterplan). When the system processes a narrative describing a situation in which counterplanning causes a plan failure, it refines the initial (flawed) plan by explaining and generalizing the observed counterplan. The newly created counterplan explanation can be used to understand narratives describing similar failures due to counterplanning and to understand measures taken to prevent similar failures.

To illustrate the refinement process used by the ARIES system and its relation to the algorithm used by the current system, an example processed by the ARIES system will now be described. The ARIES system is given a schema describing a kidnapping plan learned by the GENESIS system. This schema assumes that other agents will not interfere with the kidnapper's actions. Next, the ARIES system processes the conceptual representation for a narrative describing how a kidnapper is arrested and imprisoned after revealing his identity to the captive. The ARIES system notes that the kidnap plan has failed because the kidnapper's preserve–freedom goal is violated. Consequently, it explains and generalizes the manner in which the captive learned the identity of the kidnapper and how this led to the arrest and emprisonment of the kidnapper. This explanation structure is added to the kidnapping schema and can now be used to understand similar failures and measures taken to prevent similar failures.

The similarities between the approach used by the ARIES system and the current approach should be quite clear. Both systems use initial schema representations with simplifications. The ARIES system assumes no counterplanning, whereas the current system makes persistence assumptions. When confronted with a goal failure, both approaches explain and generalize how the goal failure occurred. With the ARIES system, processing the narrative describing the kidnapper being jailed causes it to refine the flawed kidnapping schema. In the example presented to describe the current approach, the system notes that it has failed to produce a working widget, causing it to refine the widget plan to explain how the melted gear caused a failure.

Although the basic approach used by the ARIES system is the same as in the current approach, the current approach differs from the ARIES system in three important ways. First, the ARIES system refined schemata for understanding. The current approach involves refining schemata used in problem solving. Second, the current approach uses a more explicit representation and cleaner semantics for assumptions. Third, the ARIES system assumed no counterplanning as a simplification, whereas the current approach involves making persistence assumptions as simplifications.

One type of simplification is numerical approximation. In this area, Bennett [31] used a set of qualitative domain rules as an approximation to a complex numerical relationship, allowing learning in intractable mathematical domains. In some cases, the learned approximation can be verified by substituting back into the original quantitative formula.

Bennett's approach differs from the approach described in this chapter in two ways. Bennett's work deals with numerical simplifications, whereas this work addresses conceptual simplifications. No clear conceptual abstraction is the analogue of order of magnitude or qualitative approximation. Second, although Bennett's approximation allows for validation of approximations, there is no mechanism for repairing flawed approximations.

Hammond's CHEF system [32] also addresses the problem of refining existing flawed plans. The CHEF system plans for new problems by retrieving similar plans and modifying them to produce initial plans. When one of these modified plans fails, the CHEF system constructs an explanation for why the plan failed. CHEF then uses this explanation to classify the conditions that led to the failure under a set of *planning TOP*. Planning TOPs are general classifications of failures that suggest classes of actions to correct the failure. CHEF then repairs the plan by using a suggested fix. CHEF also creates a rule using the generalized conditions that cause the failure in order to anticipate problems in similar future situations. When subsequent plans involving the same features that caused the failure are processed, the modified plan will be retrieved due to the fact that it solves the anticipated problem.

There are several important differences between our approach and that used by the CHEF system. First, CHEF presumes a powerful problem solver that is able to solve anticipated problems. Our approach makes no such requirement and hence must learn plan repairs from observation. Second, CHEF uses a static classification of planning failures to repair plans. Our approach does not require this type of knowledge. Third, because CHEF uses an episodic memory, it can determine with absolute certainty whether a plan episode failed or succeeded. In a schema–based system, certain instantiations of a plan may succeed, while others will fail. Finally, because the CHEF system corrects plans that it generates (versus understanding an external agents behavior), CHEF has access to information from the plan generation phase (i.e., why certain operators were chosen, etc.), whereas in our approach this information must be built up by an understanding module.

Another area of related work is Doyle's work on learning causal descriptions of devices [33]. In this approach, the system has several levels of detail in its domain theory. The system uses this domain theory to explain the behavior of causal mechanisms. At the more detailed levels of the domain theory, the theory is more accurate. As predictions made by the current mechanism description are contradicted by observations made by the system, the system moves to a more detailed level of description.

Doyle's approach differs from ours in two important ways. First, Doyle's system uses schematic descriptions to explain the behavior of mechanisms, whereas in our approach a system builds explanations from a more basic domain theory of rules and operators. This means that Doyle's approach depends on a predefined abstraction hierarchy, while our approach requires no such organization. Furthermore, Doyle's system learns causal descriptions of mechanisms, whereas we are concerned mainly with understanding and refining plans.

Gupta's recent work on explanation–based failure recovery [34] addresses using failures to refine overgeneralized operator application rules in planning. In this approach the system explains failures and determines which subgoals the system was attempting to achieve while causing the failure. His system then adds to this subgoal the constraint of avoiding the failure. When his system replans for the subgoal, it will avoid the failure due to the newly learned constraint.

There are several important differences between our approach and Gupta's. First, because the Gupta system learns from its own problem solving traces, it has access to information on choices made in the plan generation process. Our approach deals with inferring the purposes of operators within the plan. Second, Gupta's approach deals with failures that restrict choice of operators to achieve goals. It does not address addition of operators to a plan to prevent a failure (as in the addition of the cooling operator to prevent the melted plastic gear failure). Additionally, it is not clear that posting constraints at choice points extends to the problem of failures involving multiple dependent choices of operators.

7. Conclusions and Future Work

This chapter has discussed an approach to learning in complex domains. The representation and methods used are general enough such that the approach can be extended to other examples or domains. However, a number of interesting research areas remain for future work:

(1)   First, a taxonomy of simplifications should be developed. Initial work toward this goal is described in [35]. A general system could then be constructed that would use meta–level reasoning to select and apply simplifications to problem solving in a wide range of application areas. Critical to this goal is the development of a uniform representation of simplifications.

(2)   A related area for work is extending the simplification–based approach to other types of defeasible inferences. Although the implemented system uses only persistence assumptions, it seems reasonable that other types of default rules could also be used.

(3)   Currently, in our approach, the system is given a set of simplifications with a domain theory. An interesting area for research would be development of techniques to allow a system to learn simplifications for use in reasoning.

(4)   Another related area for work is efficient execution monitoring and error detection. In certain cases, a system may be able to isolate a failure to a set of assumptions but not be able to further pinpoint the cause of the failure. An open research area is to develop a strategy to efficiently monitor these suspect assumptions during future problem–solving episodes. Alternatively, a system could perform some form of testing or experimentation to further investigate the nature of the flaw e.g., [36, 37].

(5)   Generalizing order of actions in plans is yet another area for research [38]. Currently, the system executes plans with the same ordering of action that was observed. However, in an environment with limited resources or parallel execution, a system should be able to reorder actions to more efficiently execute plans. For example, several steps might be executed in parallel. Or alternatively, certain machines may be available only at certain times. Efficiently dealing with either of these circumstances would require an understanding of the true constraints on order of actions in plans.

(6)   Representing plans at multiple levels of abstraction is an additional area of research. Choosing the appropriate level of

generality at which to represent plans is not an easy task [39–41].
More specific plans have the advantage of easier execution,
whereas more general plans are applicable in a wider variety of
situations. An interesting approach would be to use failures and
repairs to form different levels of abstraction at which to represent
plans.

(7) Detection and refinement of suboptimal and unnecessarily specific
plans is another area for future work. Due to limited inferences or
simplifications, it is possible that a learning system might not
notice a fortuitous side effect of certain of its actions. As a result,
it might use inappropriate or even redundant actions in a plan.
Alternatively, the system might not notice that a plan would be
applicable in a situation in which it is in fact applicable. Ideally,
a planning system would have the capability to detect and remedy
either of these situations.

(8) Our current approach presumes little problem–solving capability
for a system. It would be desirable that the system have some
ability to plan for preconditions when finding a plan that is almost
immediately applicable. The system should also have the ability
to plan to prevent at least some observed failures (presently, the
system must wait until observing a plan repair).

(9) Another area for research would be to extend the knowledge
representation to a more expressive system. For example, using
intervals instead of situations would greatly enhance the expres-
siveness of the system. Allowing specialized numerical reasoning
or noninstantaneous actions would also make a system more
powerful. However, each of these extensions would greatly
increase the complexity of the inference and refinement processes.

I have argued that planning is a computationally demanding task.
In nontrivial domains, the number of possibly useful operators and potentially relevant variables is enormous. Even in game domains, the com-
binatorics of brute–force computation are intractable.

Yet people routinely deal with this type of complexity in a wide
variety of tasks. One way in which this is accomplished is by using
simplifications in reasoning. But this requires the ability to detect and
recover from incorrect usage of simplifications.

This chapter has described an integrated approach to problem solving and learning designed to deal with complexity. In this approach, a
system uses simplifications in initially understanding observed operator

sequences in order to make the process tractable. However, this introduces the possibility of learning flawed plans. To deal with this possibility, the system monitors the usage of learned plans. When a failure to achieve a goal occurs, the system begins a refinement process to prevent repetition of the failure. Because the basic domain theory used by the system is sound, any failure must be due to a faulty simplification. The system then queries the world to pinpoint the faulty assumption in the plan. The reasons for the error in the assumption are explained and generalized using explanation–based learning techniques. The resulting failure representation allows the system to avoid repetition of the failure.

References

1. E. Sacerdoti, *A Structure for Plans and Behavior*, American Elsevier, New York, 1977.

2. D. Chapman, "Planning for Conjunctive Goals," *Artificial Intelligence 32*, 3 (1987), pp. 333–378.

3. A. Newell and H. A. Simon, "GPS, A Program That Simulates Human Thought," in *Computers and Thought*, E. A. Feigenbaum and J. Feldman (ed.), McGraw–Hill, New York City, NY, 1963, pp. 279–293.

4. R. E. Fikes, P. E. Hart and N. J. Nilsson, "Learning and Executing Generalized Robot Plans," *Artificial Intelligence 3*, 4 (1972), pp. 251–288.

5. D. Rumelhart, "Schemata: The Building Blocks of Cognition," in *Theoretical Issues in Reading Comprehension*, W. Brewer (ed.), Lawrence Erlbaum and Associates, Hillsdale, NJ, 1980, pp. 33–58.

6. G. F. DeJong, "Generalizations Based on Explanations," *Proceedings of the Seventh International Joint Conference on Artificial Intelligence*, Vancouver, B.C., Canada, August 1981, pp. 67–70.

7. G. F. DeJong and R. J. Mooney, "Explanation–Based Learning: An Alternative View," *Machine Learning 1*, 2 (1986), pp. 145–176.

8. T. M. Mitchell, R. Keller and S. Kedar–Cabelli, "Explanation–Based Generalization: A Unifying View," *Machine Learning 1*, 1 (January 1986), pp. 47–80.

9. B. Silver, "Precondition Analysis: Learning Control Information," in *Machine Learning: An Artificial Intelligence Approach, Vol. II*, R. S. Michalski, J. G. Carbonell and T. M. Mitchell (ed.), Morgan Kaufmann, 1986, pp. 647–670.

10. J. W. Shavlik and G. F. DeJong, "Analyzing Variable Cancellations to Generalize Symbolic Mathematical Calculations," *Proceedings of the Third IEEE Conference on Artificial Intelligence Applications*, Orlando, FL, February 1987.

11. A. M. Segre, "Explanation–Based Learning of Generalized Robot Assembly Plans," Ph.D. Thesis, Department of Electrical and Computer Engineering, University of Illinois at Urbana–Champaign, Urbana, IL, January 1987.

12. P. V. O'Rorke, "Explanation–Based Learning Via Constraint Posting and Propagation," Ph.D. Thesis, Department of Computer Science, University of Illinois, Urbana, IL, January 1987.

13. T. M. Mitchell, "Learning and Problem Solving," *Proceedings of the Eighth International Joint Conference on Artificial Intelligence*, Karlsruhe, West Germany, August 1983, pp. 1139–1151.

14. S. T. Kedar–Cabelli, "Formulating Concepts According To Purpose," *Proceedings of the National Conference on Artificial Intelligence*, Seattle, WA, July 1987, pp. 477–481.

15. T. M. Mitchell, S. Mahadevan and L. I. Steinberg, "LEAP: A Learning Apprentice for VLSI Design," *Proceedings of the Ninth International Joint Conference on Artificial Intelligence*, Los Angeles, CA, August 1985, pp. 573–580.

16. R. J. Mooney and G. F. DeJong, "Learning Schemata for Natural Language Processing," *Proceedings of the Ninth International Joint Conference on Artificial Intelligence*, Los Angeles, CA, August 1985, pp. 681–687.

17. P. Langley, "Data–Driven Discovery of Physical Laws," *Cognitive Science 5*, 1 (1981), pp. 31–54.

18. R. S. Michalski and R. E. Stepp, "Learning from Observation: Conceptual Clustering," in *Machine Learning: An Artificial Intelligence Approach*, R. S. Michalski, J. G. Carbonell and T. M. Mitchell (ed.), Tioga Publishing Company, Palo Alto, CA, 1983, pp. 331–363.

19. J. R. Quinlan, "Induction of Decision Trees," *Machine Learning 1*, 1 (1986), pp. 81–106.

20. S. A. Chien, "Simplifications in Temporal Persistence: An Approach to the Intractable Domain Theory Problem in Explanation–Based Learning," M.S. Thesis, Department of Computer Science, University of Illinois, Urbana, IL, August 1987.

21. J. McCarthy and P. J. Hayes, "Some Philosophical Problems from the Standpoint of Artificial Intelligence," in *Machine Intelligence 4*, B. Meltzer and D. Michie (ed.), Edinburgh University Press, Edinburgh, Scotland, 1969.

22. R. Reiter, "A Logic for Default Reasoning," *Artificial Intelligence 13*, 1–2 (April 1980), pp. 81–113.

23. J. McCarthy, "Applications of Circumscription to Formalizing Common–Sense Knowledge," *Artificial Intelligence 28*, (1986), pp. 89–116.

24. P. F. Haddawy, "A Variable Precision Logic Inference System Employing the Dempster–Shafer Uncertainty Calculus," Technical Report UIUCDCS–F–86–959, M. S. Thesis, Department of Computer Science, University of Illinois, Urbana, IL, December 86.

25. B. Falkenhainer, "Towards a General Purpose Belief Maintenance System," *Proceedings Second Workshop on Uncertainty and Probability in Artificial Intelligence*, Philadelphia, PA, August 1986.

26. R. J. Mooney and S. W. Bennett, "A Domain Independent Explanation–Based Generalizer," *Proceedings of the National Conference on Artificial Intelligence*, Philadelphia, PA, August 1986, pp. 551–555.

27. P. H. Winston, "Learning by Augmenting Rules and Accumulating Censors," in *Machine Learning: An Artificial Intelligence Approach, Vol. II*, T. M. Mitchell, J. G. Carbonell and R. S. Michalski (ed.), Morgan Kaufmann, 1986, pp. 45–61.

28. J. Doyle, "A Model for Deliberation, Action, and Introspection," Technical Report 581, MIT AI Lab, Cambridge, MA, 1980.

29. S. A. Chien, "A Failure–Driven Approach to Schema Refinement," Working Paper 81, AI Research Group, Coordinated Science Laboratory, University of Illinois, Urbana, IL, 1986.

30. S. A. Chien, "Extending Explanation–Based Learning: Failure–Driven Schema Refinement," *Proceedings of the Third IEEE Conference on Artificial Intelligence Applications*, Orlando, Florida, February 1987. (Also appears as Technical Report UILU–ENG–87–2203, AI Research Group, Coordinated Science Laboratory, University of Illinois at Urbana–Champaign.)

31. S. W. Bennett, "Approximation in Mathematical Domains," *Proceedings of the Tenth International Joint Conference on Artificial Intelligence*, Milan, Italy, August 1987, pp. 239–241.

32. K. Hammond, "Learning to Anticipate and Avoid Planning Failures through the Explanation of Failures," *Proceedings of the National Conference on Artificial Intelligence*, Philadelphia, PA, August 1986, pp. 556–560.

33. R. J. Doyle, "Constructing and Refining Causal Explanations from an Inconsistent Domain Theory," *Proceedings of the National Conference on Artificial Intelligence*, Philadelphia, PA, August 1986, pp. 538–544.

34. A. Gupta, "Explanation–Based Failure Recovery," *Proceedings of the National Conference on Artificial Intelligence*, Seattle, WA, July 1987, pp. 606–610.

35. S. A. Chien, "On Resource Constrained Inference," Working Paper 82, AI Research Group, Coordinated Science Laboratory, University of Illinois, Urbana, Il., February 1987.

36. S. Rajamoney, G. F. DeJong and B. Faltings, "Towards a Model of Conceptual Knowledge Acquisition through Directed Experimentation," *Proceedings of the Ninth International Joint Conference on Artificial Intelligence*, Los Angeles, CA, August 1985.

37. S. Rajamoney and G. DeJong, "The Classification, Detection and Handling of Imperfect Theory Problems," *Proceedings of the Tenth International Joint Conference on Artificial Intelligence*, Milan, Italy, August 1987, pp. 205–207.

38. R. J. Mooney, "A General Explanation–Based Learning Mechanism and its Application to Narrative Understanding," Ph.D. Thesis, Department of Computer Science, University of Illinois, Urbana, IL, January 1988.

39. A. M. Segre, "On the Operationality/Generality Trade–off in Explanation–Based Learning," *Proceedings of the Tenth International Joint Conference on Artificial Intelligence*, Milan, Italy, August 1987, pp. 242–248.

40. R. M. Keller, "Defining Operationality for Explanation–Based Learning," *Proceedings of the National Conference on Artificial Intelligence*, Seattle, WA, July 1987, pp. 482–487.

41. J. W. Shavlik, G. F. DeJong and B. H. Ross, "Acquiring Special Case Schemata in Explanation–Based Learning," *Proceedings of the Ninth Annual Conference of the Cognitive Science Society*, Seattle, WA, July 1987, pp. 851–860.

Chapter 5

Designing Experiments to Extend the Domain Theory

Shankar Rajamoney

1. Introduction

The performance of EBL systems is directly dependent on the quality of the domain theory: Is the knowledge contained in the domain theory adequate to provide a complete, correct explanation for the training instance? An EBL system with a superior model of the domain will yield better performance since it can provide explanations for a larger collection of training instances. Consequently, the success of EBL systems hinges on the ability to construct good models for application domains. For artificially contrived or narrowly restricted domains, an idealized perfect model can be constructed. However, for real–life nontrivial domains, the expert modeling the domain is faced with the herculean task of foreseeing all the potential applications of the domain theory in order to identify and encode the relevant knowledge. To make the task feasible and more manageable, the expert is forced to make simplifications, assumptions, approximations, incorrect generalizations, overgeneralizations, undergeneralizations, and omissions. As a consequence of these and other similar shortcuts, the resulting theories are necessarily incomplete, possibly incorrect, models of the actual domains.

A practical EBL system operating in a complicated real–life setting is severely handicapped by the limitations of its domain theory. The system may not be able to construct explanations for many training instances; therefore, it cannot learn from such examples. Worse yet, the system may construct incorrect explanations which lead to incorrect generalizations. Incorrect generalizations can have profound, detrimental ramifications on the future learning and problem–solving performance of the system. Furthermore, incorrect generalizations negate the desirable "justified–generalization" aspect of explanation–based learning. If EBL systems are to provide robust learning in a practical setting, then they must be capable of recovering from failures due to the shortcomings of the domain theory.

Problems with the domain theory have been broadly classified into three categories [1, 2]. With the first, incomplete theory problems, missing knowledge results in no explanations, incomplete explanations, or multiple, mutually inconsistent, explanations. The second category is incorrect theory problems, wherein incorrect knowledge leads to contradictions during the construction of explanations. The third category is intractable theory problems. The complexity of the theory or the lack of adequate control knowledge prevents the system from constructing explanations within the resource limits.

This chapter describes an approach called *experimentation-based theory revision* [3] that addresses the incomplete and incorrect domain theory problems. Experimentation-based theory revision extends a domain theory by analyzing the failures of the system to identify the underlying beliefs, hypothesizing various revisions to the questionable beliefs to eliminate the failures, and designing experiments to test the validity of the hypotheses. The approach consists of four steps: (1) monitoring the domain to gather observations, (2) making predictions based on the domain theory, (3) postulating hypotheses to resolve differences between the observations and predictions, and (4) designing experiments to test the hypotheses.

Experimentation-based theory revision also tackles the issue of knowledge-level learning [4] — all the knowledge learned by EBL systems is, in principle, derivable from the domain theory; consequently, EBL systems do not acquire new knowledge. Experimentation, which is a central feature of experimentation-based theory revision, enables a system to augment its domain theory by acquiring new knowledge through purposeful interaction with the domain. For example, concepts like "radioactivity" and "semipermeability" could not be originally formulated by reasoning within the existing domain theory. Instead, scientists had to resort to experimentation to investigate the phenomena. Based on the results of experiments, they formed new theories or revised earlier theories that could explain these phenomena.

Experimentation-based theory revision has been implemented in a system called ADEPT (automated design of experiments for perfecting theories). ADEPT is initially supplied with a domain theory that may be incomplete or incorrect or both. When the system fails due to problems with the domain theory, it enters a hypothesis generation and experimentation cycle to gather more knowledge about the phenomenon. The new information helps it revise the flawed domain theory and eliminate the failures.

The next section introduces a detailed example that will be used to illustrate the individual steps of experimentation–based theory revision. Sections 3, 4, and 5 describe each step in detail, Section 6 identifies some of the limitations of the approach, Section 7 discusses related research, and Section 8 presents the conclusions. The details of the implementation, ADEPT, and a sample run on the example of Section 2 are described in Chapter 12.

2. The Osmosis Example

Experimentation–based theory revision has been demonstrated on a detailed example from the domain of chemistry. ADEPT's initial domain theory includes knowledge of five physical processes: the FLOW of liquids, the ABSORPTION of liquids by solids, the EVAPORATION of liquids, the CONDENSATION of vapors, and the RELEASE of absorbed liquids. During its routine problem solving, the system encounters a novel physical phenomenon called "osmosis" that occurs when two solutions of different concentrations are connected by a "semipermeable" path and that involves a flow of solvent from the solution of lower concentration to the solution of higher concentration through the semipermeable path. None of the processes known to ADEPT entail a flow of liquids through a solid. In fact, a precondition of one of the processes, FLOW, explicitly requires a clear solid–free path for the flow of liquids. Consequently, ADEPT fails to explain the observations pertaining to osmosis and is forced to revise its initial domain theory.

In the example, ADEPT is given the task of preparing two solutions of specified amounts and concentrations. This task is to be part of an elaborate chemical experiment to be performed by the laboratory technician. The chemical experiment requires the two solutions to be mixed quickly and the time taken for the ensuing reaction to be noted. To correctly measure the initial time, large volumes of the two solutions must come into contact rapidly. Therefore the two solutions must be stored in separate compartments of a container with a removable partition. ADEPT is assigned the task of forming the required solutions and storing them in a suitable container. ADEPT, unfortunately, selects a container that has a semipermeable partition separating the two compartments. ADEPT, not knowing anything about osmosis or semipermeability of solids, does not suspect the possibility of a flow of liquid through the semipermeable partition.

The system's expected predictions of the appearance of the given amounts of the two solutions in the two compartments of the container conform to the actual observations made (Figure 5–1a). However, the real world also gives some additional unexpected observations — a decrease in the amount of the solution in the first compartment and an increase in the amount of the solution in the second compartment (Figure 5–1b). ADEPT tries to construct explanations for these observations. However, it finds that it can construct explanations only for why the amounts of the solutions in the two containers must be constant, thereby contradicting the observations. The next few sections describe how ADEPT uses experimentation–based theory revision to resolve this failure. The example eventually involves learning a new process schema for osmosis, a new property definition describing the semipermeability of solids participating in osmosis, and an experiment template to determine whether an object exhibits the new semipermeability property.

8. Contradiction Detection

Theory revision commences with the detection of problems with the existing theory. A general method for detecting incomplete and incorrect domain theory problems is *contradiction detection* — determining whether the expectations of the system based on the theory conflict with the observations made of the domain. A contradiction is the disagreement of two facts known to the system. For example, (increase amount Solution1) and (decrease amount Solution1) are contradictory. Contradictions arise when the system operates with a domain theory that is incomplete or inconsistent. They can be classified into two categories:

(1)   *Contradictions between the system and the real world.* The predictions of the system do not conform to the observations made of

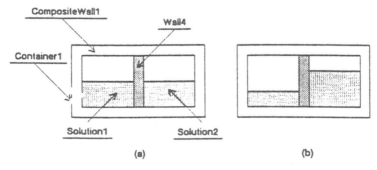

Figure 5–1:   The Scenario Before and After the Unexpected Observations.

the real–world behavior.

(2)   *Contradictions within the system.* The system makes contradictory predictions of how the real world will behave.

The following discussion concerns contradictions of the first type; contradictions within the system may be handled in a like manner with minor modifications.

Contradictions are detected by (1) monitoring the real world to gather relevant observations, (2) making predictions about how the real world will behave based on the domain theory, and (3) comparing the predictions and the observations. Differences in the observations and predictions can be classified as (1) unexpected observations — changes were observed but not predicted by the system; (2) failed predictions — changes were predicted by the system but failed to materialize; and (3) differing degree — either too much or too little of the predicted change actually occurred. Each of these differences leads to a contradiction.

The osmosis example illustrates how contradictions are used to detect incompleteness or incorrectness in domain theories. In the osmosis example, the predictions based on the system's domain theory state that the amounts of the two solutions remain constant (all the processes that can change the amounts of the two solutions are determined to be inactive due to unsatisfied preconditions). The observations provided to the system specify that the amount of the first solution decreases and the amount of the second increases. These observations contradict the predictions (Figure 5–2). With the contradiction, ADEPT discovers that its domain theory is inadequate and needs to be revised.

4. Hypothesis Formation

The next step in theory revision involves determining the beliefs underlying the contradiction and proposing changes to the questionable beliefs to eliminate the contradiction. A system operating in the real world functions under a set of beliefs — statements about how the world is organized and how it behaves. Beliefs are of many types: rules such as Newton's laws of motion, assumptions such as "friction is negligible on a smooth surface," and heuristics such as "if the sun is shining in the morning, then you may leave your umbrella at home." Beliefs generate expectations within the system about the world's behavior. The failure of these expectations leads to contradictions. *Hypotheses* are statements that identify possible reasons for the contradiction; they are derived by examining the beliefs underlying the contradiction. For example, a

almost certainly true (assuming the sensors are functioning properly). Rules are obtained from a large number of observations and are, in general, strongly believed. Heuristics, by definition, are rules of thumb and may not work in all cases. Assumptions may turn out to be wrong, depending on the situation, and are therefore less strongly believed. Experiment conclusions are based on observations from the real world and the beliefs of the domain theory used in the experiment design. Calculations can be based on assumptions, heuristics, and other beliefs of the domain theory. Therefore, the strength of secondary beliefs such as experiment conclusions and calculations are derived from the primary beliefs. All beliefs in the contradiction structure can be accordingly graded.

(2) *Depth of the node.* Assuming that the strength of the belief in each node is the same, then one way to find the false belief is to test all the leaves of the contradiction and gradually go forward to determine the path of wrong computation. The number of experiments this method requires is combinatorially explosive. A much better method is to test nodes at as high a level as possible, thereby restricting the total number of experiments required by isolating the false belief at the highest level. In this way, there will be considerable savings by avoiding tests on subtrees of true beliefs. In the osmosis example, the system constructs experiments to test whether a process is active rather than directly examining the preconditions of each process. This eliminates the testing of preconditions of those processes that can be experimentally determined to be inactive. Figure 5–3 illustrates the various levels of beliefs for the contradiction structure shown in Figure 5–2. The beliefs labeled with a lower number (and therefore less strongly believed) are tested before those with a higher number. For example, first, processes are tested to check whether they are active. Then, the preconditions of the active processes are tested to check whether they are correct. Finally, the observations or conditions that led to the failure of the preconditions are tested. However, there is no guarantee that the system can test each belief; it can test only those beliefs for which it has sufficient knowledge to construct experiments. For example, rules such as

$$(p \text{ and } (NOT\ p) \text{ implies CONTRADICTION})$$

are beyond the present experimental testing capabilities of

                    (4) (p and (NOT p) implies CONTRADICTION) (1)
(NOT (active EvaporationOfSolvent1))
            (2) (failedPrecondition EvaporationExposurePrecondition)
                    (4) (NOT (touches Vapor1 Atmosphere))
            (2) (necessary EvaporationExposurePrecondition)
    (1) (NOT (active AbsorptionOfSolution1ByWall4))

                            .
                            .
                            .

    (1) (NOT (active FlowOfSolvent1ToSolution2ViaCompositeWall1))
            (2) (failedPrecondition FlowPathPrecondition)
                    (4) (solid CompositeWall1)
            (2) (necessary FlowPathPrecondition)
            (2) (failedPrecondition FlowAgentPrecondition)
            (3) (NOT (exists FlowForceOnSolvent1FromHeightDifference))
                    (4) (equal (level Solvent1) (level Solution2))
            (3) (NOT (relevant NewForce))
            (2) (necessary FlowAgentPrecondition)
    (1) (NOT (relevant NewProcess))

Figure 5-3:   The Ordering of Beliefs into Levels Based on the Strength
              and Depth of the Belief

    ADEPT.

4.2. Hypothesis Derivation

If the dependency structure leads to a contradiction, then one (or more) of the underlying beliefs must be false or inadequate. To find the false belief, hypotheses are generated from the underlying beliefs and tested. The generation of hypotheses is a very difficult problem. Consider the earlier example of the stick immersed in water. An underlying belief is that light always travels in straight lines. Some of the hypotheses that can be derived from this belief are (1) light never travels in a straight line, (2) light travels in a straight line only in a homogeneous medium, (3) light bends whenever it moves from air to water, and (4) sticks change shape when immersed in water. Clearly, a large number of hypotheses of varying generality are possible. Obviously, a system cannot come up with every possible hypothesis to explain why a belief may be false. Experimentation-based theory revision generates hypotheses from prestored schemata describing four types of hypotheses:

(1) *Hypothesis type 1.* A belief about a calculation based on a number of objects/processes leads to a hypothesis that questions each individual object/process. In the osmosis example, the calculation (NOT (decrease amount Solution1)) is based on another calculation that states that all the processes that could decrease the amount of liquids are inactive (Figure 5–2). The hypothesis questioning the first calculation proposes one of these processes to be active.

(2) *Hypothesis type 2.* A belief based on a calculated value for a measurable quantity leads to hypotheses questioning the calculated quantity. In the osmosis example, the absence of a calculable force on Solvent1 forms the basis for believing a precondition of the FLOW process to have failed. The generated hypothesis, in this case, questions the calculation and requires the system to make a measurement to ascertain that there is no force on Solvent1.

(3) *Hypothesis type 3.* This hypothesis considers the possibility of new processes, new properties of objects, and new preconditions. For example, the system assumes that it knows all the processes that can cause a change in the amounts of liquids. This assumption need not be true. Therefore, when a contradiction based on this assumption is detected, a hypothesis that considers the possibility of a new process is generated.

(4) *Hypothesis type 4.* This hypothesis is used to find a relation between two physical quantities. In the osmosis example, the system measures a value for the magnitude of the force on Solvent1. However, it does not know how to calculate the magnitude using its domain theory. It therefore proposes a relation between the force and the properties of the objects participating in the process.

5. Experiment Design

The final step in theory revision is testing the validity of the proposed changes to the theory. An *experiment* is a directed enquiry for testing the validity of a hypothesis. It includes the following pieces of information: the hypothesis to be tested, the scenario in or conditions under which the experiment is to be performed, a set of specifications for performing the experiment, conditional results that specify the conclusion obtained from each possible observation, the actual observations made when the experiment is performed (by an external agent), and the conclusions obtained from the observation. Experimentation–based theory revision groups experiments into five classes: discrimination experiments, measurement experiments, find dependency experiments, property definition experiments, and classification experiments.

5.1. Discrimination Experiments

Discrimination experiments determine whether a process from a set of candidate processes or an object from a set of candidate objects displays specified characteristics. The desired candidate must possess observable characteristics. The purpose of discrimination experiments is to narrow the number of candidates and, if possible, to identify the desired candidate. A discrimination experiment can be characterized as follows:

> If the candidate being tested in the experiment is the desired candidate, then when the experiment is performed a specified property will behave in a particular manner.

There are four main steps in designing discrimination experiments:

(1) *Selection of a discriminant.* Any characteristic of the objects/processes that exhibits different behavior for different candidates can be used.

(2) *Formation of equivalence classes.* Candidates are grouped into mutually exclusive classes such that those within a class exhibit identical behavior with respect to the chosen discriminant. Hence, these elements are indistinguishable from one another for all experiments that use this discriminant. However, candidates in different classes can be distinguished from one another.

(3) *Construction of experiments.* Experiments are designed based on the discriminant in order to exploit the differences in behavior.

(4) *Iteration.* After the experiments are carried out, the class that conforms with the observations is further examined. If only one candidate remains in that class, it is the desired candidate. Otherwise, the candidates of the class form the current set of candidates and the above procedure is repeated. This process continues until no further discriminants are available or the desired candidate is identified.

In the osmosis example, ADEPT needs to determine which process, if any, among all the processes that can influence the amounts of liquids, is active. For example, ADEPT must determine whether one of the two different occurrences of the process FLOW, FlowOfSolvent1ToSolution2 ViaWall4 and FlowOfSolution1ToSolution2ViaWall4, is active. The system infers from the primary effects of the FLOW process (increase of amount at destination and decrease at the source) that if the first process is active, then the concentration of Solution1 increases since the proportion of the solute to the solvent increases due to a decrease in the amount of the solvent. In the case of the second process, however, the concentration of Solution1 is unaffected because the the solution flows as a whole. Thus, ADEPT uses this difference in the "effects" of the two candidates as the basis of a discrimination experiment that involves repeating the original scenario and measuring the concentration of Solution1.

A more complicated example involves distinguishing between processes of different types. In the osmosis example, ADEPT must determine which, if any, of the different occurrences of the processes FLOW, EVAPORATION, and ABSORPTION causes the observation (decrease amount Solution1). The system knows from its process models that the rate of each process depends on the geometry of the container. For example, the FLOW process depends on the cross–sectional area and length of the path, the ABSORPTION and RELEASE processes depend on the surface area of contact between the absorbing solid and the absorbed liquid, and the CONDENSATION and EVAPORATION processes depend on the surface area of contact between the liquid and its vapor. By varying these parameters, it is possible to increase or decrease the time taken to reproduce the original observations. This property forms the basis of the discrimination experiment. ADEPT tests whether EvaporationOfSolvent1 is active by specifying constraints on the geometry of the container such that the rate of this process is greatly enhanced. At the same time, the experiment is also controlled to prevent the unwanted influence of the competing processes by manipulating the geometry to inhibit their rates. (ADEPT specifies a description of the geometrical constraints on the container to be used in the experiment and assumes that a laboratory technician or a hypothetical module actually constructs the container. Figure 5–4 shows what such a container might look like.) If the experiment finds that the observations occur faster than before, then EvaporationOfSolvent1 is active. Notice that this experiment cannot distinguish between processes like FlowOfSolvent1ToSolution2ViaWall4 and FlowOfSolution1 ToSolution2ViaWall4 since they use the same geometrical path. Another discriminant, such as the effects of the process, must be used.

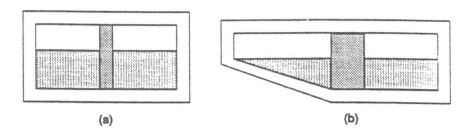

(a)   (b)

Figure 5–4:   (a) The Original Container and (b) a Container Designed
              According to the Experiment Specifications. The geometry of
              the container favors evaporation of Solvent1 and inhibits the
              FLOW and ABSORPTION processes.

5.2. Measurement Experiments

Measurement experiments involve the measurement of physical
quantities. Quantities can be measured in two ways: directly by using a
suitably calibrated meter or indirectly by measuring quantities that can
be used to compute the desired quantity. Indirect measurements involve
the specification of the indirect quantities to be measured, the function for
computing the desired quantity from the measured quantities, and the
conditions to be met when the measurements are made.

In the osmosis example, ADEPT must design an experiment to
measure the force on Solvent1 to determine whether it is zero (as
predicted by the theory). ADEPT designs an indirect measurement experiment (using a prestored experiment schema for measuring forces on
liquids) that involves exerting a measurable force opposing
ForceOnSolvent1TowardsSolution2 to stop the flow process. When the
process stops, the two forces are equal in magnitude, and thus the magnitude of ForceOnSolvent1TowardsSolution2 is determined. Figure 5–5
illustrates the experiment. The measurement conditions are obtained
from the observations that will be made if the process
FlowOfSolvent1ToSolution2ViaWall4 is stopped. The variation functions
specify that the experiment must be reproduced a number of times with
different values for the magnitude of ForceBySolid8OnSolution2. The
value that meets the measurement conditions is the desired value. The
procedure for each such experiment is the construction of scenarios such
as those depicted in Figures 5–5(b), (c).

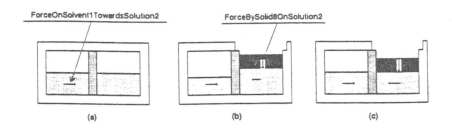

Figure 5–5: Experiments for the Indirect Measurement of the Force on Solvent1

5.3. Find Dependency Experiments

Dependency experiments determine how one physical quantity is related to other physical quantities. For example, the force causing osmosis depends on the difference in concentrations of the two solutions. Knowledge about such relations will give the system a theoretical method of computing the force from the specified concentrations. Discovering such relations involves the following steps:

(1) The identification of objects and processes whose features determine the given physical quantity.

(2) The identification of the relevant features of the selected objects and processes.

(3) The determination of the qualitative variation of the given physical quantity with respect to each selected feature.

(4) The correlation of each separate variation to generate the equation which governs the behavior of the given physical quantity expressed in terms of the selected features.

The identification of relevant objects/processes and the relevant features of these objects/processes is a very difficult problem. ADEPT uses heuristics to determine relevance; some typical heuristics are discussed in the example presented next. Once the relevant features have been identified, experiments are designed to determine how the given physical quantity varies with respect to the variation in each selected feature. If no relevant property for a relevant object can be found, then ADEPT defines a new property for the object using the property definition experiments described in the next section.

In the osmosis example, ADEPT measures the magnitude of the force, ForceOnSolvent1TowardsSolution2, a precondition of the new process, Process9 (Osmosis). The system now attempts to find a relation between the magnitude of the force and the properties of the relevant objects. To determine relevance, ADEPT uses the following heuristic:

> Heuristic1: If a physical quantity is the cause of a process, then the participants of the process are relevant objects.

This heuristic enables the system to focus on the objects — Solution1, Solution2, and Wall4 — involved in the new process. To determine the properties of these objects that may be relevant to the computation of the force, ADEPT uses the following heuristics:

(1) *Cause-effect heuristic.* If a physical quantity is the cause of a process, then the properties of objects that change as an effect of the process may be relevant. Many natural processes exhibit this effect–cause link. For example, the flow of charge from a ball of high potential to a similar ball of lower potential is caused by a difference in potentials. This flow results in a decrease in the higher potential and an increase in the lower potential. Thus the property "potential" that was affected by the process is also linked to the cause of the process.

(2) *Initial-state difference heuristic.* If a physical quantity is the cause of a process, and the process has participatory objects of similar type, then properties of these objects that initially had different values may be relevant. Examples are fluid flow due to a difference in pressures, electron flow due to a difference in potential, heat flow due to difference in temperatures, and waterfalls due to a difference in heights. If the process is directional, then the relevance of the properties may be determined by interchanging the values of the property and noting whether the direction of the process changes. Another possibility is to equate the values of the property and observe whether the process stops.

Based on the above heuristics, ADEPT generates many candidate properties and designs experiments in which these properties are varied systematically. Considerable research has already addressed the problem of discovering equations from data obtained from this type of experiment [5, 6]. The experiments designed by ADEPT are assumed to be performed and the observations analyzed by systems like BACON or ABACUS [5, 6] to produce the required equation. Based on the results from these systems, such a combined system can conclude that the desired relation is

$$\text{magnitude[ForceOnSolvent1TowardsSolution2]} =$$
$$k * (\text{concentration[Solution2]} - \text{concentration[Solution1]})$$

5.4. Property Definition Experiments

Many properties of objects define their ability to participate in a process. For example, an object is "absorbent" if it participates in the ABSORPTION process, and it is "insulating" if it does not participate in the CONDUCT–ELECTRICITY process. These properties are inherently related to the material of the object rather than the object itself. Such properties can be given a functional definition:

> To check whether an object/material exhibits the property, construct an experiment in which the role of an object/material known to exhibit the property is replaced by a test sample of the given object/material and observe if the process occurs.

5.4.1. Creating the Property Definition Experiment

When a process requires an object to be a participant, and no known property of the object can be identified as relevant to the process, then a new one must be created. This is often the case when new processes are discovered. An experiment template for the property is created by identifying six specifications. The first is an object (standard object) in a scenario that is known to exhibit the property. Second is an object (test object) that is being tested for the presence of the property. Third are associated quantities involved in defining the property. For example, the property "solubility" of a solute in the DISSOLVE process is defined with respect to the associated solvent. Fourth, it is specified how a test sample of the test object will be constructed and how it will replace the standard object in the scenario during the experiment. The specification involves the identification of the properties of the standard object relevant to its role in the scenario and the properties of the test object relevant to the test experiment. The default used by ADEPT is that the test sample is made of the same material as that of the test object and that all other properties such as shape and size are obtained from the standard object. Fifth, the scenario for performing the test experiment is specified. Finally, conditional results are stated in the following form: If the observations are such that the presence of the process is confirmed (for example, through the effects of the process), then the test object exhibits the property; otherwise it does not.

5.4.2. Using the Property Definition Experiment

The procedure to test for the property consists of three steps:

(1)   A test sample is constructed using the specifications in the property definition experiment.

(2)   The scenario described in the experiment is constructed with the standard object replaced by the test sample.

(3)   The observations are noted. If the process occurs, then the conclusion is that the test object exhibits the property; otherwise it does not.

Consider, for example, the problem of determining whether glass is absorbent. Figure 5–6(a) and (b) illustrate the original experiment performed with the standard object which is made of clay, and Figure 5–6(c) illustrates the test experiment in which a container made of glass is used. Since the level of water in the container does not decrease, the conclusion is that glass does not absorb the given liquid.

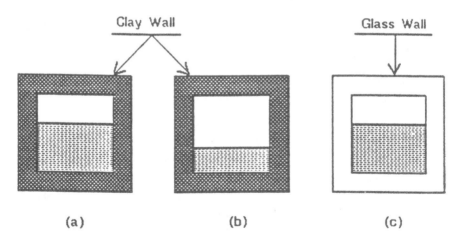

(a)   (b)   (c)

Figure 5–6:   Experiment to Determine Whether an Object is Absorbent

In the osmosis example, none of the properties of Wall4 is found to be relevant by the find–dependency experiments. Therefore, a new property that defines the role played by Wall4 in the newly formed process, Process9 ("osmosis"), must be created. The experiment template for defining the newly created property, Property22 ("semipermeability"), is shown in Figure 5–7. The variables denoted by a prefix "##" are computed when the test experiment is designed.

5.5. Classification Experiments

Often, the system needs to know:

(1)   The class of objects that exhibits a property. For example, the problem solver might need to know which objects are absorbent and which are not.

(2)   For each such object, the class of associated participants that the object interacts with while exhibiting that property. For example, a membrane may be semipermeable with respect to water and a salt solution but not with respect to alcohol and a sugar solution.

The purpose of classification experiments is to classify objects into two classes: those that exhibit a specified property and those that do not. For example, if it is required to build a container for storing liquids, then the system will have to know which materials are not absorbent and hence can be used to build such containers. Classification experiments are supplied a list of objects/materials to be classified based on their behavior to a given property as input. Each object is tested using the property definition test experiments described in the previous section. Based on the results of these test experiments, the objects are grouped into classes exhibiting or not exhibiting the specified property.

6. Limitations and Future Work

Experimentation–based theory revision has several shortcomings. The hypotheses for resolving a contradiction are derived heuristically from the beliefs underlying the contradiction structure. However, this solution is not satisfactory. The space of hypotheses defined by a set of heuristics is not easily characterizable. Also, there is a danger that such heuristics will work only for the specified examples. One approach to remedy this problem is to integrate the hypothesis generation process with the explanation construction process and to search for explanations that are supported by hypothesized revisions to the domain theory to eliminate the contradiction. Experimentation can then be used to find the

```
(DEFCLASS Property22DefinitionExperiment
        (propertyDefined        Property22)
        (processClass           Process9)
        (standardObject(Container3      (material vegetableSkin)))
        (scenario
         (Scenario42
            (objects
              (##testSample##Participant1##Participant2))
            (relations
                ((In   ##Participant1
                    (##testSample (compartment Compartment1)))
                 (In   ##Participant2
                    (##testSample (compartment Compartment2)))
                 (Closed ##testSample))))
        (sampleSpecification    ((testObject             (material))
                                 (standardObject         'everythingElse)))
        (associatedParticipants (##Participant1 ##Participant2)
              default           (Solution1 Solution2))
        (conditionalResults
         ((decrease   amount         ##Participant1)
          (increase   amount         ##Participant2)
          (increase   concentration  ##Participant1)
          (decrease   concentration  ##Participant2)))
```

Figure 5-7:   The Property Definition Experiment for "semipermeability"

correct explanation and hence the correct change required to the original domain theory.

The method for designing experiments described in this chapter involves identifying different classes of experiments to test different types of hypotheses. Five classes of experiments were identified: discrimination, find dependency, measurement, property definition, and classification experiments. These classes use domain-dependent, prestored schemata to design individual experiments. Instead, a set of domain-independent strategies for designing experiments can be developed. The results from an initial attempt in this direction were described by Rajamoney and DeJong [7].

Experimentation-based theory revision attempts to enforce theory consistency only with the observations made from the current example; it does not enforce consistency with previous observations. However, the changes to the theory that resolve the present contradiction can be incompatible with previous observations. Therefore, a notion of consistency with the previous history is essential for a robust theory revision system. Results from an initial investigation of a solution to this problem based on maintaining exemplars and prototypes was described by Rajamoney [8].

An important problem for systems that deal with both incomplete and incorrect domain theories is whether to modify the existing domain theory or to make additions to the existing domain theory. In the osmosis example, the system could either change the existing flow process to account for the observation (for example, by making a disjunctive precondition — "clear, solid–free path or semipermeable path") or it could create a new process. The present system creates a new process when there are new effects that cannot be explained by the existing process. For the osmosis example, the system chose to create a new process because there were new effects involving changes to the concentrations (discovered during experimentation) that could not be accounted for by the flow process. However, this is not a general solution to the problem. If the original domain theory had a process that was correct except for an effect, then the present system would create a new process which duplicates the old one in most respects. This can result in a proliferation of nearly identical processes in the domain theory. We are presently exploring a number of alternatives to the above method that evaluate the aesthetics of the revised theory and the ramifications of the changes [9].

Experimentation–based theory revision does not indicate how to generalize the results of the experiments. For example, the system presently generates a new schema for osmosis which involves the specific participants observed in the example — Solution1, Solution2, and Wall4. It does not have a basis for generalizing to the class of solutions or partitions. In fact, there are a number of interesting constraints that must be observed during the generalization. For example, arbitrary solutions do not participate in osmosis; only some combinations of solutions and partitions result in osmosis. One approach to this problem is to use experiments to investigate different combinations of solutions and partitions and use classification experiments to classify the combinations. The osmosis process can then be extended to cover all these combinations. An alternative approach is to make an inductive leap and generalize to arbitrary solutions and partitions; further contradictions can be used to refine the generalizations.

7. Related Work

Discovery systems like BACON [5] also propose experiments to gain crucial missing information, but they do not do so in the context of a qualitative model of the world. These systems are typically data driven; ADEPT is more theory driven. There are also important differences with the later systems of NGLAUBER [10] and STAHLP [11]. NGLAUBER uses a data–driven clustering algorithm to generate rules for observed data, and STAHLP does not perform experiments but rather relies on minimizing a cost function to decide between competing conjectures. ADEPT shares many commonalities with PHINEAS [12] since they both deal with the formation and revision of qualitative theories of the physical world. However, PHINEAS primarily depends on analogical reasoning for hypothesis generation and simulation for testing the validity of the hypotheses; ADEPT primarily relies on an analysis of the contradiction and prestored schemata of hypothesis types to generate hypotheses and experimentation to test the validity of the hypotheses. Results of an attempt to combine the two systems were described by Falkenhainer and Rajamoney [13].

A number of researchers have proposed different methods for combining EBL and similarity–based learning to address the incomplete and incorrect domain theory problems [14–18]. Typically, these methods analyze a large number of training instances to find the common features in order to construct the missing rules required to complete an explanation. Our approach uses experimentation to investigate the phenomenon and acquire the required knowledge. Laird [19] described a method for recovering from incorrect knowledge in SOAR [20]. His method focuses on modifying the decisions leading to the selection of the incorrect knowledge, whereas experimentation–based theory revision attempts to identify and rectify the incorrect knowledge. Carbonell and Gil [21] described a subsystem of PRODIGY that learns knowledge about operators through experimentation. However, their methods for designing experiments are very different from those employed by ADEPT; ADEPT generates five types of experiments — discrimination, find–dependency, measurement, property definition, and classification experiments — whereas PRODIGY designs experiments based on binary search and state comparisons to identify problematic operators, missing preconditions of operators, and missing postconditions of operators.

8. Conclusion

It is increasingly apparent that knowledge is essential for intelligent behavior. This has led to a new trend in AI toward knowledge–intensive methods such as explanation–based learning [1, 22], qualitative reasoning [23–25], and deep–model expert systems. The primary shortcoming of these approaches is not in the representation of the knowledge — a task that is relatively well understood — but in the subtleties of selecting the appropriate knowledge. The expert who is hand–coding the knowledge has to anticipate the wide range of tasks and situations for which the knowledge may be used in order to ensure that the system will function properly. Also, all AI systems that rely on a programmer–specified domain theory are fundamentally limited by their initial knowledge. For example, Utgoff [26] showed how the initial knowledge built into a learning system drastically influenced its learning capability. Consequently, a theory revision system that automatically detects and remedies problems with its domain theory is required. Such a system will free the expert from the tedious and often impossible task of hand–coding all the relevant knowledge; it will enable the use of "quick and dirty" methods to facilitate the construction of operational, but perhaps imperfect, domain theories. These domain theories can then be automatically debugged and corrected by the system.

This chapter has described experimentation–based theory revision — an approach that can be used to construct such a system. The system detects problems with the domain theory when it fails its regular tasks, analyzes the failures to identify the underlying beliefs, proposes modifications or extensions to the beliefs to eliminate the failures, and designs experiments to test the validity of the proposed changes. The approach has been implemented in a system called ADEPT and demonstrated on an example in which it learns a new process schema (osmosis), a new property of objects (semipermeability), and an experiment to determine whether an object is semipermeable. A new system called COAST [9, 27], which is much more powerful and addresses many of the limitations of the ADEPT system, is presently under development.

References

1. T. M. Mitchell, R. Keller and S. Kedar–Cabelli, "Explanation–Based Generalization: A Unifying View," *Machine Learning 1*, 1 (January 1986), pp. 47–80.

2. S. Rajamoney and G. DeJong, "The Classification, Detection and Handling of Imperfect Theory Problems," *Proceedings of the Tenth*

International Joint Conference on Artificial Intelligence, Milan, Italy, August 1987, pp. 205–207.

3. S. A. Rajamoney, "Automated Design of Experiments for Refining Theories," M. S. Thesis, Department of Computer Science, University of Illinois, Urbana, IL, May 1986.

4. T. G. Dietterich, "Learning at the Knowledge Level," *Machine Learning 1*, 3 (1986), pp. 287–316.

5. P. Langley, "Data–Driven Discovery of Physical Laws," *Cognitive Science 5*, 1 (1981), pp. 31–54.

6. B. C. Falkenhainer and R. S. Michalski, "Integrating Quantitative and Qualitative Discovery: The ABACUS System," *Machine Learning 1*, 4 (1986), pp. 367–401.

7. S. A. Rajamoney and G. F. DeJong, "Active Explanation Reduction: An Approach to the Multiple Explanations Problem," *Proceedings of the Fifth International Conference on Machine Learning*, Ann, Arbor, MI, June 1988.

8. S. Rajamoney, "Exemplar–Based Theory Rejection: An Approach to the Experience Consistency Problem," *Proceedings of the Sixth International Conference on Machine Learning*, Ithaca, NY, June 1989, pp. 284–289.

9. S. A. Rajamoney, "Explanation–Based Theory Revision: An Approach to the Problems of Incomplete and Incorrect Theories," Ph.D. Thesis, Department of Computer Science, University of Illinois, Urbana, IL, December 1988.

10. R. Jones, "Generating Predictions to Aid the Scientific Discovery Process," *Proceedings of the National Conference on Artificial Intelligence*, Philadelphia, PA, August 1986, pp. 513–517.

11. D. Rose and P. Langley, "STAHLp: Belief Revision in Scientific Discovery," *Proceedings of the National Conference on Artificial Intelligence*, Philadelphia, PA, August 1986, pp. 528–532.

12. B. Falkenhainer, "An Examination of the Third Stage in the Analogy Process: Verification–Based Analogical Learning," *Proceedings of the Tenth International Joint Conference on Artificial Intelligence*, Milan, Italy, August 1987, pp. 260–263.

13. B. C. Falkenhainer and S. A. Rajamoney, "The Interdependencies of Theory Formation, Revision, and Experimentation," *Proceedings of the Fifth International Conference on Machine Learning*, Ann,

Arbor, MI, June 1988.

14. R. Hall, "Learning by Failing to Explain," *Proceedings of the National Conference on Artificial Intelligence*, Philadelphia, PA, August 1986, pp. 568–572.

15. A. P. Danyluk, "The Use of Explanations for Similarity–Based Learning," *Proceedings of the Tenth International Joint Conference on Artificial Intelligence*, Milan, Italy, August 1987, pp. 274–276.

16. M. J. Pazzani, "Integrated Learning with Incorrect and Incomplete Theories," *Proceedings of the Fifth International Conference on Machine Learning*, Ann, Arbor, MI, June 1988, pp. 291–297.

17. M. Lebowitz, "Integrated Learning: Controlling Explanation," *Cognitive Science 10*, 2 (1986), pp. 219–240.

18. Y. Kodratoff and G. Tecuci, "Disciple–1: Interactive Apprentice System in Weak Theory Fields," *Proceedings of the Tenth International Joint Conference on Artificial Intelligence*, Milan, Italy, August 1987, pp. 271–273.

19. J. Laird, "Recovery from Incorrect Knowledge in SOAR," *Proceedings of the Seventh National Conference on Artificial Intelligence* , Saint Paul, Minnesota , August 1988, pp. 618–623.

20. J. Laird, A. Newell and P. Rosenbloom, "SOAR: An Architecture for General Intelligence," *Artificial Intelligence 33*, 1 (1987), pp. 1–64.

21. J. G. Carbonell and Y. Gil, "Learning by Experimentation," *Proceedings of the Fourth International Workshop on Machine Learning*, University of California, Irvine, June 1987, pp. 256–266.

22. G. F. DeJong and R. J. Mooney, "Explanation–Based Learning: An Alternative View," *Machine Learning 1*, 2 (1986), pp. 145–176.

23. K. D. Forbus, "Qualitative Process Theory," *Artificial Intelligence 24*, (1984), pp. 85–168.

24. J. de Kleer and J. S. Brown, "A Qualitative Physics Based on Confluences," *Artificial Intelligence 24*, (1984), .

25. B. Kuipers, "Commonsense Reasoning About Causality: Deriving Behavior from Structure," *Artificial Intelligence 24*, (1984), pp. 169–204.

26. P. E. Utgoff, "Shift of Bias for Inductive Concept Learning," in *Machine Learning: An Artificial Intelligence Approach, Vol. II*, R. S. Michalski, J. G. Carbonell and T. M. Mitchell (ed.), Morgan

Kaufmann, 1986, pp. 107–148.

27. S. A. Rajamoney,, "A Computational Approach to Theory Revision," in *Computational Models of Scientific Discovery and Theory Formation*, J. Shrager & P. Langley (ed.), Lawrence Earlbaum Associates, Hillsdale, N.J., 1990.

Chapter 6

Some Aspects of Operationality

Scott W. Bennett and
Jude W. Shavlik

1. Introduction

Operationality has proven to be a troublesome facet of EBL. Two complementary approaches to the operationality problem are presented here. The first involves constructing and remembering partial generalizations called *special cases* in addition to the standard EBL generalization. The second comprises a theory of *linear operationality*.

One of the earliest definitions of *operationalization* for machine learning was given by Jack Mostow: "convert[ing] knowledge about a task domain into procedures useful in performing the task" [1]. The term was especially useful in representing where "learning" was taking place in EBL. As work toward a unifying framework for explanation–based learning progressed around 1986, a simple binary notion of operationality was in use. Mitchell marked specific predicates as operational, a system's goal being to express the concept in terms of those operational predicates [2]. DeJong and Mooney pointed out two disadvantages of using this approach [3]. First, no method is prescribed for how operational predicates are so designated. In effect, the procedure for marking predicates as operational is nonoperational. Second, it is undesirable to mark predicates as operational regardless of arguments. It may well be possible to judge whether a predicate can be achieved with one type of argument while impossible with another. Operationality is also dependent on the current state of the system and should therefore be dynamic, not static as the earlier definition proposes. Finally, the binary definition lacks any way to express a preference between two different, yet operational, ways in which the system may achieve a goal.

Keller offered a revised definition of operationality for concept recognition tasks. Operationality is based on *usability* and *utility*. For a concept to be usable, "it must be expressed in terms of capabilities possessed by the system, and in terms of data that is known or computable by the system" [4]. The usability component of Keller's definition is in line with the earlier binary notion of operationality. However, for a concept to be utile, it must be *worth* using as defined by the system's performance objectives. The usability component is what the previous binary definition lacked. In principle, it overcomes the objections to binary operationality. Thus far, in systems like Keller's MetaLEX [5], the utility component is measured empirically by judging what efficiency gains are achieved with a new concept description without a deterioration in system effectiveness. Utility is a very general term. Can one break down the term further and yet yield a meaningful system–independent definition for operationality? This is one of the open questions in EBL research.

In using operationality to mean "cost of using some piece of knowledge," an important trade–off is that between operationality and generality. Something expressed in a very general way is often costly to use, and something very inexpensive to apply is often very specific. The first part of this chapter explores an approach for managing this trade–off through learning several rules at different levels of generality. In the second part of the chapter, a new comprehensive definition is proposed for *linear operationality*, a measure of the worth of a specific rule taken in isolation from other rules in the system. It has become increasingly apparent that many important factors are involved in determining how *worthwhile* a piece of knowledge is beyond those entertained in traditional definitions of operationality. For instance, when working with uncertainty, it becomes important to have a system which can function in spite of this uncertainty and hence have plans which are uncertainty tolerant. Linear operationality offers a criterion useful in deciding which of several rules to learn or to apply for problem solving. Several factors involving generality, economy, and real–world uncertainty make up the definition for linear operationality.

2. A Special–Case Approach to the Operationality/Generality Trade–Off

There usually is a trade–off between the operationality and the generality of concepts [2, 3, 6–9]. For example, suppose one has the goal of alleviating his or her hunger. Compare two possible schemata for satisfying this goal. One schema might be *eat-at-Chez-Jean*, which specifies that eating at an expensive restaurant would suffice. This schema includes such preconditions as being hungry for French food, having a lot of money, wanting to eat after 7:00 P.M. (when the restaurant opens), and having three hours to spare for dinner. A second problem–solving schema is *eat–at–restaurant*. It applies to many different restaurants. Preconditions are specified as constraints among potential bindings for schema variables rather than actual values. Thus, instead of specifying French food, 7:00 P.M., and three hours, it states the mutual interdependence among the restaurant chosen, quality of food, type of food, and price.

The second schema is more general than the first. One can apply the second at *McDonald's, Pop's Malt Shop,* and *China Inn,* as well as *Chez Jean.* Although subsumed by the second, the first schema is more efficient to apply. If one knows that applying the *Chez–Jean* schema leads to a satisfactory solution, one need not solve the potentially difficult constraint satisfaction problem posed by the precondition structure of the more general restaurant schema.

What underlies this generality? It is achieved by calling the problem solver to create and select among consistent sets of alternative variable bindings needed to satisfy the schema's preconditions. This problem solving must be done at the time the schema is applied. It cannot be "precompiled" since binding any of the schema variables reduces the schema's applicability. *Internal problem solving* refers to this kind of "application–time" problem solving. Performing internal problem solving is not free. It requires resources of time and effort. Thus, the more internal the problem solving, the greater the potential generality but the less operational the resulting schema.

In learning a new schema, it would seem that a learning system must weigh operationality against generality. However, this need not be the case. By acquiring several schemata, operationality can be preserved without sacrificing generality. In addition to the general schema, specializations of the concept, called *special–case schemata,* are formed and stored. These special cases are the result of composing the new, general schema with a small number of problem–solving schemata. A successful composition results in a specialization that is guaranteed to work using the composed problem–solving technique. This frees the problem solver from performing the planning that would otherwise be required to elaborate the general schema to fit the current problem–solving episode. The system can, of course, always resort to its collection of maximally general schema. This chapter presents a method for forming special cases that guarantees improved operationality and yields schemata with potentially high utility.

An example (discussed further in a later section) of this idea involves momentum conservation, a fundamental concept in physics. The explanation–based generalization of a sample collision problem leads to a physics formula that describes how external forces change a system's momentum. This general schema is broadly applicable, but ascertaining that it will lead to the solution of a given problem requires a good deal of work. The constructed special case states that when there are no external forces, momentum is conserved.

Although the motivation for this intermediate level of generalization is computational, the use of this level helps to reconcile the approach with a variety of psychological evidence showing that problem solvers use highly specific schemata [10–13]. Much of expertise consists of rapidly choosing a tightly constrained schema appropriate to the current problem. However, the difference between the knowledge of an expert and a novice cannot be explained on the basis of number of schemata alone. The scope and organization of these schemata have been shown in psychological experiments to be qualitatively different [12, 14, 15]. In representing a problem, novices make great use of the specific objects mentioned in the problem statement, whereas experts first categorize according to the techniques appropriate for solving the problem.

The intermediate–level schemata generated are similar in scope of applicability to those that human experts appear to possess. For example, the conservation of momentum problem results in a special case schema characterized by the absence of external forces and the specification of a *before* and *after* situation. These features are those cited by experts as the relevant cues for the principle of conservation of momentum (see Table 12 of [14]).[1]

2.1. Learning Special Cases

The method for automatically acquiring schemata of the intermediate level of generality requires that a system's schemata be organized into two classes:

(1)   Schemata that represent general problem–solving knowledge, which apply across many application domains (e.g., a schema for utilizing a conserved quantity to solve a problem).

---

[1] It should be noted that it was not the explicit intent to model these psychological data. Rather, computational efficiency considerations led to a system that produced results matching these empirical data.

(2)   Schemata that represent declarative knowledge of the domain of application (e.g., Newton's laws).

People with mature problem–solving backgrounds possess the first type of schema and are told schemata of the second type when introduced to a new domain. Through study they acquire a large collection of schemata that combine aspects of both types, thereby increasing their problem–solving performance in the domain. Combining general problem–solving techniques with domain–specific knowledge produces schemata that, when applied, lead to the rapid solution of new problems.

Figure 6–1 contains an overview of the approach. It is assumed that a known problem–solving schema is used to understand a solution to a specific problem. The explanation–based analysis of the solution may lead to the construction of a new broadly applicable schema. The generalization process often produces a new schema that, in its fullest form, is not usable by the originally applied problem–solving schema. Constraining the general result so that this problem–solving schema does apply produces a special case. In the special–case schema, the constrained schema, its constraints, and the original problem–solving schema are packaged together to produce a specialized problem–solving strategy.[2]

Figure 6–2 shows the relation between a general schema and its special cases. Although not shown in the figure, there can be special cases of the special cases. The properties that distinguish the special cases from

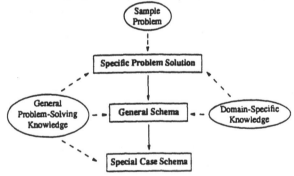

Figure 6–1:   Overview of the Special–Case Learning Model

---

[2] Only one special case is constructed. At the end of this section, methods for producing multiple special cases from one problem are discussed.

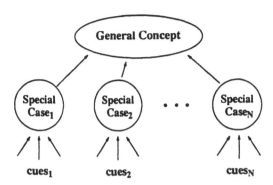

Figure 6-2:   Interschema Organization

their general cases are recorded.[3] If the indexed special case is not applicable, the general concept is then accessed. Besides being constructed when the general case is acquired, a new special case may be created whenever the general case is used to solve a later problem.

To construct a special case, the preconditions of the problem-solving schema used in the specific problem must first be satisfied. The newly acquired general schema and any of the characteristics of the specific problem can be used during this process. The resulting proof tree is generalized using a standard explanation-based learning algorithm. The leafs of the generalized proof tree constitute the necessary requirements for using the problem-solving schema with the new general schema. Those general preconditions not known to be always true, nor known to be easily derivable, are combined with the preconditions of the general schema to produce the special case's preconditions.

There are a number of ways that special cases can be constructed from a general schema. One approach would be to try combining *all* known problem-solving schema with the general result and then storing all successful combinations. However, a focus in this research is to avoid such exhaustive algorithms. Another approach would be to take advantage of the hierarchy of problem-solving schemata and consider only schemata within some arbitrary distance of the schema actually used. Since no theoretically acceptable way to limit this distance has been

---

[3] The method of using these special-case cues to select the appropriate schema is not addressed in this chapter. Possible indexing techniques include approaches based on *discrimination nets* [16–18] and approaches based on *spreading activation* [19, 20].

developed, attention will focus only on the schema used in the specific problem–solving episode.

The properties of the sample problem that allowed the problem–solving schema to apply are used to characterize the special case schema. This can be more restrictive than the most general special case. For example, in the momentum problem, all that is needed is that the external forces *sum* to zero, not that there be *no* external forces. However, in the sample problem, the integration of the external forces is supported by the fact that the external forces are individually zero, and this property is used to build the special case. This relates to the EBL idea of sample problems being representative of future problems and to the goal that the preconditions of special cases be easily evaluated (and also matches psychological data). One extension of the approach taken would be to store both the most general special case (i.e., the special case that results from constraining the general schema just enough so that the previously used problem–solving schema applies) and the special case that results by seeing how the preconditions for the most general special case are satisfied in the specific problem. Given an indexing scheme that has access time logarithmic in the number of schemata, the storage of extra schemata should not substantially hinder future problem solving.

In addition to improving a problem solver's efficiency, special cases also indicate good assumptions to make. For instance, if the values of the external forces are not known, assume they are zero, as this will allow easy solution to the problem. Physics problems often require one to assume things such as "there is no friction," "the string is massless," and "the gravity of the moon can be ignored." Problem descriptions given in textbooks contain cues such as these, and students must learn how to take advantage of them. Facts in the initial problem statement suggest possible problem–solving strategies, and any additional requirements of the special–case situations indicate good assumptions to make (provided they do not contradict anything else that is known).

The next section presents examples of the construction of general and specific case schemata in the domain of classical physics.

2.2. An Application in Classical Physics

A psychologically plausible model of the process by which a mathematically sophisticated student becomes a better problem solver in a new domain has been implemented [21]. In particular, the transition from novice to expert problem solver in the field of classical physics has been investigated. The model, implemented in a computer system named

P101, assumes the student has an understanding of mathematics through introductory calculus.

There are three main components of the model. The first is a model of how operators are chosen during problem solving [22]. The second explores the processes by which one can understand and generalize solutions to novel problems [23]. The third, the topic of this chapter, addresses the process of storing learned results so that they can be used to improve subsequent problem solving [9]. (Additional aspects of the P101 system are discussed in Chapter 11.)

The next sections discuss two sample problems analyzed by Physics 101. One involves momentum conservation, and the other energy conservation. The general schema produced in these two cases, the resulting special cases, and their selection cues are presented.

The schema that makes use of conserved quantities during problem solving is shown in Table 6–1. (Terms beginning with a question mark are universally instantiated variables.) It says that one way to solve for an unknown is to find an expression containing the unknown that is constant with respect to some variable, instantiate this expression for two different values of the variable, create an equation from the two instantiated expressions, and then solve the equation for the unknown. If the values of all but one variable at these two points are known, simple algebra can be used to easily find the unknown.

Table 1:   Conserved Quantity Schema

Preconditions

CurrentUnknown(?*unknown*) $\wedge$ ConstantWithRespectTo(?*expression*, ?*x*) $\wedge$
SpecificPointOf(?x_1, ?*x*) $\wedge$ SpecificPointOf(?x_2, ?*x*) $\wedge$?$x_1 \neq$?x_2 $\wedge$
?*leftHandSide* = InstantiatedAt(?*expression*, ?x_1) $\wedge$
?*rightHandSide* = InstantiatedAt(?*expression*, ?x_2) $\wedge$
?*equation* = CreateEquation(?*leftHandSide*, ?*rightHandSide*) $\wedge$
ContainedIn(?*unknown*, ?*equation*)

Schema Body

SolveForUnknown(?*equation*, ?*unknown*)

2.2.1. Momentum Conservation Example

One of the problems presented to P101 involves a collision among three balls. In this one–dimensional problem (shown in Figure 6–3), there are three balls moving in free space, without the influence of any external forces. Nothing is specified about the forces between the balls. Besides their mutual gravitational attraction, there could be, for example, a long–range electrical interaction and a very complicated interaction during the collision. In the initial state (state A) the first ball is moving toward the two stationary ones. Some time later (state B) the second and third balls are recoiling from the resulting collision. The task in this problem is to determine the velocity of the first ball after the collision.

A teacher's solution to Figure 6–3's problem is analyzed by Physics 101. The teacher's solution uses the concept of momentum ($mass \times velocity$) conservation to solve the problem. Since this is a con-

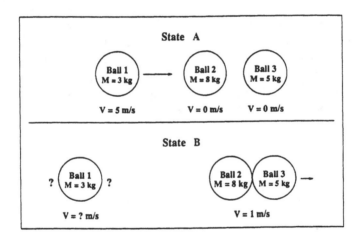

Figure 6–3:   A Three–Body Collision Problem

---

[4] In Figure 6–3 and the following figures, the following abbreviations are used: A – acceleration, F – force, M – mass, and V – velocity. There are four kinds of forces. There is the *net* force on an object, F_{net}. This force has two components – F_{int}, the *internal* force on an object due to other objects within a physical system, and F_{ext}, the *external* force on an object due to external fields. The net force itself has several components, one due to every other object in the physical system. These are called *interobject* forces and are denoted by $F_{i,j}$.

servation law, the time between the two states need not be known.[5]
(Another important attribute of momentum conservation is that the properties of the interobject forces need not be provided.) In verifying the
provided solution, the system applies a problem–solving schema in which
a constant function is equated at two different points. In accordance with
the explanation–based learning approach, the system's justification of the
provided solution is generalized as far as possible while maintaining the
veracity of the solution technique. This results in the general schema
presented in Table 6-2. (See Chapter 11 or [21] for more details on the
construction of this schema.)

The explanation–based approach results in a formula that applies to
situations significantly different from the sample problem. In addition to
not being restricted to problems containing exactly three objects, the
newly acquired formula is not restricted to situations where the external
forces are all zero. Instead, an understanding of how the external forces
affect momentum is obtained. This process also determines that there is
no constraint that restricts this formula to the x direction. It applies
equally well to the y and z components of velocity. Hence, the acquired
formula is a vector law. The mathematical operations used in the specific
solution require, for the solution strategy to be valid, that all objects have

Table 2:   The General Momentum Law

Equation

$$\frac{d}{dt} \sum_{i \in ObjectsInWorld} M_i\, V_{i,\,?c}(t) = \sum_{i \in ObjectsInWorld} F_{ext,\,i,\,?c}(t)$$

Preconditions

IsaComponent(?c) $\land$

$\forall\, i \in ObjectsInWorld$ NOT(ZeroValued(M_i)) $\land$

$\forall\, i \in ObjectsInWorld$ IndependentOf(M_i, t)

Eliminated Terms

$\forall\, i\ \forall\, j{\neq}i\ \ F_{i,\,j,\,?c}(t)$

---

[5] When the interstate time is unknown, simply solving the equations of motion resulting from Newton's laws is not possible.

nonzero mass and that these masses be constant over time. Finally, the generalization algorithm determines that the interobject forces need not be known, since they are algebraically cancelled during the derivation of the momentum law.

Notice that the result in Table 6–2 is *not* a conservation law. It describes how the momentum of a system evolves over time. Although this new formula applies to a large class of problems, recognizing its applicability is not easy. The external forces on the system must be summed, and a possibly complicated differential equation needs to be solved. Applying this law requires more than using simple algebra to find the value of the unknown.

A portion of the proof that the originally used problem–solving schema can be used with the new general formula appears in Figure 6–4.[6] For the conserved quantity schema to be applicable to this new formula, it must be the case that momentum be constant with respect to time. This means that the derivative of momentum be zero, which leads to the requirement that the external forces sum to zero. This requirement is satisfied in the specific solution because each external force is individually zero, and this property is used to characterize the special case. When this

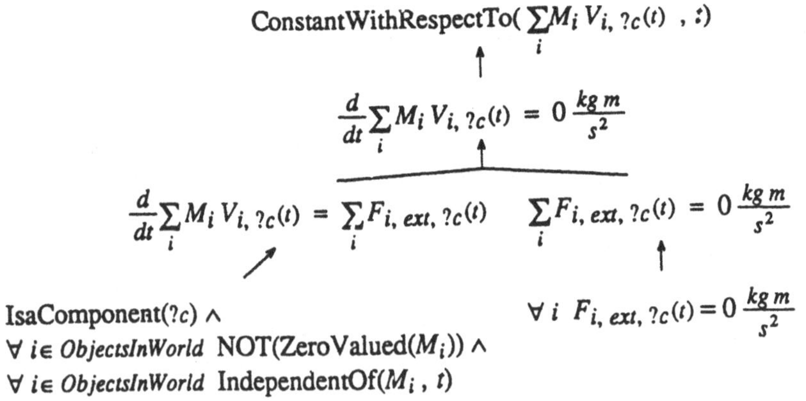

$$\text{ConstantWithRespectTo}(\sum_i M_i \, V_{i, \, ?c}(t) \, , \, t)$$

$$\uparrow$$

$$\frac{d}{dt}\sum_i M_i \, V_{i, \, ?c}(t) = 0 \, \frac{kg \, m}{s^2}$$

$$\uparrow$$

$$\frac{d}{dt}\sum_i M_i \, V_{i, \, ?c}(t) = \sum_i F_{i, \, ext, \, ?c}(t) \qquad \sum_i F_{i, \, ext, \, ?c}(t) = 0 \, \frac{kg \, m}{s^2}$$

$$\nearrow \qquad\qquad\qquad \uparrow$$

IsaComponent(?c) $\wedge$ $\qquad\qquad\qquad\qquad \forall i \; F_{i, \, ext, \, ?c}(t) = 0 \, \frac{kg \, m}{s^2}$

$\forall i \in \textit{ObjectsInWorld}$ NOT(ZeroValued(M_i)) $\wedge$

$\forall i \in \textit{ObjectsInWorld}$ IndependentOf(M_i , t)

Figure 6–4: Satisfying the Second Precondition of the Conserved Quantity Schema

---

[6] Arrows run from the antecedents of an inference rule to its consequents.

occurs, the momentum of a system can be equated at *any* two distinct states. The special case schema for momentum conservation is contained in Table 6-3. Since this is a conservation schema, the time at which each state occurs need not be provided in a problem for this schema to apply.

2.2.2. Energy Conservation Example

A second problem (Figure 6-5) presented to P101 involves a brick falling under the influence of gravity. Again, information at two different states is presented. The mass of the brick, its initial velocity, and its height in the two states are provided. The goal is to find its velocity in the second state. The teacher's solution to this problem uses energy conservation. The kinetic energy ($(1/2)$ *mass* $\times$ *velocity*^{2}) plus the potential energy (*mass* $\times$ *g* $\times$ *height*) in the two states is equated. The general law P101's produces by analyzing the sample solution is presented in Table

Table 6-3:   The Special Case Momentum Law

Equation

$$\sum_{i \in ObjectsInWorld} M_i V_{i, ?c}(t) = constant$$

Preconditions

IsaComponent($?c$) $\wedge$
$\forall\, i \in ObjectsInWorld$ NOT(ZeroValued(M_i)) $\wedge$
$\forall\, i \in ObjectsInWorld$ IndependentOf(M_i , t)

Special Case Conditions

$\forall\, i \in ObjectsInWorld$ $F_{ext, i, ?c}(t) = 0$

Problem Solving Schema Used

conserved-quantity-schema

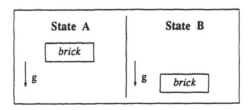

Figure 6-5:   A Falling Brick

6–4.

The general energy conservation law applies whenever the total force on an object is known. Notice, though, that a rather complicated vector integral involving the scalar (dot) product of two vectors needs to be computed if this general law is to be used. To use this formula, it is not sufficient to possess knowledge of the values of variables at two different times. A problem solver must also know how the net force depends on position for a continuum of times. In the specific problem, there is a *constant* net force (gravity). When the force is constant, the problem is greatly simplified. Integrating a constant force leads to a potential energy determined by that constant force multiplied by the object's position. The position needs to be known only at the two distinct times, not for *all* intervening times. The special case schema for energy conservation is contained in Table 6–5. Again, since this is a conservation schema, the time at which each state occurs need not be known.

2.3. Similarity–Based Approaches to Learning Special Cases

A common induction scheme is to posit that learners compare particular instances of a concept (such as specific problems of a problem type) and abstract out those aspects that are common to both problems [20, 24–26]. The fact that problem solvers use highly specific schemata supports such a view, since these schemata would arise whenever two problems from an intermediate–level problem type are compared. Although similarity–based generalization is an important means of learning, especially for novices [27–29], the research described in this chapter shows that many of these highly specific schemata can arise from an explanation–based approach. Even some strong proponents of example comparison learning have begun to incorporate some explanation–based

Table 6–4:   The General Energy Law

Equation

$$\frac{d}{dt} \left[\frac{1}{2} M_{?i} V^2{}_{?i, ?c}(t) - \int F_{net, ?i, ?c}(t) dX_{?i, ?c} \right] = 0 \; \frac{kg \, m^2}{s^3}$$

Preconditions

Object(?i) IsaComponent(?c) IndependentOf($M_{?i}$, t) NOT(ZeroValued($M_{?i}$))

Table 6-5:   The Special Case Energy Law

Equation

$$\frac{1}{2} M_{?i} V^2_{?i}(tsub) + M_{?i} \, g \, X_{?i, ?c}(t) \ = \ constant$$

Preconditions

Object($?i$) $\wedge$ IsaComponent($?c$) $\wedge$

IndependentOf($M_{?i}$, t) $\wedge$ NOT(ZeroValued($M_{?i}$))

Special Case Conditions

$$\overline{F}_{net, \, ?i}(t) \ = \ M_{?i} \, g \, ?c$$

Problem Solving Schema Used

conserved-quantity-schema

ideas in order to account for how much is learned from one example [30].

Because explanation–based learning requires extensive domain knowledge, it clearly is not appropriate for all learning in a new domain. However, it may be useful even in early learning if the new domain relies heavily on a domain for which the novice does have substantial knowledge. Because mathematics underlies many other domains, a novice with some mathematical sophistication may be able to make use of explanation–based techniques without extensive knowledge of the new domain.

2.4. Conclusions on the Operationality/Generality Trade–Off

Much of expertise in problem–solving situations involves rapidly choosing a tightly constrained schema that is appropriate to the current problem. The paradigm of explanation–based learning is used to investigate how an intelligent system can acquire these "appropriately general" schemata. Although the motivations for producing these specialized schemata are computational, results reported in the psychological literature are corroborated by the fully implemented computer program.

A major issue in explanation–based learning concerns the relationship between operationality and generality. A schema whose relevance is easy to determine may be useful only in an overly narrow range of problems. Conversely, a broadly applicable schema may require extensive work before a problem solver can recognize its appropriateness. Other approaches to selecting the proper level of generality involve pruning easily reconstructable portions of the explanation structure. This chapter's approach to this problem is to produce as general a schema as .possible from the analysis of a specific solution and then to construct a *special case* of this general schema. A special case is produced by constraining a general schema in such a way that its relevance is easily checked. This results in additional features that a situation must possess if the special case is to apply.

Acquiring these special-case schemata involves combining schemata from two different classes. One class contains domain-independent problem-solving schemata, and the other class consists of domain-specific knowledge. In the approach taken, learning by analyzing sample problem solutions produces broadly applicable schemata that, often, are not usable by the originally applied problem-solving schemata. Special-case schemata result from constraining these general schemata so that the originally used problem-solving techniques are guaranteed to work. This significantly reduces the amount of planning that the problem solver would otherwise need to perform elaborating the general schema to match a new problem-solving episode.

This section demonstrated that these highly specific schemata can arise in an explanation-based fashion. Explanation-based learning requires extensive knowledge and seems particularily suited for modeling learning by experts. Although all learning cannot be of this type, explanation-based learning can prove useful even in early learning in a new domain. This can occur if the new domain relies heavily on another domain in which the novice learner has substantial abilities.

3. A Theory of Linear Operationality

3.1. The Model

We propose a definition of linear operationality that overcomes current shortcomings and includes several more specific components which should have meaning for all learning systems. To define linear operationality, a set-theoretic model for viewing plans is used.

When a system uses approximate values in constructing a plan, what the system believes the plan will accomplish and what the plan will actually accomplish when carried out in the real world can be two different things. In the model, three mappings are used. Mapping 1 is carried out under the believed functional mapping, and mappings 2 and 3 are under the actual functional mapping.

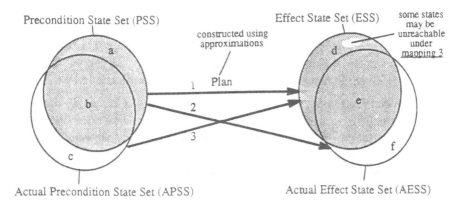

Figure 6-6: Representing the Use of a Plan

Figure 6-6 illustrates how a plan is viewed. The precondition state set (PSS) is the set of world states where the plan's preconditions are satisfied. The effect state set (ESS) is the set of states reached under mapping 1 from states in the PSS. The system treats a plan as a mapping between these two sets (mapping 1), which are illustrated by the shaded circles in the diagram. This mapping is characterized as

(1)   *functional* in that it maps an x∈PSS to one and only one y∈ESS,

(2)   *noninjective* (not *one-to-one*) in that many states in the PSS may map to the same state in the ESS,

(3)   *surjective* (*onto*) in that all states in the ESS are achievable under mapping 1 from states originating in the PSS.

The shaded circles represent the system's belief about the plan. Since, the preconditions and effects to the plan were constructed using approximations, the actual mapping may behave differently when carried out in the real world. Two additional sets are introduced for this purpose. The first is the actual precondition state set (APSS) and is the set of states from which the plan may be carried out in the real world and will result in a state which is a member of the ESS. The second is the actual effect state set (AESS) and is the set of states which result from application of the plan in the real world to states contained in the PSS. The plan's real-world mapping between the PSS and AESS (mapping 2) is characterized as functional, noninjective, and surjective. The plan's real-world mapping between the APSS and ESS (mapping 3) is characterized as functional, noninjective, and potentially *nonsurjective* in that some states in the ESS may not be achievable as a result of using approximations.

Figure 6–6 also illustrates six regions lettered a through f. With respect to real–world mappings 2 and 3: States in region b (PSS∩APSS) map to states in region e (ESS∩AESS), states in region a (PSS APSS) map to states in region f (AESS–ESS), and states in region d (ESS–AESS), if achievable, can be mapped from states in region c (APSS–PSS).

The system treats the plan as though it were a mapping between the PSS and ESS as described earlier. The plan is believed to be useful when the system's current goal has a nonempty intersection with the plan's ESS (regions d2 and e2 in Figure 6–7). Note that the goal may also intersect with region f2. However, the system incorrectly believes (Table

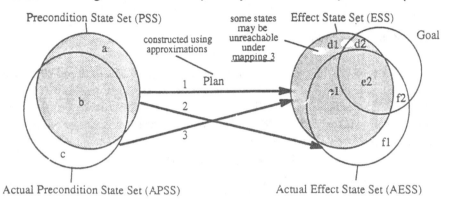

Figure 6–7:   Unifying a Goal with a Plan

Table 6–6:   State Set Descriptions

State Set	Region Description
Universe	(0≤x≤10 ∧ 0≤y≤10)
PSS	(1≤x≤3 ∧ 1≤y≤3)
ESS	(6≤x≤8 ∧ 6≤y≤8)
APSS	(1≤x≤1.5 ∧ 1≤y≤3) ∨ (2≤x≤4 ∧ 2≤y≤4)
AESS	(5.5≤x≤7 ∧ 5≤y≤7) ∨ (6≤x≤6.5 ∧ 5≤y≤8)
Goal	((y≥5) ∩ (x≥6.5) ∧ (y≤9) .∧ (y≤17−x) ∧ (y≥1.5x−5.5)) ∨ (6.25≤x≤6.5 ∧ 5≤y≤7) ∨ (5.75≤x≤6.25 ∧ 5≤y≤6)

6–6) that states in region f2 aren't reachable from the PSS. Eight possible cases may arise in determining plan preconditions and subsequently applying the plan to achieve the goal (see Table 6–7).

There are also two unexpected success cases where the system would not have considered the rule applicable: from a state originating in region c and achieving a state in region $d2$ and from a state outside both the PSS and APSS and achieving a state inside the goal but outside the ESS and AESS.

3.2. An Example

Before using the model to define linear operationality, let us introduce a simple example which can be used to illustrate both the model just defined and the aspects of linear operationality. Figure 6–8 illustrates the example domain and plan. The universe of states consists of the set of points in the 10–unit rectangle with (0,0) in the lower left and (10,10) in the upper right. The system believes that an ADD5 plan can successfully achieve states in the illustrated ESS region ($6 \leq x \leq 8$, $6 \leq y \leq 8$) from those in the illustrated PSS region ($1 \leq x \leq 3$, $1 \leq y \leq 3$). The figure also illustrates some difficulties the plan encounters with respect to the real world which the system is unaware of. Whenever the plan is applied to those states contained in the shaded–L in the lower left of the diagram, the plan successfully adds 5 units to the X and Y coordinates of

Table 6–7: Sample States Illustrating Different Cases

Case #	Goal Type	Possible Precondition Type	Possible Resultant ESS Regions
1	d2 (6.75,7.5)	a (1.75,2.5)	f1 – Failure (5.75,6.5)
2	d2 (7.25,6.75)	a (2.25,1.75)	f2 – Success (6.25,5.75)
3	d2 (7.2,7.5)	b (2.2,2.5)	e1 – Failure (6.2,6.5)
4	d2 (7.75,7.5)	b (2.75,2.5)	e2 – Success (6.75,6.5)
5	e2 (6.7,6.75)	a (1.7,1.75)	f1 – Failure (5.7,5.75)
6	e2 (6.8,6.75)	a (1.8,1.75)	f2 – Success (5.8,5.75)
7	e2	b	e1 – Failure (Not Possible Here)
8	e2 (6.3,6.5)	b (1.3,1.5)	e2 – Success (6.3,6.5)

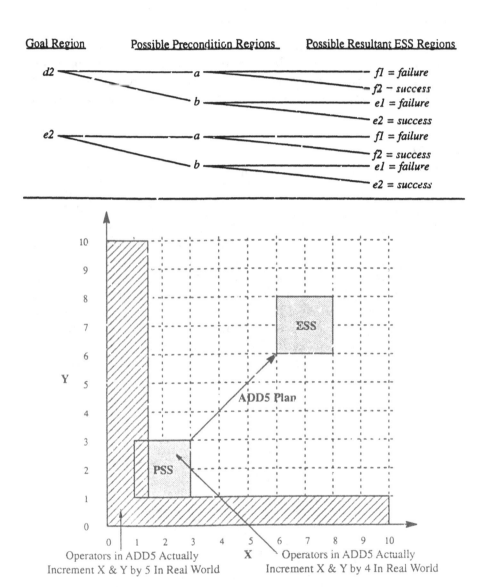

Figure 6–8:   A Simple Plan with Real–World Difficulties

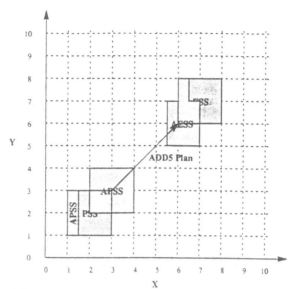

Figure 6-9: ADD5 Plan with PSS, APSS, ESS, and AESS

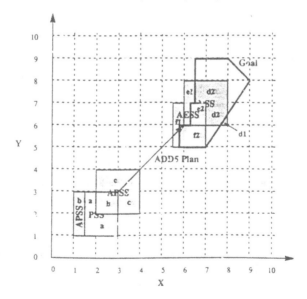

Figure 6-10: Using the Plan to Satisfy a Goal

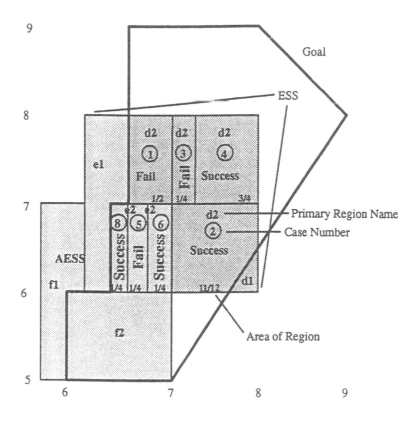

Figure 6–11: Cases Mapped to ESS Subregions

the point. However, with all other states the ADD5 plan succeeds only in adding 4 units to the X and Y coordinates. These simulated difficulties with the real world will give rise to a situation such as that described in the model and hence to the APSS and AESS regions illustrated in Figure 6–9. Expressions for all the state sets are given in Table 6–6. Table 6–7 demonstrates the different possible cases with respect to the goal illustrated in Figure 6–10. Figure 6–11 shows the cases as different regions within the ESS. Specific points which achieve the goal are used to show the different cases.

3.3. Aspects of Linear Operationality

Linear operationality will be treated here as a continuous notion comprised of nine aspects. Each of the aspects is a scalar value normalized to [0,1]. Each is expressed in such a way that linear operationality improves as the aspect approaches 1 (holding everything else constant). In general, adjusting the plan parameters to force an improvement in one of the aspect values results in a deterioration in several of the other aspect values. The user defines a nine–array function of the different aspects of linear operationality which is used to give the overall linear operationality determination.

After the aspects have been defined, a method is proposed for managing linear operationality in the context of reasoning with approximation. The definitions presented here assume world states to be equally likely as goals. The major components of linear operationality follow.

8.8.1. Generality Aspects

Precondition Generality (G_p)	$\dfrac{|PSS|}{|universe|}$

Precondition generality (G_p) refers to the broadness of a set of circumstances under which the plan can be applied. This is indicated by the ratio of the size of the precondition state space to the size of the universe of possible states.

It is important to note that we are defining theoretical terms here, not attempting to propose specific methods for measuring them. Ultimately, working values must be computed for these constructs. It may be tractable only to approximate these measures. That is, it is also necessary to have a way of characterizing the plan independent of the specific state to which it will be applied. Some aspects of linear operationality which will be discussed, such as *applicability economy,* may depend on the precise state of the world in which one is testing the applicability of the plan. This is clearly much less desirable than having adequate approximations which are less dependent on the precise situation.

Effect Generality (G_e)	$\dfrac{|ESS|}{|universe|}$

Effect generality (G_e) describes how large a set of world states a plan can achieve. For example, suppose plan A and plan B both have equal precondition generality. Further suppose that plan A can achieve only half as many world states as plan B. Therefore, assuming the states for both plans in the ESS are equally likely to be goals, the system would find plan B preferable. The G_e measure is necessary to express such a preference.

3.3.2. Economy Aspects

Applicability Economy (E_a)	$\dfrac{1}{1 + \text{cost}(\omega \in \text{PSS})}$

Deciding when a plan can be applied requires the system to test its preconditions. In the proposed framework, this amounts to testing whether the current world state is a member of the plan's PSS. There is always some cost associated with this operation. Plans with a low cost for this test (high *applicability economy* (E_a)) should be favored.

Effect Economy (E_e)	$\dfrac{1}{1 + \text{cost}(\omega \in \text{ESS})}$

In part, system performance also depends on how rapidly the current goal can be tested against available plans. This amounts to a membership test for a desired state in the ESS and is called *effect economy* (E_e).

Plan Economy (E_p)	$\dfrac{1}{1 + \text{cost(plan)}}$

The other major cost associated with a plan is the cost of execution. A plan may have a high E_a but still be very slow. The *plan economy* (E_p) measure is designed to reflect how inexpensively a plan's actions can be performed after it has been deemed applicable.

3.3.3. Real–World Aspects

In specifying formulas for the following real–world aspects, the following functional notations are used:

map1(x)	with x∈PSS	*the resulting state in the ESS under mapping 1*
map1(X)	with X⊆PSS	$\bigcup_{\text{oppAx}\in X}\text{map1}(x)$
revmap1(x)	with x∈ESS	*the set of states in the PSS which can result in x under mapping 1*
revmap1(X)	with X⊆ESS	$\bigcup_{\text{oppAx}\in X}\text{revmap1}(x)$
map2(x)	with x∈PSS	*the resulting state in the AESS under mapping 2*
map2(X)	with X⊆PSS	$\bigcup_{\text{oppAx}\in X}\text{map2}(x)$
revmap2(x)	with x∈AESS	*the set of states in the PSS which can result in x under mapping 2*
revmap2(X)	with X⊆AESS	$\bigcup_{\text{oppAx}\in X}\text{revmap2}(x)$
dist(x,y)	*with states x & y*	*a measure of the difference in certainty between an expected state x and some other state actually observed y*

An important consideration for every system is *probability of success*. This measure is based on the system's own estimation of the quality of the approximations in use. As better approximations are used, the probability of success increases. This is evident from the above definition because mapping 2 becomes closer to mapping 1 as approximations improve. How significantly probability of success is weighted depends on the degree to which the system can tolerate failure. One can envision a scenario, like picking up a beaker containing a toxic chemical, where probability of success may be treated as the most important aspect of linear operationality. On the other hand, picking up a small unbreakable object may be best done with a quick, easy grabbing action.

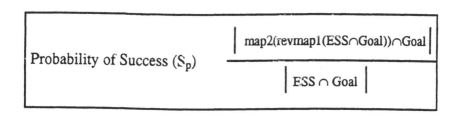

$$\text{Probability of Success } (S_p) \quad \frac{|\text{map2(revmap1(ESS}\cap\text{Goal))}\cap\text{Goal}|}{|\text{ESS}\cap\text{Goal}|}$$

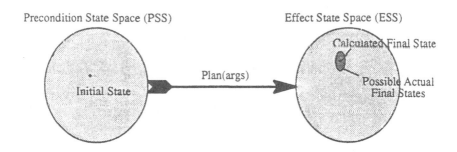

Figure 6–12: A View of Result Accuracy

$$
\text{Result Accuracy } (R_a) \qquad \frac{\big|\, PSS \,\big|}{\big|\, PSS \,\big| \;+\; \displaystyle\sum_{\forall\, p \,\in\, PSS} \text{dist}(\text{map1}(p),\text{map2}(p))}
$$

If the plan's approximations are sufficiently tight, differences between what the plan accomplishes in the real world and what the system believes the plan will accomplish can be made arbitrarily small. There must exist some specification of how large this disparity is for a particular set of approximations. This measure is referred to as *result accuracy* and is depicted graphically in Figure 6–12.

Let P_g = members of the PSS which achieve the goal in the real–world
$\quad$ = revmap2(map2(revmap1(ESS $\cap$ Goal) $\cap$ Goal)

$$
\text{Uncertainty Tolerance } (U_t) \qquad \frac{\displaystyle\sum_{\forall\, p \,\in\, P_g} \left[\; \underset{\forall\, p2 \,\in\, (Universe - P_g)}{MIN} \Big[\, \text{dist}(p,p2) \Big] \right]}{\big|\, P_g \,\big| \;\; \underset{\forall\, p \,\in\, P_g}{MAX} \left[\; \underset{\forall\, p2 \,\in\, (Universe - P_g)}{MIN} \Big[\, \text{dist}(p,p2) \Big] \right]}
$$

Uncertainty tolerance refers to the ability of a plan to achieve a goal despite uncertainties present due to a lack of knowledge about the initial world state and/or resulting from approximations in the plan. Achieving uncertainty tolerance doesn't imply that uncertainty is reduced or even reasoned about, merely that the goal can be achieved in spite of bad knowledge. Specifically, uncertainty tolerance is the maximum amount of initial uncertainty such that the goal can be achieved. With respect to our example, those states in the PSS from which the goal can be achieved are illustrated in Figure 6–13. The definition for U_t is an average of the

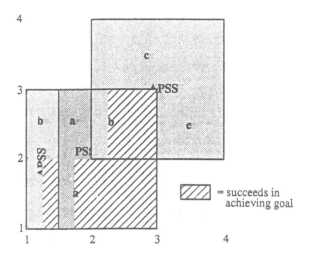

Figure 6–13: States in the PSS Which Achieve the Goal in the Real World

maximum amount by which each state in the PSS capable of achieving the goal can deviate according to the *dist* function before it fails to achieve the goal. This is then normalized to a value between 0 and 1 by dividing by the maximum possible deviation of any of these states.

$$\boxed{\text{Uncertainty Reduction } (U_r) \qquad\qquad U_t - R_a}$$

Uncertainty reduction takes place when a plan performs actions which serve to reduce uncertainty. It measures the "funneling" that takes place from an initially less certain situation to a later more certain situation. As with all the measures, high uncertainty reduction is preferred to the extent it does not sacrifice other aspects of linear operationality. Negative U_r is also possible and represents a plan which, when applied, leads to a less certain situation. Specifically, U_r is the difference between measures of certainty in the final situation (R_a) and those in the initial situation (U_i).

3.4. Measuring Linear Operationality with Our Example

In our example, the cost of a numeric comparison is 1 and the cost of an addition is 2. The different aspects of linear operationality can be calculated with respect to our example as follows:

$$G_p = \frac{|PSS|}{|universe|} = \frac{4}{100} = 0.04$$

$$G_e = \frac{|ESS|}{|universe|} = \frac{4}{100} = 0.04$$

$$E_a = \frac{1}{1 + cost(\omega \in PSS)} = \frac{1}{1 + 4\,cost(numeric\_comparison)} = \frac{1}{5}$$

$$E_e = \frac{1}{1 + cost(\omega \in ESS)} = \frac{1}{1 + 4\,cost(numeric\_comparison)} = \frac{1}{5}$$

$$E_p = \frac{1}{1 + cost(plan)} = \frac{1}{1 + 2\,cost(addition)} = \frac{1}{5}$$

(areas of regions from figure 11)

$$S_p = \frac{\left| map2(revmap1(ESS \cap Goal)) \cap Goal \right|}{\left| ESS \cap Goal \right|} = \frac{\frac{11}{12} + \frac{3}{4} + \frac{1}{4} + \frac{1}{4}}{\frac{11}{12} + \frac{3}{4} + \frac{1}{4} + \frac{1}{4} + \frac{1}{4} + \frac{1}{4} + \frac{1}{2}} = \frac{13}{19}$$

$$R_a = \frac{\left| PSS \right|}{\left| PSS \right| + \displaystyle\sum_{\forall p \in PSS} dist(map1(p), map2(p))} = \frac{4}{4 + (\ 1 \cdot 0 + 3 \cdot \sqrt{2}\ )} = \frac{4}{4 + 3\sqrt{2}}$$

result of integrating MIN function over regions illustrated in Figure 13

$$U_t = \frac{\displaystyle\sum_{\forall p \in P_g} \left[\displaystyle\operatorname*{MIN}_{\forall p2 \in (Universe - P_g)} \left[dist(p, p2) \right] \right]}{\left| P_g \right| \displaystyle\operatorname*{MAX}_{\forall p \in P_g} \left[\displaystyle\operatorname*{MIN}_{\forall p2 \in (Universe - P_g)} \left[dist(p, p2) \right] \right]} = \frac{\boxed{}}{2\frac{1}{4} \cdot \frac{\sqrt{65}}{8}}$$

$$U_r = U_t - R_a$$

3.5. Variability, Granularity, and Certainty

Keller outlined several features important in characterizing operationality definitions: variability, granularity, and certainty [4]. *Variability* is either *dynamic* or *static*, indicating whether the rating of a predicate as operational can change as the performance environment of the system changes. Whether our definition is dynamic depends on the specific techniques chosen to calculate the various aspects. As mentioned earlier, various approximations may be used to ease calculation of these measures. It is, however, desirable to have the measures linked to the environment in which the system operates. That is, they should not be linked to any specific state the plan is operating from but to the environment in general. This includes factors such as what objects are available in the world and what actions are possible. Therefore, measures such as E_a and E_e, which represent the cost of testing membership for preconditions and effects, are typically calculated based on the environment. For instance, as the number of facts, relevant or not, increases, E_a and E_e will tend to decrease as the overhead of individual predicate tests increases. Also, R_a, U_t, and U_r will be affected, as they depend on the likelihood of encountering certain states, a factor which is often empirically measured and will change as the system engages in problem solving.

Granularity reflects whether operationality is defined as being *continuous* or *binary*. Our definition is a continuous one which permits determining among multiple operational plans which one is the most operational.

Certainty indicates whether performance is *guaranteed* or *unguaranteed* by the operationality assessment. Although a guaranteed operationality assessment is ideal, seldom is it possible to tractably make this guarantee. One would have to anticipate all the situations in which the plan might be used and test them all to determine operationality. The components of linear operationality in our definition are measured using approximate means, therefore making the assessment tractable but the result unguaranteed.

3.6. The Influence of Representation

One should not overlook the effect that the predicate language in which the states are expressed strongly biases aspects of operationality. For instance, increasing the fraction of states in the universe from which a plan can work (G_p) may or may not affect precondition economy (E_p). Whether it does depends on how easily the new set of states can be expressed as opposed to the former set. It also should be pointed out that in some fine–grained representations, the size of a state set such as the PSS or ESS may contain a very large or perhaps infinite number of states. Ideally, the representation should be course grained enough to promote tractable reasoning about operationality.

3.7. Dependence on the Performance Element

As Keller has observed, operationality is a function of the system's performance element [4]. In our definition, we have sought to be as general as possible and not tie it to any specific system's performance element. Therefore, in applying this definition for use with a specific system, the various aspects of operationality must be weighted in accordance with the performance element. If a system has a very low tolerance for failures, it may lend the greatest importance to probability of success (S_p). If it needs to deal with noisy data, it may place a premium on uncertainty tolerance (U_t) and possibly uncertainty reduction (U_r).

3.8. Conclusions on Linear Operationality

Linear operationality is a measure of an individual rule's *worth* independent of the other rules present in the system. Another important area for future work is developing a better understanding of how the worth of one rule in a system is related to that of other rules present. A total theory of worth for a rule must include some combination of the factors involved in linear operationality, as presented here, in combination with a factor expressing the complex interactions among rules in the system. The linear operationality measure is a comprehensive one taking into consideration several aspects of generality, economy, and uncertainty. To facilitate calculation of the various measures of linear operationality in complex domains, approximations will need to be employed. The breakdown given by the aspects of linear operationality provides a more concrete framework than traditional operationality definitions. It is also much better suited for evaluating rules in real-world domains where uncertainty plays an important role.

Acknowledgments

This chapter was greatly influenced by discussions with Gerald DeJong and Brian Ross (of the University of Illinois Department of Psychology). The research was partially supported by the National Science Foundation under grant NSF IST 85-11542, by the Office of Naval Research under grant N00014-86-K-0309, by University of Illinois Cognitive Science/Artificial Intelligence Fellowships, and by a grant from the University of Wisconsin Graduate School.

References

1.   D. J. Mostow, "Machine Transformation of Advice into a Heuristic Search Procedure," in *Machine Learning: An Artificial Intelligence Approach*, R. S. Michalski, J. G. Carbonell, T. M. Mitchell (ed.), Tioga Publishing Company, Palo Alto, CA, 1983, pp. 367-404.

2.   T. M. Mitchell, R. Keller and S. Kedar-Cabelli, "Explanation-Based Generalization: A Unifying View," *Machine Learning 1*, 1 (January 1986), pp. 47-80.

3.   G. F. DeJong and R. J. Mooney, "Explanation-Based Learning: An Alternative View," *Machine Learning 1*, 2 (1986), pp. 145-176.

4.   R. M. Keller, "Defining Operationality for Explanation-Based Learning," *Proceedings of the National Conference on Artificial Intelligence*, Seattle, WA, July 1987, pp. 482-487.

5. R. M. Keller, "Concept Learning in Context," *Proceedings of the Fourth International Workshop on Machine Learning*, University of California, Irvine, June 1987, pp. 91–102.

6. A. M. Segre, "On the Operationality/Generality Trade–off in Explanation–Based Learning," *Proceedings of the Tenth International Joint Conference on Artificial Intelligence*, Milan, Italy, August 1987, pp. 242–248.

7. R. M. Keller, "Deciding What To Learn," submitted to *Proceedings of the National Conference on Artificial Intelligence*, New Brunswick, NY, August 1986.

8. R. Keller, "Operationality and Generality in Explanation–Based Learning: Separate Dimensions or Opposite Endpoints?," *Proceedings of the AAAI Symposium on Explanation–Based Learning*, Stanford, CA, March 1988, pp. 153–157.

9. J. W. Shavlik, G. F. DeJong and B. H. Ross, "Acquiring Special Case Schemata in Explanation–Based Learning," *Proceedings of the Ninth Annual Conference of the Cognitive Science Society*, Seattle, WA, July 1987, pp. 851–860.

10. W. G. Chase and H. A. Simon, "Perception in Chess," *Cognitive Psychology 4*, (1973), pp. 55–81.

11. D. A. Hinsley, J. R. Hayes and H. A. Simon, "From Words to Equations: Meaning and Representation on Algebra Word Problems," in *Cognitive Processes in Comprehension*, P. A. Carpenter and M. A. Just (ed.), Lawrence Erlbaum and Associates, Hillsdale, NJ, 1977, pp. 89–105.

12. A. H. Schoenfeld and D. Herrmann, "Problem Perception and Knowledge Structure in Expert and Novice Mathematical Problem Solvers," *Journal of Experimental Psychology: Learning, Memory, and Cognition 8*, 5 (1982), pp. 484–494.

13. J. Sweller and G. A. Cooper, "The Use of Worked Examples as a Substitute for Problem Solving in Learning Algebra," *Cognition and Instruction 2*, 1 (1985), pp. 59–89.

14. M. T. Chi, P. J. Feltovich and R. Glaser, "Categorization and Representation of Physics Problems by Experts and Novices," *Cognitive Science 5*, 2 (1981), pp. 121–152.

15. J. H. Larkin, J. McDermott, D. P. Simon and H. A. Simon, "Models of Competence in Solving Physics Problems," *Cognitive Science 4*, 4 (1980), pp. 317–345.

16. E. A. Feigenbaum, "The Simulation of Natural Learning Behavior," in *Computers and Thought*, E. A. Feigenbaum and J. Feldman (ed.), McGraw–Hill, New York, NY, 1963.

17. R. C. Schank, *Dynamic Memory*, Cambridge University Press, Cambridge, England, 1982.

18. J. L. Kolodner, *Retrieval and Organization Strategies in Conceptual Memory*, Lawrence Erlbaum and Associates, Hillsdale, NJ, 1984.

19. M. R. Quillian, "Semantic Memory," in *Semantic Information Processing*, M. L. Minsky (ed.), MIT Press, Cambridge, MA, 1968.

20. J. R. Anderson, *The Architecture of Cognition*, Harvard University Press, Cambridge, MA, 1983.

21. J. W. Shavlik, "Generalizing the Structure of Explanations in Explanation–Based Learning ," Ph.D. Thesis, Department of Computer Science, University of Illinois, Urbana, IL, January 1988.

22. J. W. Shavlik and G. F. DeJong, "A Model of Attention Focussing During Problem Solving," *Proceedings of the Eighth Annual Conference of the Cognitive Science Society*, Amherst, MA, August 1986, pp. 817–822.

23. J. W. Shavlik and G. F. DeJong, "Building a Computer Model of Learning Classical Mechanics," *Proceedings of the Seventh Annual Conference of the Cognitive Science Society*, Irvine, CA, August 1985, pp. 351–355.

24. R. S. Michalski, "A Theory and Methodology of Inductive Learning," in *Machine Learning: An Artificial Intelligence Approach*, R. S. Michalski, J. G. Carbonell, T. M. Mitchell (ed.), Tioga Publishing Company, Palo Alto, CA, 1983, pp. 83–134.

25. T. M. Mitchell, "Version Spaces: An Approach to Concept Learning," Ph.D. Thesis, Stanford University, Palo Alto, CA, 1978.

26. M. J. Posner and S. W. Keele, "On the Genesis of Abstract Ideas," *Journal of Experimental Psychology 77*, 3 (July 1968), pp. 353–363.

27. D. Gentner, "Mechanisms of Analogical Learning," in *Similarity and Analogical Reasoning*, S. Vosniadou and A. Ortony (ed.), Cambridge University Press, Cambridge, England, forthcoming.

28. B. H. Ross, "Remindings and their Effects in Learning a Cognitive Skill," *Cognitive Psychology 16*, (1984), pp. 371–416.

29. B. H. Ross, "Remindings in Learning and Instruction," in *Similarity and Analogical Reasoning*, S. Vosniadou and A. Ortony (ed.),

Cambridge University Press, Cambridge, England, forthcoming.

30. J. R. Anderson and R. Thompson, "Use of Analogy in a Production System Architecture," in *Similarity and Analogical Reasoning*, S. Vosniadou and A. Ortony (ed.), Cambridge University Press, Cambridge, England, 1989.

Chapter 7

Empirically Evaluating EBL

Jude W. Shavlik and
Paul O'Rorke

1. Introduction

Does learning help? This is a central question for any machine learning system. It is not enough to show that a machine learning system is capable of acquiring a "correct" or even "adequate" concept. Correctness and adequacy are relatively easy to show and are insufficient to validate the learning approach. A machine learning endeavor must demonstrate that its learning has enhanced the abilities of some performance element. This is a more subtle question.

Does EBL help? Minton [1] has shown that it is possible for EBL systems to aquire knowledge that hurts performance more than it helps. Researchers have noted a similar phenomenon under certain circumstances in the SOAR system [2].

This chapter describes empirical tests performed on two EBL systems. The first, the BAGGER system, performs structural number generalization. The second is a rational reconstruction of Newell and Simon's Logic Theorist [3] augmented with explanation–based learning.

The large–scale BAGGER experiments reveal an almost uniform benefit from structural number generalization in the domain of stacking blocks. The additional cost of generalization to N is slight while the benefit can be considerable, both in reducing the time to produce a plan and in the efficiency of the produced plan. At first glance this seems to contradict empirical evaluation of other EBL systems [1, 2]. Most likely, the discrepency is due to systematic differences in domains and the complexity of problems within the domains. Indeed, a fruitful ongoing area of research is to discover the foundations of these empirical observations to enable a general analytical description of the domain conditions under which EBL helps.

The EBL LT results represent a smaller test set (92 propositional logic problems). The problems are the original Chapter 2 of *Principia Mathematica* by Russell and Whitehead [4] reported in [3] with the addition of the problems from *Principia*, Chapter 3. The empirical evaluations are more in–depth and attempt to explain the interesting discrepancies between the original non–learning LT, a version with a form of rote learning described in [3], and a version using EBL. Interestingly, the EBL LT system was able, on occasion, to prove more general versions of theorems than were stated in *Principia*. Also interesting is the observation that on occasion EBL LT was less effective than its rote–learning counterpart. This is traceable to a restriction within LT that precludes the use of acquired theorems for which IMPLIES is not the main connective. Although somewhat artificial, this is nonetheless a kind of domain attribute to which the EBL system could not automatically adapt. The domain restriction is nowhere represented in the domain theory of logic.

2. Empirical Analysis of BAGGER

This section empirically compares the performance of a system that generalizes explanation structures to a standard explanation–based generalization algorithm and to a problem–solving system that performs no learning. (See Chapter 3 for a discussion of these two types of EBL systems.) Two different strategies for training EBL systems are analyzed. Information relevant to making decisions when designing an explanation–based learning system is reported.

A major issue of this section is whether or not generalizing explanation structures is worthwhile. The recently proposed BAGGER system (Chapter 3 and [5, 6]) is compared to an EBL system that does not generalize the structure of its explanations. Generalizing explanation structures leads to acquiring more general rules, but because the resulting rules are more complicated, applying them entails more work. Hence, these experiments address the *operationality/generality* issue in EBL (see Chapter 6 and also [7–12]). This issue involves the following two considerations. A rule whose relevance is easy to determine may only be useful in an overly narrow range of problems. Conversely, a broadly applicable rule may require extensive work before a problem solver can recognize its appropriateness. A rule acquired by BAGGER will subsume several rules acquired by an EBL system that does not generalize its explanation structures. One issue the experiments are designed to investigate is whether it is better to learn the more general rule or to individually learn the subsumed rules as they are needed. The results demonstrate the efficacy of generalizing explanation structures in particular and of explanation–based learning in general.

Two experiments compare systems that learn from their own problem solving to systems that learn by observing the actions of external agents. The external agent merely solves problems, so there need not be any thought given to properly ordering the examples to facilitate learning. Hence, in this mode the learning systems can be viewed as *learning apprentices* [13], analyzing the normal actions of their users in order to absorb new knowledge. The experimental results indicate that substantially better performance gains can be achieved by observing the behavior of external agents, because the system avoids internally solving complicated problems from first principles, which dissipates much of the savings made by learning.

2.1. Experimental Methodology

The experiments reported in this chapter used blocks–world inference rules, expressed in situation calculus. (See Chapter 3 for an annotated list of all the rules.) An initial situation develops by generating 10 blocks, each with a randomly chosen width and height. One at a time, they are dropped from an arbitrary horizontal position over a table; if they fall in an unstable location, they are picked up and re–released over a new location. Once the 10 blocks are placed,[1] a randomly chosen goal height is selected, centered above a second table. The goal height is determined by adding from one to four average block heights. In addition, the goal specifies a maximum height on towers. The difference between the minimum and maximum acceptable tower heights is equal to the maximum possible height of a block. The reason for this upper bound is explained later. A sample problem situation can be seen in Figure 7–1. The goal is to place a properly supported block so that the center of its top is located within the dotted region. (Some experiments involving the

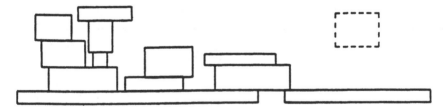

Figure 7–1:   A Sample Problem

---

[1] After the 10 blocks are dropped to construct an initial situation, the database of assertions describing the initial state is constructed. The entries in this database are randomly ordered before the experiment begins.

acquisition of plans for clearing objects are also described in this chapter. In these experiments the scene is set up as for tower–building, then an unclear block is randomly chosen as the block to be cleared.)

Once a scene is constructed, three different problem solvers attempt to satisfy the goal. The first is called no–learn, as it acquires no new rules during problem solving. The second, called sEBL, is an implementation of EGGS (Chapter 2 and [14]), a standard explanation–based learning algorithm. BAGGER (Chapter 3), a structure–generalizing EBL system, is the third problem solver. All three of these systems use a backward–chaining problem solver to satisfy the preconditions of rules. When the two learning systems attack a new problem, they first try to apply the rules they have acquired, possibly also using existing intra–situational rules. No intersituational rules are used in combination with acquired rules in order to limit searching, which would quickly become intractable. Hence, to be successful, an acquired rule must directly lead to a solution without using other intersituational rules.

During generalization, both of the learning systems prune explanation structures at terms that are either situation–independent or describe the initial state. Sample block–stacking rules produced by BAGGER and EGGS appear in Tables 3–4 and 3–5.

Two different strategies for training the learning systems are employed. In one, called *autonomous mode*, the learning systems resort to solving a problem from "first principles" when none of their acquired rules can solve it. This means that the original intersituational rules can be used, but learned rules are not used. When the proof of the solution to a problem is constructed in this manner, the systems apply their generalization algorithm and store any general rule that is produced. In the other strategy, called *training mode*, some number of solved problems (the *training set*) are initially presented to the systems, and the rules acquired from generalizing these solutions are applied to additional problems (the *test set*). Under this second strategy, if none of a system's acquired rules solve the problem at hand, the system is considered to have failed. No problem solving from first principles is ever performed by the learning systems in this mode.

Problem solving in the two modes is illustrated by Figures 7–2 and 7–3, respectively. Notice that the acquired rules are not used when constructing new explanations. This limitation is partly due to computational resource restrictions, as explained in the next paragraph. However, it is also in the spirit of schema–based problem solving, where the idea is to rapidly select and apply schemata rather than spend large amounts of

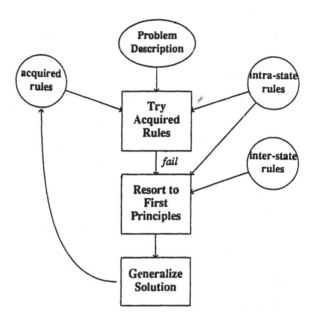

Figure 7–2:   Problem Solving in the Autonomous Mode

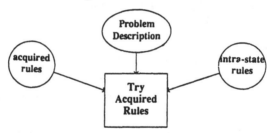

Figure 7–3:   Problem Solving in the Training Mode

time connecting many disjoint pieces of knowledge. Although it might be reasonable to consider combining a handful of schemata, unrestricted combination can be too computationally expensive. In these experiments the limiting case of allowing only one schema to be applied is followed.

All three of these systems use a backward–chaining problem solver (basically a version of Prolog [15]) to satisfy the preconditions of rules. When the two learning systems attack a new problem, they first try to apply the rules they have acquired, possibly also using existing *intra-situational* rules (rules that describe inferences that can be made about a situation). No *intersituational* rules (rules that describe inferences concerning multiple situations) are used in combination with acquired rules in order to limit searching, which would quickly become intractable.

Hence, to be successful, an acquired rule must directly lead to a solution without using other intersituational rules.

The backward–chaining problem solver used is not very sophisticated. Fortunately, the same problem–solving strategy is used by all three systems, so that improved problem solving would help each of them. However, the amount each would be helped by improvements may differ. Investigating the overall impact of problem–solving enhancements is an area for future research. On the positive side, it is possible that the gains from learning reduce the need to have a complicated problem solver.

Unfortunately, constructing towers containing more than two blocks from first principles exceeds the limits of the computers used in the experiments. For this reason, the performance of the no–learn system is estimated by fitting an exponential curve to the data obtained from constructing towers of size one and two. This curve is used by all three systems to estimate the time needed to construct towers from first principles when required, and a specialized procedure is used to generate a solution. The estimated performance curve is discussed in Section 2.8.

Data collection in these experiments is accomplished as follows. Initially, the two learning systems possess no acquired rules. They encounter a number of sample situations and thus build up their rule collections according to the learning strategy applied. (At each point, all three systems address the same randomly generated problem. For each problem, the order in which the three problem solvers address it is randomly chosen.) Statistics are collected as the systems solve problems and learn. This process continues for a fixed number of problems, constituting an experimental run. However, a single run can be greatly affected by the ordering of the sample problems. To provide better estimates of performance, multiple experimental runs are performed. At the start of each run, the rules acquired in the previous run are discarded. When completed, the results of all the runs are averaged together. The curves presented in this chapter are the result of superimposing 25 experimental runs and averaging.

Each learning system stores its acquired rules in a linear list. During problem solving, these rules are tried in order. The first successful one is used. When a rule is successful, it is moved to the front of the list. This way, less useful rules will migrate toward the back of the list. Analysis of other indexing strategies is presented later.

This indexing strategy is the reason that, in the goal, tower heights are limited. The sEBL system would sooner or later encounter a goal requiring four blocks, for which a rule would migrate to the front of its rule list. From that time on, regardless of the goal height, a four–block tower would be constructed. With a limit on tower heights, the rules for building towers of lower heights more efficiently have an opportunity to be tried. This issue would be exacerbated if the goal were not limited to small towers due to simulation time restrictions.

These experiments used six identically configured Xerox Dandelion 1108's. Each machine has 3.5 megabytes of memory and runs the Koto release of Interlisp. Random numbers for the experiments are generated using the algorithm RAN2 described by Press and colleagues [16]. The Interlisp function RAND is used to generate the seed. Timing is performed using the Interlisp function (CLOCK 2), which does not include garbage collection time. For efficiency reasons, the backward–chaining problem solvers use streams and generators [17].

Block dimensions are generated using a uniform probability distribution. The average block width is 75, while the average height is 35. The location from which blocks are dropped is uniformly distributed over a table 450 units wide. A decaying exponential distribution is used to generate tower heights. Scaling is such that the likelihood of a one–block tower is about twice that of a four–block tower.

Unfortunately, these experiments measure some quantities that grow exponentially with problem size, which leads to large variances in the results. The fact that averages are produced from a small number of experimental runs due to computational resource limitations further increases the variance. The large variances should be taken into consideration when interpreting the results presented in this chapter. Appendix B of [18] presents tables containing the numbers, along with their standard deviations, used to plot most of the curves and histograms appearing in this chapter.

2.2. Comparison of the Two Training Strategies

This section is the first of several that present experimental results. In it the operation of the two basic modes of operation — autonomous and training — are analyzed and compared. Subsequent sections analyze variations of these experiments. Rather than comparing all of the variations to one another, the two basic experiments presented in this section serve as a baseline and later experiments are compared to them.

The autonomous mode is considered first. In this mode, whenever a system's current collection of acquired rules fails to solve a problem, a solution from first principles is constructed and generalized. Figure 7–4 shows the probability that the learning systems will need to resort to first principles as a function of the number of sample problems experienced. As more problems are experienced, this probability decreases. (On the first problem the probability is always 1.) BAGGER is less likely to need to resort to first principles than is sEBL, because BAGGER produces a more general rule by analyzing the solution to the first problem.

On average, BAGGER learns 1.72 rules in each experimental run, while sEBL learns 4.28 rules. It takes BAGGER about 50 seconds and sEBL about 45 seconds to generalize a specific problem's solution. Averaging over problems 26–50 in each run (to estimate the asymptotic behavior) produces a mean solution time of 3,720 seconds for BAGGER, 8,100 seconds for sEBL, and 79,300 seconds[2] for no–learn. For BAGGER, this is a speedup of 2.2 over sEBL and 21.3 over no–learn, where speedup is defined as follows:

$$Speedup\ of\ A\ over\ B\ =\ \frac{mean\ solution\ time\ for\ B}{mean\ solution\ time\ for\ A}.$$

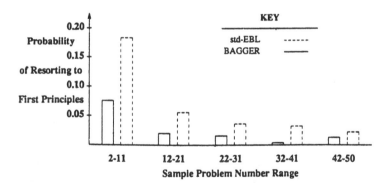

Figure 7–4: Probability of Resorting to First Principles in Autonomous Mode

---

[2] One day contains 86,400 seconds.

Figure 7–5 presents the performance during a *single* experimental run of the two learning systems in the autonomous mode. The average time to solve a problem is plotted, on a logarithmic scale, against the number of sample problems experienced. Notice that the time taken to produce a solution from first principles dominates the time taken to apply the acquired rules, accounting for the peaks in the curves.

Because the cost of solving a big problem from first principles greatly dominates the cost of applying acquired rules, the autonomous mode may not be an acceptable strategy. Although learning in this mode means many problems will be solved quicker than without learning, the time occasionally taken to construct a solution when a system's acquired rules fail can dominate the performance. The peaks in the right side of Figure 7–5 illustrate this. A long period may be required before a learning system acquires enough rules to cover all future problem–solving episodes without resorting to first principles.

The second learning mode provides an alternative. If an expert is available to provide solutions to sample problems and an occasional failure to solve a problem is acceptable, this mode is attractive. Here, a number of sample solutions are provided and the learning systems generalize these solutions, discarding new rules that are variants[3] of others

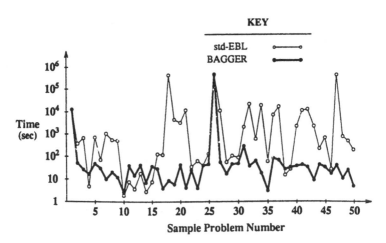

Figure 7–5:   Performance Comparison of the Autonomous Problem Solvers

already acquired. After training, the systems use their acquired rules to solve new problems. No problem solving from first principles is performed when a solution cannot be found using a system's acquired rules.

The performance results in the training mode are shown in Figure 7-6. After 10 training problems, the systems solve 20 additional problems. In these 20 test problems, the two learning systems never resort to using first principles. BAGGER takes, on average, 36.6 seconds on the test problems (versus 3,720 seconds in the autonomous mode), sEBL requires an average of 828 seconds (versus 8,100 seconds), and no–learn averages 68,400 seconds (versus 79,300 seconds).

Since no–learn operates the same in the two modes, these statistics indicate the random draw of problems produced an easier set in the second experiment. The substantial savings for the two learning systems (99% for BAGGER and 90% for sEBL) are due to the fact that in this mode these systems spend no time generating solutions from first

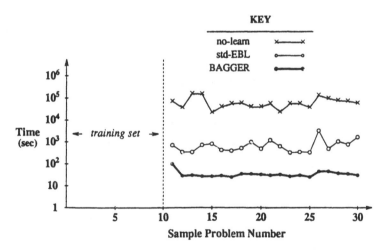

Figure 7–6:   Performance Comparison of the Trained Problem Solvers

---

3 The algorithm for detecting variants determines whether two rules exactly match, given some renaming of variables. This means, for instance, that $a \wedge b$ and $b \wedge a$ are *not* variants. Hence, semantically equivalent rules are not always considered variants. A more sophisticated variant algorithm would reduce the number of saved rules. However if the variant algorithm considered associativity and commutativity, it would be much less efficient [19].

principles. In this experiment, BAGGER has a speedup of 22.6 over sEBL (versus 2.2 in the other experiment) and 1,870 over no–learn (versus 23).

One of the costs of using the training mode is that occasionally the learning systems will not be able to solve a problem. Figure 7–7 plots the number of failures as a function of the size of the training set. In each experimental run used to construct this figure, 20 test problems are solved after the training examples are presented. With 10 training solutions, both of the systems solve over 98.5% of the test problems.

The final figure in this subsection, Figure 7–8, summarizes the performance of the three systems in the two training modes. Note that a logarithmic scale is used. Both of the experiments demonstrate the value of explanation–based learning and also show the advantages of the BAGGER system over standard explanation–based generalization algorithms. BAGGER solves most problems faster than do the other two systems, its overall performance is better, and it learns fewer rules than does sEBL. Comparing the two training modes demonstrates the value of external guidance to learning systems. If a system solves all of its problems on its own, the cost of occasionally solving complicated problems from first principles can dissipate much of the gains from learning. The remainder of this chapter investigates variants on these experiments, comparing the results to the data reported in this section.

2.3. Effect of Increased Problem Complexity

The results in the previous subsection describe the behavior of the three systems for a class of problems, namely, the construction of towers

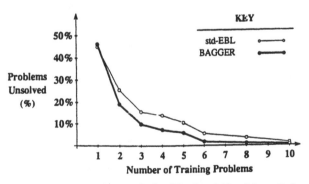

Figure 7–7:   Failure Comparison of the Trained Problem Solvers

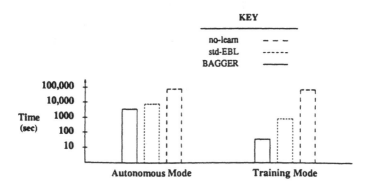

Figure 7-8:   Performance of the Three Systems in the Two Modes

containing from one to four blocks. An interesting question is how the relative performance of the three systems depends on the variability of the problems addressed. This subsection investigates performance as a function of problem complexity. Experiments are run on successively more complicated problem spaces, where complexity is varied by increasing the range of goal heights. Goals specify heights calculated by randomly summing from one to N average blocks. The computational resources available restrict the maximum N to five.

One of the negative effects of learning new rules is that problem-solving time can often be wasted trying to apply them [1, 20]. This occurs when the preconditions of a new rule are checked but no successful binding of the rule's variables can be found. The experiments in this subsection address this issue, because all of the acquired rules build towers but often no binding of a rule's preconditions can construct a tower of a given height. For example, there may be no way to bind the variables in an sEBL rule for building four-block towers such that the resulting tower is as tall as one average block. However, substantial time can be wasted discovering this. This negative effect also occurs for BAGGER rules. If BAGGER only learns that originally clear blocks can be moved to construct a tower, substantial time may be wasted before it finds out that there are not enough clear blocks in the initial state to achieve the specified height.

The figures in this subsection show how the performance of the three problem solvers depends on the magnitude of the range of possible goal heights. Figure 7-9 plots mean solution time, under both training modes, as a function of problem complexity. Since BAGGER learns no rules when the goal only involves moving one block, points are not plotted for the case when the maximum number of blocks in a tower is one. In all cases, the learning systems outperform the problem solver that does not learn. There is no evidence that, on average, learning degrades performance.

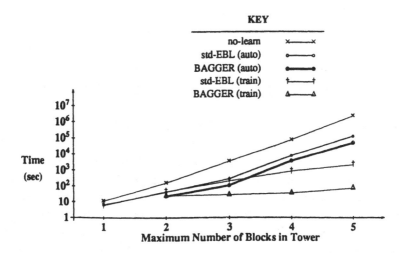

Figure 7–9:   Mean Solution Time as a Function of Problem Complexity

Table 1:   Speedup as a Function of Problem Complexity

Tower Size Range	BAGGER over sEBL	BAGGER over No-Learn	sEBL over No-Learn
autonomous mode			
1-1	–	–	1.73
1-2	1.81	7.01	3.87
1-3	2.75	30.20	11.00
1-4	2.18	21.30	9.79
1-5	2.25	39.00	17.30
training mode			
1-1	–	–	1.97
1-2	1.92	6.35	3.32
1-3	6.69	110.00	16.40
1-4	22.60	1,870.00	82.60
1-5	27.10	24,100.00	889.00

Table 7-1 reports the various speedups produced by comparing the various systems. The data demonstrate that the performance difference among the various system configurations generally widens as the complexity of the problem space increases. The trend is not monotonic in the autonomous mode, possibly due to the disproportionate effect of the infrequent need to construct a solution from first principles. Since resorting to first principles occurs infrequently, statistical fluctuations strongly affect the speedup ratios. The advantage of the training mode over the autonomous mode becomes more pronounced as problem complexity increases, because as larger towers are called for, the cost of building a solution from first principles becomes more dominant.

The experiments reported in this subsection demonstrate that the gains of explanation–based learning increase as the range of potential problems increases. They provide no evidence for the conjecture that learning can impede overall problem–solving performance. Rather, they indicate that as the range of problems increases, learning is increasingly beneficial. In addition, the relative performance of BAGGER over sEBL grows as the range of possible problems increases. Finally, these experiments strengthen the argument that the training mode is preferable to the autonomous mode of operation.

2.4. Operationality and Generality

An issue in explanation–based learning is deciding which portions of a specific problem's explanation can be considered easily reconstructable and, hence, disregarded when the explanation is generalized. Allowing such reconstruction during problem solving produces a more *general* rule since alternative reconstructions are possible, but the resulting rule is less *operational* [21] because significant effort can be expended recalculating.

In the prior three experiments, a term is considered easily evaluated if it is expressed in terms of the initial state only. A more restricted definition, one that incorporates all of the constraints in the explanation, is to consider a node acceptable only if it is a leaf node in the explanation. Being a leaf node means it is either an axiom or a term used to specify the initial state. In the latter case, it is reasonable to assume that these terms will also be specified in future problems and will require minimal effort to test.

The learning systems can be instructed to construct more operational rules. Basically, this entails not pruning any of the nodes in an explanation. This subsection describes the effect on both BAGGER and

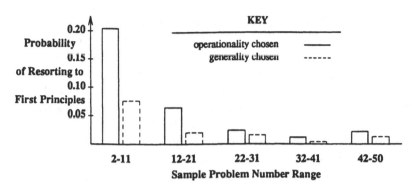

Figure 7–10: Operationality Results in Autonomous Mode for BAGGER

sEBL of not pruning nodes.

Performance in the autonomous mode under this condition appears in Figures 7–10 and 7–11. When constructing more operational rules, the learning systems more frequently resort to solving problems from first principles. This occurs because the more operational rules, being less general, are more likely to fail. Figure 7–12 compares the operational and general versions in the training mode. The advantage of the operational version is clearly visible for sEBL.

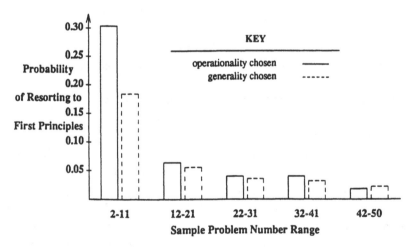

Figure 7–11: Operationality Results in Autonomous Mode for Standard EBL

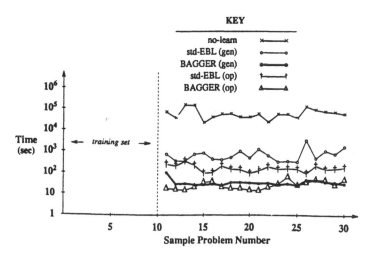

Figure 7-12: Operationality and Generality Results in Training Mode

Table 7-2 summarizes the major differences between the operational and general versions. Results from the two cases are presented for various statistics, along with the ratio of the two results. The results indicate that, although more rules are learned and used, the fact that they are evaluated faster leads to quicker overall solutions. The one exception to this is BAGGER in autonomous mode. Here the need for more solutions from first principles eliminates the gain from the more rapid evaluation of the operational rules.

The probability of a successful rule application is defined by

$$Probability(success) = \frac{\sum_{rules} successful\ applications}{\sum_{rules} attempted\ applications}$$

The average number of rules tried when solving a problem is inversely proportional to this number. Hence, the data in Table 7-2 show that more rules are evaluated, on average, when solving problems with the operational rules.

The final point in this subsection is that, in training mode, the probability that the test problem is not solved is higher in the operational version, because a higher number of operational rules are needed to cover the same number of future problems. Thus, for the operational version to be attractive, the training set must contain a highly representative sample of future problems.

2.5. Rule Access Strategies

The vast majority of machine learning research has focused on how a new concept can be learned. The question of how acquired concepts should be organized (and possibly later reorganized) has been largely neglected. However, the order in which acquired concepts are accessed can greatly affect problem–solving performance. The issue of organizing learned concepts will become a central one when machine learning systems begin to learn large numbers of concepts. This subsection describes eight strategies for organizing newly acquired concepts and reports empirical studies of their performance. Some of the strategies only address where a newly acquired concept should be placed in relation to previously acquired ones, whereas others also involve dynamically reorganizing acquired concepts as problem–solving experience is accumulated. Hence, the strategies in the second category address another aspect of machine learning — learning how to better organize a collection of acquired concepts.

Although the experiments reported in this subsection involved EBL systems, the results are also applicable to other methods of learning the concepts being organized. What is important is that the results of learning be used in later problem solving. The results are dependent on the type of concepts learned in one important sense. Two categories of acquired concepts are compared. The first, called *standard* concepts, are those that only involve a fixed number of actions or entities (e.g., a rule for moving one block onto another). The second type are called *number-generalized* concepts because they involve an indefinite number of actions or entities (e.g., a rule for constructing towers containing any number of blocks). See Chapter 3 for further discussion of these two types of concepts.

The primary strategy used to organize acquired rules is to keep them in a linear list, moving a rule to the front of this list whenever it successfully solves a problem. During problem solving, the rules are tried in order. The ordering of the rules in this list can greatly affect problem–solving performance. Seven additional strategies for accessing acquired rules have also been investigated. After describing the eight strategies for selecting the order of rule implementation, their performance is compared.

This subsection largely investigates a question of problem solving, rather than one of learning. The issue is how the results of learning

Table 2:   Operationality versus Generality Results

Description	Operationality Chosen	Generality Chosen	Ratio (Op/Gen)
Mean Solution Time			
autonomous mode			
std-EBL	6790 sec	8100	0.83
BAGGER	6660	3720	1.79
training mode			
std-EBL	155(174)	779(828)	0.20
BAGGER	27(29)	36(37)	0.75
Rules Learned			
autonomous mode			
std-EBL	5.52	4.28	1.29
BAGGER	2.60	1.72	1.51
training mode			
std-EBL	6.88	5.96	1.15
BAGGER	3.24	2.01	1.61
Probability of Successful Application			
autonomous mode			
std-EBL	0.50	0.56	0.89
BAGGER	0.90	0.99	0.91
training mode			
std-EBL	0.41	0.59	0.69
BAGGER	0.79	0.99	0.79
Percentage Solved			
training mode			
std-EBL	91.4%	98.5	0.93
BAGGER	94.0	99.4	0.95

Numbers in parentheses indicate mean solution time for *all* problems, including problems *not* solved.

would be best organized to increase the efficiency of problem solving. The access strategies investigated have no effect on the number of rules learned or on the probability of a successful solution. All that differs is the order the rules are checked. If necessary, all of them will be tried.

In all of the strategies, acquired rules are organized in a linear list. More complicated data structures, such as discrimination networks [17], can improve problem–solving performance. However, all of the rules organized in these experiments satisfy the same goal, namely, the construction of a tower. Since they all contain the same predicates in their consequent, it is reasonable to assume that they are all grouped at the same node in a discrimination net. Hence, the results of these experiments are relevant to more complicated data structures and even to parallel architectures, provided at some point a group of candidates are serially visited.

2.5.1. Strategy Descriptions

Eight strategies for ordering rules are presented roughly in order of complexity. These access strategies can be divided into two qualitative groups. The first four strategies are independent of problem–solving performance and thus avoid the complication of collecting statistics during problem solving. The second four strategies dynamically depend on the examples in the test set. That is, the results of problem solving continually affect the order in which rules are accessed.

Only the training mode is used in these experiments, and the training set always contains 10 problems, and the test set 20. More rules are learned, on average, in this mode, making it a better vehicle for investigating the issue of rule access strategies. In all of the experimental runs, towers are constructed and the goal height is randomly determined by summing from one to four average block heights. With a training set of 10 problems, the two learning systems both solve more than 98% of the test problems. Since problems not soluble by a given collection of rules are more likely to be anomalous, only the measurements on successful solutions are considered when collecting the data reported in this subsection.

Most Recently Learned (MRL)

In the first strategy, rules are accessed in the *reverse* order as they are learned. This process is easily implemented by pushing, during the training phase, new rules onto the front of the list of acquired rules. Unless otherwise stated, the other strategies use this method to initially insert new rules into the list of previously acquired rules.

Least Recently Learned (LRL)

In the second strategy, rules are accessed in the same order as they are learned. This process is implemented by placing new rules at the *end* of the list of acquired rules.

Sorted by Situations Traversed (SORT)

This strategy applies when using situation calculus and is only relevant to rules learned by standard explanation–based learning (i.e., non–number–generalized rules). By looking at the consequent of a new rule, the number of situations traversed by applying the rule can be determined. Once the training phase completes, the rules are sorted so that those that traverse the fewest number of states are in the front of the list of acquired rules. This list is not altered during the test phase. (This strategy shares many of the characteristics of iterative–deepening [22].) Under this strategy, BAGGER rules follows the MRL strategy.

Randomly Selected (RAND)

In this strategy, the order in which rules are accessed is randomly determined by randomizing the list of acquired rules before *each* test problem, then trying to apply them in their randomized order.

Most Recently Used (MRU)

In the MRU strategy, which is the access strategy used elsewhere in this chapter, the order in which rules are accessed depends on the last time they are successfully applied. Following a successful application, the successful rule is moved to the front of the list of rules. The hypothesis of this strategy is that the more useful a rule is, the more likely it will be tried early.

This and the next three strategies can be viewed as though each rule were somehow scored and these scores were used to sort the rules so that highest scoring rules are at the front of the list. The implementations of the following three strategies use such a sorting strategy, although, as described in the above paragraph, MRU does not. For MRU, no statistics are associated with each rule. The expressions used for predicting a rule's future value under each strategy follow each description.

$$Value_{MRU} = \textit{time of last successful application}$$

Most Frequently Used (MFU)

In this strategy, the order in which rules are accessed depends on how often they have been successfully applied. Unlike MRU, this strategy (and the following two strategies) requires that additional information be recorded. In this case, each rule records the number of time it is used to solve a problem. After each successful solution, MFU sorts the list of acquired rules so that the one with the highest number of successful applications is tried first.

$$Value_{MFU} = \textit{number of successful applications}$$

Most Successfully Used (MSU)

This strategy orders rules according to the *a posteriori* probability they are useful, which is calculated by dividing the number of successful applications of the rule by the number of times the rule is tried. Rules never tried are ordered after rules successfully applied and before rules tried without success. This strategy requires that two statistics be kept for each rule.

$$Value_{MSU} = \frac{\textit{number of successful applications}}{\textit{number of attempts to apply rule}}$$

Most Efficiently Used (MEU)

This strategy involves another way to get previously useful rules near the front of the list of acquired rules. Here the measure of a rule is determined by recording the total amount of time spent trying to satisfy the rule's preconditions and then dividing this time by the number of successful applications of the rule. This strategy measures the time spent per successful application, and the lower this number the more promising the rule. Hence, this measurement is inversely proportional to the value of the rule. Rules never tried are ordered as in MSU. Again, two statistics must be kept.

$$Value^{-1}{}_{MEU} = \frac{total\ time\ spent\ trying\ this\ rule}{number\ of\ successful\ applications}$$

2.5.2. Results

For each strategy for accessing rules, Figure 7–13 presents its performance on the problems in the training set. In this figure, the strategies are organized so that the most efficient one (for sEBL) is on the left and the least efficient one is on the right. There is about an eightfold difference between the best and the worst. The speedup of BAGGER over sEBL ranges from 5 to 40.

Many of the results in this experiment differ by only a small amount. To eliminate the possibility that these small variances are due to machine differences, the timing data in this subsection are determined by counting the search tree nodes visited during problem solving. For no–learn this is estimated by extrapolating results on small problems in. the same manner as done to estimate problem–solving time. The count of nodes is incremented whenever the consequent of a rule or an axiom unifies with the current goal.

To give a better perspective on the results in Figure 7–13, in the next histogram (Figure 7–14), the performances of the strategies are compared with respect to the performance of MFU. (The strategy involving sorting rules by the number of situations traversed (SORT) is not

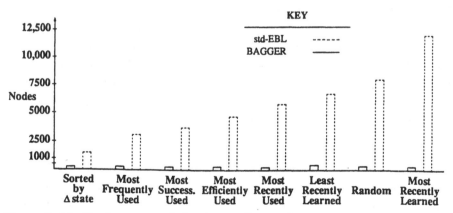

Figure 7–13: Performance of the Access Strategies

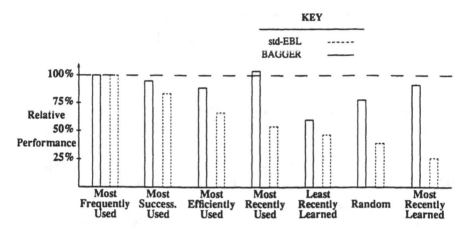

Figure 7–14: Performance of the Access Strategies Normalized Relative to MFU

included in this figure because it is not relevant for BAGGER.) Relative performance is determined by

$$Relative\ Performance\,(strategy)\ =\ \frac{nodes_{MFU}}{nodes_{strategy}}$$

Of the access strategies, the best performer for sEBL is SORT, because the time to check the preconditions of a rule can increase exponentially with the number of situations traversed. SORT also works well because the most likely goal specifies the height of one average block.

The strategies that depend on previous problems, dynamically altering the order in which rules are accessed, prove beneficial. Keeping a count of the number of times a rule is successfully used works well, whereas the method of trying the most recently used rule first works less well. If the occurrence of an intricate, rare example requires the use of a complicated rule, moving it to the front of the queue may be a bad idea because on the next problem, substantial time may be spent discovering it is not applicable. It is better to have rules work their way forward by successfully solving several problems. However, as evidenced by SORT, it can be advantageous to first try rules whose preconditions can be rapidly checked, even if they are likely to solve fewer problems [8]. This topic is further discussed in Shavlik [18], where data on the distribution of solution lengths (in terms of the number of states traversed) are presented.

Somewhat surprisingly, while LRL works better than MRL for sEBL, the opposite is true for BAGGER. The reason is that earlier rules result from more typical examples, whereas later rules result from examples that are less likely to occur again soon. In sEBL it is best to first try the rules that result from the most probable situations. However, BAGGER often learns more from the more complicated, less likely, examples, and the acquired rule usually covers the simpler, more likely, examples. This indicates that, even if one of the dynamic strategies is used, new rules should be added to the *end* of sEBL's list of acquired rules, but they should be added to the *front* of BAGGER's collection.

Each test set contains 20 problems. An interesting question is which access strategies organize rules so that performance improves as more and more problems are solved. The next histogram contains data relevant to this issue. Each strategy's performance on the first 10 test problems is compared to its performance on the second 10. Figure 7–15 presents the results. The ratio of performance on the two groups of test problems is theoretically unity for no–learn, since it only depends on the random draw of desired tower heights. The ratio should also be unity for SORT, LRL, RAND, and MRL, because the order in which they apply rules is not affected by the results of previous test problems. The heights of these bars provide an indication of the variability due to statistical fluctuations. This figure demonstrates that the strategies in which rules are continually reorganized during problem solving improve performance, especially in sEBL, where more rules are learned on average.

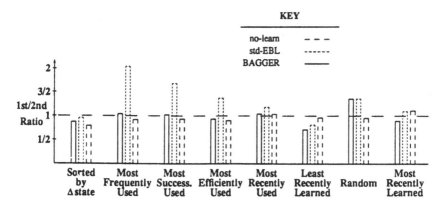

Figure 7–15: Temporal Improvement Under Each Access Strategy

Increasing the size of the training set decreases the probability that a test problem will not be solved. However there are three costs of increasing the training set size: (1) the training period takes longer to complete, (2) more rules will be acquired, and (3) more time can be spent applying the acquired rules. The law of diminishing returns applies here. Incremental gains in the probability of future success may not be worth the increase in the mean time to solve a problem.

Figure 7–16 presents data relevant to this issue. A measure of average performance on the 20 test problems is plotted as a function of the size of the training set. Results are presented for sEBL under two conditions. As they are learned, new rules are added either to the front or to the back of the list of previously acquired rules. In all cases, the MRU strategy is used during the test phase. (Note that the case where sEBL combines LRL and MRU is not one of the eight previously described strategies.) This experiment measures time rather than nodes. Timing is performed using the Interlisp function (CLOCK 2), which does not include garbage collection time. Normalized solution time, defined below, is plotted as a function of the training set size:

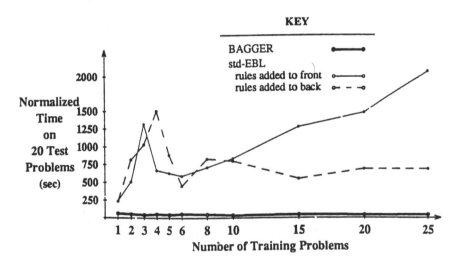

Figure 7–16: Effect of Excessive Training

$$Normalized\ solution\ time\ =\ \frac{Mean\ solution\ time}{Probability\ of\ successful\ solution}$$

Normalizing by the probability of a successful solution partially compensates for the fact that quickly solving only a few problems is not desirable.

Figure 7–16 shows that too much training can be detrimental. Due to the broad coverage of the rules it learns, BAGGER is not affected by the additional training. But excessive training clearly causes a decrease in the performance of sEBL if the most recently learned rules are tried first. However, this problem can be reduced by adding new rules to the *back* of the collection of acquired rules.

The experiments in this subsection investigate various strategies for determining the ordering of rules. The results also provide additional evidence of the value of BAGGER over standard explanation–based learning. Under various strategies for deploying rules, BAGGER always outperforms sEBL. The most successful access strategy for sEBL is to sort rules according to the number of states traversed, a technique applicable if situation calculus is being used. If this type of sorting is not possible, the order of rule access should depend on the examples experienced. Trying the most frequently successful rule first substantially improves performance. Finally, for sEBL new rules should be added to the *end* of the list of acquired rules, whereas for BAGGER they should be added to the *front*.

2.6. Clearing Blocks

This subsection reports the performance of the three systems on a different problem. In this case, initial situations are constructed in the same manner as for tower building, but the goal instead specifies a block to be cleared. After the 10 blocks are randomly dropped, one of the unclear blocks is randomly chosen as the goal block to be cleared. To keep the two experiments comparable, a new goal block is chosen if the goal block supports, directly or indirectly, more than four other blocks.

Figure 7–17 contains the performance, in the training mode, of the three systems on this task. In this case, the learning systems outperform no–learn by 4–5 orders of magnitude, several orders of magnitude better than in the tower–building experiments. One interpretation is that clearing is a much more "local" operation than is tower building. Clearing a block involves moving nearby blocks, blocks coupled to the goal block by relations such as On and Supports. However, when building a tower,

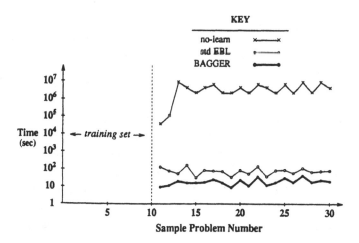

Figure 7–17: Performance Results for Clearing Blocks

blocks located anywhere in a scene can be used. In general, there is less to constrain the choice of which block to move when building a tower. For these reasons, the advantages of explanation–based learning, which collects the essential constraints in an example, become more pronounced.

Table 7–3 presents a comparison of the three problem solvers on the two types of problems. The speedup of BAGGER over sEBL is about one–fifth for clearing as it is for building towers. This may be due to the fact that, on average, less blocks are moved in the clearing problems.[4] As reported in Subsection 2.3, the speedup of BAGGER over sEBL increases as the complexity of the problem space increases.

Table 7–3 also contains the results from an experiment where *both* clearing and tower–building goals are generated. The type of goal is chosen randomly, and the training set contains 20 problems, rather than the usual 10, so that on average 10 of each type are experienced. The results are largely the average of those from the two types of experiments, except that more rules are learned and the probability of a successful rule application is decreased. The extra rules do not significantly hinder the problem solvers because the consequents of the two rule types are different enough that a rule for the wrong goal can be quickly disregarded.

---

[4] The distributions of solution lengths for the various experiments are reported in Shavlik [18].

These experiments involving clearing provide further support for the claims that explanation-based learning is beneficial and that BAGGER outperforms sEBL.

2.7. Alternative Modes of Operation

The two modes of operation investigated so far — autonomous and training — are at opposite ends of a spectrum. In one, the learning systems are completely independent of external guidance. In this mode, learning occurs whenever none of the acquired rules suffice to solve the current problem, whereas in the other all of the learning occurs during an initial training phase, where sample solutions are provided by an external

Table 3:   Comparison of Tower Building and Clearing in Training Mode

Description	No-Learn	Std-EBL	BAGGER
Mean Solution Time			
Clearing	4,200,000 *sec*	58(86)	15(20)
Tower-Building	68,400	779(828)	36(37)
Both	1,790,000	601(607)	31(33)
Speed-Up Over No-Learn			
Clearing	–	72,400	280,000
Tower-Building	–	88	1,900
Both	–	2,980	57,700
Percentage Solved			
Clearing	100.0%	84.6	85.2
Tower-Building	100.0	98.5	99.4
Both	100.0	93.4	94.8
Rules Learned			
Clearing	0.00	3.96	1.36
Tower-Building	0.00	5.96	2.00
Both	0.00	9.09	3.59
Probability of Successful Application			
Clearing	–	0.37	0.81
Tower-Building	–	0.59	0.99
Both	–	0.25	0.60

Numbers in parentheses indicate mean solution time for *all* problems, including problems *not* solved.

agent. The cost of producing explanations from first principles in the autonomous mode can be prohibitive. Conversely, the training set of problems may not be fully representative of future problems, which means that some future problems may not be soluble.

This subsection considers some ways of combining the strengths of the two approaches. The results are especially relevant to the design of expert systems that dynamically acquire new rules by observing expert behavior. Consider the following two ways to utilize external expertise that are alternatives to the training mode.

(1)   The expert can be continually on call. When one of the learning systems cannot solve a problem using its collection of acquired rules, the expert produces a solution. This solution is then explained, and any new rule that results is added to the collection of acquired rules. As more rules are learned, the mean time between requests for the expert will increase.

(2)   Again an expert is always available, except here he or she is not called until a time threshold is exceeded by one of the three systems. Time can be spent both checking acquired rules and building solutions from first principles. With this method, relatively simple problems can be solved from first principles, thereby decreasing the load on the expert, especially during the early stages of learning. However if the threshold is set too low, the expert will be unnecessarily called on problems that are soluble by the acquired rules.

These techniques mitigate the expense of solving from first principles. If the failure to solve a problem is unacceptable, combinations of these two techniques with the training mode are also possible. For example, the expert can provide solutions to an initial set of problems, then provide additional solutions during the test phase whenever the rules learned during the training phase prove insufficient. Alternatively, during the test phase solutions can be derived from first principles as done in the autonomous mode.

Table 7–4 compares the results of these approaches with the standard autonomous and training modes. All of the averages under the autonomous mode are for problems 26–50. BAGGER's performance, with and without combining it with sEBL, is also reported. One interesting point is that the two hybrid approaches perform about equally well for sEBL because it is possible for sEBL to spend more than 10,000 seconds checking its acquired rules.

The results in this subsection indicate that these hybrid approaches significantly exceed the performance of the fully autonomous approach but still guarantee solutions to all problems. The cost of this approach is that an expert must be available at all times but should be needed less

Table 4:   Comparison of Operation Modes

Mode of Operation	Mean Solution Time (sec)
Autonomous	
Std-EBL	8100(7580)
BAGGER	
w/o std-EBL	3720
with std-EBL	58
Autonomous *(external solutions after 10,000 sec)*	
Std-EBL	1290(949)
BAGGER	
w/o std-EBL	133
with std-EBL	52
Autonomous *(external solutions if all rules fail)*	
Std-EBL	1470(920)
BAGGER	
w/o std-EBL	40
with std-EBL	36
Trained	
Std-EBL	827(988)
BAGGER	
w/o std-EBL	37
with std-EBL	46

Numbers in parentheses are from runs where BAGGER used standard EBL.
The differences are due to randomness in the problem generator.

frequently as time progresses.

2.8. Estimating the Performance of the No–Learn System

Due to computational resource limits, the performance of no–learn is estimated. The equations used to estimate the performance of no–learn appear In Figure 7-20. N is the number of blocks to be moved. These equations are constructed by measuring the system's performance on 250 problems where $N = 1$ or 2, then using the curve–fitting algorithm [16]. Problems with $N = 3$ occasionally exhaust the available memory. The successful cases where $N = 3$ are consistent with the estimations.

2.9. BAGGER Evaluation Summary

The empirical results presented in this chapter demonstrate the value of generalizing the structure of explanations in particular and explanation–based learning in general. Three different problem solvers are compared. Two of them learn, BAGGER (see Chapter 3) and sEBL (an implementation of the EGGS explanation–based generalization algorithm; see Chapter 2). The other, called no–learn, performs no learning. In the experiments investigated, BAGGER and sEBL perform substantially better than the system that performs no learning, by up to five orders of magnitude. BAGGER, a system that generalizes explanation structures, also outperforms the standard EBL system.

Investigation of two training modes demonstrates the importance of external guidance to learning systems. In the autonomous mode, where the systems must solve all problems on their own, the high cost of problem solving when no learned rule applies dissipates much of the gains

$$time_{tower}(N) = 0.32 \times 10^{1.54 \times N} \; seconds$$

$$time_{clear}(N) = 0.25 \times 10^{2.08 \times N} \; seconds$$

$$nodes_{tower}(N) = 5.45 \times 10^{1.35 \times N}$$

$$nodes_{clear}(N) = 2.68 \times 10^{1.95 \times N}$$

Figure 7-18: Estimated Performance of No–Learn

from learning. Substantial gains can be achieved by initially providing solutions to a collection of sample problems and having the learners acquire their rules by generalizing these solutions. The usefulness of this method depends on how representative of future problems the training samples are and how acceptable are occasional failures. Since BAGGER requires less training examples and produces more general rules, it addresses these issues better than does standard explanation–based learning.

The BAGGER algorithm leads to the acquisition of fewer rules, because one of its rules may subsume many related rules learned using standard explanation–based learning. In this chapter, experiments demonstrate that acquiring fewer rules decreases the likelihood that time will be wasted on rules that appear to be applicable.

A number of additional statistics are reported. Eight strategies for determining the order in which to access acquired rules are analyzed. Dynamically organizing rules so the most recently or frequently used ones are tried first proves beneficial. If situation calculus is used, sEBL benefits most by ordering rules according to the number of situations they traverse. For BAGGER, new rules should be added to the front of its collection of rules, while for sEBL they should be added to the back. Rules that are more operational perform better when the training mode is used. Additionally, fewer training examples are needed for BAGGER to acquire a sufficient set of new rules, and excessive training examples affect BAGGER less severely than sEBL. The advantages of BAGGER over standard explanation–based learning magnify as the range of potential problems is increased.

Other researchers have also reported on the performance improvement of standard explanation–based learning systems over problem solvers that do not learn [1, 20, 23–26]. One major issue is that, as more new concepts are learned, problem–solving performance can *decrease*. This occurs because substantial time can be spent trying to apply rules that appear promising but ultimately fail [1, 20]. Although the non–learning system outperforms the learning systems on some problems, in the experiments reported in this chapter the overall effect is that learning is beneficial. Significantly, as the complexity of the problem space increases, so does the improvement achieved by explanation–based learning.

Another potential performance degradation can occur when a new broadly applicable rule, which can require substantial time to instantiate, blocks access to a more restricted yet often sufficient rule whose

preconditions are easier to evaluate and implement [8, 18]. Evidence for
this is found in the experiments involving the sEBL system. When building towers that contain, on average, two blocks, rules that specify moving
three blocks are preferentially chosen. This occurs because these three–
block rules, although less efficient than rules for moving two blocks, cover
a larger collection of the possible problems.

Although experiments herein indicate that learning increases overall
problem–solving performance, evidence is also presented that too much
learning can be detrimental. Techniques for forgetting or reorganizing
acquired rules are necessary. The experiments investigating rule access
strategies demonstrate the value of dynamically organizing rules. The
idea of organizing acquired rules so that rapidly evaluated special cases of
more general rules are tried first is presented here and by Shavlik et al.
[8]. An untested approach to forgetting was presented by Fikes et al.
[27], where it was suggested that statistics be kept on the frequencies
acquired rules are learned, discarding those that fall below some threshold. This idea was successfully tested by Minton [1]. To prevent the
accumulation of an excessive number of rules, it is also important to
wisely decide when to acquire a new rule. Some general heuristics have
been proposed that estimate when it is a good idea to construct the generalization of a specific explanation. For example, Minton [1] proposed
selectively generalizing those solutions that initially progress away from
the direction indicated by a hill–climbing measure. A similar idea was
proposed by Iba [28]. Only solutions that achieve *thematic* goals [29] are
generalized in the GENESIS system [30]. Additional conditions for generalization were presented by DeJong [31].

It may seem that largely investigating only tower–building problems unfairly favors explanation–based learning. An alternative would be
to investigate a more diverse collection of problems. However, the negative effects of learning are manifested most strongly when the acquired
concepts are closely related. If the effects of some rule support the satisfaction of a goal, substantial time can be spent trying to satisfy the
preconditions of the rule. If this cannot be done, much time is wasted.
To the sEBL system, a rule for stacking two blocks is quite different from
one that moves four blocks. Frequently, a rule that appears relevant
fails. For example, often sEBL tries to satisfy a rule that specifies moving
four blocks to meet the goal of having a block at a given height, only to
fail after much effort because all combinations of four blocks exceed the
limitations on the tower height. On average, sEBL tries about 1.5 rules
before solving a problem. When the effects of a rule are unrelated to the

current goal, much less time is wasted, especially if a complicated data structure is used to organize rules according to the goals they support.

While providing a major test of standard EBL and structure–generalizing EBL under a variety of conditions, it is not clear how much the results of these experiments depend on the peculiarities of the specific domain chosen. A domain–independent analysis is needed. One approach would be to randomly generate rules, initial states, and goals. Since an underlying assumption of EBL is that past problems are indicative of future problems, and hence the generalizations of their solutions are worth saving, with excessive randomness it is unlikely that learning will prove beneficial. However, varying such properties as the ratio of the number of different predicates to the number of domain rules may indicate the domains in which standard and structure–generalizing explanation–based learning algorithms perform well. Other properties to vary include the average number of antecedents in a rule, the number of different consequents, the probability that a predicate in the antecedents also appears in the consequents, and the probability that a variable appears in more than one antecedent of a rule. Finally, to complement empirical analyses of EBL, theoretical analyses are needed, as has been done for similarity–based learning [32–35]. An approach that applies Valiant's learning framework [32] to an aspect of explanation–based learning is described in [36].

These experiments demonstrate that explanation–based learning can improve problem–solving performance, that learning by observing the intelligent behavior of an external agent can be advantageous (even when a system can solve the problem by itself), and that the ability to generalize explanation structures is a valuable characterisitic of an explanation–based learning system.

3. LT Revisited: An Empirical Study

This section reports on an EBL experiment in a logical domain. The experiment involves complete machine learning systems built around one of the earliest, simplest AI problem solvers: Newell, Shaw, and Simon's LOGIC–THEORIST (LT). Results of a comparison of the performances of three versions of LT (corresponding to *non–learning, rote learning*, and *explanation–based learning*) on a large number of problems are given.

3.1. The Domain: *Principia Mathematica*

The domain of this experiment is the propositional calculus of Alfred North Whitehead and Bertrand Russell's *Principia Mathematica* [4]. The calculus deals with a set of expressions or well–formed propositional formulae built on a set of variables that are supposed to stand for arbitrary propositions such as "Agrippina killed Claudius." Complex propositions are built up by using connectives such as NOT (¯) , AND (∧), OR (∨), and IMPLIES (⊃).

Valid propositions are called theorems. It turns out that the theorems of the propositional calculus can be built up from an initial set of theorems called axioms, such as $(P \lor P) implies P$.[5] Other theorems are derived from the axioms by applying rules of inference. *Detachment*, or modus ponens, is a rule of inference that allows one to infer B if one has A and $A \supset B$. Another rule allows substitution of any expression for a variable in any theorem. Another allows replacement of definitions for defined connectives (e.g., $\overline{P} \lor Q$ for $P \supset Q$).

A derivation of a theorem is called a proof. A proof of a desired theorem can be written as a sequence ending in that theorem, where each step in the sequence is either an axiom or else follows from previous steps by a rule of inference. Alternatively, the proof can be depicted as a tree whose root is the desired theorem where each node in the tree is either an axiom or follows from its predecessors by an inference rule.

The particular theorems of interest in this chapter are from the second and third chapters of Part One of *Principia* [4].

One of the advantages of propositional logic is an advantage of mathematics in general, namely, *high levels of abstraction and generality*. When one learns arithmetic one is learning something that will apply to an extremely wide range of tasks from the mundane (e.g., choosing best buys at the grocery store) to the esoteric (e.g., performing basic calculations in the astrophysics of black holes). Similarly, propositional logic is an abstract, general theory of deduction. One can apply logic in infinitely many definite, specific domains by specifying propositions that provide details about particular subjects. Any learning that takes place at the logical level can thus be applied in many domains.

---

[5] Complete lists of the axioms and of the problems from *Principia* used in the experiments are provided in O'Rorke [37].

Another advantage of logic is that the number of schemata required for complete coverage is small. This feature facilitates the execution of large–scale experiments because it isn't necessary to hand–code large amounts of knowledge in new schemata in order to introduce new examples.

The particular logic system of *Principia Mathematica* offers the added advantage of a very simple and natural theorem prover that can be used as the problem–solving performance element in learning experiments.

3.2. The Performance Element: LT (The Logic Theorist)

According to Donald Loveland's "Automated Theorem–Proving: A Quarter–Century Review" [38], Newell, Shaw, and Simon's LOGIC THEORIST [3] was the first computer program to prove theorems automatically. The program (hereafter LT) proved some theorems in the propositional calculus of *Principia Mathematica* [4]. This subsection is a brief description of how a simple version of LT works, in the terminology of schema–based problem solving.

3.2.1. Schemata

In this context, a *schema* is merely a collection of related descriptions. Each LT schema has three descriptions (well–formed formulae of propositional calculus) related by a logical dependency. The dependency states that one description (the *consequence* of the schema) is true if both of the others (the *antecedents*) are true. LT only uses two schemata: a *detachment* schema and a *chaining* schema (see Figure 7–19). The detachment schema captures *modus ponens* and is comprised of X, Y, and

Figure 7–19: The Detachment and Chaining Schemata

$X \supset Y$, where Y depends on $X \supset Y$ and X. The chaining schema captures the *transitivity of implication* and is comprised of $X \supset Y$, $Y \supset Z$, and $X \supset Z$, where $X \supset Z$ is true if both $X \supset Y$ and $Y \supset Z$ are true.

3.2.2. Problem Solving

LT's mission is to construct a proof of a given conjecture: building it out of detachment and chaining schemata, axioms, and previously proven theorems. The resulting proof is a linear tree as shown in Figure 7–20. The leaves (labelled $T_0 \cdots T_{n+1}$) are all taken from the set of known theorems. Each schema (labeled S_i) corresponds to a step in the proof and can be considered to reduce a problem (P_i) to a simpler one (P_{i+1}) as in Figure 7–21.

Figure 7–21 shows what happens, in general, during one step in the construction of a proof. Given a problem P_i, LT chooses a schema S_i and a known theorem T_i, such that the problem is an instance of the schema's conclusion C_i and the theorem T_i is compatible with one of the schema's antecedents A_i. The other antecedent B_i (viewed in the context of identifications between C_i and P_i and between A_i and T_i) becomes the

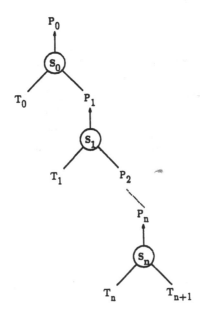

Figure 7–20: The Structure of LT's Proofs

New Problem P_{i+1} is $B_i \theta$,

where θ is the MGU of C_i with P_i and of A_i with T_i

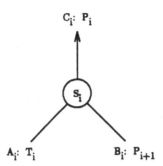

C_i: P_i

S_i

A_i: T_i B_i: P_{i+1}

Figure 7–21: One Step in the Construction of a Proof

new problem P_{i+1}.

LT is only allowed to extend the proof by means of a detachment schema in one way: Given a problem, LT looks for a known implication whose conclusion subsumes the problem. If such a theorem is found, its antecedent becomes the new problem (see Figure 7–22). This amounts to

New Problem P_{i+1} is $X \theta$

where θ is the MGU of Y with P_i and of $X \supset Y$ with T_i

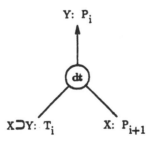

Y: P_i

dt

$X \supset Y$: T_i X: P_{i+1}

Figure 7–22: A Detachment Step

applying a detachment *operator* corresponding to modus ponens, run backward.

The chaining schema can be used in two ways to extend the proof, so in effect LT has two chaining operators corresponding to transitivity of implication inference rules. Both operators attempt to prove an implication of the form $X \supset Z$. *Chaining forward* (Figure 7-23) involves trying to show that an immediate consequence of X implies Z. In contrast, *chaining backward* (Figure 7-24) tries to show that X implies an immediate antecedent of Z.

For a concrete example, consider the operation of LT on *Principia-*2.17: $(\bar{Q} \supset \bar{P}) \supset (P \supset Q)$. This is the *only if* part of an important tautology called *contraposition* [39], which states that the contrapositive $\bar{Q} \supset \bar{P}$ holds if and only if the implication $P \supset Q$ holds.

LT proves *Principia-*2.17 by chaining forward (see Figure 7-25): It proves that the contrapositive $\bar{Q} \supset \bar{P}$ implies an intermediate result that eventually leads to the original implication $P \supset Q$. The first link of the chain is supplied by an instance of the axiom *Principia-*1.4: $(A \vee B) \supset (B \vee A)$. With A bound to $\bar{Q}$ and B bound to $\bar{P}$, this yields $(\bar{Q} \vee \bar{P}) \supset (\bar{P} \vee \bar{Q})$. By the definition of the implication connective, $\bar{P} \vee \bar{Q}$ is the same as $P \supset \bar{Q}$; this serves as the intermediate step in the chain from $\bar{Q} \supset \bar{P}$ to $P \supset Q$. Chaining forward transforms the initial problem

New Problem P_{i+1} is $Y \supset Z \; \theta$,
where θ is the MGU of $X \supset Y$ with T_i and of $X \supset Z$ with P_i

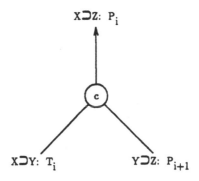

Figure 7-23: A Chaining Forward Step

New Problem P_{i+1} is $X \supset Y$ θ,
where θ is the MGU of $Y \supset Z$ with T_i and of $X \supset Z$ with P_i

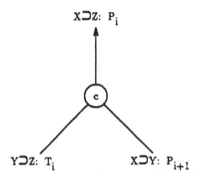

Figure 7-24: A Chaining Backward Step

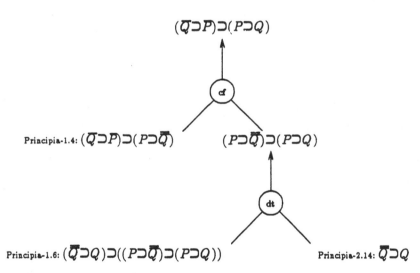

Figure 7-25: The Proof of *Principia*-2.17

into the problem of proving $(P \supset \overline{\overline{Q}}) \supset (P \supset Q)$.

Next, the detachment operator is used. The detachment operation amounts to performing modus ponens backward, so a theorem is needed whose conclusion subsumes the current subproblem. The conclusion of axiom *Principia*-1.6 — $(A \supset B) \supset ((C \vee A) \supset (C \vee B))$ — meets this requirement. With C bound to $\overline{P}$, A bound to $\overline{\overline{Q}}$, and B bound to Q, the axiom becomes $(\overline{\overline{Q}} \supset Q) \supset ((P \supset \overline{Q}) \supset (P \supset Q))$. Detachment on *Principia*–1.6 transforms the problem of proving $(P \supset \overline{Q}) \supset (P \supset Q)$ into the problem of proving $\overline{Q} \supset Q$. Assuming *Principia*–2.14 is known, $\overline{Q} \supset Q$ is the final subproblem because it is an instance of *Principia*–2.14.

3.3. LT Plus Rote Learning

In *Human Problem Solving*, Newell and Simon describe experiments on LT augmented with simple forms of learning. They mention that perhaps the simplest learning method is to make LT's list of known theorems variable, modifying LT so as to add any new theorem it proves to the list, so that "in proving a sequence of theorems, LT would gradually become more capable" [3]. This form of learning is well suited for relatively uncontrolled situations such as *learning by discovery*, where conjectures are made that may prove to be false and problems are posed that may not be solvable. In more controlled learning situations such as *learning from a teacher*, sequences of problems are often carefully selected so that all of the problems are solvable. In fact, they are usually sequenced in order of increasing difficulty. The problems from *Principia* form just such a carefully constructed sequence. LT was allowed (in both the original and the present studies) to use all prior theorems in its attempts on each new theorem, whether it had succeeded in proving them or not.

When solved problems are stored, each new problem is reduced to one that has been solved before. When all problems are stored, each new problem is reduced to one that has been seen before. In both cases, problems encountered are simply added to memory and one is left with the distinct impression that no "understanding" or "thinking" is taking place. For this reason, one can consider these strategies to be forms of *rote learning*.

3.4. LT Plus Explanation–Based Learning

One problem with rote learning systems is that they tend to be very sensitive to the particular form of the examples they observe. They retain extraneous details, as well as essential facts, of specific examples and therefore fail to recognize that a solution to one problem can also be used for another problem because the problems differ in trivial ways. One would prefer to forget about the extraneous details and to remember only the essentials of an example. The basic idea of explanation–based learning is that one can do this by constructing and using explanations. When one conducts an analysis and constructs an explanation of how and why a solution solves one particular problem, one is better prepared to see the general class of problems to which the method can be successfully applied.

LT can be augmented with EBL by focusing on explanations instead of problems. The explanations are LT's proofs, considered as structures built out of schemata. The EBL version of LT ignores the specific theorem that gave rise to a proof and considers each proof in its full generality in order to compute the most general theorem based on the proof. The generalized conclusion of an LT proof can be defined recursively as follows. The generalized conclusion of an elementary proof (a proof that states that the desired conclusion is an instance of a known theorem) is simply the known theorem itself. The generalized conclusion of a complex proof is the result of viewing the conclusion of the topmost schema in the context of identifications (unifications) between one antecedent and a known theorem, and between the other antecedent and the generalized conclusion of the subproof (see Figure 7–26).

In particular, the generalized conclusion of a proof by detachment is the result of viewing the conclusion Y of the detachment schema in the context of the unification of one of its antecedents $(X \supset Y)$ with some known theorem (T_i) and of the other antecedent X with the generalized conclusion (G_{i-1}) of the subproof (see Figure 7–27). In forward–chaining, $X \supset Y$ is unified with a known theorem while $Y \supset Z$ is unified with the generalized subconclusion to obtain a substitution that is applied to

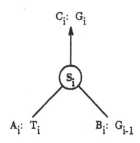

Generalized Conclusion G_i is $C_i\,\theta$,
where θ is the MGU of A_i with T_i and of B_i with G_{i-1}

$C_i:\ G_i$

S_i

$A_i:\ T_i$ $B_i:\ G_{i-1}$

Figure 7–26: The Generalized Conclusion of One Step of a Proof

Generalized Conclusion G_i is $Y\,\theta$,
where θ is the MGU of $X\supset Y$ with T_i and of X with G_{i-1}

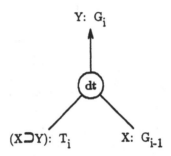

Figure 7–27: The Generalized Conclusion of a Detachment Proof

$X \supset Z.$

For a concrete example, reconsider the proof of *Principia*–2.17, $(\overline{Q} \supset \overline{P}) \supset (P \supset Q)$. Recall that the proof involved two steps: Chaining forward on *Principia*–1.4 reduced the original problem to a subproblem that was solved by detachment on *Principia*–1.6 and *Principia*–2.14. Computing the generalized conclusion also involves two steps: First the generalized conclusion of the detachment subproof must be computed, then the generalized conclusion of the overall chaining forward proof can be determined.

The generalized conclusion of the detachment step is computed by identifying *Principia*–2.14 $D \supset D$ with the antecedent $A \supset B$ of *Principia*–1.6, $(A \supset B) \supset ((C\vee A) \supset (C\vee B))$. This identification binds A to D, and B to D. The conclusion of *Principia*–1.6 *in this context* becomes the generalized conclusion of the detachment step, namely $(C\vee D) \supset (C\vee D)$. The generalized conclusion of the entire proof is computed by chaining forward on *Principia*–1.4 $(E\vee F) \supset (F\vee E)$ and the generalized conclusion of the subproof $(C\vee D) \supset (C\vee D)$.

The conclusion of *Principia*–1.4 plays the role of the middleman and is identified with the antecedent of the generalized conclusion of the detachment. That is, $F\vee E$ is unified with $C\vee D$: F is bound to C while E is bound to D. The generalized conclusion of the chaining forward step

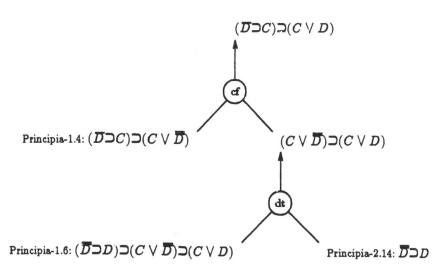

Figure 7–28: The Generalized Conclusion of the Proof of *Principia*–2.17

kicks out the middleman and goes directly from $E \vee F$, the antecedent of *Principia*–1.4, to $C \vee D$, the conclusion of the generalized conclusion of the detachment step, in light of this identification. Substituting C for F and D for E in $(F \vee E) \supset (C \vee D)$, the generalized overall conclusion is $(\overline{D \vee C}) \supset (C \vee D)$. By the definition of implication, this can also be seen as $(D \supset C) \supset (C \vee D)$, as shown in Figure 7–28.

Comparing the generalized conclusion of the proof of *Principia*–2.17 to the particular problem,

$$Principia\text{–}2.17\text{: } (\overline{Q} \supset \overline{P}) \supset (P \supset Q) \text{ Generalized}$$
$$\text{Conclusion: } (D \supset C) \supset (C \vee D)$$

one can see that the proof is strictly more general than the problem because the problem contains an extraneous negation. The NOT in $\overline{P}$ is not really necessary.

3.5. Methodology

The experiment reported here involves the application of three different versions of LT to propositional logic problems from *Principia Mathematica*. All three versions of LT start with the same axioms (the same initial set of known theorems). However, the first (non–learning) version of LT is not allowed to learn from its successes or failures. No new theorems are added to the list of known theorems. The non–learning LT attempts to solve each new problem by reducing it to one of the original axioms. The second version is allowed a form of rote–learning: Problems are added to the list of known theorems whether they are solved or not. The rote–learning LT attempts to solve new problems by reducing them to problems it has seen before. The third version augments the basic LT by the simple form of explanation–based learning described earlier. Of course, EBL is useless when the search for a proof fails, so rote–learning is resorted to in this case. However, when a novel theorem is proved, the generalized conclusion of the proof is added to the list of known theorems.[6]

The main questions asked on each *Principia* problem are:

- What is the nature of the search for a solution?
- What is the quality of the solution found?
- What is the quality of the learning?

3.5.1. Characterizing the Search for a Solution

For each problem in *Principia*, a record is made concerning whether each version of LT solves or fails to solve the problem in a limited search. LT does breadth–first search, maintaining a queue of untried problems. Before a problem is added to the queue, it is checked to see whether it is an instance of a known theorem. Problems are dequeued and attempted by applying LT's operators: First the detachment operator is applied, followed by chaining–forward and then chaining–backward. Each of these operators may produce new subproblems which may be added to the queue of untried problems. LT restricts the search by limiting the number of problems attempted.

Whether the problem is solved or not, the total number of subproblems generated and the number of problems attempted in each search for a solution are recorded and used to compute the average branching factor (the number of subproblems generated divided by the number of prob-

---

[6] It is important to note that the same basic problem–solving machinery (LT) is being used in each version. LT is admittedly primitive by modern standards of theorem proving, but our main interest is in differences in performance among non–learning, rote–learning, and EBL systems, not in the particular performance element. All the learning and non–learning systems are handicapped by LT's lack of sophistication.

lems attempted) for each problem.

3.5.2. Evaluating the Results of Problem Solving and Learning

If a proof of a theorem is found, a measure of the size of the proof is recorded. To facilitate comparison of rote versus explanation–based learning, the theorems learned by the EBL version of LT are recorded. These degenerate to the input theorem in cases when no proof is found. When a nontrivial proof is found, the generalized conclusion is computed and the generality of the result is compared to the generality of the corresponding result of rote–learning.

3.6. Limited Search Under the IMPLIES Restrictions

Our initial experiments involve severely limited search. To be exact, the number of subproblems LT is allowed to attempt in its effort to solve each *Principia* problem is limited to 15.

3.6.1. Results on Search Performance

Average Branch, New Problems Attempted ≤ 15, IMPLIES Restrictions, Unsolved

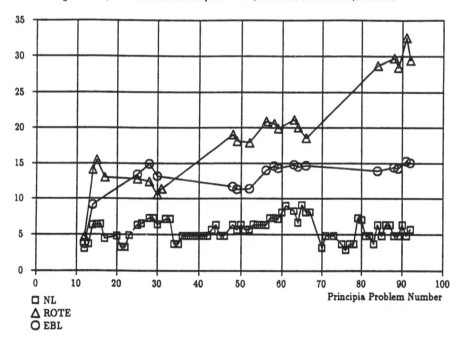

□ NL
△ ROTE
○ EBL

Figure 7–29: Limited Search Performance on Unsolved Problems

Figure 7–29 shows the search behavior of three versions of LT on the problems they fail to solve. The figure gives the "average branching factor," the number of problems generated in the search divided by the number of problems attempted. In the case of unsolved problems, the number of problems attempted is a constant, since this parameter is limited to 16 (15 subproblems and the original problem) and search has to be abandoned at that point when LT fails to find solutions. Thus, the average branching factor is the number of problems generated divided by 16.

The number of points on the curves indicates that LT solves far more problems with learning than without and that the learning versions are roughly comparable in this respect. The fact that the RL curve is generally above the EBL curve and that both are always above the NL curve indicates that, in most cases, RL does more search than EBL, which does more search than NL.

Turning to solved problems, consider the search behavior of no–learning as opposed to rote. The NL system solves 22 problems, including one problem not solved by RL (problem 31, *Principia* 2.41). RL solves 69 problems, including 48 problems not solved by NL. When both systems

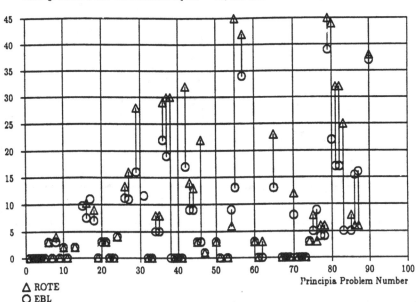

Average Branch, New Problems Attempted ≤ 15, IMPLIES Restrictions, Solved

△ ROTE
○ EBL

Figure 7–30: Rote versus EBL on Solved Problems in Limited Search

solve a problem, RL never attempts more subproblems than NL, and RL almost always generates fewer (or the same number of) subgoals before a solution is found.

Figure 7–30 shows the search behavior of rote versus EBL on the solved problems. There are no isolated circles, but three isolated boxes indicate that EBL solves everything that rote solves and more. (EBL picks up problem 31 and thus also solves everything NL solves as well.) In general, EBL does less search than rote, as measured in terms of problems attempted, subproblems generated, and in terms of average branching factors. However, there are a significant number of exceptions to this rule, for example, problems 86 and 87.

3.6.2. Results on the Quality of the Solutions

Figure 7–31 shows the quality of the solutions delivered under NL versus RL, and Figure 7–32 compares the quality of the RL solutions versus those provided by EBL. Rote provides solutions that are always at least as good as NL, often better. However, the differences in quality between RL and EBL are mixed. They often get the same proof, but

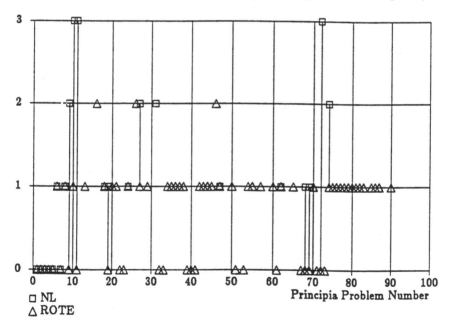

Figure 7–31: Quality of Solutions of NL versus Rote in Limited Search

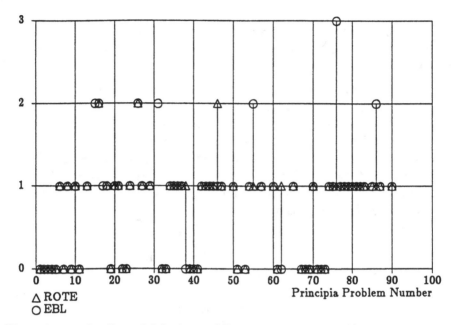

Figure 7–32: Quality of Solutions of Rote versus EBL in Limited Search

sometimes RL finds a shorter one, sometimes vice versa.

3.6.3. Discussion of Search Performance

In general, problems solved by the non–learning LT are also solved by the rote–learning version, and problems solved by the rote–learning LT are also solved by the EBL version. Some exceptions to this rule are explained by new theorems leading the learning systems astray, so that they use up their limited search resources before finding a solution.

Looking at the number of subproblems generated and attempted by each version of LT, in some cases one sees increases in the amount of search in going from non–learning to learning and drops in other cases. The drops indicate that some learned theorem is useful in solving a problem efficiently. The increases are due to the fact that learned theorems increase the number of possible next steps in proofs. The learning versions of LT generally have more ways of attempting to solve a problem. When one of the early attempts succeeds, the problem is solved immediately and less search is done. Otherwise, more attempts are made before a solution is found or search is abandoned.

Relationships between the average branching factors are especially clear in the unsolved problems: They are relatively low for the non–learning system, much higher in both learning systems, but significantly lower in EBL than in rote–learning. The branching factors appear to be relatively constant in NL but increase with learning more quickly in RL than in EBL.

It may seem odd that the no–learning performance is poor (it solves far fewer problems) as compared to the learning systems when it seems to have a less difficult search space (lower branching factor) to contend with. There are several reasons for this. First, learned theorems enable the learning versions of LT to "see more deeply into the search space." Search is limited, and there are problems that cannot be solved without learning just because the required search exceeds the limit. The learning versions of LT may be able to effectively exceed the limit because search done in constructing the proof of learned solutions is not counted against searches that apply these earlier solutions to solve later problems.

Another reason for the drastic improvement in performance in learning as compared to non–learning has to do with LT's limited control strategy. LT is restricted to producing linear proofs: Each operator (detachment and chaining) uses a known theorem to reduce a problem to a new subproblem. However, the learning systems add to the initial axioms theorems that follow from the initial axioms by one or more operations. This has the effect of allowing the learning versions of LT to break out of this restriction so that the search for a solution is taking place in a radically different search space, one which contains solutions that cannot be generated by the non–learning version of LT. Figure 7–33 shows an example of a proof that is within the search space of the learning systems but denied to the NL LT. Although NL does manage to construct an equivalent proof, using chaining forward as a mirror image of chaining backward, this is done at the cost of extra search.

An additional source of the improvement in performance in learning is that learned solutions can increase the set of problems that can be solved. It is known that LT is an incomplete theorem prover; in other words, there are theorems that it cannot prove in principle (even ignoring any limitations of the amount of search allowed). For example, *Principia* problem 2.13 cannot be solved by LT. Adding such problems to the list of known results covers for incompleteness in the theorem prover and leads to solutions of problems that otherwise could not be solved.

Focusing on search performance differences between the learning systems, we note that sometimes problems are solved by the EBL version alone (for example, in this experiment, *Principia*–2.16 and *Principia*–2.18). Also, it is often the case that EBL finds proofs with less search than RL, measuring the amount of search in terms of problems attempted, subproblems generated, and average branch. One reason for improvements in performance in EBL as opposed to RL is the improved generality of the results of explanation–based learning. Another reason for this improvement is that the rote–learning LT adds instances of known theorems to the list of known theorems. This violates a general principle of explanation–based learning that might be paraphrased: *Only novel solutions to problems are worth remembering* [10]. Even without invoking EBL, however, there is no point in adding instances of known theorems to the list of known theorems, because any "indirect" instance of an instance X of Y is also a "direct" instance of Y. Adding instances hurts by increasing the branching factor of the search but provides no benefits, since the instances are added to the end of the list of known theorems, rather than the beginning.

Sometimes the search performance of EBL is inferior to RL. For example, if this experiment is run with a limit of 200 rather than 15, rote solves *Principia*–2.37 but EBL misses it. Occasionally, one might expect a more general result learned by EBL to get in the way of finding the correct proof, but it turns out that this anomalous behavior is actually due to the fact that LT is too restrictive in its use of problem–solving operators. It requires subproblems to have IMPLIES as their top–level connective before it will attempt to reduce them using forward– or backward–chaining. In addition, the known theorem used must also have IMPLIES as its top–level connective [3, 40].[7] The conclusion to be drawn here is that it is necessary to have a reasonably "smart" matcher in order to take full advantage of the improved generality of explanation–based learning; otherwise, one may wind up with degradation in performance rather than improvement! In fact, the overall number of problems solved can be lower in EBL with a "dumb matcher" than in rote–learning because of this effect.

3.6.4. Discussion of the Quality of the Solutions

Turning to the quality of the solutions found by LT, the proofs discovered by the rote–learning LT are always at least as short as the proofs discovered by the non–learning LT. This is a consequence of the fact that the rote–learning LT needs only to reduce a problem to a previously seen problem, whereas the non–learning LT has to reduce it to one of the original axioms.

---

[7] The resulting subproblem is, by definition, an explicit implication, but it may ground in (match with) a known theorem that is not an implication.

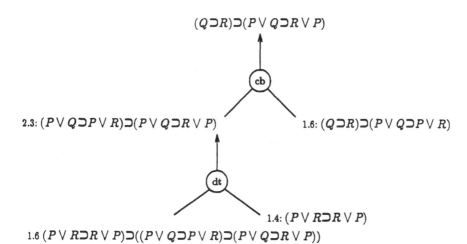

Figure 7–33: Rote–Learning and EBL Proof of *Principia*–2.36

The rote and EBL proofs are of comparable quality, the same proofs being found in most cases. Sometimes (viz *Principia*–2.49, *Principia*–2.56, and *Principia*–2.8) EBL produces shorter proofs. However, in other cases (namely, *Principia*–2.68, *Principia*–3.24, and *Principia*–3.41) the rote proofs are shorter. We shall see that this is due to the IMPLIES restriction. Once again, with a "dumb" matcher, EBL can actually hurt performance as much or more than it improves it.

3.7. Limited Search Without the IMPLIES Restrictions

In this subsection, we examine some effects of lifting the IMPLIES restrictions.

3.7.1. Results on Search and Quality of Solutions

Turning to solved problems, Figure 7–34 shows the search behavior of rote versus EBL. There are no isolated circles, but three isolated boxes indicate that EBL solves everything that rote solves and more. Furthermore, EBL does less search than rote on every problem now, as measured by problems generated, subproblems attempted, and by average branching factors. The exceptions observed in the initial experiments no longer occur once the IMPLIES restrictions are lifted.

Figure 7–35 shows the quality of the solutions provided by RL versus EBL. Note that RL no longer gets superior solutions, once the

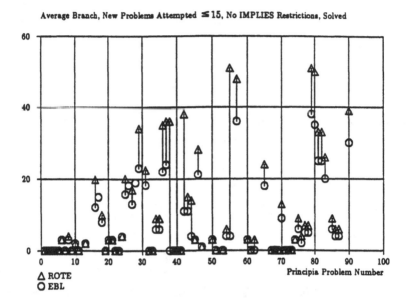

Average Branch, New Problems Attempted ≦ 15, No IMPLIES Restrictions, Solved

△ ROTE
○ EBL

Figure 7–34: RL versus EBL Without the IMPLIES Restrictions

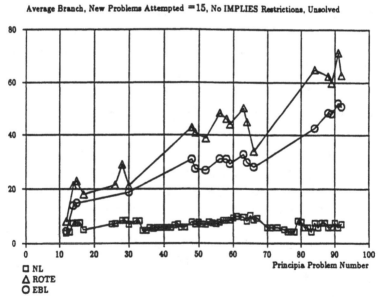

Average Branch, New Problems Attempted ═ 15, No IMPLIES Restrictions, Unsolved

☐ NL
△ ROTE
○ EBL

Figure 7–35: Search Behavior Without the IMPLIES Restrictions

IMPLIES restrictions are lifted.

3.7.2. Discussion on the Effects of Lifting the IMPLIES Restrictions

Lifting the IMPLIES restrictions tends to increase branching factors, as reflected in the numbers of problems generated in limited attempts on the unsolved problems. However, this is offset by the fact that the new subproblems generated sometimes lead to early proofs. This sometimes makes the difference, in limited search, between solving or not solving a problem. In other cases it means that a shorter proof is found.

Since problems must be reduced to the initial axioms when learning is disallowed, changes in behavior noted in the non–learning system are due solely to the fact that chaining is allowed to work on subproblems that are no longer required to be implications (the initial axioms are always implications). In rote learning, changes are due to both types of IMPLIES restrictions, but the effect of the requirement that known theorems be implications is muted by the fact that almost all of the *Principia* problems are implications. Thus, once they are learned, they can be

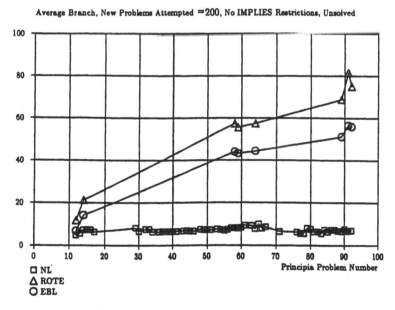

Figure 7–36: Search Behavior on Unsolved Problems in Extended Search

used even under the IMPLIES restrictions. In the EBL system, however, lifting the IMPLIES restrictions leads to much more pronounced changes in performance, because many of the theorems learned are not implications.

EBL does significantly more search than rote in some cases due to the fact that the IMPLIES–restricted LT fails to put the results of explanation–based learning to full use. LT only uses the chaining schema to solve problems when they have the form of implications. In addition, it only uses known implications in chaining, in order to transform problems into new subproblems. These restrictions effectively prevent the EBL LT from finding some legitimate proofs by preventing LT from using some of the theorems learned by EBL.[8] Thus, in the remaining experiments discussed in this chapter, the IMPLIES restrictions are lifted.

3.8. Extended Search Experiments

What happens when the search limits are relaxed? In this subsection, we abandon the implies restrictions and loosen the limits on search. Instead of only attempting the first 15 subproblems, we now allow 200 subproblems to be attempted.

3.8.1. Search Performance

Figure 7–36 shows the search behavior of NL, RL, and EBL on the problems they fail to solve. With extended search, the learning methods each fail to solve only 8 out of 92 problems. As in limited search, NL solves far fewer problems than the learning methods. The branching factor observed in NL seems to be roughly constant and much lower than the sharply increasing branching factors of the learning systems. Again, EBL's branching factors are uniformly below those of RL. With extended search, there is no difference in the number of problems solved by the learning systems, but RL does more search as indicated by subproblems generated and attempted, and faces higher branching factors in all cases as shown in Figure 7–37.

3.8.2. Quality of Learning

A comparison of the quality of the results learned by RL versus those learned by EBL is shown in Table 7–5. Note that EBL was not attempted in many cases, specifically when the original problem was an

---

[8] Some of the theorems learned by EBL are disjunctions more general than implications; they can be specialized to implications.

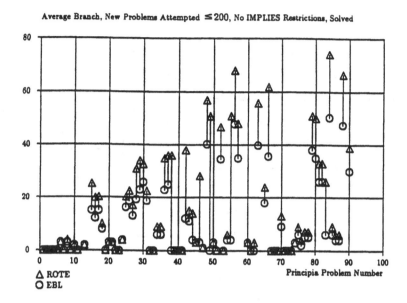

Figure 7–37: Rote versus EBL on Solved Problems in Extended Search

instance of a known theorem and when no proof was found. The following is a discussion of the theorems learned by EBL versus rote–learning in
the remaining cases.

A priori, one can see that when EBL works at all, it provides
theorems that are at least as general as the original problems. *The original problems are always instances of the generalized conclusions of their
proofs.*

From the experiment, one sees that although many theorems (25 of
57, or about 44%) learned via EBL were no more general than the given
problems, in many cases (32 of 57, about 56%) the theorem added by
EBL was strictly more general than the theorem added by rote–learning.

How are the results of EBL more general? In many cases (e.g.,
Principia–2.06) EBL produced a variant of the original problem, minus
an extraneous negation. The EBL version of LT acquires the theorem
$P \vee Q \vee (Q \supset R \vee (P \vee R))$ from the solution of *Principia*–2.06. The problem, $(p \supset q) \supset ((q \supset r) \supset (p \supset r))$, is an instance of this theorem with Q
bound to q, R bound to r, and P bound to $\bar{p}$. (This is the meaning of the
difference substitution in the theta column of Table 7–5.) The rote–

learning LT demands a negation that is not required by the proof.

Table 5: Comparison of Theorems Learned by EBL versus Rote

Problem	EBL vs ROTE	Theorem Learned by EBL	θ
2.06	>	$P \vee Q \vee (\overline{Q} \vee \overline{R} \vee (P \vee R))$	$\{P/\overline{p}, Q/q, R/r\}$
2.08	=	$P \supset P$	
2.11	=	$P \vee P$	
2.14	=	$\overline{P} \supset P$	
2.16	>	$P \vee Q \supset \overline{Q} \vee P$	$\{P/\overline{p}, Q/q\}$
2.17	>	$\overline{P} \vee Q \supset Q \vee P$	$\{P/p, Q/\overline{q}\}$
2.18	=	$(\overline{P} \supset P) \supset P$	
2.2	=	$P \supset P \vee Q$	
2.24	>	$P \vee (\overline{P} \vee Q)$	$\{P/\overline{p}, Q/q\}$
2.25	=	$P \vee (P \vee Q \supset Q)$	
2.3	=	$P \vee (Q \vee R) \supset P \vee (R \vee Q)$	
2.31	=	$P \vee (Q \vee R) \supset (P \vee Q) \vee R$	
2.32	=	$(P \vee Q) \vee R \supset P \vee (Q \vee R)$	
2.36	=	$(P \supset Q) \supset (R \vee P \supset Q \vee R)$	
2.37	=	$(P \supset Q) \supset (P \vee R \supset R \vee Q)$	
2.38	=	$(P \supset Q) \supset (P \vee R \supset Q \vee R)$	
2.4	=	$P \vee (P \vee Q) \supset P \vee Q$	
2.41	=	$P \vee (Q \vee P) \supset Q \vee P$	
2.45	=	$\overline{P \vee Q} \supset P$	
2.46	=	$\overline{P \vee Q} \supset \overline{Q}$	
2.47	>	$\overline{P \vee Q} \supset P \vee R$	$\{P/p, Q/q, R/q\}$
2.48	>	$\overline{P \vee Q} \supset R \vee \overline{Q}$	$\{P/p, Q/q, R/p\}$
2.521	>	$\overline{P \vee Q} \vee (\overline{Q} \vee R)$	$\{P/\overline{p}, Q/q, R/p\}$
2.53	=	$P \vee Q \supset (\overline{P} \supset Q)$	
2.54	=	$(\overline{P} \supset Q) \supset P \vee Q$	
2.55	=	$\overline{P} \supset (P \vee Q \supset Q)$	
2.56	=	$\overline{P} \supset (Q \vee P \supset Q)$	
2.6	>	$P \vee (\overline{Q} \vee (R \vee Q))$	$\{P/\overline{p}, Q/q, R/\overline{p} \vee q\}$
2.61	>	$P \vee Q \supset \overline{P} \vee \overline{Q} \vee Q$	$\{P/\overline{p}, Q/q\}$
2.621	=	$(P \supset Q) \supset (P \vee Q \supset Q)$	

Table 5 Continued

Problem	EBL vs ROTE	Theorem Learned by EBL	θ
2.64	=	$P \lor Q \supset (P \lor \overline{Q} \supset P)$	
2.67	>	$\overline{P \lor Q} \lor R \lor (\overline{P} \lor R)$	$\{P/p, Q/q, R/q\}$
2.68	>	$\overline{P} \lor Q \lor R \lor (P \lor R)$	$\{P/p, Q/q, R/q\}$
2.69	>	$\overline{P} \lor Q \lor R \supset \overline{R} \lor \overline{P} \lor P$	$\{P/p, Q/q, R/q\}$
2.73	=	$(P \supset Q) \supset ((P \lor Q) \lor R \supset Q \lor R)$	
2.76	=	$P \lor (Q \supset R) \supset (P \lor Q \supset P \lor R)$	
2.81	=	$(P \supset (Q \supset R)) \supset (S \lor P \supset (S \lor Q \supset S \lor R))$	
2.83	>	$\overline{P} \lor (\overline{Q \lor R}) \lor (\overline{P \lor (R \lor S)}) \lor (P \lor (Q \lor S)))$	$\{P/\overline{p}, Q/\overline{q}, R/r, S/s\}$
2.85	>	$\overline{P \lor Q} \lor (R \lor S) \supset R \lor (\overline{Q} \lor S)$	$\{P/p, Q/q, R/p, S/r\}$
3.12	>	$P \lor (Q \lor \overline{P \lor Q})$	$\{P/\overline{p}, Q/\overline{q}\}$
3.21	>	$P \lor (Q \lor \overline{Q \lor P})$	$\{P/\overline{p}, Q/\overline{q}\}$
3.22	>	$\overline{P \lor Q} \lor \overline{Q} \lor P$	$\{P/\overline{p}, Q/\overline{q}\}$
3.24	>	$\overline{P} \lor P$	$\{P/\overline{p}\}$
3.26	>	$\overline{P \lor Q} \lor P$	$\{P/p, Q/q\}$
3.27	>	$\overline{P \lor Q} \lor Q$	$\{P/\overline{p}, Q/q\}$
3.3	>	$\overline{P \lor Q} \lor R \supset P \lor (Q \lor R)$	$\{P/\overline{p}, Q/\overline{q}, R/r\}$
3.31	>	$P \lor (Q \lor R) \supset \overline{P \lor Q} \lor R$	$\{P/\overline{p}, Q/\overline{q}, R/r\}$
3.33	>	$\overline{P \lor Q} \lor \overline{Q} \lor R \lor (P \lor R)$	$\{P/\overline{p}, Q/q, R/r\}$
3.34	>	$\overline{P \lor Q \lor \overline{R} \lor P} \lor (R \lor Q)$	$\{P/p, Q/q, R/\overline{r}\}$
3.35	>	$\overline{P \lor P \lor Q} \lor Q$	$\{P/\overline{p}, Q/q\}$
3.37	>	$\overline{P \lor Q} \lor R \supset P \lor \overline{R} \lor Q$	$\{P/\overline{p}, Q/\overline{q}, R/r\}$
3.4	>	$\overline{P \lor Q} \lor (R \lor Q)$	$\{P/\overline{p}, Q/q, R/\overline{p}\}$
3.41	>	$\overline{P \lor Q} \lor (\overline{P} \lor R \lor Q)$	$\{P/p, Q/q, R/\overline{r}\}$
3.42	>	$\overline{P \lor Q} \lor (\overline{R \lor P} \lor Q)$	$\{P/p, Q/q, R/\overline{r}\}$
3.43	>	$\overline{P \lor Q \lor P \lor R} \lor (P \lor \overline{Q} \lor R)$	$\{P/\overline{p}, Q/q, R/r\}$
3.45	>	$P \lor Q \supset \overline{P \lor R} \lor \overline{Q} \lor R$	$\{P/\overline{p}, Q/q, R/\overline{r}\}$

The EBL version of LT offers only modest improvements over rote–learning in such examples because it is well known that one can reverse the sign of a literal everywhere in a theorem to get a new theorem. One could easily modify the rote–learning LT to take advantage of the fact that whenever a literal appears only negatively in a *Principia* problem, one can safely delete the negative sign to obtain a logically equivalent but syntactically more general problem.

In a number of cases, however, there is no such simple fix that the rote–learning LT could use to obtain theorems as general as those acquired by the EBL version. For example, in a number of cases, rote–learning unnecessarily collapses two or more variables into one. Problem

36, *Principia*–2.47, is $\overline{p \vee q} \supset (p \supset q)$. The EBL version of LT acquires $P \vee Q \supset (P \vee R)$ from the proof. The problem is obtained as an instance by substituting p for P and by binding both Q and R to q.

In other cases rote–learning results in more interesting overspecializations. In these examples, variables are not simply collapsed by rote–learning but are required to be related logically in complicated ways when they really should be completely independent.

In Problem 42, one variable is made to be the negation of another when they should be independent and neither need be a negation. The problem (*Principia*–2.521) is $p \supset q \supset (q \supset p)$, the generalized conclusion of the proof is $P \vee Q \vee (\overline{Q} \vee R)$. These match with bindings of P to $\overline{p}$, Q to q, and R to p.

In Problem 47, three independent variables are specialized by effectively making one into a negation of an implication between the others and by requiring one to be a double negative. The problem (*Principia*–2.6) is $\overline{p} \supset (q \supset ((p \supset q) \supset q))$ and the generalized conclusion of the proof is $P \vee (Q \supset (R \vee \underline{Q}))$. These match with P bound to $\overline{\overline{p}}$, Q bound to q, and R bound to $p \supset q$.

With LT's IMPLIES restrictions loosened, the improved generality afforded by EBL leads to performance that is superior to that of the rote–learning version of LT.[9] Sometimes the EBL system solves problems that could not be solved by the rote system due to limits on search. Sometimes both RL and EBL solve the problem, but the EBL solution is found earlier in the search. In some of these cases, the EBL solution is of higher quality in that it is simpler than the solution provided by RL. The quality of solutions found by the learning systems in extended search is not discussed in this subsection. Instead, this comparison will take place in the next subsection, in the context of a comparison between EBL and a version of rote learning that produces the same solutions as the present rote–learning system using a more efficient search.

8.9. On the Effects of Adding Instances in–Rote Learning

In discussing future work, O'Rorke [24] stated that it would be interesting to factor out the sources of the improved performance of the EBL version of LT. The improved generality of learned solutions helps, as does the fact that the EBL system does not add instances of known

---

[9] For examples of how EBL improves performance, see the appendix to this chapter.

theorems. In this subsection, we report on an experiment that isolates these sources of improvement by allowing the rote–learning LT to avoid adding problems that are instances of known theorems.

Figure 7–38 shows the search behavior of RL without adding instances on unsolved problems superimposed on that of the systems previously studied. Figure 7–39 illustrates the search performance of the improved RL system versus EBL on solved problems. The differences in numbers of problems attempted are very similar to differences shown between the number of subproblems generated.

The results on search behavior indicate that adding instances accounts for much of the decrease in branching factors that occurs in going from the original rote to EBL. Although EBL does uniformly less search than the original RL system on both solved and unsolved problems, it tends to do slightly more search than the improved RL method. This is always the case on the unsolved problems and often the case in solved problems as well. However, exceptions in the solved problems occur when EBL pays off by enabling the problem solver to hit upon a solution earlier in the search. As a result, EBL generates 2,791 fewer subproblems than the improved RL method and attempts 84 fewer problems

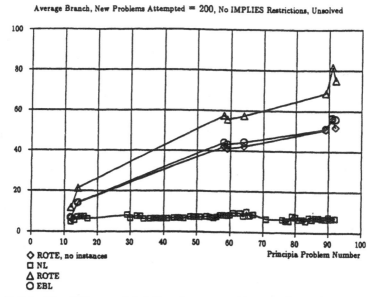

Figure 7–38: The Effects of Adding Instances During Rote–Learning

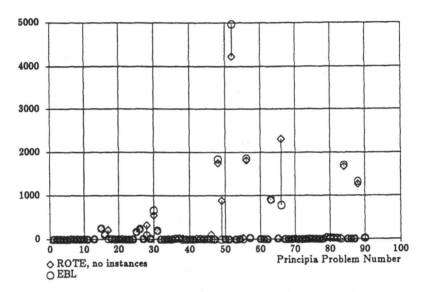

Figure 7–39: Subgoals Generated by Improved Rote versus EBL on Solved
Problems

overall on the problems solved by both methods.

RL should never produce shorter proofs than EBL since the
theorems learned by EBL are always at least as general as those learned
by RL. Figure 7–40 shows that some of the proofs discovered by EBL are
shorter than those provided by the improved RL system. The bottom
line seems to be that, for a small increase in search on most problems, one
can buy large decreases in search and improved solutions on some problems by using EBL rather than the improved rote–learning procedure.

3.10. Conclusions

This chapter discussed an experimental study of explanation–based
learning (EBL), using a significant number of examples. The examples
were uncontrived in the sense that the problem set used in this experiment was designed for entirely different purposes roughly a half–century
ago — long before electronic computers existed and with no consideration
of machine learning experiments in mind. Nevertheless, the experimental
results presented here provide support for some claims about machine
learning. For example, the experiments show that both EBL and rote–
learning are much better than no learning at all on the *Principia* problems.

Average Branch, New Problems Attempted ≤ 200, No IMPLIES Restrictions, Solved

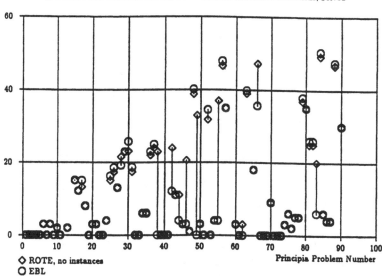

◇ ROTE, no instances
○ EBL

Figure 7–40: Quality of Solutions Provided by (Improved) Rote versus EBL

The experiments focused on the difference between EBL and rote–learning in an abstract, purely logical setting, using very general problems, where neither learning method is allowed an advantage in "turning constants to variables." Before these experiments were done, it was hypothesized that generalization and performance would not improve in going from rote to EBL on purely logical problems because neither learning system is allowed to make inductive leaps from concrete propositions such as "it is raining" or "today is Monday." It seems harder for EBL to "win big" on the *Principia* problems because any improvements of EBL over rote–learning are forced to occur at a very high level of abstraction. Indeed, the experiments can be interpreted as supporting this hypothesis, because rote–learning is "roughly comparable" to EBL on the *Principia* problems in the sense that the difference between the learning systems is small when compared with the large differences between non–learning and learning.

Ignoring non–learning, however, the experimental data focusing on the differences between the learning systems clearly show that EBL is significantly more effective than rote–learning even in highly abstract settings. The experiments show that even in this context EBL learns strictly more general results quite frequently and that — *provided the matcher is* "*smart*" *enough* — EBL's superior generalization contributes to superior problem–solving performance.

The caveat that the matcher should be "smart" is critical. The experiments reported here include all problems from Chapter 3 of *Principia*, thus going beyond the 52 problems from Chapter 2 used in Newell, Shaw, and Simon's work and our early work reported in [24]. We were surprised to find that, in a reversal of our earlier results, EBL's overall performance was actually worse than rote in some experiments involving the new problems. The explanation proved to be that, although the matcher supplied to our version of LT was capable of decoding $P \supset Q$ using its definition in terms of $\bar{P} \vee Q$, it was short–circuited by LT's "IMPLIES restrictions." These restrictions forced problems and known theorems to have IMPLIES as the main connective, rendering unusable some of the generalizations of problems learned by EBL. Thus it was found that LT's IMPLIES restrictions can cause EBL to be *less effective* than rote–learning. This is an instance of a more general observation, that it is important not to restrict matching unnecessarily in EBL.

When one considers the goals of the designers of a logical system such as the one found in *Principia Mathematica*, it may seem surprising that the EBL LT (with the IMPLIES restrictions removed) performs significantly better than rote–learning on the *Principia* problems. Surely, the authors of *Principia* must have intended each problem to be as general as possible. Imagine Whitehead and Russell creating their sequence of theorems. Assume they have proposed a certain problem as the next theorem in the sequence. If they found a proof for this problem that actually proved a more general theorem than the problem they began with, they should have crossed out the proposed theorem, replacing it with the more general one. With this in mind, one can view the superior generalizations produced by the EBL version of LT as suggesting improvements on the logical system of *Principia Mathematica*.

8.11. Relation to Previous Work

This chapter is part of the growing body of work on explanation-based learning. Other work [10, 11, 14] provides overviews and pointers into the EBL literature. It should be noted that the way explanation-based generalization contributes to future problem solving in the present study is a bit nonstandard. In contrast to standard EBG macro–learning methods (see, e.g., [41]), only generalized conclusions are learned in the EBL LT. The leaves of the "generalized" proof tree are thrown away; they are not needed because they are (always true) theorems.

Disregarding these details, the present chapter is basically an experimental study of EBL versus no–learning and rote–learning in a particular "domain," a logic where rote–learning was expected to do well because of the generality of the problems. Other experimental studies of EBL involving relatively large numbers of examples have been done recently in a number of other task domains, including planning [42]. Mooney's Ph.D. thesis [43] reports on experiments with a general EBL system solving examples from a number of task domains such as planning, recognition, and so on. Shavlik's Ph.D. thesis [18] contains the results of a number of experiments on planning and physical reasoning tasks, and Segre's Ph.D. thesis [44] contains experimental work on applications of EBL in robotics.

This work is also related to work on macro–operators and can be viewed as a step toward viewing theorem proving as a process that can benefit from the acquisition of macro–operators (as suggested, for example, by Korf [45]).

Another way to view the work presented here is as evidence bearing on the relative value of methods for generalizing examples by turning constants into variables versus EBL methods of generalizing examples by specializing existing general knowledge. Thus, this work may be viewed as providing experimental evidence that conversions such as the one described in Rosenbloom and Laird [46] should lead to improved performance.

3.12. Future Work

More experiments should be done involving complete explanation-based learning systems and large numbers of examples. Several possible extensions to the experiments reported here suggest themselves. For example, we have recently completed new experiments involving reversals and random permutations of the problem sets, in an effort to determine how changes in the order of the *Principia* problems affect the learning methods. In another experiment, we have disallowed learning of unsolved problems in order to address concerns that this strategy, while perhaps appropriate for highly structured learning situations, is not appropriate in general. The results of these experiments will be presented in a follow–on paper.

It would be interesting to see how much of the improvement in going from non–learning to rote–learning and EBL is due to the limited control structure of LT requiring that proofs be linear. How much of the improvement is due to macro–learning? It might also be interesting to augmenting the simple EBL version of LT with subgoal learning. This could yield results on how much improvement occurs in between trial learning. The original LT would have to be modified to produce non–linear proof trees in order to get results on the effectiveness of within trial learning.

The results on the *Principia* problems presented in this chapter are part of an effort to provide a baseline characterization of the performance of learning methods such as rote and basic EBL on these problems. It is hoped that this will make it possible to use the *Principia* problems as a benchmark for testing improved EBL methods, just as problems like the eight puzzles have been considered the *Drosophila* or fruit fly of research on search in AI [47].

If one looks at the theorems learned by EBL in the present study, it is obvious that they could stand some improvement. Many of these theorems are still less general than they could be (e.g., some contain double negations). It would be interesting to see how performance changes when basic EBL is augmented by a system designed to transform learned expressions into their most general form.

Finally, the present domain seems like an ideal candidate for studies on search utility measures and their uses in improving learning. It would be interesting to see whether Minton's results on search utility in planning [42] can be replicated in the purely logical domain of *Principia*. This domain should also serve as a useful testbed for experiments with different strategies for organizing learned results.

Acknowledgments

Some of the results presented here were originally published in the *Proceedings of the Fourth International Workshop on Machine Learning* [24]. The research presented here grew out of a discussion with Pat Langley at the Cognitive Science Conference held at the University of California, Irvine, in the summer of 1985. Early work was carried out by the author when he was a member of Gerald DeJong's Explanation–Based Learning Research Group at the University of Illinois at Champaign–Urbana. Special thanks to Gerald DeJong and Scott Bennett at Illinois, to Ray Mooney (now at the University of Texas at Austin), and also to Pat Langley, Tony Wieser, and Heping He at Irvine. Wieser provided a great deal of research assistance to the author, including reimplementation of the author's LISP systems in PROLOG, as well as having discovered that the IMPLIES restriction forced the EBL LT's performance to deteriorate in the extended experiments first reported here. Heping He provided programming support and assisted in the analysis and presentation of the data. This research was supported in part by the National Science Foundation under grant NSF IST 83–17889, by a Cognitive Science/AI Fellowship from the University of Illinois, and by a McDonnell–Douglas University External Relations award to UCI.

Appendix: Examples of Improvements in Performance Due to EBL

The superior generality of EBL contributes to superior problem–solving performance in two main ways. Sometimes it enables the problem solver to solve problems that could not be solved before. Alternatively, when both rote–learning and EBL systems solve a problem, the EBL solution is sometimes found more quickly and is sometimes simpler than that provided by rote–learning.

For an example of an EBL system solving more problems as a result of improved generality, note that the EBL version of LT found a proof for Problem 17 (*Principia*–2.18), while the rote–learning version failed to find a proof in small search (with the subproblems attempted limited to 15). The proof found by EBL involves the theorem learned from Problem 16 (*Principia*–2.18). It was obtained by chaining forward on the learned theorem and axiom *Principia*–1.2 (see Figure 7–41). The generalized conclusion of this proof of *Principia*–2.18 is $(A \supset A) \supset A$. The proof is not constructed by rote–learning because of the extraneous NOT in *Principia*–2.17.

Chaining forward on the result of rote–learning on *Principia*–2.17 yields the less general conclusion $(A \supset \overline{A}) \supset A$ (Figure 7–42). *Principia*–2.18 $(P \supset P) \supset P$ is not an instance of this conclusion.

Concrete examples of EBL constructing simpler solutions as a result of improved generality also occurred in the experiments (see Figure 7–43). While both learning versions of LT solve Problem 38 (*Principia*–2.49), the EBL version recognizes it as an instance of the class of problems solved by a previous solution, and the rote–learning version has to regenerate that

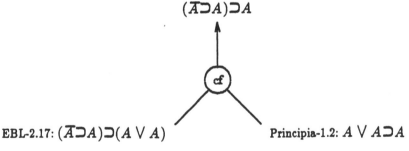

$$(\overline{A} \supset A) \supset A$$

EBL-2.17: $(\overline{A} \supset A) \supset (A \lor A)$ Principia-1.2: $A \lor A \supset A$

Figure 7–41: The Proof of *Principia*–2.18

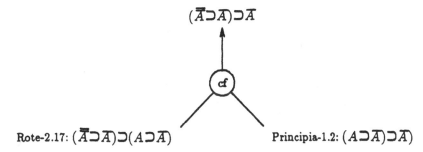

Figure 7–42: Inferiority of Rote–Learning on *Principia*–2.18

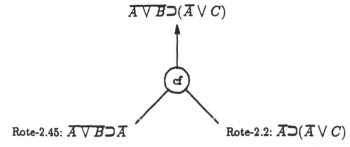

Figure 7–43: Rote–Learning Proof of *Principia*–2.47 and 2.49

solution. The problem is $\overline{P \vee Q} \supset (\overline{P} \vee \overline{Q})$, an instance of the generalized conclusion_ of the proof of Problem 36 (*Principia*–2.47), namely $A \vee B \supset (A \vee D)$. This proof is not constructed during rote–learning because *Principia*–2.47 identifies B and D, but Q and $\overline{Q}$ are incompatible. It turns out that to prove *Principia*–2.49, the rote–learning LT winds up having to prove the theorem that the explanation–based learning LT extracted from *Principia*–2.47. That is, it regenerates the same proof that it used before on *Principia*–2.47 because it failed to learn all it could from this proof. This is a clear case of rote–learning losing because it simply stores problems instead of generalizing and computing the class of problems that a novel solution solves.

References

1. S. Minton, "Selectively Generalizing Plans for Problem–Solving," *Proceedings of the Ninth International Joint Conference on Artificial Intelligence*, Los Angeles, August 1985, pp. 596–599.

2. M. Tambe and A. Newell, "Some Chunks are Expensive," *Proceedings of the 1988 International Machine Learning Conference*, Ann Arbor, June 1988, pp. 451–458.

3. A. Newell and A. H. A. Simon, "The Logic Theorist: An Example ," in *Human Problem Solving* , Prentice–Hall, Inc. , Englewood Cliffs, New Jersey , 1972, pp. 105–140 .

4. A. N. Whitehead and B. Russell, *Principia Mathematica*, Cambridge University Press, Cambridge, England, 1913.

5. J. W. Shavlik and G. F. DeJong, "BAGGER: An EBL System that Extends and Generalizes Explanations," *Proceedings of the National Conference on Artificial Intelligence*, Seattle, WA, July 1987, pp. 516–520.

6. J. W. Shavlik, *Extending Explanation–Based Learning by Generalizing the Structure of Explanations*, Pitman, London, 1990.

7. A. M. Segre, "On the Operationality/Generality Trade–off in Explanation–Based Learning," *Proceedings of the Tenth International Joint Conference on Artificial Intelligence*, Milan, Italy, August 1987, pp. 242–248.

8. J. W. Shavlik, G. F. DeJong and B. H. Ross, "Acquiring Special Case Schemata in Explanation–Based Learning," *Proceedings of the Ninth Annual Conference of the Cognitive Science Society*, Seattle, WA, July 1987, pp. 851–860.

9. R. M. Keller, "Defining Operationality for Explanation–Based Learning," *Proceedings of the National Conference on Artificial Intelligence*, Seattle, WA, July 1987, pp. 482–487.

10. G. F. DeJong and R. J. Mooney, "Explanation–Based Learning: An Alternative View," *Machine Learning 1*, 2 (1986), pp. 145–176.

11. T. M. Mitchell, R. Keller and S. Kedar–Cabelli, "Explanation–Based Generalization: A Unifying View," *Machine Learning 1*, 1 (January 1986), pp. 47–80.

12. R. Keller, "Operationality and Generality in Explanation–Based Learning: Separate Dimensions or Opposite Endpoints?,"

Proceedings of the AAAI Symposium on Explanation-Based Learning, Stanford, CA, March 1988, pp. 153–157.

13. T. M. Mitchell, S. Mahadevan and L. I. Steinberg, "LEAP: A Learning Apprentice for VLSI Design," *Proceedings of the Ninth International Joint Conference on Artificial Intelligence*, Los Angeles, CA, August 1985, pp. 573–580.

14. R. J. Mooney and S. W. Bennett, "A Domain Independent Explanation-Based Generalizer," *Proceedings of the National Conference on Artificial Intelligence*, Philadelphia, PA, August 1986, pp. 551–555.

15. W. F. Clocksin and C. S. Mellish, *Programming in Prolog*, Springer Verlag, Berlin, 1984.

16. W. H. Press, B. P. Flannery, S. A. Teukolsky and W. T. Vetterling, *Numerical Recipes: The Art of Scientific Computing*, Cambridge University Press, Cambridge, England, 1986.

17. E. Charniak, C. Riesbeck and D. McDermott, *Artificial Intelligence Programming*, Lawrence Erlbaum and Associates, Hillsdale, NJ, 1980.

18. J. W. Shavlik, "Generalizing the Structure of Explanations in Explanation-Based Learning ," Ph.D. Thesis, Department of Computer Science, University of Illinois, Urbana, IL, January 1988.

19. D. Benanav, D. Kapur and P. Narendran, "Complexity of Matching Problems," *Proceedings of the First International Conference on Rewriting Techniques and Applications*, Dijon, France, May 1985.

20. R. J. Mooney, "A General Explanation-Based Learning Mechanism and its Application to Narrative Understanding," Ph.D. Thesis, Department of Computer Science, University of Illinois, Urbana, IL, January 1988.

21. D. J. Mostow, "Machine Transformation of Advice into a Heuristic Search Procedure," in *Machine Learning: An Artificial Intelligence Approach*, R. S. Michalski, J. G. Carbonell, T. M. Mitchell (ed.), Tioga Publishing Company, Palo Alto, CA, 1983, pp. 367–404.

22. R. E. Korf, "Depth-First Iterative-Deepening: An Optimal Admissible Tree Search," *Artificial Intelligence 27*, 1 (1985), pp. 97–109.

23. R. E. Fikes, P. E. Hart and N. J. Nilsson, "Learning and Executing Generalized Robot Plans," *Artificial Intelligence 3*, (1972), pp. 251–

288.

24. P. V. O'Rorke, "LT Revisited: Experimental Results of Applying Explanation–Based Learning to the Logic of Principia Mathematica," *Proceedings of the Fourth International Workshop on Machine Learning*, University of California, Irvine, June 1987, pp. 148–159.

25. A. E. Prieditis and J. Mostow, "PROLEARN: Towards a Prolog Interpreter that Learns," *Proceedings of the National Conference on Artificial Intelligence*, Seattle, WA, July 1987, pp. 494–498.

26. D. Steier, "CYPRESS–Soar: A Case Study in Search and Learning in Algorithm Design," *Proceedings of the Tenth International Joint Conference on Artificial Intelligence*, Milan, Italy, August 1987, pp. 327–330.

27. R. E. Fikes, P. E. Hart and N. J. Nilsson, "Learning and Executing Generalized Robot Plans," *Artificial Intelligence 3*, 4 (1972), pp. 251–288.

28. G. A. Iba, "Learning by Discovering Macros in Puzzle Solving," *Proceedings of the Ninth International Joint Conference on Artificial Intelligence*, Los Angeles, CA, August 1985, pp. 640–642.

29. R. C. Schank and R. P. Abelson, *Scripts, Plans, Goals and Understanding: An Inquiry into Human Knowledge Structures*, Lawrence Erlbaum and Associates, Hillsdale, NJ, 1977.

30. R. J. Mooney and G. F. DeJong, "Learning Schemata for Natural Language Processing," *Proceedings of the Ninth International Joint Conference on Artificial Intelligence*, Los Angeles, CA, August 1985, pp. 681–687.

31. G. F. DeJong, "Acquiring Schemata through Understanding and Generalizing Plans," *Proceedings of the Eighth International Joint Conference on Artificial Intelligence*, Karlsruhe, West Germany, August 1983, pp. 462–464.

32. L. G. Valiant, "A Theory of the Learnable," *Communications of the Association for Computing Machinery 27*, 11 (November 1984), pp. 1134–1142.

33. M. Kearns, M. Li, L. Pitt and L. G. Valiant, "Recent Results on Boolean Concept Learning," *Proceedings of the Fourth International Workshop on Machine Learning*, University of California, Irvine, June 1987, pp. 337–352.

34. D. Haussler, "Learning Conjunctive Concepts in Structural Domains," *Proceedings of the National Conference on Artificial Intelligence*, Seattle, WA, , pp. 466–470.

35. B. Natarajan, "Learning Functions from Examples," Technical Report CMU–TR–87–19, Department of Computer Science, Carnegie–Mellon University, Pittsburgh, PA, 1987.

36. S. Mahadevan and P. Tadepalli, "On the Tractability of Learning from Incomplete Theories," Working Paper 71, Department of Computer Science, Rutgers University, New Brunswick, NJ, October 1987.

37. P. V. O'Rorke, "Explanation–Based Learning Via Constraint Posting and Propagation," Ph.D. Thesis, Department of Computer Science, University of Illinois, Urbana, IL, January 1987.

38. D. W. Loveland, "Automated Theorem Proving: A Quarter–Century Review ," in *Proceedings of the Special Session on Automatic Theorem Proving at the American Math. Soc. Annual Meeting* , 1 (ed.), Denver, Colorado, January 1983.

39. H. B. Enderton, *A Mathematical Introduction to Logic* , Academic Press, Inc. , New York , 1972.

40. E. Stefferud, "The Logic Theory Machine: A Model Heuristic Program ," Memorandum RM–3731–CC , The Rand Corporation , Santa Monica, CA , June, 1963.

41. S. T. Kedar–Cabelli and L. T. McCarty, "Explanation–Based Generalization as Resolution Theorem Proving," *Proceedings of the Fourth International Workshop on Machine Learning*, University of California, Irvine, June 1987, pp. 383–389.

42. S. Minton, "Quantitative Results Concerning the Utility of Explanation–Based Learning ," *Proceedings of the Seventh National Conference on Artificial Intelligence* , Saint Paul, Minnesota , August 1988, pp. 564–569 .

43. R. J. Mooney, "A General Explanation–Based Learning Mechanism and its Application to Narrative Understanding," Ph.D. Thesis, Department of Computer Science, University of Illinois, Urbana, IL, January 1988. (Also appears as UILU–ENG–87–2269, AI Research Group, Coordinated Science Laboratory, University of Illinois at Urbana–Champaign.)

44. A. M. Segre, "Explanation–Based Learning of Generalized Robot Assembly Tasks," Ph.D. Thesis, Department of Electrical and

Computer Engineering, University of Illinois, Urbana, IL, January 1987. (Also appears as UILU–ENG–87–2208, AI Research Group, Coordinated Science Laboratory, University of Illinois at Urbana–Champaign.)

45. R. E. Korf, *Learning to Solve Problems by Searching for Macro-Operators* , Morgan Kaufmann, Palo Alto, CA , 1985.

46. P. S. Rosenbloom and J. E. Laird, "Mapping Explanation–Based Generalization onto SOAR ," *Proceedings of the National Conference on Artificial Intelligence* , Philadelphia, PA , August 1986.

47. R. E. Korf, "Search: A Survey of Recent Results ," in *Exploring Artificial Intelligence: Survey Talks from the National Conferences on Artificial Intelligence* , Howard E. Shrobe (ed.), Morgan Kaufmann, San Mateo, CA , 1988, pp. 197–237 .

Chapter 8

Psychological Studies of Explanation–Based Learning

Woo–Kyoung Ahn and William F. Brewer

1. Introduction

This chapter reviews traditional psychological theories of concept acquisition. Almost all of these theories assume that concepts are learned through the repeated occurrence of similar instances. This broad framework will be referred to as repeated similarity–based learning (RSBL). We contrast these psychological theories with the recent work in artificial intelligence on explanation–based learning (EBL) that makes strong use of the learner's background knowledge. In addition, we report the results from a series of experiments which show that humans carry out EBL of new information when exposed to single instances of material from knowledge–rich domains.

2. Traditional Concept Learning Models in Psychology

Although there is a long tradition in psychology of studying concept formation, few models seem to be able to answer an apparently simple question such as, How do we learn concepts such as MARRIED or BANKRUPT? A close examination of earlier research reveals that some of the models called concept learning models actually do not include a learning component. This section of the chapter will (1) review the assumptions about the representation of concepts and the learning of concepts for each class of models and (2) point out the difficulties with each of these models. Following Smith and Medin's classification, the psychological models are categorized into three basic classes: rule models, probabilistic models, and exemplar models [1]. In addition to the models for concept learning, this section will review the accounts for the acquisition of complex knowledge provided by schema theory and connectionist theory.

2.1. Rule Models

Rule models assume that a concept consists of a set of defining rules. Their main focus was on how defining rules are discovered through experience with multiple examples and what kinds of strategies subjects use to find a rule that is true of all the examples [2–5].

The critical problem for these models is that most natural concepts do not have singly sufficient and jointly necessary defining features [1, 6]. For example, one cannot provide a precise definition of GAME which includes all kinds of games and excludes all nongames. Even concepts which may have sufficient and necessary defining features (e.g., a BACHELOR is "an unmarried man") are probably not learned by observing numerous instances of the concept as was typically the case in the experiments carried out in this tradition. Instead, it is more likely that people learn such concepts by being directly told their definitions.

2.2. Probabilistic Models

Probabilistic models postulate that the representation of a concept is a summary description of its exemplars (often called a prototype). Abstract information about a concept is assumed to be represented not in terms of defining features but in terms of characteristic features, which have a high probability of occurring in instances of concepts but are not logically required. The details of the prototype constructs and its acquisition process vary from model to model. Smith and Medin [1] classified the probabilistic models into three classes depending on their representational assumptions: featural models, dimensional models, and holistic models.

2.2.1. Featural Approach

In featural models, category representation consists of the modal features that occur in instances of the concept. Learning a concept consists of recording frequency information about the features in examples and abstracting the modal features from them. For example, if one has been exposed to three 3–foot trees and one 5–foot tree which belong to the same category, the prototype TREE is 3 feet high. Models which adopt the featural approach are [7] and [8].

2.2.2. Dimensional Approach

The dimensional approach, like the featural approach, assumes that concepts are represented by characteristic features. The difference between the two approaches is that in the dimensional approach, each feature has a value in a continuous dimension and the prototype consists of mean values of its exemplars. The acquisition process consists of simply averaging values in the same dimensions across the entire exemplars. For example, in case of the concept mentioned above, the prototypical TREE would be 3.5 feet high [i.e., $((3 \times 3 \text{ ft}) + (1 \times 5 \text{ ft}))/4$]. This approach was suggested in Reed [9] and in the earlier works of Rosch [10].

One obvious problem with this approach is that prototypes may prove to be nonexisting objects as a result of the averaging process. For example, if you average a chair with four legs and a chair with three legs, the prototype CHAIR will have 3.5 legs.

2.2.3. Holistic Approach

In the holistic approach, a probabilistic concept is represented by a single holistic property such as a template or an image. The basic idea of this approach can be traced back to Galton's "composite photograph" theory [11]. Galton attempted to derive the general concept HUMAN FACE by making a composite photograph from a great number of pictures of different faces. Similarly, in a more recent experiment [12], a prototype dot pattern (corresponding to Galton's composite photograph) was distorted in various ways to generate examples of each prototype. The subjects in these experiments were good at recognizing the prototype, even though they had never seen it before. However, this kind of mechanism is very limited in that it can be applied only to concrete objects with very similar spatial characteristics. It is not clear how it could work for an abstract concept such as TRUTH or object concepts such as FURNITURE.

2.2.4. General Problems with Probabilistic Models

The probabilistic models were developed to deal with evidence demonstrating prototype effects. For example, typical examples of a concept are judged to be members of the concept faster than atypical examples [13], prototypicality determines speed of learning [10], and children learn typical examples before atypical ones [14]. These findings have been interpreted as evidence for the assumption that concept representation is based on central tendency because both the central tendency and typical examples contain features shared by many other members. Although much evidence has been presented to show that concepts behave as though they were prototypes, Rosch noted that the prototype construct is not a model of process, representation, or learning [14]. However, interpretation of prototypical effects as direct reflection of category representation led to the use of prototypical theories as concept formation theories (see [15] for a different interpretation of prototypical effects).

Another problem that applies to the featural and dimensional forms of the probabilistic model is their lack of constraint on what is to count as a feature [16]. Psychologists have tended to avoid the issue of how the learner is able to select the relevant features in concept learning. Since indefinitely large numbers of features and feature combinations can occur in an object or an event, it appears that learners must make use of some form of inductive bias to choose appropriate features for generalization.

Furthermore, Rosch [14] argued that features may not objectively exist in the world but rather vary relative to our knowledge about the world. For example, "some attributes such as 'large' for the object 'piano' seemed to have meaning only in relation to categorization of the object in terms of a superordinate category — piano is large for furniture but small for other kinds of objects such as buildings" (p. 42). Rosch also pointed out that some attributes were functional attributes that required knowledge about other concepts.

In addition, the featural and dimensional models do not seem to consider the underlying structure of features. Simply learning a list of characteristic attributes such as "has feathers, eats worms, has two legs, etc." is not equivalent to understanding the concept BIRD. A simple list of independent features for a concept such as BIRD is not the same as the actual concept because it does not contain information about the relationships between the category features [17].

2.3. Exemplar Models

Exemplar models assume that concepts are represented in the form of a unique memory of its exemplars rather than as abstracted information and that people categorize new exemplars based on the similarity to the old exemplars [18, 19]. Consequently, in these models, a learner simply stores exemplars with information about the categories to which they belong.

The problem with the exemplar models is their lack of elaborated assumptions about encoding and storage of exemplars. Clearly, previous experience and knowledge can affect, for example, at which level of abstraction an example is encoded or which features become salient. Human beings are active interpreters of stimuli rather than passive receivers, so what a learner knows is more than what is physically experienced.

2.4. Schema Theories

A schema is a type of knowledge representation usually used for complex forms of knowledge, such as the knowledge involved in representing complex spatial scenes, sequences of actions, or sequences of events [20, 21]. Schema theorists have not been precise about the mechanisms for learning schemata but have tended to take the RSBL approach.

For example, Schank and Abelson [22] assumed that scripts are acquired through repetition: Events repeated in a second experience are reinforced and become a part of the script, whereas events that do not occur again are variabilized. Rumelhart and Norman outlined three ways of learning and modifying a schema [23]. They stated that schema acquisition is carried out through a process of schema restructuring which is the creation of new schemata through either patterned generation or schema induction. Patterned generation is similar to learning by analogy, whereas schema induction is similar to learning in frequency models in that co–occurring configurations of information give rise to a new schema. Van Dijk and Kintsch proposed that situation models are the specific global representation of narratives constructed when a particular text is understood [24]. They suggested that if a situation model is used frequently, it becomes decontextualized, forming a script.

2.5. Connectionist Models

Recently, a connectionist model of schema acquisition was proposed [25]. For a schema such as ROOM, these researchers assume that there are collections of units which represent objects such as a refrigerator, a television, and so on. Units have connections and interact by sending signals to each other. The strength of transmission between units depends on the weights that have been assigned to the connections between each unit. During learning, if two units tend to co–occur, the weights of the connection between them becomes positive and the relationship between the units is excitatory. On the other hand, if the occurrence of one aspect of a schema inhibits that of another, the weight of the connection between them becomes negative. After experience with multiple examples, the network reaches a stable state which is a schema. According to this model, schemata are not "things" but emerging patterns as a result of the interaction of units constrained by their weighted connections.

The basic learning mechanism of this connectionist model is similar to that in the Hayes–Roth [8] model in that co–occurrence of features is the crucial aspect for learning. Therefore, this model is subject to the same criticism as that model: There is no constraint on what counts as a feature or a weight.

3. General Problems with Traditional Concept Learning Models

All of the models presented earlier seem to face an additional set of problems. First, these models do not consider the interaction between learning mechanisms and types of domains. Second, the models are insufficient because they do not give sufficient weight to the role of learner's knowledge about the domain to which a concept belongs. Third, they do not consider the distinction between explanatory and non-explanatory information. Fourth, they are vulnerable to spurious correlations among examples. Finally it is not clear how these models could represent a concept that contains a universal. Each of these issues will be discussed in more detail.

3.1. Simple Stimuli

Traditional concept formation models have frequently assumed that learning mechanisms operate in the same way regardless of what is to be learned and that laws found in simple situations will enable us to understand complex situations. Thus, the experimenters in this tradition tended to use only simplified experimental materials, such as dot patterns or a list of descriptions of club members. Consequently, subjects had limited opportunity to bring their knowledge into use. With this type of stimuli it appears that the subjects adopt a strategy of looking for matching and mismatching attributes, which is the basic mechanism of RSBL. The use of simplified experimental materials can be seen as a residual of the earlier behaviorist paradigm which focused researchers' attention on superficial and physical attributes. With simple material, often varying only along some physically specifiable dimension, there was little possibility for EBL or learning by analogy to occur. These theories typically did not specify whether RSBL was the only learning mechanism, and they did not specify situations to which the RSBL mechanism should have been applied.

3.2. Background Knowledge

Many experiments have demonstrated the effects of context on concept acquisition caused by various types of background knowledge such as category information, goal, or domain–specific knowledge. Barsalou [26] showed that examples sharing no apparently correlated properties (e.g., children, dog, stereo, and blanket) can be listed as members of a concept (e.g., "things to take from one's home during a fire") because of people's knowledge about the goal of the concept. Roth and Shoben [27] showed that the gradient structure of a concept changes depending on the context in which the concept is used. These studies show the importance of background knowledge in concept formation. However, traditional models have not taken into consideration the obvious fact that people's learning is affected by what they already know.

3.3. Explanatory Versus Nonexplanatory Information

One reason why traditional models have adopted repetition–based models is that they have focused on the nonexplanatory aspects of concepts or schemata. The nonexplanatory aspects of concepts and schemata are the features or the events that occur with no underlying explanatory structure. In human actions, they are often the conventions of society. For example, in an American restaurant schema, the fork is set on the left side of the plate and the salad is served before the main course. The explanatory aspects of concepts or schemata are the features or the events that have an explanatory framework such as physical causality for physical objects and intentional action for human agents. For example, in a restaurant schema the diner might tear open a pink packet and put the contents in his coffee or hand the waiter a plastic card after the meal is over. Each of these actions (using an artificial sweetener or paying for the meal with a credit card) is embedded in a complex explanatory framework. It seems to us that although the nonexplanatory aspects of schemata may be learned by a mechanism based on repetition of similar examples, the explanatory aspects require some more complex form of EBL. Note that in the examples given above, it would be possible to learn the two nonexplanatory aspects of the restaurant schemata by observing many examples of people eating at restaurants, but it is unlikely that mere observation of multiple examples of the explanatory events would lead to the successful acquisition of these aspects of the schemata. We think that if traditional theorists had focused on the explanatory aspects of complex knowledge, they would have been less likely to adopt RSBL theories.

8.4. Spurious Correlations

The traditional models are vulnerable to spurious correlations caused by the co-occurrence of irrelevant aspects of the schema. For example, in a KIDNAPPING schema, if a kidnapper was wearing blue jeans in all instances, "wearing blue jeans" is generalized as a constraint of the schema although it is irrelevant to the goal of the schema [28].

8.5. Universal Constraints

The traditional models cannot explain how a concept containing a universal (e.g., "all birds have feathers") can be learned because these models are based on purely inductive mechanisms. Given 100 examples of birds, all we know for certain is "100 birds have feathers," not "all birds have feathers." Pure induction of instances does not guarantee that the 101st bird will also have feathers. On the other hand, one can impart this type of universal information with a single symbolic instance (e.g., "all birds have feathers"). An interesting issue here that needs additional research is that after a 100 instances people may, in some cases, treat this knowledge as a true universal.

4. Explanation-Based Learning

Recently, a new approach to concept learning has been suggested by researchers in the area of artificial intelligence. This approach, called explanation-based learning, uses domain knowledge to construct explanations that separate relevant features from irrelevant ones [29]. (See the other chapters in this book for more details.) For example, GENESIS [30] analyzes novel plans in a knowledge-rich domain and develops an explanation by causally connecting the instantiations of the lower-level schemata from a schema library of background knowledge. If the achieved goal in the plan is a general one that is likely to be encountered again, the learning process starts by generalizing the explanation. The generalization process changes constants to variables subject to the constraint that the structure of the explanation remains intact. Finally, the system acquires the schema, which consists of a set of variables (slots which can be instantiated differently) and a set of constraints that specify necessary properties of variables and necessary relationships between variables.

The term *EBL* has been used in two different ways. Some researchers have used it to refer to any learning mechanism involving background theories or beliefs [31]. Researchers in AI have tended to use the term in a more restricted fashion and limit it to generalized explanatory structures that separate relevant features from irrelevant ones in specific representations of exemplars [29].

As mentioned earlier, researchers in the psychology of concept formation focused almost exclusively on nonknowledge–based learning mechanisms. Although some psychologists emphasized the role of background knowledge in comprehension [32, 33], they did not develop explicit models of learning. Essentially all of the psychological theories were RSBL theories, and therefore there do not appear to have been any empirical studies investigating the possibility that concepts can be learned in a single trial as is assumed in the EBL systems in AI. We have carried out three experiments to investigate EBL in humans. These experiments show that one example is enough to learn a schema if the example has a causal structure and if people have appropriate background knowledge. The next section summarizes the procedure and results of these experiments, which have been presented elsewhere in more detail [34, 35].

5. Psychological Experiments on EBL

Ahn and colleagues [36] carried out three experiments to test both the psychological validity of EBL and its limitations. This section will summarize the results of those experiments. The three experiments were similar in their overall design but differed in the specific tasks used to test how well the subjects learned the underlying schema.

Our basic goal in these studies was to show that human beings carry out EBL when exposed to single instances of material from knowledge–rich domains. To carry out these experiments, we developed two types of written passages. One set of materials was designed to enable EBL to occur (EBL passages). These texts were examples of complex schemas which were not known to our undergraduate subjects but which made use of their background knowledge. The other set of materials was designed to restrict the possibility of EBL (non–EBL passages). These texts were examples of complex schemas unknown to our subjects and required background knowledge not known to them.

Our basic strategy was to have each subject read a specific passage which described an instance of a complex schema and then assess what kind of knowledge the subject had acquired from reading the passage. We developed a variety of psychological tasks (e.g., asking subjects to generate a new instance of the schema) to give us information about what types of knowledge our subjects had acquired.

We compared the knowledge acquired from reading a single instance of an EBL passage with that acquired from reading a single instance of a non–EBL passage and compared both with the knowledge acquired from reading an abstract passage which overtly described the complex schema.

5.1. Hypotheses

Each experiment had two conditions: an EBL condition and a non–EBL condition. The EBL condition made use of plan schemata in knowledge–rich domains and was used to test whether or not subjects could acquire an abstract schema from a single example. It was predicted that the subjects would be able to acquire a schema from a single example if they had sufficient domain knowledge and if the schema had explanatory constraints. The non–EBL condition was designed to examine schema acquisition with materials for which the subjects did not have the appropriate background knowledge. It was predicted that the subjects would fail to develop an explanatory structure for these instances and consequently would fail to acquire the schemata in this condition.

5.2. Materials

5.2.1. EBL Passages

Three schemata were chosen for this condition: (1) Kyeah, a Korean cooperative system, (2) a schema for forging art, and (3) a schema for a particular con game. The following passage was used as the instance of the Kyeah schema:

> Tom, Sue, Jane, and Joe were all friends who each wanted to make a large purchase as soon as possible. Tom wanted a VCR, Sue wanted a microwave, Joe wanted a car stereo, and Jane wanted a compact disk player. However, they each had only $50 left at the end of each month after paying their expenses. Tom, Sue, Jane, and Joe all got together to solve the problem. They made four slips of paper with the numbers 1, 2, 3, and 4 written on them. They put them in a hat and each drew out one slip. Jane got the slip with the 4 written on it, and said, "Oh darn, I have to wait to get my CD player." Joe got the slip with the 1 written on it and said, "Great, I can get my car stereo right away!" Sue got number 2, and Tom got number 3. In January, they each contributed the $50 they had left for the month. Joe took the whole $200 and bought a Pioneer car stereo at Service Merchandise. In February, they each contributed their $50 again. This time, Sue used the $200 to buy a Sharp 600 watt 1.5 cubic foot microwave at Service Merchandise. In March, all four again contributed $50. Tom took the money and bought a Sanyo Beta VCR with wired remote at Service Merchandise. In April, Jane got the $200 and bought a Technics CD player at Service

Merchandise.

5.2.2. Non–EBL Passages

For the non–EBL condition, we attempted to find complex schemata for which most undergraduate subjects would not have the relevant background knowledge. Two schemata were chosen: (1) a potlatch schema (a Northwestern American Indian ceremony) and (2) a Korean wedding ceremony schema. The following passage was used as the instance passage for the potlatch schema:

> Yanagi is a Kwakiutl chief and a descendant of Monaga. One day, Yanagi decided to hold a potlatch and invited Kaoka, the chief of a tribe whose ancestor is Monaga, and four of his followers. Yanagi's family gathered fresh and dried fish, berries, and animal skins. On June 6th, the appointed day, the guests paddled up to the host's village and went into Yanagi's house. There they gorged themselves on salmon and wild berries while dancers masked as beaver gods entertained them. While Yanagi's wife and daughter–in–law, wearing seashell necklaces, were busy serving food to the guests, Yanagi and his cousins, Egulac and Hiipe, arranged in neat piles the wealth they had gathered. Kaoka, the guest chief, stared at Yanagi as Yanagi danced up and down, telling the visitors about how much he was about to give them. As he counted out the boxes of berries and fish, Yanagi said Kaoka was poor. Yanagi's followers said, "Do not make any noise, tribes. Be quiet or we shall cause a landslide of wealth from our chief, the overhanging mountain." At the climax of the potlatch Yanagi and his first son, Managi, stood up and started burning animal skins. Yanagi's wife, hugging her son, watched their destruction. Finally, Yanagi, Joam, and Hiipe gave the remaining piles of gifts to Kaoka and his first son. Laden with gifts, the guests paddled back to their own village.

5.3. General Methods for Assessing Schema Acquisition

To assess how well subjects acquired a schema, we used the concept of constraints and variables which have been used by many schema theorists (e.g., [23]) and also in GENESIS [37]. Variables in schemata are slots that can be changed to represent particular situations. The constraints specify the range of objects that can fill the slots and the relationship between the variables. Since constraints and variables are core components of schemata, it was assumed that testing subjects on constraints and variables would be a clear test of the quality of the schemata that the subjects had acquired.

For each schema used in each condition, a list of constraints and variables was developed before the experiments. For example, in the

"Kyeah" schema, the number of participants, the amount of money, and so on are variables while the statement "the method should be fair to all the participants" is a constraint. Note that these experiments used more natural and structured experimental materials than those in traditional concept formation experiments. Consequently, judgment of how well subjects formed the concept was based on relational properties of the concept (i.e., constraints and variables), not on independent features.

5.4. Procedure and Design

Three different tasks were developed to measure the degree to which subjects were able to acquire a schema from a single instance.

5.4.1. Tasks for Experiment 1

In Experiment 1, the subjects were given instance passages and then asked to generate a general description of the specific text they read with the instance passage still available. This task was designed to be a direct test of the reader's ability to overtly state the general schema.

After the experiment, two judges independently scored the subjects' generated abstract schema in terms of the correctness of constraints and variables in their schemata. The details of the scoring methods are described in Ahn [34]. Basically, a subject received credit if his or her description contained generalized variables or statements consistent with the preestablished list of constraints. For example, descriptions of the Kyeah schema were scored as correct if they contained a statement such as, "each person in the group contributed the same amount of money (constraint)" or "by using random selection (variable for 'drawing slips')."

5.4.2. Materials and Schema Assessment for Experiment 2

In Experiment 2, half of the subjects were given instance passages and asked to generate new instances of a schema. We reasoned that an individual who had developed a general schema for a specific instance should be able to use that schema to generate a new specific instance.

The rest of the subjects read an abstract version of each schema. The abstract passages were generalized versions of each instance passage so that if there were "four people" in the instance passage (for a variable), for example, the abstract passage would say "some people." The abstract group's ability to generate a new specific instance served as a criterion for which the performance of the instance group could be compared since the abstract group received explicit overt information about the schemata. The abstract passage for the Kyeah schema is as follows:

Suppose there are a number of people (let the number be n), each of

whom wants to make a large purchase but does not have enough cash
on hand. They can cooperate to solve this problem by each donating
an equal small amount of money to a common fund on a regular basis.
(Let the amount donated by each member be m.) They meet at regular
intervals to collect everyone's money. Each time money is collected,
one member of the group is given all the money collected $(n \times m)$ and
then with that money he or she can purchase what he or she wants. To
be fair, the order in which people are given the money is determined
randomly. The first person in the random ordering is therefore able to
purchase the desired item immediately instead of having to save the
needed amount of money. Although the last person does not get to buy
the desired item early, this individual is no worse off than if he or she
had saved the money.

For the schemata in the non–EBL condition, the abstract passages
included both the cultural conventions in the ceremony and the explanation for the goal and procedures of the ceremony. The abstract passage
for potlatch schema is as follows:

One of the most famous of the institutions described by ethnographers
is the potlatch ceremony of the native Indians of the northern Pacific
Coast of North America. Potlatching tribes included the Coast Salish
of Washington and British Columbia and the Kwakiutl, who live farther north. The potlatch was generally a festive event. When the chief
of a tribe is not content with the amount of respect he was getting from
his own followers and from neighboring chiefs, he held a potlatch. The
family titles to which the chief lays claim belong to his ancestors, and
there are other people who can trace descent from the same ancestors
and so they were entitled to vie with him for recognition as a chief.
Every chief therefore feels the obligation to justify and validate his
chiefly status. The prescribed manner for doing this is to hold a potlatch. Each potlatch is given by a host chief and his followers to a
guest chief and his followers. The object of the potlatch is to show that
the host chief is truly entitled to chiefly status and that he is more ex-
alted than the guest chief. To prove this point, the host chief gives the
rival chief and his followers quantities of valuable gifts. The sponsor's
prestige grows directly with the magnitude of the potlatch, the volume
of goods given away in it. The guests' status is reduced by receiving
gifts but they have no choice but to receive the gifts. During the
ceremony, various kinds of food are served while dancers masked as
several gods entertain the guests. Sometimes, the host chief destroys
the valuables in front of the guests.

After the experiment, the subjects' new instances were scored in the
same manner as in Experiment 1 except for the following changes. Since
the task was to write a specific story which was as different from the

given example as possible, variables were scored as correct only if the subjects in the instance group changed the value of the variables (e.g., "three people" instead of "four people"). However, in the abstract group, no score for variables was possible because there were no constants whose values could be changed as there was in the instance group.

5.4.3. Materials and Schema Assessment for Experiment 3

In Experiment 3, subjects were given either EBL passages or non-EBL passages and asked direct yes/no questions about all the constraints and variables of the schema to be acquired. This procedure ensured that the subjects would be asked explicitly about every constraint and variable in the passages and avoided the difficulty of interpretation that occurred when subjects omitted information in their written response as was possible in the open–ended tasks of Experiments 1 and 2.

An example of a yes/no question for the a priori constraint *each participant donates the same amount* is "Can some people consistently donate less than others and have the system work?" (correct answer is no). An example of the yes/no question for a variable *number of participants does not matter* is "Is there any particular number of people required for this plan?" (correct answer is no).

Abstract passages were included as a control group by having one group of subjects read an abstract passage with explicit information about the schema and asking them the same yes/no questions we had used for the instance group. Since all the yes/no questions were written in general terms, the same questions could be use for both abstract and instance groups. Subjects' answers were scored according to the preestablished criteria which would be expected as a result of a full understanding of the schema.

Table 8–1 gives a summary of tasks and type of passages that each group received.

Table 1. Overview of Tasks and Passages in Experiments 1, 2, and 3	
Task	Type of Passages
Experiment 1:Generating a general description	Instances of EBL schemata Instances of Non–EBL schemata
Experiment 2: Producing a new instance of a schema	Instances of EBL schemata Instances of Non–EBL schemata Abstract of EBL schemata Abstract of Non–EBL schemata
Experiment 3: Answering yes/no questions about a general schema	Instances of EBL schemata Instances of Non–EBL schemata Abstract of EBL schemata Abstract of Non–EBL schemata

5.5. Results of Experiments 1, 2, and 3

The results of all three experiments consistently showed that the subjects could acquire a schema from a single example if its structure was causally determined and if the appropriate background knowledge was known to the subject. However, if these two preconditions were not satisfied, subjects could not carry out EBL and failed to acquire the new schema.

Table 8-2 gives an overview of the results from these experiments.

Table 2. Percent Correct Responses in Experiment 1, 2, and 3					
Task	Constraint/ Variable	Instance EBL	Instance Non–EBL	Abstract EBL	Abstract Non–EBL
Experiment1: General	C	74.9	18.1	–	–
description	V	89.3	75.4	–	–
Experiment 2: New	C	78.8	11.4	73.6	61.0
instance generation	V	66.3	72.9	–	–
Experiment 3: Yes/no	C	86.1	59.4	82.7	86.7
questions	V	84.7	55.6	79.3	85.6

5.5.1. Results of Experiment 1

When subjects in the EBL condition were asked to write a general description of an instance, 74.9% of the constraints were explicitly mentioned. However, in the non–EBL condition, only 18.1% of the possible constraints were correctly mentioned. In case of variables, subjects in the EBL condition identified 89.3% of the variables in their description, and those in the non–EBL condition identified 75.4%. The apparently good performance of the non–EBL condition may be due to the high omission rate (66.1%) compared to that of the EBL condition (32.9%). In other words, the subjects in the non–EBL condition appear to have omitted for the items for which they were less confident.

An example of one of the descriptions of the Kyeah schema in the EBL condition follows:

> Suppose in a group of people each person would like to buy something expensive, but over a period of time, each person cannot earn enough to buy what he would like. By using random selection, each person could be assigned a number. When the group had saved enough money together to purchase an item, the person with the first number would get his item. This would continue for the rest of the group until everyone had gotten what he wished.

5.5.2. Results of Experiment 2

When subjects were asked to generate a new instance of a schema, the subjects reading the EBL passages also showed evidence for schema acquisition. In the EBL condition, the average percent correct for constraints in the instance group was 78.8%, while it was 73.6% for the group given the schema in overt form. However, in the non-EBL condition, the average percent correct for constraints in the instance group was much worse, only 11.4%, while the abstract group showed performance similar to that of the EBL group, 61.0%.

There was no difference between the two conditions for variables, but the instance group in the non-EBL condition omitted many more variables. If the items were mentioned in their new stories, the instance group in the EBL condition correctly changed 66.3% of the variable items and the instance group in the non-EBL condition correctly changed 72.9%. However, the instance group in the non-EBL condition omitted 61% of the variables, whereas the instance group in the EBL condition omitted only 21% of the variables.

An example of a new instance of the Kyeah schema written by a subject in the instance group of the EBL condition follows:

> Bill, Kim, John, and Mary were all business associates. Bill wanted some land in northern Illinois, Kim wanted a new house in Switzerland, John wanted a new Porsch 928S with all accessories, and Mary wanted to take a trip around the world. The only problem was they each had only $25,000 left unspent at the end of each month. They all got together and picked random variables on Bill's business computer. Mary was furthest from her variable, so she would have to wait till last to get her trip around the world. John nailed his variable and jumped enthusiastically saying, "Yeah, I get to get my new Porsch 928S right now." They each talked with their banker and drew the $25,000 out and pooled it after the first month, and the next day John drove up in his new, black, 928S with all accessories. At the end of the next month they again pooled their money and Kim got her chalet in Switzerland. Again at the end of the next month they pooled their money and Bill got his land in northern Illinois. Finally, after the fourth month they pooled their money together and Mary left for her trip around the world.

5.5.3. Results from Experiment 3

The results from yes/no questions follow the same pattern as the other tasks. In the EBL condition there was no difference between the abstract group and the instance group in performance combining variable and constraint scores (81.1% and 85.4%), whereas in the non–EBL condition the instance group's performance was much poorer than the abstract group's (57.5% and 86.2%, respectively).

5.5.4. Overview of Results

To summarize the results, the subjects who read only a single example acquired a schema as did the subjects who read an abstract description of the schema if the domain of the example had an explanatory structure and the background knowledge was known to subjects. On the other hand, nonexplanatory structures and lack of background knowledge prevented the instance group from acquiring a schema in a single trial.

6. Discussion

The results of these experiments raise a number of new issues that need to be addressed in future research.

6.1. When Does Generalization Occur?

In most EBL systems (e.g., GENESIS [38]), generalization occurs as soon as explanation structures are constructed. However, the experiments presented here do not show whether the subjects in the instance group acquired a generalized schema when they read and understood the examples or while they were carrying out the experimental tests. Additional research will be needed to understand when humans actually carry out the generalizations.

6.2. Learning in the Non–EBL Conditions

Another interesting issue is how learning occurs in the non–EBL conditions. If one were to expose subjects to multiple examples as is assumed in RSBL, then one could contrast RSBL and EBL. For example, if repeated features in additional examples were irrelevant for a schema, the subjects in an EBL condition would still be able to identify the irrelevant features as variables regardless of how frequently those features appeared. On the other hand, subjects unable to carry out EBL would probably consider the repeated features to be constraints because they would have no knowledge that would allow them to distinguish irrelevant features from relevant ones. This type of stimulus exposure is what psychologists studying rule–learning behaviors have traditionally used.

6.3. EBL for Non-EBL Materials

Some of the data obtained in our experiments indicate that the subjects in the non-EBL conditions were not using just RSBL. The analysis of the individual items in the instance group of the non-EBL condition suggests that the subjects did not store the intact specific example. Instead, it appears that they tried to apply their background knowledge to understand the example even though they did not, in fact, have the required background knowledge to understand the passage correctly. For example, in the Korean wedding ceremony passage, the subjects' knowledge of Western culture led them to infer (incorrectly) that rings are essential in the Korean wedding ceremony. Similarly, in the potlatch narrative, subjects assumed that the chief's giving of valuables was a benevolent action and concluded that the recipient was poor. Considering these phenomena, it would appear that the subjects in the non-EBL condition were not performing pure RSBL. That is, it does not look as though these subjects were adopting the strategy of simply storing the specific example. Instead, they appeared to use their background knowledge to make a tentative generalization before they saw any additional examples of the same concept. In other words, the subjects in the non-EBL conditions were sometimes also trying to do EBL.

This finding supports Bartlett's hypothesized process of "effort after meaning" [32]. He observed that people rationalized an unfamiliar story, "The War of the Ghosts." When asked to remember it accurately, his subjects reconstructed the story to make it more consistent with their cultural expectations and tended to interpret information in terms of previously acquired concepts.

Our subjects' approach to dealing with specific instances of non-EBL materials is quite different from Lebowitz's AI system, which stores all the specific examples without making any generalization until it finds communality among these specific instances [39]. However, our subjects' approach is somewhat more similar to that of OCCAM [40], in which prior causal theories are used first in preference to correlational data.

Currently, we are carrying out more research on the issue of how people learn a new schema when they have insufficient domain knowledge or when the structure of their domain knowledge is too complex to find relevant information; we hope to provide clear evidence about how humans carry out both EBL and RSBL.

7. Conclusion

We believe this work is a good example of the powerful impact that the ideas from one discipline can have on another within the cognitive sciences. There have been a large number of different theories of concept acquisition in psychology. However, it appears that they all implicitly worked within a general framework in which concepts were derived by induction from repeated examples of instances. These psychological theories were then tested with relatively simple stimuli that typically varied along various surface (physical) dimensions.

When researchers in the area of artificial intelligence began to work on the problem of learning, many came from a tradition that focused on complex knowledge structures. Some of these researchers developed approaches to knowledge acquisition such as the EBL work in this book that enabled machines to use the knowledge that they already possessed to construct new knowledge.

The EBL approach to machine learning leads directly to the basic issue of this chapter: Do humans carry out EBL? Our work strongly suggests that humans do carry out EBL when the conditions are right. In fact, it appears that this may be an important area of human learning that was overlooked because of the implicit theoretical biases of psychological research in this area. Clearly, the infusion of a new set of ideas from our colleagues in the area of artificial intelligence has provided an important stimulus to research in the area of human learning.

References

1. E. E. Smith and D. L. Medin, *Categories and concepts*, Harvard University, Cambridge, MA, 1981.

2. L. E. Bourne, Jr. and F. Restle, "Mathematical theory of concept identification," *Psychological Review 8*, (1959), pp. 278–296.

3. G. Bower and T. Trabasso, "Concept identification," in *Studies in mathematical psychology*, R. C. Atkinson (ed.), Stanford University, 1964, pp. 32–94.

4. J. S. Bruner, J. J. Goodnow and G. A. Austin, *A study of thinking*, Wiley, New York, 1957.

5. M. Levine, "Hypothesis behavior by humans during discrimination learning," *Journal of Experimental Psychology 71*, (1966), pp. 331–338.

6. L. Wittgenstein, *Philosophical investigations*, Macmillan, New York, 1953.

7. P. G. Neumann, "An attribute frequency model for the abstraction of prototypes," *Memory and Cognition 3*, (1974), pp. 241–248.

8. B. Hayes–Roth and F. Hayes–Roth, "Concept learning and the recognition and the classification of exemplars," *Journal of Verbal Learning and Verbal Behavior 16*, (1977), pp. 321–338.

9. S. K. Reed, "Pattern recognition and categorization," *Cognitive Psychology 3*, (1972), pp. 382–407.

10. E. Rosch, C. Simpson and R. S. Miller, "Structural bases of typicality effects," *Journal of Experimental Psychology: Human Perception & Performance 2*, (1976), pp. 491–502.

11. F. Galton, *Inquiries into human faculty and its development*, J. M. Dent and Sons, London, 1907.

12. M. J. Posner and S. W. Keele, "On the Genesis of Abstract Ideas," *Journal of Experimental Psychology 77*, 3 (July 1968), pp. 353–363.

13. E. E. Smith, E. J. Shoben and L. J. Rips, "Structure and process in semantic memory: A feature model for semantic decisions," *Psychological Review 81*, (1974), pp. 214–241.

14. E. Rosch, "Principles of categorization," in *Cognition and categorization*, E. Rosch and B. B. Lloyd (ed.), Erlbaum, Hillsdale, NJ, 1978, pp. 27–48.

15. G. Lakoff, "Women, Fire, and Dangerous Things: What Categories Reveal About the Mind," in press, University of Chicago Press, Chicago, IL, 1986.

16. G. L. Murphy and D. L. Medin, "The Role of Theories in Conceptual Coherence," *Psychological Review 92*, 3 (July 1985), pp. 289–316.

17. W. D. Wattenmaker, G. L. Nakamura and D. L. Medin, "Relationships Between Similarity–based and Explanation–based Categorization," in *Contemporary Science and Natural Explanations: Common Sense Concepts of Causality*, D. Hilton (ed.), Harvester Press, Sussex, England, 1987, pp. 205–241.

18. L. Brooks, "Nonanalytic concept formation and memory for instances," in *Cognition and categorization*, E. Rosch and B. B. Lloyd (ed.), Erlbaum, Hillsdale, NJ, 1978, pp. 169–211.

19. D. L. Medin and M. M. Schaffer, "Context theory of classification learning," *Psychological Review 85*, (1978), pp. 207–238.

20. W. F. Brewer and G. V. Nakamura, "The Nature And Functions of Schemas," in *Handbook of Social Cognition: Volume 1*, R. S. Weyer, T. K. Srull (ed.), Lawrence Erlbaum and Associates, Hillsdale, NJ, 1984, pp. 119–160.

21. D. E. Rumelhart and A. Ortony, "The representation of knowledge in memory," in *Schooling and the acquisition of knowledge*, R. C. Anderson, R. J. Spiro, and W. E. Montague (ed.), Lawrence Erlbaum, Hillsdale, NJ, 1977.

22. R. C. Schank and R. P. Abelson, *Scripts, Plans, Goals and Understanding: An Inquiry into Human Knowledge Structures*, Lawrence Erlbaum and Associates, Hillsdale, NJ, 1977.

23. D. E. Rumelhart and D. A. Norman, "Accretion, Tuning, and Restructuring: Three Modes of Learning," in *Semantic Factors in Cognition*, J. W. Cotton & R. L. Klatzky (ed.), Lawrence Erlbaum and Associates, Hillsdale, NJ, 1978.

24. T. A. van Dijk and W. Kintsch, *Strategies of discourse comprehension*, Academic Press, New York, 1983.

25. D. E. Rumelhart, P. Smolensky, J. L. McClelland and G. E. Hinton, "Schemata and Sequential Thought Processes in PDP Models," in *Parallel Distributed Processing: Explorations in the Micro–Structure of Cognition, Vol. II*, D. E. Rumelhart and J. L. McClelland (ed.), MIT Press, Cambridge, MA, 1986, pp. 7–57.

26. L. W. Barsalou, "Ad hoc categories," *Memory and Cognition 11*, (1983), pp. 211–227.

27. E. M. Roth and E. J. Shoben, "The effect of context on the structure of categories," *Cognitive Psychology 15*, (1983), pp. 346–378.

28. G. F. DeJong, "An Approach to Learning from Observation," in *Machine Learning: An Artificial Intelligence Approach, Vol. 2* , Ryszard S. Michalski, Jaime G. Carbonell, and Tom M. Mitchell (ed.), Morgan Kaufmann , Los Altos, California , 1986, pp. 571–590

29. T. M. Mitchell, R. Keller and S. Kedar–Cabelli, "Explanation–Based Generalization: A Unifying View," *Machine Learning 1*, 1 (January 1986), pp. 47–80.

30. G. F. DeJong, R. E. Stepp, R. J. Mooney, P. V. O'Rorke, S. A. Rajamoney, A. M. Segre and J. W. Shavlik, "Current Research in Machine Learning," Working Paper 04, AI Research Group, Coordinated Science Laboratory, University of Illinois, Urbana, IL, June 1985.

31. D. L. Medin, W. D. Wattenmaker and R. S. Michalski, "Constraints and Preferences in Inductive Learning: An Experimental Study of Human and Machine Performance," *Cognitive Science 11*, 3 (1987), pp. 299–239.

32. F. C. Bartlett, *Remembering*, Cambridge University Press, Cambridge, England, 1932.

33. J. D. Bransford, *Human cognition: Learning, understanding and remembering*, Wadsworth Publishing Company, Belmont, CA, 1979.

34. W. Ahn, "Schema Acquisition from a Single Example," M.A. Thesis, Department of Psychology, University of Illinois, Urbana, IL, October 1987.

35. W. Ahn, W. F. Brewer and R. J. Mooney, Schema Acquisition From a Single Example, , submitted, 1990.

36. W. Ahn, R. J. Mooney, W. F. Brewer and G. F. DeJong, "Schema Acquisition from One Example: Psychological Evidence for Explanation–Based Learning," *Proceedings of the Ninth Annual Conference of the Cognitive Science Society*, Seattle, WA, July 1987.

37. A. M. Segre and G. DeJong, "Explanation–Based Manipulator Learning: Acquisition of Planning Ability Through Observation," *Proceedings of the IEEE International Conference on Robotics and Automation*, St. Louis, MO, March 1985, pp. 555–560.

38. G. F. DeJong and R. J. Mooney, "Explanation–Based Learning: An Alternative View," *Machine Learning 1*, 2 (1986), pp. 145–176.

39. M. Lebowitz, "Generalization from natural language text," *Cognitive Science 7*, (1983), pp. 1–40.

40. M. Pazzani, M. Dyer and M. Flowers, "The role of prior causal theories in generalization," *Proceedings of the Fifth National Conference on Artificial Intelligence*, 1986, pp. 545–550.

Chapter 9

Case Study 1 — ARMS:
Acquiring Robotic Assembly Plans

Alberto Maria Segre

1. An Overview of the ARMS System

The ARMS system is an *explanation-based learning-apprentice system* operating in a robot assembly domain. ARMS is a *learning-apprentice system* because it learns, in part, by analyzing an external agent's solution to a given problem, as opposed to a solution produced by an internal weak-method problem solver.

The ARMS domain consists of a prototypical industrial robot arm maneuvering pieces in a finite three-dimensional workspace. Assembling an object that exhibits a known mechanical behavior breaks neatly into two subproblems: the *design problem*, involving transforming a specification of an assembly's mechanical function into physical descriptions of the assembly and its constituent parts, and the *assembly problem*, which determines a sequence of executable actions that result in the construction of an assembly from given initial conditions. Both of these problems are characterized by very large search spaces that would quickly overwhelm weak-method problem solvers (see Figure 9–1).

Explanation-based learning is applied in both of these search spaces to acquire general problem-solving macro-operators based on sample solutions. For the assembly problem, ARMS relies on a *nonpredictive*

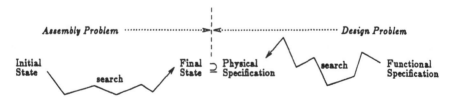

Figure 9–1:   The ARMS Problem Space

understanding process to construct a generalizable structure while observing the external agent's problem–solving behavior. For the design problem, a deductive *verification* process starts with the structure produced in the assembly space and uses a naive kinematic domain theory to derive a generalizable structure in the design space.

Other learning–apprentice systems (e.g., the LEAP system [1]) rely on extensive querying of the expert by the system to construct a generalizable explanation of the expert's problem–solving behavior. The ARMS nonpredictive understanding process quietly observes the expert's behavior without interruption, on the premise that more obtrusive interactions force (possibly inaccurate) introspection on the part of the expert and perturb the expert's problem–solving performance. Thus we say ARMS is guided by the principle of *unobtrusiveness*.

The ARMS mechanical assembly environment ideally consists of physical pieces manipulated by a real robot arm. As one might expect, this involves solving a great number of engineering problems which, although interesting in their own right, are not terribly relevant to AI or machine learning. To sidestep these engineering problems (arm control, kinematics, sensors, path planning, tolerances), we use instead a software simulation of a robot arm moving through a modeled workspace. The use of the simulator insulates ARMS from sensor and control problems.[1]

2. ARMS Architecture

The ARMS architecture is shown in Figure 9–2. ARMS consists of two independent components: a *learning element* and a *performance element*. Each component accesses *domain knowledge* stored in the *schema library*. The performance element uses domain knowledge from the schema library to construct solutions for new design and assembly problems. The learning element uses existing domain knowledge to produce new entries for the schema library that improve the system's performance.

---

[1] Although the research reported here relies on the use of the simulator, the ARMS system was in fact also used in conjunction with a real–world robot arm [2].

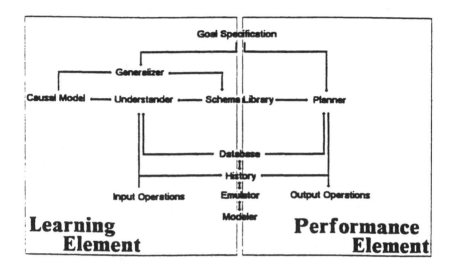

Figure 9-2:   The ARMS Architecture

2.1. Knowledge Representation

A *schema* [3-6] is a data structure that encodes generalized knowledge about a particular concept or topic. *State schemata* are used to represent relations in the world, and *operator schemata* are used to describe the actions the system can apply to effect changes in the world. A *schema instance* is a fully specified prototype of a schema, and *descriptors* are used to represent the physical objects manipulated by the system.[2]

Descriptors make use of a solid modeler to describe the geometric properties of the pieces they represent. A *piece* is a rigid solid object that has no moving parts. Different pieces can be combined to form *joints* or *assemblies* by inserting parts of one piece into holes in others. Depending on the relative sizes and shapes of the inserted portions, these assemblies

---

[2] In the traditional STRIPS framework [7], states are represented as predicate calculus wffs and operators are given as transition specifications (packaged as add and delete lists of wffs). Schema instances are analogous to propositions of these states and operators. Descriptors are constants along with assertions about the properties of the objects they denote. As we shall soon see, the ARMS knowledge representation more naturally supports geometric reasoning about physical objects.

exhibit different mechanical behaviors.

The current *world state* is described by a collection of state schema instances, each a partial description of the world state. There are five primitive operator schemata corresponding to the physical capabilities of the robot arm. These five parameterized primitive operators represent what changes the arm (modeled as an idealized disembodied two–fingered gripper) can effect on the world state:[3]

(1) *Open:* Open the gripper fingers to the widest possible extent.

(2) *Close:* Close the gripper fingers as far as possible, stopping when they meet or when any intervening piece obstructs further movement.

(3) *Translate (unitVector, delta):* Move the gripper from its present position in a straight line along the given axis by delta units while maintaining the orientation of the gripper.

(4) *Rotate (unitVector, theta):* Rotate the gripper about the given axis by theta degrees while maintaining the current location of the gripper.

(5) *MoveTo (newPosition):* Move the gripper from its current position to newPosition along any collision-free path. Note that newPosition specifies both the location and orientation of the gripper.

While this command set is not that of any particular industrial robot arm, nearly any arm possessing the minimum requisite degrees of freedom (six plus gripper) can be made to implement these five commands, at least within some restricted workspace envelope.

Nonprimitive operator schemata are composed from other operator and state schemata. Instances of composite operator schemata refer to descriptors as well as to other state or operator schema instances. A composite operator contains a set of *preconditions*, a partial ordering on a set of *subgoals*, a *body*, and a set of *goals*. The goals are state schema instances that describe some (but not necessarily all) of the effects of successfully applying this operator. The preconditions are state schema instances describing what conditions must be true in the world for this

---

[3] Note that these five parameterized operators define the assembly space which would have to be searched by a weak–method problem solver. Given continuously valued parameters in three–dimensional space, this problem space can be considered to have an essentially infinite branching factor.

operator to be applicable. The subgoals are a partially ordered set of state schema instances that must be achieved before applying the body, a single operator schema instance. If the subgoals are achieved and the body applied in the context of the precondition states being true, the new world state will at least contain the goal states.

The initial collection of state and operator schemata constitute a domain theory for the assembly problem. ARMS uses a separate domain theory (a naive theory of kinematics), also encoded in the form of schemata, for the design problem. The learning element acquires new composite operator schemata which describe novel solutions to assembly problem instances as well as new state schemata which embody novel solutions to design problem instances. Once added to the schema library, learned schemata are indistinguishable from original built-in knowledge. Acquired schemata are used by the performance element when planning solutions to new assembly problems, as well as by the learning element when analyzing later observed episodes. For ARMS, the advantages of learning are twofold: Not only will the system's performative component be more efficient, but the learning component will also improve its learning capability.

2.2. Naive Kinematic Domain Theory

The ARMS naive kinematic domain theory attempts to account for relative piece motions (loosely based on Tilove [8]). The theory describes the aggregate behavior of individual pieces as they are combined in assemblies. Starting from simple mechanical behaviors inferred from the geometric properties of pairs of pieces in direct contact (*simple joints*), it is possible to determine the more complicated mechanical behavior of complex assemblies. An *open kinematic chain* is a transitive relation between two pieces not directly related by a simple joint. Such a chain spans two or more simple joints and forms a *composite joint*.

The rules for determining mechanical behavior rely on the notion of a *degree of freedom*. A degree of freedom describes motion along a given axis. It may be *prismatic* (a translation along the axis) or *revolute* (a rotation about the axis). Two unrelated (and therefore unconstrained) pieces have six degrees of freedom between them — three revolute and three prismatic — along three mutually orthogonal axes. There are zero degrees of freedom between two rigidly connected bodies.

Each degree of freedom specifies upper and lower limits for the motion it allows. These boundary conditions can be of two different types, depending on the physical instantiation of the joint. A *hard bound* corresponds to a physical limit imposed by the mechanism. Such a bound occurs when two surfaces collide. For example, imagine a square tab sliding back and forth in a slot: A hard bound on either end limits its travel. A *soft bound* corresponds to a limit that may be physically exceeded by the mechanism, but if exceeded it will cause the joint to fail. A soft bound fails when the tab mentioned above is pulled straight out from the slot.

We can distinguish between knowledge about the mathematics of joint behavior and knowledge about how a particular instance of a joint is physically realized. *Abstract joint schemata* are special state schemata that contain the first kind of knowledge. Given that only a finite number of degrees of freedom exist between two pieces, there are only a finite number of abstract joint schemata. A subset of these are built into ARMS. *Physical joint schemata* are a different type of state schemata that contain information about the physical realization of abstract joint behavior. Each physical joint schema is associated with an abstract joint schema that describes its behavior. This indexing describes a mapping of the information in one schema onto the information in the other. Since there may be many different ways to physically implement a particular joint, the mapping from abstract joint schemata to physical joint schemata may be one–to–many.

Physical joint schemata corresponding to simple joints are pre–encoded in the ARMS system, but, as we shall see below, the others are acquired. Acquired physical joint schemata correspond to generalized solutions to particular instances of the design problem.

3. The Widget Assembly Example

Consider the assembly shown in Figure 9-3. This particular assembly, which we shall call a *widget* for convenience, consists of three pieces: a peg, a washer, and a block. The three pieces in this particular widget will be represented by the descriptors $Peg1, $Washer1, and $Bored-Block1, respectively.[4] The widget is constructed by inserting the shaft of $Peg1 through the hole in $Washer1 into the socket of $BoredBlock1.

---

[4] We shall adopt a leading "$" character as a notational convention to flag descriptor and schema names. Descriptors and schema instance names will have the leading "$" as well as a trailing number. Thus $RevoluteJoint55 names an instance of the schema $RevoluteJoint, and $Peg1 names a descriptor.

Figure 9-3:   Exploded View of Widget Assembly

The relative sizes of the shaft of $Peg1 and the hole in $Washer1 ensure that $Washer1 may spin freely (i.e., there exists a revolute degree of freedom between $Peg1 and $Washer1). $Peg1 and $BoredBlock1 are designed to fit together snugly; thus we can say that there exist no degrees of freedom between $Peg1 and $BoredBlock1 and that they are constrained to move rigidly together. Finally, we note that $Washer1 is free to slide (e.g., a prismatic degree of freedom) along $Peg1, constrained, of course, by collisions with the underside of the head of $Peg1 and the top of $BoredBlock1.

We call the kind of mechanical behavior embodied by the widget a *revolute joint* (one revolute degree of freedom) between $Washer1 and $BoredBlock1. Closer examination reveals that this revolute joint behavior results from the composition and subsequent interaction of two simple joints: a *cylindrical joint* (a prismatic degree of freedom and a revolute degree of freedom about the same axis) between the washer and the peg, and a *rigid joint* (zero degrees of freedom) between the peg and the block.

We encode knowledge about the expected function of the joint in the abstract joint schema $RevoluteJoint. This knowledge indicates that the joint should permit one revolute degree of freedom between the two base pieces of the assembly (in this case, $Washer1 and $BoredBlock1).

The $RevoluteJoint schema does not specify *how* the assembly is put together. The physical realization of $RevoluteJoint for the widget requires first creating an instance of $CylindricalJoint between $Peg1 and $Washer1 and then constraining (via the imposition of a hard bound) the prismatic degree of freedom with an instance of $RigidJoint between $Peg1 and $BoredBlock1. An analysis of the assembly indicates the existence of an open kinematic chain between the block and the washer (via the peg) which exhibits only a single revolute degree of freedom.

Given this analysis, the system will acquire a new physical joint schema, $RevoluteJointA, that describes one way of implementing the functional behavior described in the abstract joint schema $RevoluteJoint. In other words, $RevoluteJointA contains a generalized solution to the design problem for $RevoluteJoint. Note that $RevoluteJoint relates only the two base pieces, whereas $RevoluteJointA must mention the third piece (i.e., $Peg1) involved in the assembly.

3.1. Specifying the Widget Assembly Problem

Consider the initial configuration of widget component pieces shown in Figure 9–4. $BoredBlock1 is on the right, with its socket also facing toward the right. $Washer1 is in the foreground, with $Peg1 stacked on top of it. In addition, there is a fourth piece (hereafter $Block1) in the left rear part of the workspace. The robot arm is shown as a disembodied

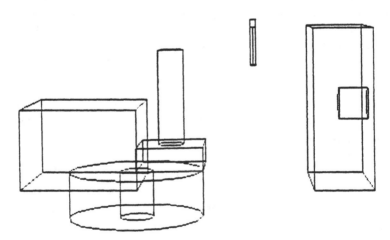

Figure 9–4:   Initial State for Widget Assembly Problem

two–fingered gripper in its home position.[5]

This particular placement is one of an infinite number of legal initial piece placements possible for these four pieces. The piece descriptors (i.e., their geometric specifications), along with their positions relative to the workspace frame of reference, constitute the *initial state* specification for the system. The *goal state* is given as a partially specified abstract joint schema instance, $RevoluteJoint0122, that describes the mathematical relationship between the descriptors $Washer1 and $BoredBlock1. Note that it does not mention $Peg1 at all.

3.2. Attempting to Solve the Problem

The performance element attempts to achieve the goal state. The ARMS performance element consists of a *schema planner*, similar to Friedland's *skeletal planner* [9], that performs a two–phase depth–first search with limited backtracking. The first phase is a search through the *design space* to find a fully instantiated physical joint schema that is consistent with the partially specified abstract joint schema instance given as the goal. The design phase may produce more than one physical joint schema instance; these can be thought of as a set of alternate goals, attaining any of which is enough to attain the goal specification. The *planning phase* is a search through the *assembly space* to produce a *plan*, or sequence of primitive robot arm commands, to achieve one of the physical joint schema instances found in the design phase.

The design process begins by fleshing out the partially specified abstract joint schema instance, being careful to honor any constraints pertaining to interdependencies of the degrees of freedom attached to the abstract joint schema. From the fully instantiated abstract joint schema instance, the system indexes a set of partially specified physical joint schema instances which represent all known possible physical implementations consistent with this joint behavior. Constraints attached to the physical joint schemata representing the physical features as well as interdependencies of various pieces used in the assembly are used to complete the specification of the physical joint schema instances.

---

[5] All of the examples in this chapter are taken from the December 1986 version of the system. The figures are the product of the robot arm simulator and are reproduced without modification.

The planning process uses a physical joint schema instance produced by the design phase to index any operator schemata listing this joint schema as a goal. If an operator is found, it is expanded, causing subgoals to be generated and suboperators to be applied. The process continues recursively until it bottoms out with a robot arm command sequence. The ARMS executive applies the robot arm commands by handing them to the simulator. Unlike more traditional planning systems, the ARMS planner and executive are interleaved; thus the executive may be applying operators before the planner has specified a complete sequence of primitive operators.

For our example, although the system possesses the abstract joint schema $RevoluteJoint, it has no corresponding physical joint schema. Lacking a general solution to this design problem, the planner simply gives up.

3.3. Observing the Expert's Plan

When the performance element fails to discover a way of realizing the specified goal, control passes to the learning element. An external agent — presumably an assembly domain expert — is asked to lead the robot arm through a solution by providing a series of primitive operator schema instances.[6] As each input is read in, the simulator models the changing workspace by executing each arm command. The learning element consists of two modules: an *understander*[7] and a *generalizer*. The purpose of the understander is to construct a *causal model* of the observed problem-solving behavior. An analysis of how the observed solution meets

---

[6] On the factory floor, the solution sequence would presumably be given by a skilled factory worker via a teach-pendant. Thus the user interface of an ARMS implementation for a real robot arm would be identical to the user interface of robot teach-by-guiding systems currently in industrial use. Note that any sequence produced in this manner would probably contain many superfluous primitive actions. These extra inputs would arise naturally from the expert's successive approximation of the proper position. The ARMS system is insensitive to this kind of noise.

[7] Apologies to McDermott:

  We should avoid, for example, labeling any part of our programs an "understander." It is the job of the text accompanying the program to examine carefully how much understanding is present, how it got there, and what its limits are [10].

In this case, the alternative term *causal model builder*, while perhaps more acceptable from McDermott's point of view, conflicts with our goal of descriptive simplicity. We choose to stick with the simpler, more intuitive, terminology even at the risk of fooling ourselves.

the goal specification serves as an *explanation* and may result in the construction of a new physical joint schema. An explanation of how the expert's plan transforms the initial state into the final state is analyzed by the generalizer and used to construct a new composite operator schema.

For this example, the expert's solution is a sequence of 30 fully instantiated primitive operator schemata, roughly divided as follows:

(1) Position $BoredBlock1 so that its socket is pointed upward (seven robot arm commands).

(2) Grasp $Peg1 and clear it from the top of $Washer1, placing it on top of $Block1 (nine commands).

(3) Grasp the newly liberated $Washer1 and place it on top of $BoredBlock1 so that their holes are aligned (seven commands).

(4) Return to $Peg1, presently on top of $Block1, and grasp it by the head. Position it directly above $Washer1 and $BoredBlock1 so that the shaft of $Peg1 is aligned with the holes of $Washer1 and $BoredBlock1 (four commands).

(5) Move $Peg1 along a straight line, inserting it through $Washer1 into $BoredBlock1 (one command).

The solution presented by the expert contains several less than-optimal subsequences. In particular,

(1) While removing $Peg1 from of the top of $Washer1, the expert chooses to move the arm using four $Translate commands (along Z, X, Y, and negative Z axes, respectively). A single $MoveTo would do as well. Due to the implementations of these primitives on most industrial arms, the computational expense of a $MoveTo is usually much less than a $Translate.[8]

(2) $Peg1 is transferred to the top of $Block1 rather than simply placing it directly on the workspace surface. This would condemn a normal teach–by–guiding robot arm to reliance on the presence of the redundant piece $Block1.

---

[8] A $MoveTo through uncluttered space corresponds to joint–interpolated motion on many arms. This requires a single kinematic solution for the arm. $Translate is usually approximated by finding many intermediate kinematic solutions along the trajectory and using joint–interpolated motion along these points in sequence.

(3)   Before grasping $Washer1, the expert directs the arm to execute a
       $Rotate command, twisting the gripper 90 degrees around the
       vertical axis. This twist is redundant, since by the symmetry of
       $Washer1, it makes no difference what two points on its exterior
       surface are grasped by the robot gripper as long as they are
       diametrically opposed.

Note that these subsequences do not affect the correctness of the
solution. One would hope, however, that a composite operator schema
acquired by the system that can be used to solve this problem would produce a better solution, that is, one that doesn't rely on these quirks of the
expert's plan.

As the input sequence is processed, the understanding module builds
a causal model (from which an explanation will be extracted for later use
by the generalizer) of the assembly process. The understanding process
can best be described as inferring in a bottom–up fashion, using higher
level operators, the context in which the lower level input operators
occur. The understander is similar to natural–language story-
understanding systems that attempt to describe the context of an input
story [11–14] .

For the most part, natural–language story understanding takes
place in a predictive framework. This is necessary, since the inputs to a
story–understanding system are rift and rife with gaps that must be filled
by inference chains. The understander must by necessity be to some
degree predictive, or the intervening inference chain cannot be constructed. Unlike natural–language understanding systems, learning-
apprentice systems usually do not face the problem of input gaps. A typical learning apprentice has access to every action taken by the external
problem–solving agent: Unless the operators are poorly understood, there
are never any gaps in the input sequence. In addition, the learning
apprentice need only worry about a single external problem–solving
agent, thus removing any difficulties resulting from interactions between
agents.

Nonpredictive understanding means that a schema is activated
(added to the causal model) only after the actions that it represents are
temporally completed in the observed input. This implies that the *activation conditions* for any higher–level schema can be expressed in terms of
that schema's goals. This also implies that if any schema is checked for
activation and its activation conditions are not met, it is not necessary to
retain the schema for future checking; no schema is ever checked for
activation more than once.

The ARMS understander produces a causal model that relates instances of primitive operator schemata (the observed input) to state schema instances, descriptors, and inferred composite operator schema instances. The causal model is represented as a graph making relations explicit between the objects represented by data structures. The edges of the graph relate the preconditions, subgoals, bodies, and goals to the proper inferred composite operator schema instances. Figure 9–5 shows a portion of the causal model constructed during the understanding process.

3.4. Generalizing the Expert's Solution

There are two distinct phases to the generalization process. The *verification phase* must ascertain whether the final state achieved by the expert's actions embodies the mechanical behavior stipulated by the goal specification. It is during this verification phase that a new physical joint schema may be acquired. The verification phase also provides a clue as to whether or not a new composite operator schema is worth learning; if so, we say the episode meets the *learning criteria*. If the learning criteria are

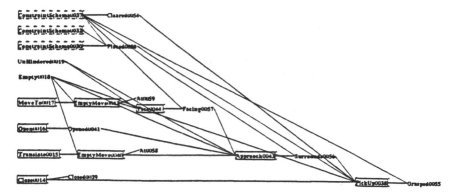

Figure 9–5: Portion of Causal Model. This figure represents a part of the causal model built (for a particular instance of $PickUp) using the nonpredictive ARMS schema activation algorithm. The unboxed nodes correspond to state schemata, the nodes in the dashed boxes are constraint schemata, and the boxed nodes correspond to operator schemata. The boxed nodes on the left edge of the figure represent the primitive operator schemata of the observed input sequence (with time increasing down the graph).

met, the *operator acquisition phase* generalizes the assembly procedure embodied in the observed input sequence to produce a new composite operator schema.

The abstract joint schema given as a goal specification characterizes the final assembly in terms of its degrees of freedom. The goal of the verification process is to find a valid physical joint schema instance which corresponds to the abstract joint schema instance partially specified by the expert. There are four cases to consider:

(1) *Goal recognized during observation*: The partially specified abstract joint schema instance matches a physical joint schema instance extant in the causal model. Since the understander was able to recognize a physical joint schema instance corresponding to the goal specification, a composite operator that characterizes the expert's plan must already exist in the schema library. This case does not meet the learning criteria, causing the generalizer to terminate. This case corresponds to the system having a solution to both the design and assembly problems, and will never arise if the system is always given a chance to solve the problem first.

(2) *Known physical joint schema verified*: The partially specified abstract joint schema instance is used to index a set of partially specified physical joint schema instances, one of which can be proven to hold using the ARMS kinematic domain theory. In this situation, the verification process completes successfully, using existing joint schema knowledge. This case corresponds to the system having a solution to the design problem but no solution to the assembly problem; the learning criteria are met and a new composite operator schema is constructed.

(3) *New physical joint schema constructed and verified*: There is no known physical joint schema that can be used to explain that the assembly episode achieves the instantiated abstract joint schema. In this situation, the current joint schema knowledge is too weak to account for the mechanism's behavior. The ARMS kinematic domain theory is applied to the other joints in the causal model to deduce an explanation of the assembly's behavior. A new physical joint schema is constructed to account for the operation of the realized mechanism; in addition, the learning criteria are met and a new composite operator schema is constructed.

(4) *Assembly cannot be analyzed*: The goal is not verifiable using current joint schemata. It is possible that this same example might

be verifiable after acquiring other schemata. It is also possible that the mechanism really does not meet the goal specification. This case does not meet the learning criteria, causing the generalizer to terminate.

We can thus summarize the ARMS *learning criteria* as follows: If an episode achieves a verifiable goal, and the physical joint schema which corresponds to the goal specification was not recognized by the understander, then the episode meets the learning criteria and a new composite operator schema will be constructed.

In some episodes, the verification process itself produces an explanation, based on the ARMS kinematic domain theory, of how the assembled mechanism achieves the specified behavior (case 3). This explanation can be generalized to yield a new physical joint schema. For every episode that meets the learning criteria (cases 2 and 3), a (different) explanation is extracted from the causal model during the operator acquisition phase. This explanation can be generalized to produce a new composite operator schema. The widget example falls under case 3; that is, there is no physical joint schema that can be used to show that the abstract joint schema given as the goal specification was realized. The system will therefore be able to apply explanation–based learning in both places, acquiring two new schemata.

3.5. Building a New Physical Joint Schema

It is up to the verification process to construct some explanation, using the kinematic domain theory, of how this assembly fulfills the function specified by the goal specification. The first step in this analysis is to look for a kinematic chain linking the two end pieces specified by the abstract joint \$RevoluteJoint0122, the goal specification.

During the course of the understanding process, the system was able to recognize two physical joint schema instances, \$RigidJointA0301 and \$CylindricalJointA0311. Recognition of these two joints was accomplished by the activation of two operator schema instances, \$NewSchemaA0298 and \$NewSchemaB0308, both of which are instances of operator schemata acquired by ARMS in the course of previous learning episodes. These two recognized joints provide a chain between \$Washer1 and \$BoredBlock1 via \$Peg1. In this example, this kinematic chain is the only one between the desired end pieces.

The verifier examines all the degrees of freedom in the chain, computing all of their soft bounds by taking into account the presence of the

other pieces in the chain. In this example, there are two degrees of freedom present: the prismatic and revolute degrees of freedom contributed
by $CylindricalJointA0311.

The revolute degree of freedom has no bounds that could be affected
by the other pieces in the kinematic chain. On the other hand, the
prismatic degree of freedom undergoes some modification when incorporated into the kinematic chain. This degree of freedom has a hard
bound imposed by a collision between the underside of $Peg1's head and
the top surface of $Washer1. The other bound was originally a soft bound
limited only by the length of the shaft of $Peg1. When the entire
kinematic chain is considered, a collision between the underside of
$Washer1 and the top surface of $BoredBlock1 transforms the soft bound
into a hard bound. The remaining range of motion on this degree of freedom is so small as to fall below a systemwide tolerance value indicating
when a degree of freedom ceases to be significant.

The collected degrees of freedom of the kinematic chain are finally
mapped onto the expected degrees of freedom of the goal specification's
abstract joint schema. In this case, the remaining revolute degree of freedom corresponds to the single expected degree of freedom of $Revolu-
teJoint0122. The prismatic degree of freedom is canceled by the newly
imposed bounds.

The explanation constructed by the verifier is used as the basis for a
new physical joint schema $RevoluteJointA that is added to the schema
library. The new schema represents a particular physical realization of
the joint function described by the abstract joint schema $RevoluteJoint.
This is *explanation–based learning*: learning of an implementation of
$RevoluteJoint guided by an explanation inferred deductively using the
system's kinematic domain theory. The explanation is generalized to produce $RevoluteJointA.

$RevoluteJoint is associated with $RevoluteJointA, making the
latter accessible from the former later. The indexing scheme specifies a
mapping of the contents of an instance of $RevoluteJoint to its
corresponding instance(s) of $RevoluteJointA. $RevoluteJointA describes
how appropriate instances of $CylindricalJointA and $RigidJointA can be
combined to form the target behavior. It refers to partial descriptions of
all of the pieces involved (including internal chain pieces such as $Peg1),
as well as the constraints that govern their physical interrelations (e.g.,
shape and size interpiece constraints) and the cancellation of the
prismatic degree of freedom. Finally, an instance of the new physical
joint schema $RevoluteJointA0354 is created to represent the achieved

goal state.

3.6. Building a New Operator Schema

The verifier has proven, using the system's domain theory, that the construction of the revolute joint relies on $CylindricalJointA0311, $RigidJointA0301, and various constraints on their interaction. This information is contained in the new physical joint schema instance $RevoluteJointA0354. The operator acquisition process will now construct a new composite operator schema that achieves the goal $RevoluteJointA.

The new composite operator schema will be extracted from an explanation derived from the causal model.[9] The verifier has identified two physical joint schema instances in the causal model ($CylindricalJointA0311 and $RigidJointA0301) as the substantiating evidence that the example has met the goal specification. The first step is to analyze any dependencies between the top–level subgoals in order to produce a partial ordering on the subgoal set. In this case, the analysis is simple since one of the two joints, $RigidJointA0301, imposes constraints on the degrees of freedom of the other joint, $CylindricalJointA0311. Hence, $CylindricalJointA0311 must be achieved before $RigidJointA0301. The explanation can now be identified by tracing the dependencies from these top–level subgoals back through the causal model. Any causal model elements that are not contributing to the achievement of these top–level subgoals are easily identified and flushed.

The new schema will be a generalized version of a cross–section or *fringe* of the explanation. The lowest fringe corresponds to the observed input sequence, and the highest most abstract fringe is simply the top subgoal relationship already described. The ARMS operator acquisition process is capable of producing two different operator schemata: a more general new schema (the highest possible fringe) or a more operational new schema (an intermediate fringe). The more general new schema will likely cover a greater number of future examples but is more expensive to use in planning than the more operational version. For an empirical performance analysis of planning behavior using these two schemata, see Segre [15]. For this discussion, we limit ourselves to the more operational version.

---

[9] This explanation is distinct from the explanation used to acquire $RevoluteJointA in Section 3.5.

Determining where to take the fringe of the explanation to produce the more operational composite operator schema is accomplished by using a heuristic on the syntactic structure of the explanation. We note that achieving $RigidJointA and $CylindricalJointA both require grasping InterimPiece1 ($Peg1 in this example). There should be no need to duplicate planning effort for this grasping operation. This is the insight that enables a more operational new schema to be produced. The operator acquisition process descends the causal model until there are no more shared subplans that achieve identical repeated subgoals and creates a new schema at that level of representation. A new schema at this level is more operational since there will not be any wasted planning effort during application of the schema: The details of the manipulation of Interim-Piece1 will be worked out only once.

The shared substructure analysis continues until the top–level subgoal set has been transformed into a new subgoal set with its members having no common subgoals. The analysis is order–preserving; hence the top–level subgoal set ordering imposed by the joint dependency analysis is carried through to the ordering of the new subgoal set.

Preconditions are collected from the members of the new subgoal set. The last element of the set is used to determine the body of the new schema. The remaining subgoals become the subgoals of the newly acquired schema.

The schema produced, $NewSchemaC, is shown in Figure 9–6. It essentially states

> In order to achieve an instance of $RevoluteJointA, given the subgoal $Placed that describes the position of InterimPiece1, begin by achieving an instance of $BracedHoles for Piece1 and Piece2 of the joint. Next achieve a $Grasped of InterimPiece1 from its $Placed position, avoiding obstructing any surfaces of InterimPrimitive1, and achieve a $MultiAligned between InterimPrimitive1 and the previously braced holes. Finally, execute a $FullMove to translate InterimPiece1 by a distance computed from the combined hole depth and the alignment offset.

The process of acquiring new composite operator schemata is a second example of explanation–based learning. The system extracts an explanation from the causal model, constructed on the basis of a domain theory embodied by the schema library *in toto*. The system relaxes the explanation while maintaining its correctness, in this case its ability to achieve an instance of $RevoluteJointA. The result is a composite operator schema capable of producing an entire class of assembly plans that construct   different   instances   of   the   physical   joint   schema

```
((Supers OperatorSchema)
 (TypeSlots
  (Goals (($RevoluteJointA          (Piece1 Piece1)
                                    (Piece2 Piece2)
                                    (Primitive1 Primitive1)
                                    (Primitive2 Primitive2)
                                    (Orientation Orientation)
                                    (DOF1 DOF1)
                                    (InterimPiece1 InterimPiece1)
                                    (InterimPrimitive1 InterimPrimitive1)
                                    (DOF2 DOF2))))
   (SubGoals ((($Placed             (Piece InterimPiece1)
                                    (SupportSurface NewSlot2)))
              ($BracedHoles         (Piece1 Piece2)
                                    (Primitive1 Primitive2)
                                    (Hole1 NewSlot3)
                                    (Piece2 Piece1)
                                    (Primitive2 Primitive1)
                                    (Hole2 NewSlot4)
                                    (Depth NewSlot5))
              ($Grasped             (Piece InterimPiece1)
                                    (OldSupportSurface NewSlot2)
                                    (FreePrimitives InterimPrimitive1))
              ($MultiAligned        (Piece1 InterimPiece1)
                                    (Primitive1 InterimPrimitive1)
                                    (Piece2 Piece2)
                                    (Primitive2 Primitive2)
                                    (Hole2 NewSlot3)
                                    (Piece3 Piece1)
                                    (Primitive3 Primitive1)
                                    (Hole3 NewSlot4)
                                    (Depth NewSlot5)
                                    (Delta NewSlot1))))
  (Body ($FullMove                  (Piece InterimPiece1)
                                    (Delta NewSlot1))))
 (TokenSlots
  (Piece1 NIL                doc (* From goalSchema))
  (Piece2 NIL                doc (* From goalSchema))
  (Primitive1 NIL            doc (* From goalSchema))
  (Primitive2 NIL            doc (* From goalSchema))
  (Orientation NIL           doc (* From goalSchema))
  (DOF1 NIL                  doc (* From goalSchema))
  (InterimPiece1 NIL         doc (* From goalSchema))
  (InterimPrimitive1 NIL     doc (* From goalSchema))
  (DOF2 NIL                  doc (* From goalSchema))
  (NewSlot1 NIL              doc (* Promoted slot))
  (NewSlot2 NIL              doc (* Promoted slot))
  (NewSlot3 NIL              doc (* Promoted slot))
  (NewSlot4 NIL              doc (* Promoted slot))
  (NewSlot5 NIL              doc (* Promoted slot))
```

Figure 9-6: $NewSchemaC

$RevoluteJointA.

3.7. Solving the Same Problem After Learning

We now present the system with the same problem a second time
after schema acquisition, giving as a goal exactly the same information as
before, this time as the partially specified abstract joint schema instance
$RevoluteJoint0776. As before, the design process consists of fleshing out

the abstract joint schema given as a goal specification and producing a corresponding physical joint schema instance.

A single instantiated physical joint schema, $RevoluteJointA0966, is constructed by the design process. Starting from the abstract joint schema instance $RevoluteJoint0776, the design process accesses the newly acquired physical joint schema $RevoluteJointA and creates a new instance $RevoluteJointA0966, carrying information across the mapping specified in $RevoluteJoint. $RevoluteJointA0966 mentions all three pieces in the assembly, not just the two mentioned in the goal specification.

Selection of the third piece to fill the InterimPiece1 slot is made in accordance with the constraints of the $RevoluteJointA schema. Recall these constraints were established on the basis of interpiece relations which were found to be necessarily true during joint verification. In this case, such constraints mandate, among other things, that the shaft size of InterimPiece1 match the diameter of the hole in $BoredBlock1 and be slightly smaller than the diameter of the hole in $Washer1.

There are only two pieces ($Block1 and $Peg1) in the initial state not already included in the goal specification. Both are tested for conformance with the constraint set. $Peg1 is the only piece that can be used to fill the role of InterimPiece1.

After the design phase terminates, the planner looks for a way to achieve $RevoluteJointA0966. It finds $NewSchemaC by indexing from $RevoluteJointA. A new instance $NewSchemaC0971 is created with information mapped over from $RevoluteJointA0966, and this is recursively expanded to generate and operator sequence.

The operator sequence produced from $NewSchemaC0971 has 24 steps, arranged, roughly, as follows:

(1)   Brace $BoredBlock1 such that its socket is pointing upward.

(2)   Clear $Peg1 off of $Washer1, placing it directly on the workspace surface in some free spot.

(3)   Grasp $Washer1 and stack it on top of $BoredBlock1 with the hole of $Washer1 aligned with the socket of $BoredBlock1.

(4)   Grasp $Peg1 in such a way as not to occlude its shaft, and align it with the holes in $Washer1 and $BoredBlock1.

(5)   Translate $Peg1 along the negative z axis a distance corresponding to the alignment offset plus the minimum of the $Peg1 shaft length and the combined $Washer1 hole/$BoredBlock1 socket

depth.

Note that, unlike the observed plan, the resulting operator sequence does not rely on the presence of $Block1. In addition, extraneous commands in the observed plan that do not figure in the explanation from which $NewSchemaC was derived do not occur in the new plan.

3.8. Solving Similar Problems

$NewSchemaC can be applied in other problem situations to produce a successful assembly sequence. As long as the goal specification can be realized as an instance of $RevoluteJointA, $NewSchemaC may well be applicable. For the initial states of Figures 9-7 and 9-8, the goal specification remains the same as our previous example. Using $NewSchemaC, for the initial state of Figure 9-7, the performance element produces a 12-step assembly sequence, while 30 steps are generated for that of Figure 9-8.

A more interesting example is shown in Figure 9-9. In this case, the goal specification is an abstract joint schema instance that relates the descriptors $Washer3 and $BoredCylinder1. Note that the desired assembly has quite a different physical aspect than that of the widget in the learning episode. Functionally, however, the structure demonstrates

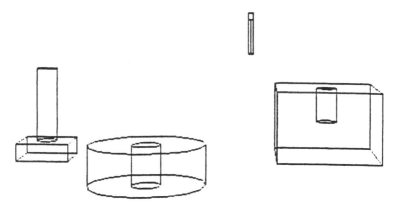

Figure 9-7: First Alternate Initial State for Widget Assembly Problem. The robot gripper is located in the center of the picture with fingers closed. $BoredBlock1 is to the right, $Peg1 is to the left, and $Washer1 is in the foreground just left of center.

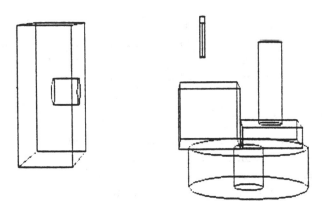

Figure 9–8:   Second Alternate Initial State for Widget Assembly Prob-
              lem. The robot gripper is located in the center of the pic-
              ture with fingers closed. $BoredBlock1 is to the left. $Wash-
              er1 is to the right, with $Block2 and $Peg1 stacked on top of
              it.

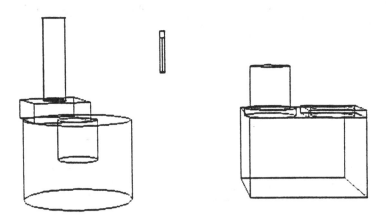

Figure 9–9:   Third Alternate Initial State for Widget Assembly Problem.
              The robot gripper is located in the center of the picture with
              fingers closed. $BoredCylinder1 is to the left, with $Peg1
              stacked on top of it. $Peg3 and $Washer2 are stacked (from
              left to right) on top of $Block1 on the right side of the
              workspace.

exactly the same joint behavior.

The design process properly selects $Peg2 over $Peg1 to fill the role of InterimPiece1. This selection is based on the interpiece constraints associated with $RevoluteJointA. The planning process produces an assembly sequence of 18 steps that achieves the goal specification.

3.9. Observing the Same or Similar Problems Again

After $NewSchemaC is integrated into the schema library, it can be used for planning (as previously) or recognized bottom–up during the course of future observation processes. This has two important implications:

(1)   More complicated joints using an instance of $RevoluteJointA as a part of their structure can now be understood and learned from. An analogous situation arises in this episode: Both $Cylindrical-JointA0311 and $RigidJointA301 are recognized using previously acquired instances of $NewSchemaB and $NewSchemaA, respectively. Note that these physical joint schema instances might still have been analyzable on the basis of $CylindricalJoint and $Rigid-Joint, but the presence of $NewSchemaC reduces the computational burden placed on the verifier.

(2)   Other observed episodes with functionally identical goals when achieved in the same physical manner lead to the bottom–up assertion of an instances of $RevoluteJointA via instances of $NewSchemaC. Such episodes no longer meet the learning criteria, so no effort is wasted in attempting to learn from them.

4. Summary and Discussion

ARMS is an *explanation–based learning–apprentice system* that addresses the *robot retraining problem*. This problem can be reduced to two subproblems — a *design problem* and an *assembly problem* — each characterized by very large search spaces. ARMS represents a novel type of learning–apprentice system, one that is governed by the principle of unobtrusiveness.

ARMS attacks the design problem by applying explanation–based learning. A known more abstract concept (e.g., $RevoluteJoint) is mapped to a realizable new concept (e.g., $RevoluteJointA), guided by an explanation constructed by a deductive inference procedure using a naive kinematic domain theory.

ARMS addresses the assembly problem through explanation–based learning of new composite operators. These new macro–operators are produced by analyzing an explanation derived from the causal model constructed by the system of an external expert's observed problem–solving behavior. The causal model is constructed by a novel *nonpredictive understanding* explanation–construction method. This strictly bottom–up technique is used to construct a generalizable structure in the assembly problem space. This is a viable alternative to the top–down methods used in other explanation–based learning work.

Finally, we note that ARMS constructs composite operators at differing levels of generality, thus providing an opportunity to experiment with several different operators acquired from the same example and measure their effect on performance.

Many open problems remain. In particular, the ARMS domain does not take *uncertainty* (e.g., what to do when the real world doesn't work as expected) into account. Traditionally, AI research has simply ignored this problem, reducing real–world planning problems to idealized problem–solving domains. The unspoken assumption is that problem–solving techniques can eventually be abstracted and applied in more challenging real–world situations. This assumption is open to question; much current planning research is meant to address such less well behaved worlds [16].

Work on nonpredictive understanding as an explanation–construction technique was driven by a particular problem domain. Other real–world domains may in fact suggest novel explanation–construction methods; such methods should be more efficient than the simplistic weak–method problem solvers typically used in explanation–based learning research.

The explanation–based learning algorithms used in ARMS rely on both domain–specific and domain–independent (e.g., explanation syntax) information when constructing a new schema. Exactly which is the best possible new schema remains an open question; much attention has been given to a facet of this question [15, 17–20], but the deeper issue remains. We are currently experimenting with a new explanation–based learning system which allows us to isolate schema–construction heuristics and compare their performance [21]. This new system also allows us to experiment with extensions to what is typically thought of as explanation–based learning which are not deductive, thus supporting other kinds of learning within a uniform explanation–based learning framework.

If we take our eventual goal to be the application of machine–learning techniques to real–world problems, then ARMS is a promising, albeit admittedly small, first step. ARMS' greatest contributions lie in its novel explanation–construction methodology, its integration of explanation–based learning in more than one space, its nontrivial robotic assembly domain, and its investigation of differing levels of generality in constructing new operators.

References

1. T. M. Mitchell, S. Mahadevan and L. I. Steinberg, "LEAP: A Learning Apprentice for VLSI Design," *Proceedings of the Ninth International Joint Conference on Artificial Intelligence*, Los Angeles, CA, August 1985, pp. 573–580.

2. B. Gustafson, "Development of Localized Planner for Artificial Intelligence–Based Robot Task Planning System," M.S. Thesis, University of Illinois at Urbana–Champaign, Urbana, IL, October 1986.

3. W. Chafe, "Some Thoughts on Schemata," *Theoretical Issues in Natural Language Processing 1*, Cambridge, MA, June 1975, pp. 89–91.

4. E. Charniak, "On the Use of Framed Knowledge in Language Comprehension," *Artificial Intelligence 11*, 3 (1978), pp. 225–265.

5. M. L. Minsky, "A Framework for Representing Knowledge," in *The Psychology of Computer Vision*, P. H. Winston (ed.), McGraw–Hill, New York, NY, 1975, pp. 211–277.

6. R. C. Schank and R. P. Abelson, *Scripts, Plans, Goals and Understanding: An Inquiry into Human Knowledge Structures*, Lawrence Erlbaum and Associates, Hillsdale, NJ, 1977.

7. R. E. Fikes, P. E. Hart and N. J. Nilsson, "Learning and Executing Generalized Robot Plans," *Artificial Intelligence 3*, (1972), pp. 251–288.

8. R. Tilove, "Extending Solid Modeling Systems for Mechanism Design and Kinematic Simulation," *IEEE Computer Graphics and Applications 3*, 3 (May 1983), pp. 9–19.

9. P. E. Friedland, "Knowledge–based Experiment Design in Molecular Genetics," Technical Report 79–771, Computer Science Department, Stanford University, Palo Alto, CA, 1979.

10. D. McDermott, "Artificial Intelligence Meets Natural Stupidity," *SIGART Newsletter 57*, (April 1976), pp. 4–9.

11. E. Charniak, "MS. MALAPROP, A Language Comprehension System," *Proceedings of the Fifth International Joint Conference on Artificial Intelligence*, Cambridge, MA, August 1977.

12. R. E. Cullingford, "Script Application: Computer Understanding of Newspaper Stories," Technical Report 116, Department of Computer Science, Yale University, New Haven, CT, January 1978.

13. G. F. DeJong, "An Overview of the FRUMP System," in *Strategies for Natural Language Processing*, W. G. Lehnert and M. H. Ringle (ed.), Lawrence Erlbaum and Associates, Hillsdale, NJ, 1982.

14. R. W. Wilensky, "Understanding Goal-Based Stories," Technical Report 140, Ph.D. Thesis, Department of Computer Science, Yale University, New Haven, CT, September 1978.

15. A. M. Segre, "On the Operationality/Generality Trade-off in Explanation-Based Learning," *Proceedings of the Tenth International Joint Conference on Artificial Intelligence*, Milan, Italy, August 1987, pp. 242–248.

16. J. Turney and A. M. Segre, "A Framework for Learning in Planning Domains with Uncertainty," 89-1009, CUCS, May 1989.

17. D. J. Mostow, "Machine Transformation of Advice into a Heuristic Search Procedure," in *Machine Learning: An Artificial Intelligence Approach*, R. S. Michalski, J. G. Carbonell, T. M. Mitchell (ed.), Tioga Publishing Company, Palo Alto, CA, 1983, pp. 367–404.

18. R. M. Keller, "Defining Operationality for Explanation-Based Learning," *Proceedings of the National Conference on Artificial Intelligence*, Seattle, WA, July 1987, pp. 482–487.

19. H. Hirsh, "Explanation-Based Generalization in a Logic-Programming Environment," *Proceedings of the Tenth International Joint Conference on Artificial Intelligence*, Milan, Italy, August 1987, pp. 221–227.

20. S. Minton and J. G. Carbonell, "Strategies for Learning Search Control Rules: An Explanation-based Approach," *Proceedings of the Tenth International Joint Conference on Artificial Intelligence*, Milan, Italy, August 1987, pp. 228–235.

21. C. Elkan and A. M. Segre, "Not the Last Word on EBL Algorithms," 89-1010, CUCS, May 1989.

Chapter 10

Case Study 2 — GENESIS:
Learning Schemata for Narrative Text Understanding

Raymond J. Mooney

1. Introduction

The ability to "understand" natural language text is a very difficult task requiring a large amount of world knowledge. Systems for understanding narrative text e.g., [1–3] generally encode relevant world knowledge in terms of *scripts* or *schemata* [4], that is, abstract descriptions of common plans and events. The amount of world knowledge represented in terms of schemata largely determines the performance of such a system. Experience with the FRUMP system [3] indicated that robustness of a text–understanding system is directly related to the number of schemata it possesses. However, anticipating and encoding all of the schemata required for a robust natural–language system is impossible for both theoretical and practical reasons. Theoretically, texts can display novel concepts unknown to the implementors of a natural–language system. If the natural–language system is to respond properly, it must discover such new concepts automatically. Practically, the number of schemata required to cover most natural–language domains is prohibitively large and prevents manual programming of all of the necessary concepts. Once again, automatic schema acquisition is essential.

GENESIS is a natural–language text–understanding system which, during its normal course of operation, uses explanation–based learning to acquire new plan schemata. Such schemata are acquired by explaining and generalizing specific single instances of plans executed by characters in a narrative. Characters' actions are explained in terms of later actions they enable and in terms of ultimate goals they achieve. When the system detects that a character has achieved an important goal by combining actions in a novel and unfamiliar way, it generalizes the specific explanation for how the goal was achieved into a general plan schema. Generalization is performed by the EGGS system (see Chapter 2), which removes

irrelevant information while maintaining the validity of the explanation.[1]
The resulting schema is then retained by the system and indexed so that
it can be subsequently retrieved and used to aid in the understanding of
future narratives.

The remainder of this chapter describes the GENESIS system and
presents examples illustrating its learning abilities. The overall organization of the system is presented in Section 2, and an example of its performance is given in Section 3. Sections 4, 5, and 6 present some details on
representation, understanding, and learning in GENESIS. Section 7
presents information on GENESIS' ability to learn meanings for schema-
related words. Finally, Section 8 compares GENESIS to other EBL systems and draws some conclusions. A more in depth description of the
entire system is given in Mooney [7].

2. Organization of the GENESIS System

A diagram illustrating the architecture of the complete GENESIS
system is shown in Figure 10–1. In the diagram, circles represent declarative data structures and rectangles represent procedural subsystems.
First, English input is parsed into predicate calculus using an adaptation
of McDYPAR [2] (a reduced version of the parser used in the BORIS narrative processing system). However, parsing is not the focus of the current
system and alternative techniques could be employed for this task e.g.,
[8–10]. The parsed input is passed to the *understander*, which uses
schematic knowledge in the *schema library* to causally connect the inputs
and fill in missing information. The embellished representation constructed for a narrative is called the *causal model*. An *explanation* for a
particular goal achievement is the subset of the causal model that supports the given goal state. The representation of actions used in
GENESIS is an enhanced STRIPS–like representation [11] and is discussed in Section 4. The techniques used in the understanding process are
similar to those used in previous work in narrative understanding [1–3,
12–14] and are discussed in Section 5.

GENESIS also has a number of components for demonstrating its
understanding. The question–answerer (Q/A) takes questions from the
user after they have been parsed and employs a number of heuristics for
retrieving answers from the causal model. Since the focus of the system is

---

[1] A previous implementation of GENESIS [5, 6] was built before the development of
EGGS and used a special–purpose generalizer.

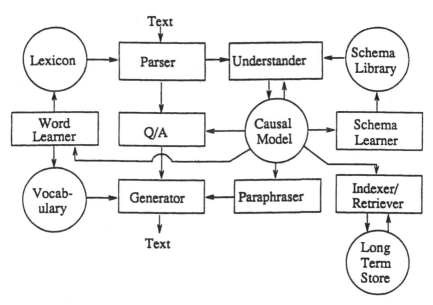

Figure 10–1: Architecture of GENESIS

on the construction of generalizable explanations, this subsystem is primarily built to answer questions about why a character performed a certain action or why a particular state exists. The system also has a *paraphraser* which uses the most comprehensive schemata instantiated in the causal model to produce a paraphrase of the text. The paraphraser can also produce English descriptions of abstract schemata from the schema library. The output of both the question–answerer and paraphraser are translated from predicate calculus to natural language by the *generator*, which is an adaptation of McMUMBLE [13] (a reduced version of the generator use by the TALE–SPIN narrative generating system [15]).

The *schema learner* analyzes the causal model built by the understander in order to learn new plan schemata. It monitors the causal model and detects when a character has achieved an important goal in a novel manner. The explanations for how such goals are achieved are used to learn new schemata. In addition to deciding when to learn, this subsystem includes an *explanation pruner*, *generalizer*, and *packager* as defined in Chapter 2. After the explanation for the goal achievement is extracted from the causal model, a special pruning function is used to remove actions and states that only support the goal through more abstract concepts. The pruned explanation is then generalized using the EGGS explanation–generalization algorithm. Next, an enhancement of the procedure for building partially ordered macro–operators discussed in Chapter 3 is used to package the generalized explanation into a schema. Finally, this schema is stored in the schema library and indexed so that it can aid the understanding of future narratives. The pruning, packaging, and indexing procedures as well as the procedure that decides when to learn are discussed in Section 6.

GENESIS also has the ability to learn word meanings for schema–related terms and to use the schemata it learns to index and retrieve specific instances. The word–learning process involves detecting the conceptual role that an unknown word fills in the schema that is being learned. After a word is associated with a slot in a new schema or with the new schema itself, a definition for the new word is constructed for both the parser's lexicon and the generator's vocabulary. This allows both the parser and generator to use the new word for understanding narratives and answering questions. GENESIS' ability to learn new words is briefly discussed in Section 7. After processing a narrative, the *indexer* stores the causal model constructed for the text in the *long–term store* and indexes it under the most comprehensive schemata used in interpreting the story. When answering questions about a particular narrative, the *retriever* can be instructed to retrieve past episodes that are indexed under the same schema used to interpret the current text. These modules allow GENESIS to function as a conceptual retrieval system [16] which, during normal operation, automatically learns new ways to index events. Further details on this aspect of GENESIS are given in [7, 17].

2.1. The Importance of the Complete System

Although GENESIS is primarily a tool for exploring learning, this section has revealed that it contains a large number of components that have no direct connection to learning, such as a parser, question–answerer, paraphraser, and so on. An important question concerns the relevance of these additional components. Though the nonlearning components in GENESIS certainly make the learning system easier to test and debug, they also serve a more important purpose. The primary goal of learning is to improve the performance of an overall system in some relevant task domain. Several AI researchers have stressed the importance of viewing learning in the context of a performance system [18–20]. The requirement of improving overall system performance often imposes important constraints on a learning system. As a result, certain degrees of freedom are eliminated that could otherwise be unfairly manipulated to bias the performance of an isolated learning system.

For example, in GENESIS, the same explanations that support learning must also be used to answer questions about the text, and the schemata produced by the learning mechanism must be able to aid the understanding of future narratives as well as support reasonable paraphrases. Many representations suitable for learning are unsuitable for performing these other tasks. Most EBL systems do not use the explanations they construct for any task other than to support generalization. In fact, most do not even retain the entire generalized explanation but rather extract only a macro–rule or macro–operator that summarizes the overall preconditions and post–conditions. These data structures do not generally contain information on the substructure that composes and justifies them.[2] In GENESIS, the entire generalized explanation must be retained in order to use the learned schema to understand future narratives and answer questions about them.

Complementing the impact of the understanding system on the learning system is the impact of the learning system on the understanding system. Building explanations sufficient to support generalization and schema acquisition is an important test of how well a text–processing system has actually "understood" a piece of text. Previous tasks that have been used to test understanding are question–answering [21], paraphrasing [1, 3], and summarizing [22]. Unlike these tasks, the ability to construct an explanation sufficient for generalization is a crucial test of how well the system has comprehended the global causal structure of a piece of text. Answering "why" and "how" questions is a good way of testing comprehension of *local* causal structure; however, unlike question–answering, generalization requires the construction of a globally consistent causal model. Paraphrasing and summarizing require having an adequate global structure for the text; however, they do not generally test the understanding of *causal* structure. For example, FRUMP [3] produced summaries of newspaper articles using *sketchy scripts* which contain only temporally ordered lists of events with very little causal information. In summary, for many narratives, it is fair to say that a system has not truly "understood" the text unless it has the ability to produce an explanation that could be generalized into a schema using EBL techniques. Therefore, the ability to learn a schema from a narrative can be

---

[2]The generalized triangle tables retained by STRIPS do contain much of this information. This knowledge is used to detect and correct problems encountered during execution monitoring.

viewed as an additional test of the understanding abilities of a natural-language system.

8. Sample Performance

A standard procedure is used to test GENESIS' ability to learn a schema from a single instance. This procedure illustrates both the schema learning process itself as well as the ability of the learned schema to improve system performance. First, the system is given a *test narrative* which presents a sparse description of an instance of the schema. This description is missing one or more actions that are crucial to the overall plan. Consequently, the narrative is not detailed enough for the system to construct a causally complete explanation for characters' actions without a schema to supply missing actions and inferences. The system is therefore unable to answer questions that require making default inferences about what must have taken place, and it is unable to produce an adequate paraphrase of the narrative. Next, the system is given a *learning narrative* which describes in detail a complete instance of the schema and which contains the crucial actions and other information that were lacking in the test narrative. Using its existing knowledge, GENESIS is able to construct a causally complete explanation for this narrative and can therefore answer questions about why actors performed certain actions as well as produce an adequate paraphrase of the text. Since the narrative presents a novel plan that achieves an important goal, the system generalizes its explanation of how the goal was achieved into a new plan schema. Finally, GENESIS is given the test narrative again. This time, it can use the schema it has just learned to fill in missing information, and as a result, it can now answer questions that it was previously unable to answer as well as produce a better paraphrase of the text.

The remainder of this section is dedicated to presenting the trace produced by GENESIS as it learns a "kidnapping for ransom" schema [5, 23–27]. This is currently the most complicated example on which GENESIS has been tested. GENESIS has also learned schemata for "murder for inheritance," "arson for insurance," and "solicitation entrapment." Details on these other examples are given in Mooney [7]. Before processing the narratives used in the kidnapping example, the system has knowledge about bargaining, capturing and confining, threatening, and a number of other concepts; however, it does not have any knowledge about the concept of kidnapping for ransom nor any knowledge of the words *kidnap, kidnapper,* or *ransom*. To illustrate the system's current ignorance of kidnapping and how this lack of knowledge affects its ability to understand certain kidnapping narratives, the system is first given a test narrative. Below is the actual I/O trace produced by the system:

Input: Ted is Alice's husband. He won 100000 dollars in the lottery. Bob imprisoned Alice in his basement. Bob got 75000 dollars and released Alice.

Thematic goal achieved: Ted is happy that Ted has the $100000.

Ready for questions:

>Summarize
Ted won $100000 in a lottery. Bob captured Alice and locked her in a basement. Bob released Alice.

>Why did Bob lock Alice in his basement?
Cannot find sufficient reason.

>How did Bob get the money?
Cannot find sufficient cause.

>Why did Bob release Alice
Cannot find sufficient reason.

>How did Ted get the money?
Ted won the $100000 in the lottery.

Notice that this narrative does not mention how Bob got the money or why Bob imprisoned Alice and then released her. Since the system does not have a schema for kidnapping, it cannot infer the missing information and causally connect the actions in the input. Consequently, its paraphrase of the narrative is very poor and it is unable to answer many questions about it. Next, GENESIS is given the following more detailed narrative:

Input: Fred is Mary's father and is a millionaire. John approached Mary and pointed a gun at her. She was wearing blue jeans. He told her if she did not get in his car, then he would shoot her. He drove her to his hotel and locked her in his room. John called Fred and told him John was holding Mary captive. John told Fred if Fred gave him 250000 dollars at Trenos, then John would release Mary. Fred paid him the ransom and the kidnapper released Mary. Valerie is Fred's wife and he told her that someone had kidnapped Mary.

Thematic goal achieved: John is happy that John has the $250,000.
Explanation suitable for generalization.
Pruning...Generalizing...Packaging...
Creating New Schema:
(CaptureBargain ?x55 ?a34 ?b9 ?c4 ?r5 ?y5 ?l11)

?b9 is a person. ?c4 is a location. ?r5 is a room. ?c4 is in ?r5. ?x55 is a character. ?b9 is free. ?x55 captures ?b9 and locks him/her in ?r5. ?a34 is a character. ?x55 contacts ?a34 and tells it that ?b9 is ?x55's captive. ?y5 is a valuable. ?x55 wants to have ?y5 more than it wants ?b9 to be ?x55's captive. ?a34 has a positive relationship with ?b9. ?a34 has ?y5. ?x55 and ?a34 carry out a bargain in which ?x55 releases ?b9 and ?a34 gives ?x55 ?y5 at ?l11.

Unknown word 'ransom' refers to ?y5 in CaptureBargain
Unknown word 'kidnapper' refers to ?x55 in Capture-Bargain

Having: ?x55 captured ?b9. suggest CaptureBargain
Having: ?x55 contacted ?a34 and told it that ?b9 was ?x55's captive. suggest CaptureBargain
Having: ?x55 and ?a34 carried out a bargain in which ?x55 released ?b9 and ?a34 gave ?x55 ?y5 at ?l11. suggest CaptureBargain

Unknown word '?x55 kidnap ?b9' refers to CaptureBargain

Ready for questions:

>Summarize Mary was free. John captured Mary and
locked her in a room. John contacted Fred and told
him that Mary was John's captive. John wanted to
have $250000 more than he wanted Mary to be John's
captive. Fred had a positive relationship with Mary.
Fred had the $250000. John and Fred carried out a
bargain in which John released Mary and Fred gave
John the $250000 at Trenos.

>Why did John approach Mary?
So John could aim the gun at Mary.

>Why did John aim the gun at Mary?
So John could threaten to shoot Mary with the gun unless Mary went from John into the car.

>Why did Mary get into the car?
Because Mary wanted not to be shot and because Mary
believed that if Mary did not go from John into the car
then John would shoot Mary with the gun.

>Why did John threaten to shoot Mary unless she got
in the car?
So John could drive Mary to the hotel in the car.

>Why did John drive Mary to the hotel?
So John could move Mary from the hotel into the
room.

>Why did John move Mary into the room?
So John could confine Mary in the room.

>Why did John confine Mary in the room?
So John could call Fred and could tell him that Mary
was John's captive and so John and Fred could carry
out a bargain in which John released Mary and Fred
gave John the $250000 at Trenos.

>Why did John tell Fred that John was holding Mary
captive?
So John and Fred could carry out a bargain in which

John released Mary and Fred gave John the $250000 at Trenos.

>Why did Fred give John the money?
Because Fred believed that if Fred gave John the $250000 at Trenos then John would release Mary and because Fred wanted Mary to be free more than he wanted to have the $250000.

>Why did Fred have $250000?
Because Fred had millions of dollars.

>Why did Fred believe that John was holding Mary captive?
Because John called Fred and told him that Mary was John's captive.

>Why did Fred want Mary free?
Because Fred was Mary's father.

>Why did John release Mary?
Because John wanted to have the $250000 more than he wanted Mary to be John's captive and because John believed that if John released Mary then Fred would give John the $250000 at Trenos.

Unlike the first narrative, this one is detailed enough to allow GENESIS to causally connect the characters' actions. Specifically, the crucial bargain that took place between the kidnapper and the ransom payer is alluded to more directly. As a result, the system is able to answer numerous questions about why certain characters performed certain actions. The resulting explanation for how John got the $250,000 is generalized into a new schema for kidnapping for ransom (which GENESIS calls CaptureBargain based on the names of two existing schemata that compose the new schema).

A few important aspects of the learned schema should be pointed out. First, it does not contain any facts or actions that are irrelevant to the workability of the plan. For example, the fact that the victim is wearing blue jeans is not included. A similarity–based learning system that was given a number of examples of kidnapping in which the victim was always wearing blue jeans is liable to include this fact in its representation of the concept. Second, the exact manner in which the component plan schemata (e.g., Capture) were decomposed into subgoals and executed in the example is not included in the schema. For example, the facts that the kidnapper executed the Capture by threatening the victim with a gun and then driving her to a hotel and that he contacted the ransom payer by telephone are not a part of the CaptureBargain schema. Third, the generalization process eliminates facts that are causally relevant to the plan only because they are specializations of more general facts. For example, the fact that the ransom payer was the victim's father is relevant to the plan since it motivated him to pay the ransom; however, the more important fact is the more general one, that he had a positive emotional relationship with the victim and consequently valued her freedom more than personal possessions. This generalization is important since the schema should be able to handle alternative relationships between the ransom payer and victim such as the husband–wife relationship in the test narrative.

After learning CaptureBargain, the system indexes the new schema so that if it subsequently encounters a narrative in which someone captures someone or exchanges someone's freedom for a valuable item, it will be reminded of CaptureBargain and attempt to use it to help understand the narrative. The system also acquires preliminary definitions for three unknown words which occurred in the story: *kidnapper*, *ransom*, and *kidnap*.

Finally, GENESIS is given the test narrative once again. This time, Alice's imprisonment reminds it of CaptureBargain, and it uses this newly acquired schema to infer the missing actions and explain how Bob got the money. Consequently, its ability to answer questions and paraphrase the text is greatly improved.

> Input: Ted is Alice's husband. He won 100000 dollars in the lottery. Bob imprisoned Alice in his basement. Bob got 75000 dollars and released Alice.
>
> Thematic goal achieved: Ted is happy that Ted has the $100000.
> Thematic goal achieved: Bob is happy that Bob has the $75000.
>
> Ready for questions:

>Summarize
Alice was free. Bob captured Alice and locked her in a basement. Bob contacted Ted and told him that Alice was Bob's captive. Bob wanted to have $75000 more than he wanted Alice to be Bob's captive. Ted had a positive relationship with Alice. Ted had the $75000. Bob and Ted carried out a bargain in which Bob released Alice and Ted gave Bob the $75000.

>Why did Bob lock Alice in his basement?
So Bob could contact Ted and could tell him that Alice was Bob's captive and so Bob and Ted could carry out a bargain in which Bob released Alice and Ted gave Bob the $75000.

>Why did Bob release Alice?
Because Bob wanted to have the $75000 more than he wanted Alice to be Bob's captive and because Bob believed that if Bob released Alice then Ted would give Bob the $75000.

>How did Bob get the money?
Bob kidnapped Alice.

>Who gave Bob the money?
Ted gave Bob the $75000.

>Why did Ted give him the money?
Because Ted believed that if Ted gave Bob the $75000 then Bob would release Alice and because Ted wanted Alice to be free more than he wanted to have the $75000.

>Why did Ted want Alice free?
Because Ted was Alice's husband.

>Why did Ted believe that Bob was holding Alice captive?
Because Bob contacted Ted and told him that Alice was Bob's captive.

While answering questions about this narrative for the second time, it is interesting to note that the system used the newly learned word *kidnap* to refer to the CaptureBargain schema in its answer to the question, "How did Bob get the money?" This is because the state in question is an effect of the new schema and since it knows how to refer to this schema in English, it considers it to be an appropriate answer.

4. Representation in GENESIS

All domain–specific knowledge in GENESIS is represented declaratively in the schema library. This knowledge is divided into information about *objects, attributes, states,* and *actions* which are further organized into taxonomic hierarchies. The hierarchies under each of these classes of knowledge support abstraction inferences such as Isa(?x, Gun) $\rightarrow$ Isa(?x, Weapon), Father(?x, ?y) $\rightarrow$ Parent(?x, ?y), and Poison(?x, ?y) $\rightarrow$ Murder(?x, ?y). Attributes refer to facts about an object that are not affected by actions, and states refer to other static facts about objects. Attributes and states can both have backward–chaining and forward–chaining Horn clause rules associated with them. For example, the following rule is used in a backward–chaining fashion to infer that someone possesses a particular amount of an object if he or she possesses a larger amount of that object:

$$\text{Amount}(?y,?g,?u) \wedge \text{Possess}(?a,?y) \wedge \text{Amount}(?x,?l,?u) \wedge \text{Isa}(?x,?t)$$
$$\wedge \text{Isa}(?y,?t) \wedge \text{LessThan}(?l,?g) \rightarrow \text{Possess}(?a,?x)$$

In this rule, Amount(?x,?l,?u) specifies that the object ?x consists of a number, ?l, of units, ?u (e.g., Amount(Money1, 100, dollars)).

Most of GENESIS' knowledge is in the form of action definitions. Actions are represented using an enhancement of the STRIPS–like representation presented in Chapter 3. The first modification is that preconditions are divided into constraints, preconditions, and motivations. *Constraints* are required attributes or classes of the arguments of an action and therefore cannot be achieved by other actions. *Preconditions* are physical states of the world that enable an action and can be achieved by other actions. *Motivations* are mental states of the actor, such as goals, goal priorities, and beliefs, that motivate the person to perform a volitional action. Together, constraints, preconditions, and motivations are called the *supports* of an action. As in the representation in Chapter 3, *effects* are states, possibly negated ones, resulting from the execution of an action. An action definition includes only the supports and effects unique to that particular action. Supports and effects that are inherited from more abstract actions are defined at that level. As an example, the supports and effects of the Murder action and one of its specializations (Poison) are shown in Table 10-1. The effect stating that the victim is dead is specified only in the definition of Murder. The preconditions that the actor must possess a poisonous food and the victim must be hungry and the effects that the poisonous food is inside the victim and no longer possessed by either the actor or victim are specific to Poison and are specified only in its definition. Knowledge about an action may also include information about its *expansion*, that is, its decomposition into more primitive actions. In this case, an action is recursively defined as a macro–operator that has an expansion in terms of other actions. The expansion of an action specifies the set of *subactions* which comprise the macro–operator and may also include other information such as temporal ordering constraints on the subactions (see Chapter 3).

5. Understanding in GENESIS

A substantial body of research in natural–language processing has addressed the problem of "understanding" narrative text. Most of the research in narrative understanding has focused on constructing explanations for characters' actions and inferring missing actions that are only implicitly mentioned [13, 28, (Chapter 10)]. Although these are difficult problems which are far from completely solved, a reasonable amount of progress has been made and a number of useful mechanisms have been developed.

In the work on narrative understanding, a distinction can be made between schema–based (also called script–based) and plan–based understanding mechanisms [4]. A *schema-based* understanding mechanism attempts to directly and efficiently access a relatively specific knowledge structure (a schema) that accounts for the actions in the text. This schema can then be efficiently used to causally connect actions in the

Table 1: Sample Definition of Action Supports and Effects			
Action	Constraints	Preconditions	Effects
Murder(?a,?v) "?a murdered ?v"	Isa(?a,Character) Isa(?v,Person)		Dead(?v)
Poison(?a,?v,?p) "?a poisoned ?v with ?p"	Poisonous(?p) Food(?p)	Possess(?a,?p) NeedSustenance(?v)	Inside(?p,?v) ¬Possess(?a,?p) ¬Possess(?v,?p)

narrative and fill in missing actions. In terms of problem solving, it is analogous to using a macro–operator to solve a particular problem in one step. Examples of systems that use schema–based understanding are SAM [1] and FRUMP [29].

A *plan–based* understanding mechanism, on the other hand, can be used for understanding novel situations. It involves searching for a set of missing actions that causally connect to observed actions to form a plan that achieves a character's goal. PAM [30] is an example of a system that does plan–based understanding. In terms of problem solving, this approach is more like doing search–intensive planning to achieve a goal. In Newell's terminology [31], plan–based understanding is primarily a *weak method* whereas schema–based understanding is primarily a *strong method.*

Since a robust understanding system must be able to deal with both mundane and novel situations, several recent understanding systems perform both schema– and plan–based understanding. For example, BORIS [2] and FAUSTUS [14, 32] are systems that use both of these understanding mechanisms. GENESIS also employs both schema– and plan–based mechanisms in its understanding process. First, the system tries to find an action schema that will directly explain the characters' actions. If this fails, it resorts to trying to causally connect individual actions in a plan–based manner. However, the search it performs during plan–based understanding is very limited to prevent it from spending an inordinate amount of time performing combinatorially explosive search through the space of all possible explanations. Consequently, GENESIS cannot produce adequate explanations for certain narratives although it theoretically could understand them given an exhaustive search algorithm and unlimited time and space. Nevertheless, the system's limited ability to do plan–based understanding allows it to construct explanations for many novel plans presented in narratives. The system then uses the EGGS generalizer to perform explanation–based learning on these explanations in order to learn new schemata which allow it to understand future instances of the plan using schema–based understanding. Explanation–based learning in GENESIS can therefore be viewed as the acquisition of schemata that allow the system to process narratives using efficient schema–based techniques which previously could have been understood only by using inefficient, search–intensive, plan–based understanding.

5.1. Schema Selection

If a schema–based mechanism is to be able to process a broad range of texts, it must have access to a large number of schemata. Therefore, to avoid repeated searching through the entire database of schemata, it must also have an efficient method for selecting the particular schemata that are applicable to the current input. This process is frequently referred to as *schema selection* or *frame selection*. It is a difficult problem and has been the subject of several research efforts [3, 32–35].

In GENESIS, the process of selecting a schema has two stages: *suggestion* and *determination*. An action, A, in a narrative *suggests* a schema, B, if A is a subaction of B. Each suggested schema is *instantiated* (i.e., a unique instance is created with the appropriate variable bindings) and monitors the inputs to find confirming evidence in the form of additional inputs which match states or actions in its expansion. When all of the subactions of a suggested schema have been observed or inferred as filling a gap in a causal chain of events, it is *determined* and its complete expansion is added to the causal model.[3]

5.2. Causally Connecting Actions Without a Schema

If, while processing a narrative, GENESIS encounters an input action that does not match part of an existing or suggested schema nor suggest any schemata, it attempts to explain the action in a more plan–based fashion by attempting to causally connect the new action to previous actions. The procedure GENESIS uses to connect actions without a schema is based on the plan verification algorithm given in Chapter 3. Basically, the system tries to deduce, by the effects of previous actions, how the preconditions of each action are met.

The implicit goal of the understanding procedure is to determine an action or connected set of actions taking place in the narrative that achieve a character's ultimate goal. Since narratives rarely explicitly mention characters' ultimate goals, the system must have a way of inferring them. *Thematic goals* [4] are defined as goals that arise from basic human wants and needs and therefore require no further explanation. GENESIS has a set of inference rules that determine when a thematic goal has been achieved. For example, the following inference rule defines

---

[3]The term *determination* is taken from Norvig [32], where it is used to refer to a similar process in FAUSTUS.

the thematic goal of wanting to possess valuable items:

$$\text{Possess}(?x,?y) \wedge \text{Valuable}(?y) \rightarrow \text{ThemeGoalMet}(?x, \text{Possess}(?x,?y))$$

GENESIS checks input actions and determined schemata to see whether they can be explained as achieving a thematic goal for some character.

Notice that GENESIS does not conduct an expensive search for missing actions that would create a causal chain of actions that achieves a thematic goal. Rather, it simply tries to verify that an existing set of actions causally connect together to achieve such a goal. Therefore, the system is incapable of constructing appropriate explanations for narratives that have missing actions and do not suggest known schemata. For example, consider the processing of the kidnapping test narrative *before* the system learns a kidnapping schema. Since there is no mention of the bargain that took place between Bob and Ted, the system is incapable of explaining Bob's actions and therefore cannot appropriately answer most questions about them. Understanding this narrative without a kidnapping schema using plan–based techniques would require independently inventing or discovering the notion of kidnapping for ransom.

5.3. Understanding the Kidnap Learning Narrative

As an example of the understanding process, this section summarizes GENESIS' processing of the learning narrative for the kidnapping example. First, the input facts that Fred is Mary's father and the owner of millions of dollars are simply added to the causal model. An effect of John's action of approaching Mary is that they are both at the same location. A precondition of John aiming a gun at Mary is that he have a line of sight path to her which is inferred from the fact that they are at the same location. John telling Mary that he would shoot her if she didn't get in the car suggests a Threaten schema. Since John driving Mary to the hotel requires as a precondition that Mary be in the car and since this state is the effect of the successful completion of the Threaten, the Threaten schema is determined. This in turn adds the assertion that Mary got in the car because she didn't want to be shot and causes the effect of the Aim to be equated to a precondition of the Threaten. John driving Mary to the hotel brings them both to the hotel's location. John confining Mary in the hotel room suggests a complete Capture schema, which is immediately determined since the Confine action is the final subaction in the causal chain of events defining Capture. This determination adds the assertion that John must have moved Mary into the room, which in turn is connected to the fact that she was already at the hotel. John calling Fred suggests a Telephone schema, which is subsequently determined when John tells Fred he is holding Mary captive. This Telephone instance is possible because John believes that he is holding Mary captive as an effect of the Capture. It should be noted that GENESIS has a very naive view of communication in which believing a proposition is a precondition for communicating it and in which everyone believes everything that they are told. Next, John telling Fred that he would release Mary if Fred gave him $250,000 suggests a Bargain schema, which is determined when both of these actions take place. Preconditions of the completed Bargain include that John have Mary held captive (which matches an effect of the Capture), that Fred have the $250,000 (which is inferred from the fact that he is a millionaire), that Fred believe that John has Mary (which matches an effect of the Telephone), and that Fred value Mary's freedom more than $250,000 (which is inferred from the fact that he is her father). Finally, the Bargain is found to achieve John's thematic goal of possessing $250,000. Figure 10-2 shows the final explanation constructed for this narrative. This explanation is called a *highest-level* explanation because it does not include the expansions of its component actions (e.g., Capture, Telephone, and Bargain). The complete explanation constructed for this narrative allows the system to answer the questions shown in the trace in Section 3.

6. Learning Schemata in GENESIS

If the understander is capable of constructing an explanation for how a goal was achieved, GENESIS may be able to use EGGS to generalize this explanation and learn a new schema which can aid in the understanding of future narratives. First, the system decides whether or not an explanation is worth generalizing. Second, a special pruning procedure eliminates overly specific parts of the explanation. Third, the EGGS generalizer is used to generalize the resulting explanation. Fourth, a special packager constructs a new schema from the generalized explanation and indexes the schema so that its subactions suggest it. The following subsections elaborate each of the steps in this process.

6.1. Deciding When to Learn

If every explanation GENESIS encountered were generalized into a new schema, the system would soon become overloaded with rarely used schemata. Most actions would suggest a large number of schemata, and selecting among these would require an excessive amount of processing

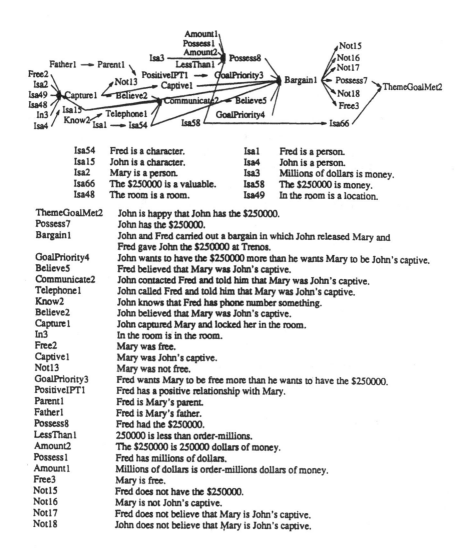

Figure 10-2: Kidnap Example— Specific Explanation (Highest Level)

Isa54	Fred is a character.	Isa1	Fred is a person.
Isa15	John is a character.	Isa4	John is a person.
Isa2	Mary is a person.	Isa3	Millions of dollars is money.
Isa66	The $250000 is a valuable.	Isa58	The $250000 is money.
Isa48	The room is a room.	Isa49	In the room is a location.

ThemeGoalMet2	John is happy that John has the $250000.
Possess7	John has the $250000.
Bargain1	John and Fred carried out a bargain in which John released Mary and Fred gave John the $250000 at Trenos.
GoalPriority4	John wants to have the $250000 more than he wants Mary to be John's captive.
Believe5	Fred believed that Mary was John's captive.
Communicate2	John contacted Fred and told him that Mary was John's captive.
Telephone1	John called Fred and told him that Mary was John's captive.
Know2	John knows that Fred has phone number something.
Believe2	John believed that Mary was John's captive.
Capture1	John captured Mary and locked her in the room.
In3	In the room is in the room.
Free2	Mary was free.
Captive1	Mary was John's captive.
Not13	Mary was not free.
GoalPriority3	Fred wants Mary to be free more than he wants to have the $250000.
PositiveIPT1	Fred has a positive relationship with Mary.
Parent1	Fred is Mary's parent.
Father1	Fred is Mary's father.
Possess8	Fred had the $250000.
LessThan1	250000 is less than order-millions.
Amount2	The $250000 is 250000 dollars of money.
Possess1	Fred has millions of dollars.
Amount1	Millions of dollars is order-millions dollars of money.
Free3	Mary is free.
Not15	Fred does not have the $250000.
Not16	Mary is not John's captive.
Not17	Fred does not believe that Mary is John's captive.
Not18	John does not believe that Mary is John's captive.

time. This problem is analogous to the performance deterioration noticed in problem–solving systems which learn too many useless macro–operators [36]. To help avoid this problem, GENESIS has criteria for selectively learning schemata. Below are the set of criteria that GENESIS uses to determine whether an explanation is worth generalizing:

(1)   It should be an explanation of how a thematic goal was achieved.

(2)   The highest–level explanation for the goal achievement should not be simply an instantiation of a known schema.

(3)   All actions in the highest–level explanation should rely on the character whose thematic goal was achieved.

The first criterion is crucial for ensuring that the acquired schema will be a useful one. A method for achieving a state that satisfies normal human wants and desires is likely to make a schema that will arise again and again. Therefore, an explanation is considered to be worth generalizing into a new schema only if it achieves a thematic goal. In the Kidnapping example, the explanation shown in Figure 10–2 satisfies this criterion since it achieves John's goal of possessing a valuable item.

The second criterion is the obvious one of not already possessing a schema for the combination of actions that achieves the goal. This simply involves checking the highest–level explanation for the goal achievement to make sure it contains several different actions. If the system already had a schema for this case, it would have used it in processing the narrative and the goal achievement would be explained at the highest level by an instance of this schema instead of by a combination of actions. In the Kidnapping example, the highest–level explanation satisfies this criterion since it is composed of a Capture, a Communicate, and a Bargain.

The third and final criterion ensures that the schema that is learned from the explanation is a volitional action that a character can use to achieve his or her own thematic goal. Let the term *main character* refer to the character whose thematic goal was achieved. If the learned schema is to represent a plan that can be executed by the main character to achieve the thematic goal, actions in the explanation that are not volitionally performed by the main character should at least be motivated by actions that he or she performs. The Kidnapping example also satisfies this criterion since all of Mary's and Fred's actions in the explanation are motivated by John's actions as part of his Capture and Bargain plans. If the third criterion were not used, the system could learn schemata that contain serendipitous actions over which the main character has no control. For example, assume GENESIS had the knowledge to explain the following narrative but did not have the third learning criterion:

> John's rich uncle was killed in an earthquake.
> John inherited a million dollars.

Such a system would acquire an EarthquakeInherit schema (or possibly a NaturalDisasterInherit schema) from its explanation of this narrative.

Such a nonvolitional schema would probably not be that useful for understanding later narratives.

6.2. Pruning the Explanation

If an explanation meets all three learning criteria, GENESIS proceeds to generalize it into a new schema. To increase to the generality and applicability of the resulting schema, GENESIS has a pruning procedure that removes unnecessarily specific branches from the explanation prior to generalization. If such pruning were not performed, the system would frequently learn schemata that are too restrictive to be useful (operational). For example, if the explanation for the kidnapping narrative were not pruned, the resulting schema would only cover cases in which the ransom payer was the victim's father.

The pruning procedure removes from an explanation units which only support the thematic goal achievement through a more abstract action or state as defined by the taxonomic hierarchy. For example, in the Kidnapping example, the fact that the ransom payer is the victim's father only supports the eventual goal achievement through a more abstract state stating that the ransom payer has a positive interpersonal relationship with the victim (PositiveIPT1). Therefore, the following two rules are pruned from the explanation structure:

$$\text{Father}(?x, ?y) \rightarrow \text{Parent}(?x, ?y)$$
$$\text{Parent}(?x, ?y) \rightarrow \text{PositiveIPT}(?x, ?y)$$

This process also prunes the fact that the kidnapper communicated with the ransom payer by means of the Telephone schema since its only contribution to the thematic goal achievement is through the more abstract Communicate schema.

6.3. Generalizing and Packaging the Explanation

Once an explanation is pruned, it is generalized using the EGGS generalization algorithm (see Chapter 2). The generalized explanation for the kidnapping example is shown in Figure 10–3. The generalized explanation is then packaged into a form suitable for the schema library. The packaging process used in GENESIS is a slight enhancement of the procedure for learning partially ordered macro–operators presented in Chapter 3. First, the leaves of the generalized explanation are divided into constraints, preconditions, and motivations based on the manner in which they support actions in the generalized explanation. Temporal ordering constraints and the effects of the schema are determined using the

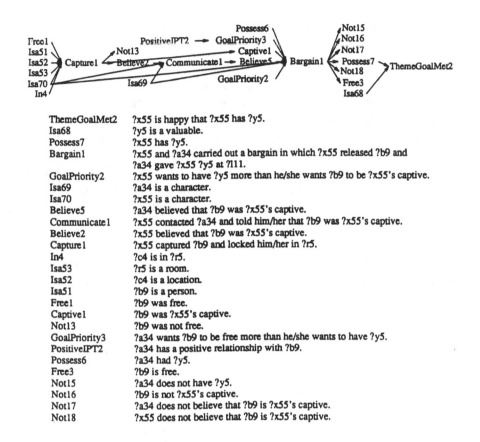

ThemeGoalMet2	?x55 is happy that ?x55 has ?y5.
Isa68	?y5 is a valuable.
Possess7	?x55 has ?y5.
Bargain1	?x55 and ?a34 carried out a bargain in which ?x55 released ?b9 and ?a34 gave ?x55 ?y5 at ?l11.
GoalPriority2	?x55 wants to have ?y5 more than he/she wants ?b9 to be ?x55's captive.
Isa69	?a34 is a character.
Isa70	?x55 is a character.
Believe5	?a34 believed that ?b9 was ?x55's captive.
Communicate1	?x55 contacted ?a34 and told him/her that ?b9 was ?x55's captive.
Believe2	?x55 believed that ?b9 was ?x55's captive.
Capture1	?x55 captured ?b9 and locked him/her in ?r5.
In4	?c4 is in ?r5.
Isa53	?r5 is a room.
Isa52	?c4 is a location.
Isa51	?b9 is a person.
Free1	?b9 was free.
Captive1	?b9 was ?x55's captive.
Not13	?b9 was not free.
GoalPriority3	?a34 wants ?b9 to be free more than he/she wants to have ?y5.
PositiveIPT2	?a34 has a positive relationship with ?b9.
Possess6	?a34 had ?y5.
Free3	?b9 is free.
Not15	?a34 does not have ?y5.
Not16	?b9 is not ?x55's captive.
Not17	?a34 does not believe that ?b9 is ?x55's captive.
Not18	?x55 does not believe that ?b9 is ?x55's captive.

Figure 10–3: Kidnap Example — Generalized Explanation

procedure presented in Chapter 3. The subactions and internal structure of the generalized explanation are also stored as part of the final result. As an example, an English summary of the CaptureBargain schema learned from the kidnapping narrative is shown in the trace in Section 3.

The final step in the packaging of a new schema is indexing the schema so that the system is "reminded" of it whenever it might be helpful in processing a future narrative. Indexing is performed by having the schema's volitional subactions suggest it. This method is appropriate because the new schema may now provide an explanation for why someone is executing the subaction. The suggestions for the CaptureBargain schema are also presented in the trace presented in Section 3. When the test narrative is processed for the second time, the fact that Bob confined

Alice in his basement suggests a Capture schema which is immediately determined and in turn suggests the new CaptureBargain schema. This suggested schema is subsequently determined when it explains how Bob got the money and why he released Alice. The resulting missing actions and connections added to the causal model due to the determination of this schema allow GENESIS to answer correctly the questions it couldn't answer when it processed the story without the schema.

7. Learning Word Meanings

As revealed in the I/O trace presented in Section 3, GENESIS also has the ability to learn provisional meanings for words from one example of their use. While processing the learning narrative for the kidnapping example, the system encounters the following unknown words: *kidnapper*, *ransom*, and *kidnap*. Based on the context in which these words appear and their relation to the overall schema that is learned, the system acquires preliminary meanings for each of these unknown words.

Previous computational models of the acquisition of word meaning [37–39] have assumed existing knowledge of the concept underlying the word to be learned. In these models, word learning is a process of using surrounding context to establish an identification between a new lexical item and a known concept. However, new words are not always encountered as labels for known concepts. When encountering a new concept in natural language text or discourse, it is quite likely that one will also come across unknown words that refer to various aspects of the new concept. Unlike previous models, word learning in GENESIS is integrated with schema acquisition and the system is capable of acquiring word meanings and their underlying concepts from the same piece of text.

The process of acquiring word meanings in GENESIS depends on whether the word is a role label or a schema label. *Role labels* are words like *kidnapper* or *ransom* which refer to the role a particular person or object fills in a schema. Schema labels are words which refer to entire plan schemata such as *kidnap* or *rob*.

Role labels are acquired in a manner similar to that employed by the FOUL–UP system [39]. If an unknown noun fills a slot in an action which is subaction of a learned schema, then this word is associated with the corresponding slot in the overall schema. For example, since the unknown word *ransom* acts as the object which is transferred from the ransom payer (?a34) to the kidnapper (?x55) in the CaptureBargain schema, it is associated with this role in the overall schema (i.e., ?y5). As a result, it is given a definition as a valuable item transferred in a CaptureBargain and is made to suggest the CaptureBargain schema. The fact that role labels suggest their related schemata allows them to aid in the understanding of future narratives. For example, the definition acquired for the word *ransom* is crucial to GENESIS' understanding of the following narrative.

Ted is Alice's husband. John took Alice into a room.
Ted paid John the ransom and John released Alice.

When the word *ransom* is encountered in this narrative, it suggests that the CaptureBargain schema might be relevant. This schema is then used in a top–down fashion to construct an explanation for the text. Since no other piece of information suggests CaptureBargain, the learned definition for *ransom* is a critical piece of knowledge used in the understanding of this narrative.

Learning meanings for schema labels is a more difficult task since the relevant context is potentially much broader. A sentence such as "John robbed the store" may be used to introduce a long piece of text elaborating the situation, to succinctly summarize a previous piece of text, or to refer to a single action in an even larger plan. A few heuristics have been developed that allow a reasonable guess to be made regarding the referent of such unknown verbs. The following one is used to resolve the meaning of "kidnap" as used in the kidnap learning narrative:

If one character informs another that some unknown action occurred and a schema whose actor is the same as this action's was recently acquired from the narrative, and this schema also has roles filled by the speaker and any direct and indirect objects of the action, then assume that the speaker is summarizing the event and that the unknown act refers to the new schema.

Specifically, since Fred tells his wife that "someone kidnapped Mary" and since both he and Mary were participants in the just completed CaptureBargain schema, GENESIS assumes that the word *kidnap* refers to CaptureBargain. The system gives it a definition stating that *kidnap* refers to an instance of CaptureBargain in which the subject of the clause is the actor (?x55) and the direct object is the victim (?b9).

It should be noted that word definitions acquired by the system are only provisional and can be removed if contradicted by later evidence. More information on GENESIS' word–learning abilities is presented in Mooney [7, 40].

8. Conclusions

GENESIS is a unique EBL system for several reasons. First, it is a complete performance system operating in a complex domain which uses a general explanation–based learning mechanism to improve performance. Other complete EBL systems operating in complex domains (e.g., ARMS, Chapter 9; PHYSICS–101, Chapter 11; LEX–2 [41]) are not based on domain–independent generalizers.

Second, GENESIS has illustrated EBL's ability to improve the performance of an understanding system. Most other EBL systems improve their ability to solve problems rather than their ability to construct explanations for observed behavior. Other than GENESIS, the only EBL system that improves its ability to understand external problem solving behavior is the ARMS system (Chapter 9). ARMS uses learned schemata to aid the understanding of assembly sequences in a robotics domain. However, the understanding system in ARMS is incapable of inferring missing actions, and therefore, unlike GENESIS, the plan schemata it learns cannot be used to fill in gaps in future observations.

Third, GENESIS has motivated psychological experiments which indicate that people can also perform explanation–based learning of schemata from novel plans presented in narrative text (see Chapter 8 and [42]). There are currently no other psychological experiments specifically directed at judging the ability of an EBL system to model human learning. Nevertheless, as reviewed by Murphy and Medin [43], there is a substantial amount of psychological research that reveals the important effect subjects' background knowledge and naive theories of the world have on the process of concept acquisition.

In conclusion, this chapter has shown that a general explanation–based learning mechanism can be used to improve the abilities of a natural–language system for narrative text comprehension. However, many schemata needed for narrative understanding cannot be learned using a purely explanation–based approach. For example, imagine a system like GENESIS trying to learn a schema for a birthday party by reading narratives about particular celebrations. Such a system could probably use its domain knowledge to explain the baking, cutting, and eating of the birthday cake since these actions are causally connected and satisfy important hunger and enjoyment goals. However, it would probably not be able to explain why someone put a particular number of candles on the cake and why someone else made a wish and then blew them out while everyone else sang. However, these components of the birthday–party schema might be learned using a similarity–based approach. Since many stereotypical actions (e.g., a wedding ceremony or a trip to the restaurant or supermarket) contain both features that are causally necessary and others that are conventional, such an approach to integrating EBL and SBL could be very useful, particularly in the domain of narrative understanding.

References

1. R. E. Cullingford, "Script Application: Computer Understanding of Newspaper Stories," Technical Report 116, Department of Computer Science, Yale University, New Haven, CT, January 1978.

2. M. J. Dyer, *In–Depth Understanding*, MIT Press, Cambridge, MA, 1983.

3. G. F. DeJong, "An Overview of the FRUMP System," in *Strategies for Natural Language Processing*, W. G. Lehnert and M. H. Ringle (ed.), Lawrence Erlbaum and Associates, Hillsdale, NJ , 1982.

4. R. C. Schank and R. P. Abelson, *Scripts, Plans, Goals and Understanding: An Inquiry into Human Knowledge Structures*, Lawrence Erlbaum and Associates, Hillsdale, NJ, 1977.

5. R. J. Mooney and G. F. DeJong, "Learning Schemata for Natural Language Processing," *Proceedings of the Ninth International Joint Conference on Artificial Intelligence*, Los Angeles, CA, August 1985, pp. 681–687.

6. R. J. Mooney, "Generalizing Explanations of Narratives into Schemata," M.S. Thesis, Department of Computer Science, University of Illinois, Urbana, IL, May 1985.

7. R. J. Mooney, "A General Explanation–Based Learning Mechanism and its Application to Narrative Understanding," Ph.D. Thesis, Department of Computer Science, University of Illinois, Urbana, IL, January 1988.

8. H. Hirst, Explanation–Based Generalization in a Logic–Programming Environment, , January 1987.

9. M. P. Marcus, *A Theory of Syntactic Recognition for Natural Language*, MIT Press, Cambridge, MA, 1980.

10. D. L. Waltz and J. B. Pollack, "Massively Parallel Parsing: A Strongly Interactive Model of Natural Language Interpretation," *Cognitive Science*, 1984.

11. R. E. Fikes, P. E. Hart and N. J. Nilsson, "Learning and Executing Generalized Robot Plans," *Artificial Intelligence 3*, (1972), pp. 251–

288.

12. E. Charniak, "MS. MALAPROP, A Language Comprehension System," *Proceedings of the Fifth International Joint Conference on Artificial Intelligence*, Cambridge, MA, August 1977.

13. R. C. Schank and C. Riesbeck, *Inside Computer Understanding*, Lawrence Erlbaum and Associates, Hillsdale, NJ, 1981.

14. R. W. Wilensky, *Planning and Understanding: A Computational Approach to Human Reasoning*, Addison–Wesley, Reading, MA, 1983.

15. J. Meehan, "The Metanovel: Writing Stories by Computer," Technical Report 74, Ph.D. Thesis, Yale University, New Haven, CT, 1976.

16. R. C. Schank, J. L. Kolodner and G. F. DeJong, "Conceptual Information Retrieval," in *Information Retrieval Research*, R. N. Oddy, S. E. Robertson, C. J. van Rijsbergen, and P. W. Williams (ed.), Butterworths, London, 1981.

17. R. J. Mooney and G. F. DeJong, "Learning Indices for Conceptual Information Retrieval," Technical Report UILU–ENG–87–2230, Coordinated Science Laboratory, University of Illinois at Urbana–Champaign, Urbana, IL, May 1987.

18. H. A. Simon, "Why Should Machines Learn?," in *Machine Learning: An Artificial Intelligence Approach*, R. S. Michalski, J. G. Carbonell and T. M. Mitchell (ed.), Tioga Publishing Co., Palo Alto, CA., 1983, pp. 25–37.

19. T. M. Mitchell, "Learning and Problem Solving," *Proceedings of the Eighth International Joint Conference on Artificial Intelligence*, Karlsruhe, West Germany, August 1983, pp. 1139–1151.

20. B. G. Buchanan, T. M. Mitchell, R. G. Smith and C. R. Johnson, "Models of Learning Systems," in *Encyclopedia of Computer Science and Technology, Vol. 11*, J. Belzer, A. G. Holzman, & A. Kent (ed.), Marcel Dekker, New York, NY, 1977, pp. 24–51.

21. W. Lehnert, *The Process of Question Answering*, Lawrence Erlbaum and Associates, Hillsdale, NJ, 1978.

22. W. G. Lehnert, "Plot Units: A Narrative Summarization Strategy," in *Strategies for Natural Language Processing*, W. G. Lehnert and M. H. Ringle (ed.), Lawrence Erlbaum and Associates, Hillsdale, NJ, 1982, pp. 375–414.

23.   G. F. DeJong, "Generalizations Based on Explanations," *Proceedings of the Seventh International Joint Conference on Artificial Intelligence*, Vancouver, B.C., Canada, August 1981, pp. 67–70.

24.   G. F. DeJong, "Automatic Schema Acquisition in a Natural Language Environment," *Proceedings of the National Conference on Artificial Intelligence*, Pittsburgh, PA, August 1982, pp. 410–413.

25.   G. F. DeJong, "Explanation Based Learning," in *Machine Learning: An Artificial Intelligence Approach, Vol. II*, R. S. Michalski, J. G. Carbonell, T. M. Mitchell (ed.), MORGAN, 1986.

26.   G. F. DeJong and R. J. Mooney, "Explanation-Based Learning: An Alternative View," *Machine Learning 1*, 2 (1986), pp. 145–176.

27.   R. J. Mooney, "Generalizing Explanations of Narratives into Schemata," in *Machine Learning: A Guide To Current Research*, T. M. Mitchell, J. G. Carbonell and R. S. Michalski (ed.), Kluwer Academic Publishers, Hingham, MA, 1986, pp. 207–212.

28.   E. Charniak and D. McDermott, *Introduction to Artificial Intelligence*, Addison–Wesley, Reading, MA, 1985.

29.   G. F. DeJong, "Skimming Stories in Real Time: An Experiment in Integrated Understanding," Technical Report 158, Ph.D. Thesis, Department of Computer Science, Yale University, New Haven, CT, 1979.

30.   R. W. Wilensky, "Understanding Goal-Based Stories," Technical Report 140, Ph.D. Thesis, Department of Computer Science, Yale University, New Haven, CT, September 1978.

31.   A. Newell, "Artificial Intelligence and the Concept of Mind," in *Computer Models of Thought and Language*, R. C. Schank & K. M. Colby (ed.), W. H. Freeman and Company, San Francisco, CA, 1973, pp. 1–60.

32.   P. Norvig, "Frame Activated Inferences in a Story Understanding Program," *Proceedings of the Eighth International Joint Conference on Artificial Intelligence*, Karlsruhe, West Germany, August 1983, pp. 624–626.

33.   E. Charniak, "With a Spoon in Hand this Must be the Eating Frame," *Theoretical Issues in Natural Language Processing 2*, Urbana, IL, 1978, pp. 187–193.

34. E. Charniak, "Context Recognition in Language Comprehension," in *Strategies for Natural Language Processing*, W. G. Lehnert and M. H. Ringle (ed.), Lawrence Erlbaum and Associates, Hillsdale, NJ, 1982, pp. 435–454.

35. S. L. Lytinen, "Frame Selection in Parsing," *Proceedings of the National Conference on Artificial Intelligence*, Austin, TX, August 1984.

36. S. Minton, "Selectively Generalizing Plans for Problem–Solving," *Proceedings of the Ninth International Joint Conference on Artificial Intelligence*, Los Angeles, August 1985, pp. 596–599.

37. M. Selfridge, "Inference and Learning in a Computer Model of the Development of Langague Comprehension in a Young Child," in *Strategies for Natural Language Processing*, W. G. Lehnert and M. H. Ringle (ed.), Lawrence Erlbaum and Associates, 1982, pp. 299–326.

38. R. C. Berwick, "Learning Word Meanings from Examples," *Proceedings of the Eighth International Joint Conference on Artificial Intelligence*, Karlsruhe, West Germany, August 1983, pp. 459–461.

39. R. H. Granger, "FOUL–UP: A Program that Figures Out Meanings of Words from Context," *Proceedings of the Fifth International Joint Conference on Artificial Intelligence*, Cambridge, MA, August 1977, pp. 172–178.

40. R. J. Mooney, "Integrated Learning of Words and their Underlying Concepts," *Proceedings of the Ninth Annual Conference of the Cognitive Science Society*, Seattle, WA, July 1987.

41. T. M. Mitchell, S. Mahadevan and L. I. Steinberg, "LEAP: A Learning Apprentice for VLSI Design," *Proceedings of the Ninth International Joint Conference on Artificial Intelligence*, Los Angeles, CA, August 1985, pp. 573–580.

42. W. Ahn, R. J. Mooney, W. F. Brewer and G. F. DeJong, "Schema Acquisition from One Example: Psychological Evidence for Explanation–Based Learning," *Proceedings of the Ninth Annual Conference of the Cognitive Science Society*, Seattle, WA, July 1987.

43. G. L. Murphy and D. L. Medin, "The Role of Theories in Conceptual Coherence," *Psychological Review 92*, 3 (July 1985), pp. 289–316.

Chapter 11

Case Study 3 — PHYSICS 101: Learning in Mathematically Based Domains

Jude W. Shavlik

1. Introduction

Mathematically based domains present several unique challenges and opportunities for machine learning. Many scientific and technical domains — physics, electronics, chemistry, and economics, for example — share the common formalism of mathematics, and much of the reasoning in these fields involves understanding the constraints inherent in mathematical descriptions. Mathematical models of real–world situations are constructed, and these mathematical abstractions are used to predict the behavior of the domain being modeled. Hence, solving quantitative problems in these domains requires a competence in symbolic mathematical manipulation. Furthermore, since mathematics is the underlying formal language, many important domain concepts can be adequately captured only through a mathematical specification. Thus, concept learning in these domains is also rooted in mathematics.

The research reported here focuses on learning new concepts from examples in mathematically oriented domains, using the explanation-based learning paradigm. A computer system, PHYSICS 101, has been developed that embodies the theories of learning and problem solving developed. It is intended to model, in a psychologically plausible manner, the acquisition of concepts taught in a first–semester college physics course [1-3] — hence the name PHYSICS 101. The model assumes competence in mathematics at the level of someone who has completed a semester of calculus.

Mathematically based domains are an area where the strengths of explanation–based learning are particularly appropriate, because explanation–based learning supports the construction of large concepts by analyzing how smaller concepts can be pieced together to solve a specific problem. Combining small concepts to form larger ones is the basis of progress in mathematical domains.

Because explanation–based learning requires extensive domain knowledge, it clearly is not appropriate for all learning in a new domain.

However, it may be useful even in early learning if the new domain relies heavily on a domain for which learner does have substantial knowledge. Because mathematics underlies many other domains, a novice with some mathematical sophistication may be able to make use of explanation-based techniques without extensive knowledge of the new domain.

The focus of the PHYSICS 101 implementation is not physics per se. Very little knowledge about physics is in the system. In fact, all of its initial physics knowledge is contained in a half–dozen or so formulae, which are listed later in this chapter. None of the system's algorithms utilize knowledge about physics, except that which is captured in these initial physics formulae. Rather, the focus is on mathematical reasoning, and the domain of physics is used as a testbed, since it is an elegant domain that stresses the use of complicated mathematics.

1.1. Initial Knowledge of the System

PHYSICS 101 possesses a large number of mathematical problem-solving techniques. For example, it can symbolically integrate expressions, cancel variables, perform arithmetic, and replace terms by utilizing known formulae. Figure 11–1 contains a portion of the system's hierarchy of calculation techniques. A calculation step may either rearrange the entities in the current expression, simplify the current expression, or replace terms in the expression by substituting formulae. Rearrangement involves such things as moving constants into and out of integrals and derivatives. Simplification involves algebraic cancellation, numerical calculation, and the solving of calculus. The formulae that may be used to replace variables existing in an expression are determined by the domain being investigated. (Further details on PHYSICS 101's problem solver appear in Shavlik [4, 5].)

Figure 11–2 contains some of the general mathematical rewrite rules known to the system. Note some formulae belong to more than one category, depending on use. (Terms beginning with a question mark are universally quantified variables.)

Figure 11–3 contains the initial physics formulae provided to the system, along with the conditions on their applicability. The first two formulae in Figure 11–3 define the physical concepts of velocity (V) and acceleration (A). An object's velocity is the time rate of change of its position (X) and its acceleration is the time rate of change of its velocity. Newton's second and third laws are also included. (Newton's first law need not be included because it is a special case of his second law.) The

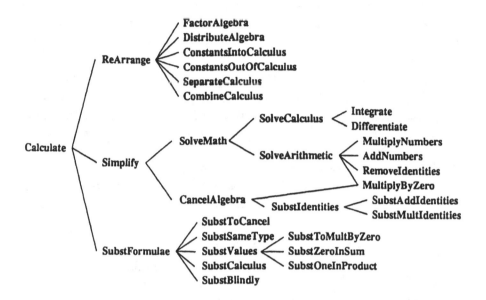

Figure 11–1: Some of the System's Mathematical Techniques

second law states that the net force (F) on an object equals its mass (M) times its acceleration (A). The net force is decomposed into two components: the external force (F_{ext}) and the internal force (F_{int}). External forces result from any external fields (e.g., gravity) that act upon objects. Object $?i$'s internal force is the sum of the forces the other objects in the world[1] exert on object $?i$. These *interobject* forces are constrained by Newton's third law, which says that every action has an equal and opposite reaction.

Position, velocity, acceleration, and force are spatial *vectors*. Hence one of their arguments $(?c)$ indicates which vector component is being discussed $(x, y, \text{ or } z)$. All of these physical variables are functions of time. Mass, however, is a time–independent scalar. It is only indexed by the physical object whose mass is being specified.

When a problem is described, the number of objects in the world is specified. At this time, summations $(\sum\text{'s})$ and products $(\prod\text{'s})$ in the

---

[1] The term *world* is used to refer to physical systems and situations. The term *system* is reserved for referring to computer programs.

$?expression - ?expression = 0$

      Problem-Solving Schema: SubstAddIdentities

$?expression + 0 = ?expression$

      Problem-Solving Schema: RemoveIdentities

$?expression / ?expression = 1$

      Problem-Solving Schema: SubstMultIdentities

      Preconditions: NOT(ZeroValued($?expression$))

$1 * ?expression = ?expression$

      Problem-Solving Schema: RemoveIdentities

$\int (?independent * ?expression) \, d\,?x = ?independent \int ?expression \, d\,?x$

      Problem-Solving Schema: ConstantsOutOfCalculus

      Preconditions: IndependentOf($?independent, ?x$)

$\int (?expression_1 + ?expression_2) \, d\,?x = \frac{d}{d\,?x} ?expression_1 + \frac{d}{d\,?x} ?expression_2$

      Problem-Solving Schema: SeparateCalculus

$\int ?expression_1 \, d\,?x + \int ?expression_2 \, d\,?x = \int (?expression_1 + ?expression_2) \, d\,?x$

      Problem-Solving Schema: CombineCalculus

$\frac{d}{d\,?x} ?expression^{?n} = ?n \, ?expression \frac{d}{d\,?x} ?expression^{?n-1}$

      Problem-Solving Schema: Differentiate

      Preconditions: Number($?n$)

$\int ?expression \, d\,?x = ?independent * ?x + constant$

      Problem-Solving Schema: Integrate

      Preconditions: IndependentOf($?independent, ?x$)

Figure 11–2: Sample Mathematical Rewrite Rules

known formulae are expanded. For instance, if there are three objects in
a world, the second from last equation in Figure 11–3 becomes:

$$F_{int,\, ?i,\, ?c}(?t) = F_{?j1,?i,\, ?c}(?t) + F_{?j2,?i,\, ?c}(?t)$$

Preconditions:

Permutation($\{?i, ?j1, ?j2\}$, *ObjectsInWorld*) $\wedge$ IsaComponent($?c$) $\wedge$ IsaTime($?t$)

Expanded equations are produced because of their greater psychological plausibility as a model of learning by a college freshman.

World–specific equations can also be provided when a new problem is posed. For example, it may be stated that the external force on object k is $M_k\, g\, X_{k,y}$. Although formulae of these types may be used in solutions to specific examples, they could unnecessarily constrain generalization, since they do not hold in *all* worlds.

$$V_{?i,\, ?c}(t) = \frac{d}{dt} X_{?i,\, ?c}(t)$$

Preconditions: Member($?i$,*ObjectsInWorld*) $\wedge$ IsaComponent($?c$)

$$A_{?i,\, ?c}(t) = \frac{d}{dt} V_{?i,\, ?c}(t)$$

Preconditions: Member($?i$,*ObjectsInWorld*) $\wedge$ IsaComponent ($?c$)

$$F_{net,\, ?i,\, ?c}(?t) = M_{?i} * A_{?i,\, ?c}(?t)$$

Preconditions: Member($?i$,*ObjectsInWorld*) $\wedge$ IsaComponent($?c$) $\wedge$ IsaTime($?t$)

$$F_{net,\, ?i,\, ?c}(?t) = F_{ext,\, ?i,\, ?c}(?t) + F_{int,\, ?i,\, ?c}(?t)$$

Preconditions: Member($?i$,*ObjectsInWorld*) $\wedge$ IsaComponent($?c$) $\wedge$ IsaTime($?t$)

$$F_{int,\, ?i,\, ?c}(?t) = \sum_{\substack{j \in ObjectsInWorld \\ j \neq ?i}} F_{j,\, ?i,\, ?c}(?t)$$

Preconditions: Member($?i$,*ObjectsInWorld*) $\wedge$ IsaComponent($?c$) $\wedge$ IsaTime ($?t$)

$$F_{?j,\, ?i,\, ?c}(?t) = -F_{?i,\, ?j,\, ?c}(?t)$$

Preconditions: Member($?i$,*ObjectsInWorld*) $\wedge$ Member($?j$, *ObjectsInWorld*) $\wedge$

$?i \neq ?j \wedge$ IsaComponent($?c$) $\wedge$ IsaTime($?t$)

Figure 11–3: The Initial Physics Formulae of the System

2. Building Explanations in PHYSICS 101

In explanation–based learning, the solution to a specific sample problem is generalized and the result saved, in the hopes of being applicable to future problems. This section addresses the construction of explanations in mathematically based domains, and the next addresses the generalization of these explanations. The focus is on understanding solutions, presented by a teacher, to problems the system could not solve on its own.[2] During this understanding process, gaps in the teacher–provided solution may need to be filled. The teacher must provide enough guidance so that the system's limited problem solver can successfully solve the problem. If the provided solution can be sufficiently well understood, a new equation may result, and the next time the system faces a problem related to the current one it may be able to solve it without the need for external assistance.

Understanding a teacher–provided solution involves two phases. First, the system attempts to verify that each of the instructor's solution steps mathematically follows. If successful, in the second phase the mathematical reasoning component of PHYSICS 101 builds an explanation of *why* the solution works. A sample collision problem illustrates these two phases.

2.1. A Sample Problem

In the one–dimensional problem shown in Figure 11–4, there are three balls moving in free space, without the influence of any external forces. (Nothing is specified about the forces between the balls. Besides their mutual gravitational attraction, there could be a long–range electrical interaction and a very complicated interaction during the collision.) In the initial state (state A) the first ball is moving toward the other two, which are stationary. Some time later (state B) the second and third balls are recoiling from the resulting collision. The task is to determine the velocity of the first ball after the collision.

---

[2] Although the emphasis is on teacher–provided solutions, much of this discussion also applies to the explanation of the system's own problem solving. It may take a substantial amount of work for PHYSICS 101 to solve a problem, even without needing external help, and this effort can be reduced in the future by creating a new equation from the analysis of its labors.

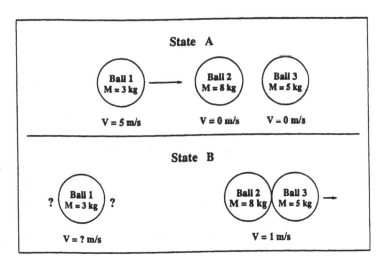

Figure 11–4: A Three–Body Collision Problem

PHYSICS 101 cannot solve this problem with only the formula shown in Figure 11–3. Initially, the formula $V = ddtX$ is tried, which leads nowhere, then the solution steps presented in Figure 11–5 are attempted. The system's problem solver is incomplete, for reasons detailed by Shavlik [4]. One source of incompleteness occurs because the problem solver never performs two unmotivated ("blind") substitutions consecutively. The problem solver possesses no motivated strategy to lead it past line 2 in Figure 11–5, and asks for a solution from its teacher.

The teacher's solution to the collision problem can be seen in Figure 11–6. Without being explicitly stated, the principle of conservation of momentum is being invoked, as the momentum $(M \times V)$ of the balls at two different times is equated. This equation is not a variation of any

$$V_{1,x}(t) \quad = \int A_{1,x}(t)\,dt$$

$$= \int \frac{F_{net,\,1,x}(t)}{M_1}\,dt$$

Figure 11–5: The Failed Solution Attempt

$$M_1 V_{1,s}(A) + M_2 V_{2,s}(A) + M_3 V_{3,s}(A) = M_1 V_{1,s}(B) + M_2 V_{2,s}(B) + M_3 V_{3,s}(B)$$

$$(3\,kg)(5\,\tfrac{m}{s}) = 3\,kg\ V_{1,s}(B) + (8\,kg)(1\,\tfrac{m}{s}) + (5\,kg)(1\,\tfrac{m}{s})$$

$$15\,\tfrac{kg\ m}{s} = 3\,kg\ V_{1,s}(B) + 13\,\tfrac{kg\ m}{s}$$

$$V_{1,s}(B) = 0.67\,\tfrac{m}{s}$$

Figure 11-6: The Teacher's Solution

formula known to the system (Figure 11-3). A physically consistent mathematical derivation is needed if PHYSICS 101 is to accept the solution provided.

2.2. Verifying a Teacher's Solution

To accept a teacher's answer, the system must verify each of the steps in the solution. Besides being mathematically correct, the calculations must be consistent with its domain-specific knowledge. To be valid, each of the solution steps must be assigned to one of the following four classifications:

(1) Instantiation of a known formula: $Force = mass \times acceleration$ is an example of this type.

(2) Definition of a new variable in order to shorten later expressions: $Resistance = voltage\,/\,current$ would fall in this category.

(3) Rearrangement of a previously used formula. These equations are mathematical variants of previous steps. The replacement of variables by their values also falls into this category.

(4) Statement of an unknown relationship among known variables. These steps require full justification, which the system performs symbolically by reasoning about algebra and calculus. Only the steps in this category are candidates for generalization.

PHYSICS 101 possesses several methods for verifying equations falling into category 4. Two are suggested when the two sides of an equation differ only as to the time at which they are evaluated (a condition satisfied by the initial equation in Figure 11-3). One method this suggests is to determine whether the common form underlying each side of the equation is constant with respect to time. This can be done by seeing whether its derivative is zero. The second suggested method is to determine how the underlying form explicitly depends on time. If time can be made explicit, it is easy to see if it is valid to equate the expression at two different times. This method can handle more situations than the first, and is the one used by PHYSICS 101 to understand the teacher's solution.

Once the system selects a method for verifying a new equation, it must perform the mathematics necessary to determine any additional information required by the method. For example, it may need to determine the derivative of an expression or legally eliminate all the terms whose time dependence is not know. In this phase, PHYSICS 101 is a mathematical problem solver.

The trace produced by PHYSICS 101 while solving the problem appears in Figure 11–7. The goal is to convert, via a series of equality–preserving transformations, the top expression into an equivalent expression whose time dependence is explicit. Once this is done, the system can determine whether Figure 11–7's equation 1 is valid. (The top expression in Figure 11–7 is called the *left–hand side* of the calculation, and the other expressions are termed *right–hand sides*.)

The annotations to the left of the expressions in Figure 11–7 are produced by the system. These annotations indicate which of PHYSICS 101's problem–solving techniques (Figure 11–1) is used to perform each calculation step.[3] In the next step, the formulae substitutions are chosen because the mass terms can be canceled. Before this cancellation can take place, however, the canceling terms must be brought together. The calculation continues in a like manner until all the unknown variables are eliminated. Then the known values are substituted and the ensuing arithmetic and calculus solved. Since the initial expression is constant, it can be equated at any two times. Equation 1 of Figure 11–7 is valid.

---

[3] Initially, the system chooses to replace the velocities by the derivative of the positions. This leads nowhere and the system backtracks. No other backtracking occurs during the calculation of Figure 11–7. The system is guided by the goal of canceling variables, which greatly reduces the amount of unnecessary substitutions during problem solving.

$$M_1 V_{1,x}(t) + M_2 V_{2,x}(t) + M_3 V_{3,x}(t)$$

(1)　SubstSameType　$= M_1 \int A_{1,x}(t)\,dt + M_2 \int A_{2,x}(t)\,dt + M_3 \int A_{3,x}(t)\,dt$

(2)　SubstToCancel　$= M_1 \int \dfrac{F_{net,\,1,\,x}(t)}{M_1}\,dt + M_2 \int \dfrac{F_{net,\,2,\,x}(t)}{M_2}\,dt + M_3 \int \dfrac{F_{net,\,3,\,x}(t)}{M_3}\,dt$

(3)　ConstsOutCalculus　$= \dfrac{M_1}{M_1} \int F_{net,\,1,\,x}(t)\,dt + \dfrac{M_2}{M_2} \int F_{net,\,2,\,x}(t)\,dt + \dfrac{M_3}{M_3} \int F_{net,\,3,\,x}(t)\,dt$

(4)　SubMultIdentities　$= 1\int F_{net,\,1,\,x}(t)\,dt + 1\int F_{net,\,2,\,x}(t)\,dt + 1\int F_{net,\,3,\,x}(t)\,dt$

(5)　RemoveIdentities　$= \int F_{net,\,1,\,x}(t)\,dt + \int F_{net,\,2,\,x}(t)\,dt + \int F_{net,\,3,\,x}(t)\,dt$

(6)　SubstSameType　$= \int (F_{ext,\,1,\,x}(t) + F_{int,\,1,\,x}(t))\,dt + \int (F_{ext,\,2,\,x}(t) + F_{int,\,2,\,x}(t))\,dt$
　　　　　　　　　　　$+ \int (F_{ext,\,3,\,x}(t) + F_{int,\,3,\,x}(t))\,dt$

(7)　SubstSameType　$= \int (F_{ext,\,1,\,x}(t) + F_{2,\,1,\,x}(t) + F_{3,\,1,\,x}(t))\,dt + \int (F_{ext,\,2,\,x}(t) + F_{1,\,2,\,x}(t) + F_{3,\,2,\,x}(t))\,dt$
　　　　　　　　　　　$+ \int (F_{ext,\,3,\,x}(t) + F_{1,\,3,\,x}(t) + F_{2,\,3,\,x}(t))\,dt$

(8)　SubstToCancel　$= \int (F_{ext,\,1,\,x}(t) + F_{2,\,1,\,x}(t) + F_{3,\,1,\,x}(t))\,dt + \int (F_{ext,\,2,\,x}(t) - F_{2,\,1,\,x}(t) + F_{3,\,2,\,x}(t))\,dt$
　　　　　　　　　　　$+ \int (F_{ext,\,3,\,x}(t) - F_{3,\,1,\,x}(t) - F_{3,\,2,\,x}(t))\,dt$

(9)　CombineCalculus　$= \int (F_{ext,\,1,\,x}(t) + F_{2,\,1,\,x}(t) + F_{3,\,1,\,x}(t) + F_{ext,\,2,\,x}(t) - F_{2,\,1,\,x}(t) + F_{3,\,2,\,x}(t)$
　　　　　　　　　　　$+ F_{ext,\,3,\,x}(t) - F_{3,\,1,\,x}(t) - F_{3,\,1,\,x}(t))\,dt$

(10)　SubAddIdentities　$= \int (F_{ext,\,1,\,x}(t) + 0\,\frac{kg\,m}{s^2} + 0\,\frac{kg\,m}{s^2} + F_{ext,\,2,\,x}(t) + 0\,\frac{kg\,m}{s^2} + F_{ext,\,3,\,x}(t))\,dt$

(11)　AddNumbers　$= \int (F_{ext,\,1,\,x}(t) + F_{ext,\,2,\,x}(t) + F_{ext,\,3,\,x}(t) + 0\,\frac{kg\,m}{s^2})\,dt$

(12)　RemoveIdentities　$= \int (F_{ext,\,1,\,x}(t) + F_{ext,\,2,\,x}(t) + F_{ext,\,3,\,x}(t))\,dt$

(13)　SubstValues　$= \int (0\,\frac{kg\,m}{s^2} + 0\,\frac{kg\,m}{s^2} + 0\,\frac{kg\,m}{s^2})\,dt$

(14)　AddNumbers　$= \int 0\,\frac{kg\,m}{s^2}\,dt$

(15)　Integrate　$= constant_1$

Figure 11–7: Verifying the First Equation in Figure 11–6

2.3. Explaining Solutions

At this point, the system has ascertained that its teacher's use of a new equation is indeed valid. Figure 11–7 can be viewed as an explanation structure. Underlying the calculation are a large number of

formulae, along with their associated preconditions. These formulae justify the transformations from one line to the next.

However, although Figure 11–7 constitutes a perfectly acceptable
explanation of the solution to the specific example of Figure 11–4, the
underlying explanation does not directly suffice to produce the proper
general concept. Applying a standard explanation–based generalization
algorithm does produce a generalization of the specific solution (see Section 4.9 of [4]), and a number of attributes of the problem are generalized. For example, the result does not only apply to colliding balls — it
applies to situations involving any type of physical object. Nor does the
problem have to be in the x direction, since none of the formulae used to
tie the calculation together constrain the component of the variables. A
third property generalized is that the external forces need not individually
be zero. All that step 15 of Figure 11–7 requires is that the external
forces sum to zero. However, since the explanation structure is not generalized, one unfortunate aspect of the specific example remains. The new
law applies only to physical situations involving *three* objects. Without
that property, adding the $M\,V$ terms of three objects will not lead to the
complete cancellation of internal forces of the objects. The preconditions
of the new equation would insist on a three–object world without external
forces, because only then will the sum of three momentum terms always
be constant across time. Unfortunately, this result is not broadly applicable. The system would need to learn separate rules when it encountered a
four–object system, a five–object system, and so on.

To produce the proper generalization, the system must determine a
reason for including each variable in this equation. This will determine
which variables are required in its general form.

In the explanation process, PHYSICS 101 determines how the value
of the current problem's *unknown* is obtained. The problem's unknown is
the expression about which the value of some property is being sought; in
the sample problem, V_1 is the unknown and its value in state B is being
sought. During this process, the system determines the role of each variable in the initial expression of the calculation.

During a calculation one of three things can happen to a variable:

(1)   Its value can be substituted.

(2)   It can be symbolically replaced during a formulae substitution.

(3)   It can be *canceled.*

Understanding and generalizing variable cancellation drives PHY-
SICS 101. The system can identify the first five of the following six types
of variable cancellations:

(1) *Additive identity.* These are algebraic cancellations of the form
     $x - x = 0$. Line 10 in Figure 11–7 contains two additive cancella-
     tions.

(2) *Multiplicative identity.* These are algebraic cancellations of the
     form $x / x = 1$. Line 4 in Figure 11–7 involves two multiplicative
     cancellations.

(3) *Multiplication by zero.* These are cancellations that result from an
     expression (which may contain several variables) being multiplied
     by zero. None appear in Figure 11–7.

(4) *Integration (to a number).* This type of cancellation occurs when
     variables disappear during symbolic integration. When integra-
     tion produces *new* variables (other than the integration constant),
     this calculation is viewed as a substitution involving the original
     terms. No cancellations of this type appear in Figure 11–7.

(5) *Differentiation (to a number).* This is analogous to cancellation
     during integration.

(6) *Assumed ignorable.* A term can be additively ignored because it is
     assumed to be approximately zero or multiplicatively ignored
     because it is assumed to be approximately equal to one.

2.4. Understanding Obstacles

Obstacles are variables appearing in a calculation but whose values
are not known. A powerful problem–solving technique is to introduce
new obstacles or regroup existing variables in such a way that, after suitable rewriting, the obstacles are *canceled*, thereby allowing the value of
the unknown to be easily determined. This type of mathematical reasoning supports many important domain concepts. This chapter describes
how PHYSICS 101 applies this technique to acquire the concept of conservation of momentum.

Primary obstacles are obstacles descended, via formula applications,
from the unknown. The primary obstacles are a set of unacceptable variables that together would allow a value to be attributed to the unknown.
The task in problem solving is to circumvent the need to know the value
of these obstacles. The additional notion of *secondary obstacles* will be
discussed later. Note for now that secondary obstacles are *not* simply

descendants of descendants of the designated unknown. These are also primary obstacles. Rather, the term *secondary obstacles* is used to refer to obstacles unavoidably introduced during the process of canceling primary obstacles.

In the momentum problem the only primary obstacles not replaced in a formula substitution are $F_{2,1}$ and $F_{3,1}$. If the value of the desired property of each of the primary obstacles were known, the value of the unknown's desired property would be specified. The system ascertains how these obstacles are eliminated from the calculation. Canceling obstacles is seen as the essence of the solution strategy, because when all the obstacles have been canceled the value of the unknown's desired property can be easily calculated.

Figure 11-8 illustrates the concept of primary obstacles. The goal in the sample problem is to determine the value of V_1. Since this is not known, the problem is transformed to that of finding A_1 (for simplicity, the integral sign is ignored here). However, the value of A_1 is not known either. This leads to the substitution of $F_{net,1}$ divided by M_1. The mass is known, but the net force is not. The net force is then decomposed into two components – a known external force and an unknown internal force. Finally, the internal force is further decomposed into its constituents. These two interobject forces are the obstacles to knowing the value of $V_{1,z}$. PHYSICS 101 needs to determine how the solution in Figure 11-6 circumvents the need to know the value of these two variables.

To understand the calculation, the system first determines that the primary obstacles $F_{2,1,z}$ and $F_{3,1,z}$ are eliminated by being *additively canceled*. Although canceled additively, these variables descended from a

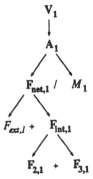

Figure 11-8: Decomposing the Unknown

multiplicative expression $(A = F/M)$. Hence, the system must determine how they are *additively isolated*. Multiplication by M_1 performed this task. So an explanation of the M_1 term in the left–hand side expression of Figure 11-7 is obtained.

The next thing to do is to determine how the terms that additively cancel $F_{2,1,z}$ and $F_{3,1,z}$ are introduced into the calculation. $F_{2,1,z}$ is canceled by a force descended from $V_{2,z}$. This $F_{2,1,z}$, too, must first be additively isolated. PHYSICS 101 discovers that the left–hand side's M_2 performs this isolation. The system now has explanations for the M_2 and the $V_{2,z}$ terms in the left–hand side. Similar reasoning determines the role of M_3 and $V_{3,z}$.

Cancellation of the primary obstacles requires the presence of additional variables on the left–hand side of the equation. These extra terms may themselves contain obstacle variables, which are called *secondary obstacles*. The system must also determine how these obstacles are eliminated from the calculation. The elimination of the secondary obstacles may in turn require the presence of additional variables in the left–hand side expression, which may introduce additional secondary obstacles. This recursion must terminate, however, as the calculation is known to have eliminated all of the unacceptable terms.

Canceling the interobject forces involving ball 1 introduced one secondary obstacle — $F_{3,2,z}$. This secondary obstacle was additively canceled by a force descended from $V_{3,z}$. Canceling this secondary obstacle produced no new obstacles.

Once the system determines how all of the obstacles in the calculation are canceled, generalization can occur. At this time, PHYSICS 101 can also report any variables in the left–hand side of a calculation that are irrelevant to the determination of the value of the unknown. Those variables not visited during the understanding of obstacle cancellation are not necessary, even though they are present in the teacher's solution.

3. Generalizing Solutions in PHYSICS 101

Once the solution to a problem is understood, it must be generalized so that it can be used to help solve similar problems in the future. In PHYSICS 101 this involves generalizing the structure of the specific problem's solution, as well as generalizing the constants in the specific example. This section presents the process by which the general version of a specific problem's solution is constructed.

The system starts with the generalized unknown, $V^{?n}{}_{?s,\,?c}(?arg)$.[4] It then performs the general versions of the specific formulae substitutions that produced the first of the primary obstacles. This can be seen, for the collision problem, in Figure 11–9.[5]

While the general formulae are being applied, a global unification list is maintained, in the manner of the EGGS system [6]. This process determines how the terms in the new general formulae used must relate to ones already in the general calculation. For example, $?arg$ in the generalized unknown is constrained to be t and $?n$ is constrained to be 1, since the first step of Figure 11–9 applies the second equation of Figure 11–3 to the generalized unknown. Unifications that are needed to satisfy the preconditions of the formulae are also maintained.

Recall from Section 2.4 that the interobject forces are *additively* canceled in the specific case. Hence, the next generalization step is to additively isolate each interobject force. $M_{?s}$ is introduced into the left–hand side of the general calculation in order to accomplish this isolation. Figure 11–10 presents this generalization step.

$$V_{?s,\,?c}(t)$$

$$(1) \quad = \int A_{?s,\,?c}(t)\,dt$$

$$(2) \quad = \int \frac{F_{net,\,?s,\,?c}(t)}{M_{?s}}\,dt$$

$$(3) \quad = \frac{1}{M_{?s}}\int F_{net,\,?s,\,?c}(t)\,dt$$

$$(6) \quad = \frac{1}{M_{?s}}\int (F_{ext,\,?s,\,?c}(t) + F_{int,\,?s,\,?c}(t))\,dt$$

$$(7) \quad = \frac{1}{M_{?s}}\int (F_{ext,\,?s,\,?c}(t) + \sum_{\substack{j\in ObjectsInWorld \\ j\neq ?s}} F_{j,\,?s,\,?c}(t))\,dt$$

Figure 11–9: Introduction of the Primary Obstacles

---

[4] The variables used in this chapter are defined in Section 1.1.

[5] The figures that follow, except Figure 11–13, are verbatim transcriptions of actual outputs of the implemented system. The numbers associated with each line refer to the calculation steps of Figure 11–7.

$$M_{?s} \, V_{?s, \, ?c}(t)$$

$$(1) \quad = M_{?s} \int A_{?s, \, ?c}(t) \, dt$$

$$(2) \quad = M_{?s} \int \frac{F_{net, \, ?s, \, ?c}(t)}{M_{?s}} \, dt$$

$$(3) \quad = \frac{M_{?s}}{M_{?s}} \int F_{net, \, ?s, \, ?c}(t) \, dt$$

$$(4) \quad = 1 \int F_{net, \, ?s, \, ?c}(t) \, dt$$

$$(5) \quad = \int F_{net, \, ?s, \, ?c}(t) \, dt$$

$$(6) \quad = \int (F_{ext, \, ?s, \, ?c}(t) + F_{int, \, ?s, \, ?c}(t)) \, dt$$

$$(7) \quad = \int (F_{ext, \, ?s, \, ?c}(t) + \sum_{\substack{j \in ObjectsInWorld \\ j \neq ?s}} F_{j, \, ?s, \, ?c}(t)) \, dt$$

Figure 11–10: Introduction of $M_{?s}$ to Additively Isolate the Primary Obstacles

$$M_{?s} \, V_{?s, \, ?c}(t) + \sum_{\substack{j \in ObjectsInWorld \\ j \neq ?s}} M_j \, V_{j, \, ?c}(t)$$

$$(1) \quad = M_{?s} \int A_{?s, \, ?c}(t) \, dt + \sum_{j \neq ?s} M_j \int A_{j, \, ?c}(t) \, dt$$

$$(2) \quad = M_{?s} \int \frac{F_{net, \, ?s, \, ?c}(t)}{M_{?s}} \, dt + \sum_{j \neq ?s} M_j \int \frac{F_{net, j, \, ?c}(t)}{M_j}$$

$$(3) \quad = \frac{M_{?s}}{M_{?s}} \int F_{net, \, ?s, \, ?c}(t) \, dt + \sum_{j \neq ?s} \frac{M_j}{M_j} \int F_{net, \, j, \, ?c}(t) \, dt$$

$$(4) \quad = 1 \int F_{net, \, ?s, \, ?c}(t) \, dt + \sum_{j \neq ?s} 1 \int F_{net, \, j, \, ?c}(t) \, dt$$

$$(5) \quad = \int F_{net, \, ?s, \, ?c}(t) \, dt + \sum_{j \neq ?s} \int F_{net, \, j, \, ?c}(t) \, dt$$

$$(6) \quad = \int (F_{ext, \, ?s, \, ?c}(t) + F_{int, \, ?s, \, ?c}(t)) \, dt + \sum_{j \neq ?s} \int (F_{ext, \, j, \, ?c}(t) + F_{int, \, j, \, ?c}(t)) \, dt$$

$$(7) \quad = \int (F_{ext, \, ?s, \, ?c}(t) + \sum_{j \neq ?s} F_{j, \, ?s, \, ?c}(t)) \, dt + \sum_{j \neq ?s} \int (F_{ext, \, j, \, ?c}(t) + \sum_{k \neq j} F_{k, \, j, \, ?c}(t)) \, dt$$

Figure 11–11: Introduction of the Cancelers of the Primary Obstacles

At this point the general versions of the primary obstacles are isolated for additive cancellation. To perform this cancellation, those terms that will cancel the intraobject forces must be introduced into the general calculation. The system determines that in the specific solution each interobject force acting on ball 1 is canceled by the equal–but–opposite interobject force specified by Newton's third law.

In the general case, *all* of the other objects in a situation exert an interobject force on object $?s$. *All* of these interobject forces need to be canceled. In the specific case, $M_2 \times V_2$ produced and isolated the additive canceler of $F_{2,1}$ and $M_3 \times V_3$ produced and isolated the additive canceler of $F_{3,1}$. So to cancel object $?s$'s interobject forces, an $M_j \times V_j$ term must come from every other object in the situation. Figure 11–11 presents the introduction of the summation that produces the terms that cancel object $?s$'s interobject forces. Notice how the goal of cancellation motivates generalizing the number of objects involved in this expression.

Once all the cancelers of the generalized primary obstacle are present, the primary obstacle itself can be canceled. This is shown in Figure 11–12, which is a continuation of Figure 11–11 (the last line of Figure 11–11 is repeated in Figure 11–12).

Now that the primary obstacles are canceled, the system checks to see whether any secondary obstacles have been introduced. As can be seen in Figure 11–12, the interobject forces *not* involving object $?s$ still remain in the expression. These are secondary obstacles. Figure 11–13 graphically illustrates these remaining forces in a situation containing N objects. All of the forces acting on object $?s$ have been canceled, while a force between objects j and k still appears whenever neither j nor k equals $?s$. This highlights an important aspect of generalizing to N. Introducing more entities may create new interactions that do not appear and, hence, are not addressed in the specific example. This issue is further elaborated in the discussion of the BAGGER system (Chapter 3).

$$(7) \quad = \int (F_{ext,\ ?s,\ ?c}(t) + \sum_{j \neq ?s} F_{j,\ ?s,\ ?c}(t))\,dt + \sum_{j \neq ?s} \int (F_{ext,\ j,\ ?c}(t) + \sum_{k \neq j} F_{k,\ j,\ ?c}(t))\,dt$$

$$(9) \quad = \int (F_{ext,\ ?s,\ ?c}(t) + \sum_{j \neq ?s} F_{j,\ ?s,\ ?c}(t) + \sum_{j \neq ?s} [F_{ext,\ j,\ ?c}(t) + \sum_{k \neq j} F_{k,\ j,\ ?c}(t)])\,dt$$

$$(10) \quad = \int (F_{ext,\ ?s,\ ?c}(t) + 0\,\frac{kg\,m}{s^2} + \sum_{j \neq ?s} [F_{ext,\ j,\ ?c}(t) + \sum_{k \neq j,\ ?s} F_{k,\ j,\ ?c}(t)])\,dt$$

Figure 11–12: Cancellation of the Primary Obstacles

PHYSICS 101 cannot eliminate the remaining interobject forces if the specific example only involves a two–object collision. The system does not detect that the remaining forces all cancel one another, since in the two–object example there is no hint of how to deal with these secondary obstacles. A collision involving three or more must be analyzed by the system to properly motivate this cancellation. More details on the reasons for this are given in [4, Chap. 7], which presents additional examples. In the three–body collision problem, the system continues as shown in Figure 11–14.

Once all obstacle cancellations of the specific example have been reproduced, PHYSICS 101 produces the final result. The preconditions of each formulae are collected, the global unification list is used to determine the final form of each variable in these preconditions, and the final result is simplified. This process produces the restrictions that the masses of the objects be constant over time (since each was factored out of a temporal integral — see Figure 11–7) and that the objects cannot have zero mass (since their masses appear in the denominator of expressions). The final result is shown in Figure 11–15. The new equation is recorded, along with its preconditions. In addition, the terms canceled in the general calculation are recorded. Although not implemented in PHYSICS 101, the eliminated terms could be used to help index the acquired formula. For example, when the interobject forces are not specified, this equation could

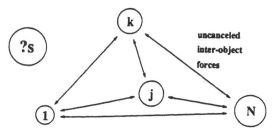

Figure 11–13: The Remaining InterObject Forces

(10) $= \int (F_{ext,\ ?s,\ ?c}(t) + 0\ \frac{kg\ m}{s^2} + \sum_{j \neq ?s} [F_{ext,\ j,\ ?c}(t) + 0\ \frac{kg\ m}{s^2}])\ dt$

(11) $= \int (F_{ext,\ ?s,\ ?c}(t) + \sum_{j \neq ?s} F_{ext,\ j,\ ?c}(t))\ dt$

Figure 11–14: Cancellation of the Secondary Obstacles

be suggested as possibly being appropriate.

In addition to not being restricted to situations containing three objects, the newly acquired formula is not restricted to situations where the external forces are all zero. Instead, an appreciation of how the external forces effect momentum is obtained. This process also determines that there is no constraint that restricts this formula to the x direction. It applies equally well to the y and z components of V. Hence, the acquired formula is a vector law. Notice that those physics variables whose values are used in the specific solution (e.g., the F_{ext}) remain in the general formula. The final equation is added to PHYSICS 101's collection of general formulae. (If PHYSICS 101 generalized the two–body collision, it would produce in an expression still containing those interobject forces that do not involve object i. However, this formula would not be kept.) The new formula says: *The rate of change of the total momentum of a collection of objects is completely determined by the sum of the external forces on those objects.* Other problems, which involve any number of bodies under the influence of external forces, can be solved by the system using this generalized result. For example, it can be used to solve a three–dimensional collision problem involving four objects, where there are external forces due to gravity.

Not all of the preconditions of the equations in a calculation appear in the final result. Each equation providing support in a calculation may have associated with it propositions that are known to be true. *Known*

Equation

$$\frac{d}{dt} \sum_{i \in ObjectsInWorld} M_i V_{i, ?c}(t) = \sum_{i \in ObjectsInWorld} F_{ext, i, ?c}(t)$$

Preconditions

IsaComponent($?c$) $\wedge$
$\forall i \in ObjectsInWorld$ NOT(ZeroValued(M_i)) $\wedge$
$\forall i \in ObjectsInWorld$ IndependentOf(M_i, t)

Eliminated Terms

$\forall i \; \forall j \neq i \; F_{i, j, ?c}(t)$

Figure 11–15: The Final Result

facts are filtered out of the final result. For example, if $\sum_{\substack{j \in ObjectsInWorld \\ j \neq \mathcal{P}i}}$ appears in a formula, that formula's known facts include $Member(j, ObjectsInWorld)$ and $j \neq \mathcal{P}i$. Preconditions of the formulae used in a calculation that match any of the known facts do not appear in the final collection of preconditions. For instance, a precondition of the equation $F_{j,\mathcal{P}i} = -F_{\mathcal{P}i,j}$ is $j \neq \mathcal{P}i$. This precondition does not appear in Figure 11–15 because the use of another equation leads to this precondition being a known fact.

4. Conclusion

PHYSICS 101 is a mathematical reasoning system, offered as a psychologically plausible model, that performs explanation–based learning in mathematically oriented domains. This system's understanding and generalization processes are guided by the manner in which variables are canceled in a specific problem. Attention focuses on how *obstacles* are eliminated in the specific problem. Obstacles are variables that preclude the direct evaluation of the unknown. Canceling these variables allows the determination of the value of the unknown. One important feature of analyzing variable cancellations is that the generalization of explanation structures is motivated. The explanation of a specific calculation closely guides the construction of a general version of the calculation, from which a new general concept is extracted.

This chapter first discussed the construction of explanations in mathematically based domains. An approach to categorizing and then embellishing teacher–provided solutions was presented. Equations in a teacher's solution that are seen as containing something significantly new were explained in detail, during which the system performs some focused problem solving. Once the system ascertains that an interesting solution step is mathematically correct, a more abstract explanation of the step is constructed. This abstract explanation is needed if PHYSICS 101 is to produce the proper generalization. Simply applying standard explanation–based learning techniques to an explanation based on the mathematical rewrite rules used is not sufficient. Rather, the fuller explanation is required to guide the construction of the general version of the calculation. In the fuller explanation, the manner by which the calculation eliminates the obstacles in the calculation is recorded. The goal of eliminating the general versions of these obstacles leads to the necessary restructuring of the original calculation and to a new, general concept.

PHYSICS 101 learns new general concepts by analyzing its solutions of specific problems. The generalization process is guided by the specific solution's *cancellation graph.* This data structure determines how the calculation is reconstructed, in a more general form. The general versions of the obstacles canceled in the specific solution are also canceled in the general calculation. Reconstruction of the calculation produces a generalization of the structure of the explanation of the original problem's solution. While this reconstruction takes place, constants in the example are converted to constrained variables using a standard explanation–based algorithm. No problem–solving search is performed during the construction of the general calculation — construction deterministically follows from the specific calculation. Hence, the process is relatively efficient.

PHYSICS 101 offers a different perspective on the process of explanation–based generalization. Rather than directly using the explanation of the specific problem's solution as is done in more standard algorithms, the explanation of a specific calculation closely guides the construction of a general version of the calculation, from which a new general concept may be extracted. The new calculation is often substantially more general, in terms of its structure as well as its variables, than the specific calculation.

There are three reasons why the structure of a generalized calculation can differ from that of the specific calculation from which it is constructed. First, certain equations — those involving indefinite summations or products — are used in different forms in the two cases. Second, some equations are problem–specific and cannot be used in the general calculation. Third, portions of the calculation that do not play any role in the elimination of obstacles do not appear in the general calculation.

From the sample collision problem used to illustrate generalization, a new equation is produced which describes how external forces affect the momentum of any collection of objects. Information about the number of entities in a situation, localized in a single physics formula, lead to a global restructuring of a specific solution's explanation. The effect of external forces is determined, even though the solution of the specific example took advantage of the fact that the external forces sum to zero. Also, the resulting equation applies to situations containing any number of physical objects, although the specific example only contained three balls. Standard explanation–based learning algorithms do not produce these generalizations. If the structure of the specific solution's explanation were not generalized, the resulting new formula would apply only to situations containing three objects and where the external forces summed to zero. A separate rule would have to be learned each time a situation contained a different number of objects.

Because explanation–based learning requires extensive domain knowledge, it clearly is not appropriate for modeling all learning in a new domain. Nevertheless, it may be useful even in early learning if the domain relies heavily on a domain for which the novice does have substantial knowledge. Because mathematics underlies many other domains, a novice with some mathematical sophistication may be able to make use of explanation–based techniques without extensive knowledge of the new domain.

Acknowledgments

The PHYSICS 101 system was greatly influenced by Gerald DeJong and the rest of the members of the artificial intelligence research group of the University of Illinois' Coordinated Science Laboratory. Their comments are thankfully acknowledged. This research was partially supported by the Office of Naval Research under grant N00014–86–K–0309, by the National Science Foundation under grant NSF IST 85–11542, by a University of Illinois Cognitive Science/Artificial Intelligence Fellowship, and by a grant from the University of Wisconsin Graduate School.

References

1. J. W. Shavlik and G. F. DeJong, "Building a Computer Model of Learning Classical Mechanics," *Proceedings of the Seventh Annual Conference of the Cognitive Science Society*, Irvine, CA, August 1985, pp. 351–355.

2. J. W. Shavlik and G. F. DeJong, "A Model of Attention Focussing During Problem Solving," *Proceedings of the Eighth Annual Conference of the Cognitive Science Society*, Amherst, MA, August 1986, pp. 817–822.

3. J. W. Shavlik, G. F. DeJong and B. H. Ross, "Acquiring Special Case Schemata in Explanation–Based Learning," *Proceedings of the Ninth Annual Conference of the Cognitive Science Society*, Seattle, WA, July 1987, pp. 851–860.

4. J. W. Shavlik, "Generalizing the Structure of Explanations in Explanation–Based Learning ," Ph.D. Thesis, Department of Computer Science, University of Illinois, Urbana, IL, January 1988.

5.   J. W. Shavlik, *Extending Explanation-Based Learning by Generalizing the Structure of Explanations*, Pitman, London, 1990.

6.   R. J. Mooney and S. W. Bennett, "A Domain Independent Explanation-Based Generalizer," *Proceedings of the National Conference on Artificial Intelligence*, Philadelphia, PA, August 1986, pp. 551-555.

Chapter 12

Case Study 4 — ADEPT: Extending the Domain Theory

Shankar Rajamoney

1. Introduction

The ADEPT system [1, 2] performs problem solving in the chemistry domain. The system manipulates liquids, solids, and gases to prepare solutions of specified concentrations, mix liquids in specified proportions, pour liquids into selected containers, and store liquids in closed containers. ADEPT's domain theory includes knowledge about liquids, solids, gases, containers, physical processes affecting these objects, and so on. However, because of the complexity of the domain, the domain theory is necessarily incomplete and incorrect. To overcome this obstacle, ADEPT is equipped with additional knowledge that enables it to detect and analyze situations where its domain theory fails. Thus, one of ADEPT's primary tasks is to handle abnormal situations. When it encounters such failures, ADEPT designs experiments to gather additional information. This information will enable the system to learn, anticipate, and overcome situations about which previously it knew nothing.

Figure 12–1 shows the architecture of the ADEPT system. The functioning of the system has been split into three main phases:

(1) The problem–solving phase in which the system plans solutions for tasks given to it.

(2) The contradiction detection and analysis phase in which the system identifies and analyzes differences between the observations made from the real world and the predictions made by the system based on its domain theory.

(3) The hypothesis formation and experimentation phase in which the system generates hypotheses to explain contradictions and designs experiments to test the validity of these hypotheses.

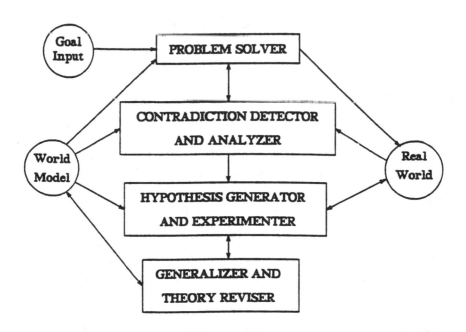

Figure 12–1: The Architecture of the ADEPT System

2. Knowledge Representation in ADEPT

ADEPT's knowledge about the domain is represented declaratively in the form of encapsulated knowledge structures called schemata. A schema (similar to a script [3] or a frame [4]) is a structured collection of typical information about objects and events. The system knows about four types of schemata: objects, operators, processes, and abstract quantities. These schemata are organized in the form of an inheritance network. Figure 12–2 shows the inheritance network for the system. Objects in the world are represented as unique instances of the class to which they belong. For example, a container in the real world may correspond to the unique instance, Container7, of the generic Container class. The representation allows attribute–value pairs with default values and constraints on the attribute values of instances. For example, Absorption14, an instance of the generic class Absorption, may have Solid7 as the value of the attribute absorbingSolid. A default value that evaluates to the container containing the absorbed liquid may also be specified. Additionally, the attribute absorbingSolid may be constrained to allow only values that are instances of the class Solid.

Figure 12-2: ADEPT's Schemata Organized in an Inheritance Network

The schemata used by ADEPT are:

(1)   *Objects.* Objects are divided into three main classes: solids, liquids, and gases. These are further classified into objects relevant to the problem–solving needs of the system. For example, some of these objects are containers, solutions, solvents, solutes, and vapors. Features for each class of objects differ. For example, the features for the object Container are its parts, volume, mass, capacity, color, material, contents, temperature, compartments, the objects it touches, and whether it is open.

(2)   *Operators.* Operators are action schemata that the system uses to bring about the required changes to the state of the world. The operators known to the system are MIXing of solutions, POURing

of liquids into containers, STOREing of liquids in containers, CHOOSEing of objects satisfying given constraints, ExertForceOnLiquid for exerting forces on liquid surfaces, and ExertForceOnSolid for exerting forces on solids.

(3) *Processes.* Apart from operators, ADEPT also knows about physical processes [5] that occur without the need of external agents and cause changes in the world. The processes known to ADEPT are the FLOW of liquids, the EVAPORATION of liquids, the CONDENSATION of vapor, the ABSORPTION of liquids by solids (like a sponge absorbing water), and the RELEASE of the absorbed liquid by solids. The features of a process are its name, participants, preconditions, effects, observable effects, and status (whether it is active). Additional features may be used to distinguish the values of features. For example, the process FLOW has a path, a source, and a destination as its participants. An instance of the process ABSORPTION is shown in Figure 12–3.

(4) *Abstract Quantities.* ADEPT also has detailed schematic knowledge about abstract quantities. This knowledge enables the system to analyze contradictions, design experiments, measure physical quantities such as forces, apply inference rules, and use heuristics.

```
(DEFINST Absorption   (AbsorptionOfSolution16ByWall13)
            (name              AbsorptionOfSolution16ByWall13)
            (participants      (Solution16 Wall13))
            (absorbingSolid  Wall13)
            (absorbedLiquid Solution16)
            (agents            NIL)
            (preconditions     (((touches? Solution16 Wall13) T)
                               ((absorbent? Wall13) T)))
            (effects           ((increase mass Wall13)
                               (decrease amount Solution16)))
            (observableEffects ((decrease amount Solution16)))
            (active?        T)
            (reverseProcess    NIL))
```

Figure 12–3: An Instance of the Process Schema Absorption

3. The Problem–Solver Phase

The problem solver consists of two parts: a planner and an executor. Tasks to be solved are input to the planner in the form of goals to be achieved by the system. The planner creates a plan that leads to the goal. This plan consists of a sequence of operators which when performed will transform the current state of the world into one in which the goal is true. The goals given to the system are simple enough to be achieved by a composition of instantiations of existing operators. The executor carries out the plan. It makes predictions about the changes to the world that will result from the successful application of each operator in the plan.

4. The Contradiction Detection and Analysis Phase

In ADEPT, the problem–solving phase provides predictions of the real–world behavior, namely, the changes that are expected when an operator is applied and the effects of processes known to be active. These predictions are compared with the observations made from the real world. Differences between the two are of the following types: extra predictions, extra observations, and differing degree. ADEPT currently handles only the first two types of differences. If differences are detected, ADEPT tries to construct an explanation to account for them. For example, if there are extra observations, ADEPT determines whether some process has become active and is causing the observations. Processes which can cause the observations and are not active due to unsatisfied preconditions are added to an explanation for why the observed quantities are not changing. If no explanation can be found, the system triggers a contradiction between the observed changes and the constructed explanation for why the quantities should not be changing.

5. The Hypothesis Formation and Experiment Design Phase

The contradiction structure is organized in a TMS–like dependency structure. Each node is supported by other nodes or is a premise. Each node forms a belief of the system. These beliefs are ordered by a combination of (1) the strength of the belief which is computed based on the type of the node (e.g., if the node represents a rule, then its strength is higher than a node representing an assumption) and (2) the level of the node in the contradiction structure. The system then derives hypotheses from the beliefs using the heuristics described in Chapter 5.

Experiments are designed to test the hypotheses level by level. The schemata for designing experiments are indexed by the type of the hypothesis. If an experiment class can be found for a given hypothesis type, the system constructs an instance of the experiment class using the variable bindings in the hypothesis. If an experiment class cannot be found, then the system cannot test the hypothesis. It will instead test the supports of the corresponding belief. Once experiments have been designed, they are assumed to be performed in the real world by an external agent and the observations are input to the system. Based on the conclusions from these observations, the system updates its hypotheses. The cycle of hypothesis generation and experiment design continues until no further hypotheses are generated.

6. Annotated Trace of the Osmosis Example

An annotated run of the system on the osmosis example described in Chapter 5 is presented:

```
Plan:  ((Store Liquid1 (Container3 (compartment Compartment1))
                       (Solution1 (amount 20) (concentration 10)))
       (Store Liquid2 (Container3 (compartment Compartment2))
                       (Solution2 (amount 20) (concentration 20))))
Executing plan.
    Executing Store:
            Predictions:         ((increase amount Solution1)
                                  (decrease amount Liquid1))
            Please enter observations.
            OBSERVATIONS:        ((increase amount Solution1)
                                  (decrease amount Liquid1))
            Observations conform with predictions.
    Executing Store:
            Predictions:         ((increase amount Solution2)
                                  (decrease amount Liquid2))
            Please enter observations.
            OBSERVATIONS:        ((increase amount Solution2)
                                  (decrease amount Liquid2))
            Observations conform with predictions.
            OBSERVATIONS:        ((increase amount Solution2)
                                  (decrease amount Solution1))
            Unexpected observations: ((increase amount Solution2)
                                      (decrease amount Solution1))
```

The system is given the goal of collecting two solutions with specified amounts and concentrations. As it happens, unknown to the system, the chosen container has two compartments separated by a semi–permeable membrane (Chapter 5, Figure 5–1a). The system's expected predictions of the appearance of the given amounts of the two solutions in the two compartments of the container conform to the actual observations made from the real world. However, the real world also gives some additional unexpected observations (Chapter 5, Figure 5–1b).

> Trying to explain the observations:
>   ((increase amount Solution2) (decrease amount Solution1))
> as an effect of some process.
> Relevant processes are:
>   (Flow Absorption Release Evaporation Condensation)
> All occurrences of processes failed.
> No explanation found for the observations.
> Constructing Contradiction Structure.

The system tries to justify the observations as an effect of one of the known processes that can influence the amounts of liquids. But it finds that each process has preconditions that are not satisfied in the current situation. FLOW requires a solid–free path and a force on the source liquid. ABSORPTION and RELEASE require the material of the container to be absorbent. CONDENSATION and EVAPORATION require exposure to the external atmosphere, but in this case the container is closed. Since all the relevant processes have failed, the system cannot generate an explanation for the observations. This leads to a contradiction. Figure 5–2 in Chapter 5 shows the contradiction structure for a decrease in the amount of Solution1:

> Generating hypotheses that may explain the observations:
> Hypotheses:
>   ((Discriminate
>   (processes
>   (FlowOfSolution1ToSolution2ViaWall4
>   FlowOfSolution1ToSolution2ViaCompositeWall1
>   FlowOfSolvent1ToSolution2ViaWall4
>   FlowOfSolvent1ToSolution2ViaCompositeWall1
>   ReleaseOfSolution2ByWall4
>   ReleaseOfSolution2ByCompositeWall1
>   ReleaseOfSolvent2ByWall4
>   ReleaseOfSolvent2ByCompositeWall1
>   CondensationOfVapor2))
>   (condition active))
>   (Discriminate
>   (processes
>   (FlowOfSolution1ToSolution2ViaWall4
>   FlowOfSolution1ToSolution2ViaCompositeWall1
>   FlowOfSolvent1ToSolution2ViaWall4
>   FlowOfSolvent1ToSolution2ViaCompositeWall1
>   AbsorptionOfSolution1ByWall4
>   AbsorptionOfSolution1ByCompositeWall1
>   AbsorptionOfSolvent1ByWall4

```
                AbsorptionOfSolvent1ByCompositeWall1
                EvaporationOfSolvent1))
          (condition active))
       (NewProcess1    (type Process)
                       (participants(Solution1 Solution2))
                       (effects
                         ((increase amount Solution2)
                          (decrease amount Solution1)))))
```

The system generates the first level of hypotheses by analyzing the dependency structure. The hypotheses are:

(1) The computation leading to the conclusion "(constant amount Solution1)" was based on computations that found each of the processes to be inactive (Chapter 5, Figure 5–2). This may be wrong and some process may in fact be active. The system suggests designing experiments that test whether a process is active. Notice that the system does not try to test the preconditions of each process to check whether they are correct, because this would require a large number of experiments. The system tests the preconditions of a process only after it finds the process to be active.

(2) A process, previously unknown to the system, may be active and may have effects that generate the unexpected observations:

```
       Testing hypotheses.
       Constructing Discrimination Experiments.
       Discrimination finished.
       Possibilities left = (FlowOfSolvent1ToSolution2ViaWall4)
       Showing sample discrimination experiment.
       (DEFINST DiscriminationExperiment
        (DiscriminationExperiment13 "JTV0.^d:.440")
              (aim
                  (discriminate (FlowOfSolvent1ToSolution2ViaWall4
                                 FlowOfSolution1ToSolution2ViaWall4)))
              (possibilities
                  (FlowOfSolvent1ToSolution2ViaWall4
                   FlowOfSolution1ToSolution2ViaWall4))
              (possibilitiesTested
                  (FlowOfSolvent1ToSolution2ViaWall4))
              (competingPossibilities
                  (FlowOfSolution1ToSolution2ViaWall4))
              (discriminant
                  effects)
              (procedure
                  ((ConstructScenario Scenario7)
                   (measure concentration Solution1)))
              (conditionalResults
```

```
(((((increase concentration Solution1))
      (FlowOfSolvent1ToSolution2ViaWall4))))
(observations
      ((increase concentration Solution1)))
(conclusions
      (FlowOfSolvent1ToSolution2ViaWall4)))
```

The system tests the first two sets of hypotheses by designing *discrimination experiments* to find active processes. These experiments are based on the difference in the behavior of properties such as the *effects* or the *parameters* (the rate at which the process runs) of the processes. The system displays a sample experiment in which the *discriminant* is the *effects* of the processes. The experiment determines which, if any, of the two different occurrences of the process FLOW — FlowOfSolvent1To Solution2ViaWall4 and FlowOfSolution1ToSolution2ViaWall4 — is active. The system finds through inferences based on the primary effects of FLOW (increase of amount at destination and decrease of amount at the source) that if the first process were to occur, then there would be an increase in the concentration of Solution1. The reason is that the proportion of solute to solvent would have increased due to a decrease in the amount of solvent. In the second process, however, there is no effect on the concentration of Solution1 because the proportion is unaffected by a decrease in the amount of the solution as a whole. Thus, this difference in *effects* forms a basis for discrimination. The system constructs an experiment to repeat the original scenario and measures the concentration of Solution1. It finds the concentration to have increased and hence concludes that a flow of Solvent1 may be taking place.

After conducting a series of discrimination experiments using various discriminants, the system finds that the process FlowOfSolvent1To Solution2ViaWall4 may be active. However, it still does not have sufficient information to choose between this process being active and the possibility of a new process causing the observations.

```
Updating Hypotheses
Generating new hypotheses:
    ((Measure ForceOnSolvent1TowardsSolution2)
    (CreateNewPrecondition NewPrecondition FlowPathPrecondition)
    (NewProcess1    (type Process)
                    (participants   (Solution1 Solution2))
                    (effects        ((increase amount Solution2)
                                    (decrease amount Solution1)
                                    (increase concentration Solution1)
                                    (decrease concentration Solution2))
                    (parameters     ((proportionalTo (crossSectionalArea
                                    (path Solvent1 Wall4 Solution2)))
```

```
                              (inverselyProportionalTo (length
                              (path Solvent1 Wall4 Solution2)))))))
```

The system now examines the reasons why the process
FlowOfSolvent1ToSolution2ViaWall4 failed. It failed because the two
preconditions — a non–zero force to cause the flow and a clear solid–free
path — were not satisfied. The first precondition failed because the system could not compute a force using its current domain theory. The only
force known to the system that can cause FLOW is based on a difference
in levels of liquids. To verify that no new force is present, the system
suggests an experiment to measure the force. The second precondition
failed since the partition, Wall4, is a solid and is in the path. The system
suggests creating a new precondition that will permit FLOW in the
specific case when Wall4 is in the path. At the same time, the system
updates the previous hypothesis, the existence of a new process, which has
not yet been ruled out. From the discrimination experiments performed,
it knows that the new process must have the *effects* and *parameters*
shown.

```
     Testing hypotheses.
     Constructing Measurement Experiments.
        Measurement Experiment:
           Quantity Measured:  ForceOnSolvent1TowardsSolution2
           Type of Experiment:  IndirectMeasurement
           Conclusions:
              ((Value (magnitude ForceOnSolvent1TowardsSolution2) 35))
        Displaying sample measurement experiment:
     (DEFINST MeasurementExperiment
              (MeasurementExperiment84 "JTV0.^d:.cf=.445")
        (aim
              measure  (magnitude ForceOnSolvent1TowardsSolution2))
        (quantityMeasured
              (magnitude ForceOnSolvent1TowardsSolution2))
        (quantitiesVaried
              (magnitude Force2BySolid8))
        (measurementConditions
              ((constant amount Solvent1)
               (constant amount Solution2)
               (constant concentration Solution1)
               (constant concentration Solution2)))
        (relationFunction
              (Equals (magnitude ForceOnSolvent1TowardsSolution2)
                (magnitude Force2BySolid8)))
        (variationFunctions
              ((type multiple)
               ((magnitude Force2BySolid8)
                (lowLimit 0)
```

```
                    (highLimit 50)
                    (stepSize 5))))
          (procedure
                ((ConstructScenario Scenario10)
                 (Vary(magnitude Force2BySolid8))))
          (observations
                ((Value (magnitude Force2BySolid8) 35)))
          (conclusions
                ((Value (magnitude ForceOnSolvent1TowardsSolution2) 35))))
      Creating new precondition:
          NewPrecondition
```

The system uses an *indirect measurement experiment* since the force on Solvent1 cannot be directly measured. The indirect measurement experiment involves exerting a measurable force to oppose the force on Solvent1. When the process stops, the two forces are equal in magnitude, and thus the magnitude of force on Solvent1 is determined. Figure 5–5 illustrates the experiment. The measurement conditions are derived from observations that will be made if the process FlowOfSolvent1ToSolution2 ViaWall4 is stopped (Figure 5–5c).

At this stage, the system has found the path precondition to be unsatisfiable and has created a new one. It has found the agent precondition to be satisfied by a force that was measured.

The system has two options now:

(1)   Modify the flow process to incorporate the new information.

(2)   Create a new process which has experimentally determined effects and parameters, new preconditions, a new agent, and new participants.

The system constructs a new process whenever there are new effects. In this case, the concentrations of the solutions change, and this change is not predicted directly by a flow process. Therefore, the system selects the second option and creates a new process.

```
Creating a new process schema:
   (NewProcess1    (type Process)
           (participants    (Solution1 Wall4 Solution2))
           (effects         ((increase amount Solution2)
                             (decrease amount Solution1)
                             (increase concentration Solution1)
                             (decrease concentration Solution2))
           (parameters      ((proportionalTo (crossSectionalArea
                             (path Solvent1 Wall4 Soltuion2)))
                             (inverselyProportionalTo (length
                             (path Solvent1 Wall4 Solution2)))))
```

```
(preconditions      (NewPrecondition FlowAgentPrecondition))
(agent              (ForceOnSolvent1TowardsSolution2
                        (magnitude 35)
                        (direction        (from     Solvent1)
                                          (to       Solution2)))))
```
Analyzing new schema for incomplete information.
        (magnitude ForceOnSolvent1TowardsSolution2) measured value.
Trying to find relation between
        (magnitude ForceOnSolvent1TowardsSolution2)
and properties of
        (Solution1 Wall4 Solution2)
Generating new hypotheses:
        ((FindDependency   (magnitude ForceOnSolvent1TowardsSolution2)
                           (Solution1 Wall4 Solution2)))

The system analyzes the newly acquired process to determine
whether any information is incomplete. It finds that it does not have a
method to compute the force on Solvent1 because the force was measured
experimentally. The system tries to relate this force to the properties of
the objects associated with the process using *find–dependency experiments.*

Testing hypotheses.
Constructing Find Dependency Experiments.
    Quantity: (magnitude ForceOnSolvent1TowardsSolution2)
    Objects: (Solution1 Wall4 Solution2)
    Running heuristics to determine relevant properties of Solution1.
            Properties: (concentration amount mass location)
    Running heuristics to determine relevant properties of Wall4.
            Properties: NIL
    Running heuristics to determine relevant properties of Solution2.
            Properties: (concentration amount mass location)
    Performing Find Dependency Experiments.
    Conclusion:
    (magnitude[ForceOnSolvent1TowardsSolution2] = k *
    (concentration[Solution2] – concentration[Solution1]))
Displaying sample Find Dependency experiment using Cause Effect Heuristic:
(DEFINST FindDependencyExperiment
 (FindDependencyExperiment10 "JTV0.^d:.cf=.473")
    (aim   (FindRelation
                             (magnitude ForceOnSolvent1TowardsSolution2)
                             (concentration Solution1)))
    (quantityRelated   (magnitude ForceOnSolvent1TowardsSolution2))
    (propertyTested   concentration)
    (objectsOwningProperty   (Solution1))
    (heuristicUsed   CauseEffectHeuristic4)
    (scenario   Scenario7)
    (procedure   ((Vary (concentration Solution1))))
```
```

```
(variationFunctions          ((type multiple)
                             ((concentration Solution1)
                             (lowLimit 0)
                             (highLimit 50)
                             (stepSize 5)
                             (direction increasing))))
(conclusions                 (proportional
                             (magnitude ForceOnSolvent1TowardsSolution2)
                                (concentration Solution1))))
```

The system uses the heuristics described in Section 5.3 to determine the properties of the objects that may be relevant to the computation of the force. Based on such heuristics, it generates a number of prospective properties. It then designs experiments in which these properties are varied systematically, and their influence on the force on Solvent1 is observed. In the experiment shown, the effect of varying the concentration of Solution1 on the force is observed. These experiments are assumed to be performed, and the data collected are assumed to be analyzed by a BACON–type system to produce the relation:

$$\text{magnitude}[\text{ForceOnSolvent1TowardsSolution2}]$$
$$= k * (\text{concentration}[\text{Solution2}] - \text{concentration}[\text{Solution1}])$$

```
Creating new property for Wall4
    Property Name: Property22
Creating Experiment Definition for Property22
Displaying Experiment Definition for Property22:
(DEFCLASS Property22DefinitionExperiment
   (propertyDefined Property22)
   (processClass     NewProcess1)
   (standardObject  (Container3   (Wall4 (material vegetableSkin))))
   (scenario         (Scenario42
                             (objects
                             (##testSample ##Participant1 ##Participant2))
                             (relations ((In ##Participant1 (##testSample
                             (compartment Compartment1)))
                              (In ##Participant2 (##testSample
                              (compartment Compartment2)))
                             (Closed ##testSample)))))
   (sampleSpecification      ((testObject             (material))
                             standardObject 'everythingElse)))
   (associatedParticipants   (##Participant1          ##Participant2)
                             default   (Solution1 Solution2))
   (conditionalResults       ((decrease amount         ##Participant1)
                             (increase   amount         ##Participant2)
                             (increase   concentration  ##Participant1)
                             (decrease   concentration  ##Participant2)))
```

Even though Wall4 is a participant of the new process, the system finds that none of its current properties are relevant to the new process. The system creates a new property, Property22 (semipermeability), that defines the role played by Wall4 in the new process. This property captures the nature of walls that can take part in the new process. It also constructs an experiment class that serves as an operational definition for the new property. When the system needs to know whether an object exhibits the new property, Property22, it creates an experiment from the preceding *property definition experiment* class. A test sample of the given object is constructed using the specifications given in the experiment, and the original partition of the container is replaced by the test sample. If the process occurs, then the object tested exhibits the property. Similarly, different objects in the world may be grouped into sets using *classification experiments*, depending on whether they exhibit given properties.

At this stage, the system has acquired through experimentation:

(1)   a new process schema, "osmosis,"

(2)   a new property, "semipermeability," of solids participating in "osmosis," and

(3)   an experiment class to determine if an object exhibits the new property, semipermeability.

7. Discussion

ADEPT is a first–pass implementation of experimentation–based theory revision. It demonstrates how experiments can be designed to gather the information required to complete or correct a domain theory. ADEPT is limited by its knowledge representation and inferencing capabilities. ADEPT's knowledge representation is tied to the liquids domain; consequently, it would be very difficult to extend the system to run on examples from other domains. Also, ADEPT does not perform complete influence resolution [5] — for example, it does not compute how an effect of one process can affect other processes. Its inference mechanism is limited to simple depth–bounded forward–chaining on the primary effects of active processes. A more general version of ADEPT called COAST [6, 7] which uses the Qualitative Process theory framework developed by Forbus [5] is presently under development. This system will have domain–independent methods for forming hypotheses and designing experiments [8] and will be demonstrated on a number of examples drawn from different domains.

References

1. S. Rajamoney, G. F. DeJong and B. Faltings, "Towards a Model of Conceptual Knowledge Acquisition through Directed Experimentation," *Proceedings of the Ninth International Joint Conference on Artificial Intelligence*, Los Angeles, CA, August 1985.

2. S. A. Rajamoney, "Conceptual Knowledge Acquisition through Directed Experimentation," in *Machine Learning: A Guide To Current Research*, T. M. Mitchell, J. G. Carbonell and R. S. Michalski (ed.), Kluwer Academic Publishers, Hingham, MA, 1986, pp. 255–260.

3. R. C. Schank and R. P. Abelson, *Scripts, Plans, Goals and Understanding: An Inquiry into Human Knowledge Structures*, Lawrence Erlbaum and Associates, Hillsdale, NJ, 1977.

4. M. L. Minsky, "A Framework for Representing Knowledge," in *The Psychology of Computer Vision*, P. H. Winston (ed.), McGraw–Hill, New York, NY, 1975, pp. 211–277.

5. K. D. Forbus, "Qualitative Process Theory," *Artificial Intelligence 24*, (1984), pp. 85–168.

6. S. A. Rajamoney, "Explanation–Based Theory Revision: An Approach to the Problems of Incomplete and Incorrect Theories," Ph.D. Thesis, Department of Computer Science, University of Illinois, Urbana, IL, December 1988.

7. S. A. Rajamoney,, "A Computational Approach to Theory Revision," in *Computational Models of Scientific Discovery and Theory Formation*, J. Shrager & P. Langley (ed.), Lawrence Earlbaum Associates, Hillsdale, N.J., 1990.

8. S. A. Rajamoney and G. F. DeJong, "Active Explanation Reduction: An Approach to the Multiple Explanations Problem," *Proceedings of the Fifth International Conference on Machine Learning*, Ann, Arbor, MI, June 1988.

Chapter 13

Case Study 5 — NONMON: Learning with Recoverable Simplifications

Steve Chien

1. Introduction

This chapter describes an implementation of *recoverable simplifications* (described in Chapter 4). This system learns general plans for constructing assemblies in a workshop domain and uses operators representing actions such as drilling, heating, and rolling of objects. The implemented system learns by analyzing plans generated by a problem-solving system or observed from an expert.

This chapter describes details of the implementation of recoverable simplifications and consists of three main parts. The first part is a modular description of the system. The second part consists of an annotated trace of the system performance on the melted–gear sequence of examples described in Chapter 4. The third part contains the operator and rule used by the system to process the melted gear sequence.

2. Architectural Organization

The architecture of the implemented learning system is shown in Figure 13–1. The system is initially given knowledge in the form of a complete and sound but intractable domain theory and simplifications. When the system is initially learning a plan, it receives as its input an initial state, operator sequence, and goal. Using the existing knowledge base of rules, facts, and operators, plus simplifications to make the understanding process tractable, the understander maintains the causal model, which is the system's description of world events. The generalizer extracts the explanation for goal achievement from the causal model and generalizes the explanation to form a plan. This plan is then analyzed with respect to previously learned failures to check for preventive measures. The resultant structure is packaged into a plan and added to the plan library.

When the system is problem solving, it receives a goal as its input. The planner selects an applicable plan from the plan library to achieve the goal. The executive then executes the plan, updating the causal model to reflect the changes in the world caused by plan execution. After

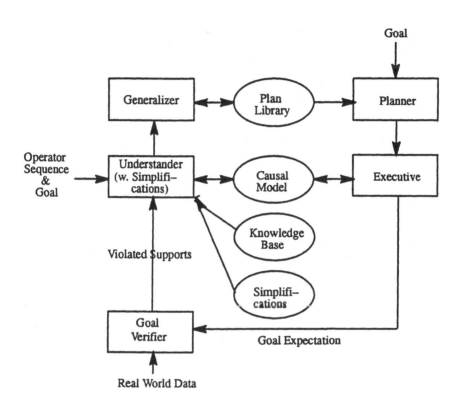

Figure 13–1: System Architecture

the plan has been completed, the goal verifier verifies the achievement of
the goal. If the plan fails to achieve the goal, the goal verifier backtraces
to find the set of violated supports responsible for the failure. Because
the domain theory is sound, these must be due to violated simplifications.
The understander explains the reasons for these violated simplifications.
The resulting explanations are then generalized and used to modify the
original plan preconditions. If the plan achieves the goal, no refinement
of plan preconditions is necessary.

3. Annotated Trace

The feasibility of this approach has been demonstrated by the implementation of a prototype learning system that uses the simplification–based approach. The current implementation has been tested on a sequence of several examples that demonstrates the systems ability to (1) learn using simplifications, (2) correct flaws due to incorrect usage of simplifications, and (3) use previously learned representations of failures to understand preventive measures. Each example takes from one to four minutes to run, the majority of the time being spent garbage collecting.

In the first training example, the system is shown a plan to construct a widget. This is a simple assembly consisting of a gear mounted on a shaft that extends through a sheet (see Figure 13–2). The system is shown a sequence of steps which include drilling holes in the gear and sheet and heating and rolling a metal rod. The rod is then cooled and inserted into the gear for a friction fit, and the rod inserted through the sheet for a fit that allows the rod to spin. In this example, the gear is plastic and the other pieces are metal. The system learns a plan in which a number of defeasible inferences are used. The system learns this plan by constructing and generalizing an explanation using numerous defeasible and numerous completely sound rules of inference. However, in this explanation, the system uses a persistence assumption to verify that the shape of the gear does not change throughout the plan. Because of this

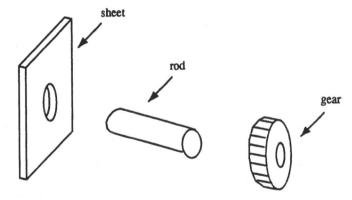

Figure 13–2: Widget Assembly

assumption, the system does not understand that if the gear is plastic, the success of the plan depends on the cooling step. The trace for this learning example is shown below.

Running: (RUN–EXAMPLE *W2*)
Initial State Consists of:
(AT R1 BENCH1)
(AT R2 BENCH1)
(AT G1 BENCH1)
(AT G2 BENCH1)
(AT P1 BENCH1)
(COMPOSITION R1 METAL)
(STATE R1 SOLID)
(STATE BASE SOLID)
(COMPOSITION G1 PLASTIC)
(SHAPE G1 GEAR)
(AT BASE BENCH1)
(SHAPE BASE SHEET)
Start state is state 0
Operator 1 is (MOVE R1 OVEN)
Operator 2 is (HEAT R1)
Operator 3 is (MOVE R1 ROLLING–STATION)
Operator 4 is (ROLL R1 10.0CM)
Operator 5 is (COOL R1)
Operator 6 is (MOVE R1 BENCH1)
Operator 7 is (MOVE G1 DRILLING–STATION)
Operator 8 is (DRILL G1 HOLE1 10.0CM)
Operator 9 is (MOVE G1 BENCH1)
Operator 10 is (MOVE BASE DRILLING–STATION)
Operator 11 is (DRILL BASE HOLE2 10.1CM)
Operator 12 is (MOVE BASE BENCH1)
Operator 13 is (INSERT R1 G1 HOLE1)
Operator 14 is (INSERT R1 BASE HOLE2)
Learning plan to achieve (WIDGET ?GEAR40645 ?PLANE37642 ?ROD41646 ?HOLE42647 ?LOC38643 ?S139644).
Generalizing...
Packaging and Indexing...
Ordering Actions...
Marking assumption intervals...
Learned new plan WIDGET776
NIL

The system then uses this newly learned plan to solve several problems with all metal pieces. It successfully constructs several widgets. A successful problem–solving trace follows.

Running: (EXECUTE–EXAMPLE EX–SOLVE)
Start state is state 0
Initial State is:
(AT ROD101 BENCH3)
(AT GEAR212 BENCH2)
(AT BASE4 BENCH4)
(COMPOSITION ROD101 METAL)
(STATE ROD101 SOLID)
(SHAPE GEAR212 GEAR)
(STATE GEAR212 SOLID)
(SHAPE BASE4 SHEET)
(COMPOSITION GEAR212 METAL)
(STATE BASE4 SOLID)
Using plan WIDGET776 to achieve goal (WIDGET GEAR212 BASE4 ROD101 HOLE3 BENCH3 ?S124752)
Operator 1 is (MOVE ROD101 OVEN)
Operator 2 is (HEAT ROD101)
Operator 3 is (MOVE ROD101 ROLLING–STATION)
Operator 4 is (ROLL ROD101 12.0CM)
Operator 5 is (MOVE ROD101 BENCH3)
Operator 6 is (MOVE GEAR212 DRILLING–STATION)
Operator 7 is (DRILL GEAR212 HOLE784 12.0CM)
Operator 8 is (MOVE GEAR212 BENCH3)
Operator 9 is (MOVE BASE4 DRILLING–STATION)
Operator 10 is (DRILL BASE4 HOLE785 12.1CM)
Operator 11 is (MOVE BASE4 BENCH3)
Operator 12 is (INSERT ROD101 GEAR212 HOLE784)
Operator 13 is (INSERT ROD101 BASE4 HOLE785)
Plan WIDGET776 completed.
Verifying achievement of functionality.
Goal achievement successfully verified.
NIL

However, the system is then requested to construct a widget with a plastic gear. The system attempts to apply the faulty plan. After the plan is executed, the system determines that the plan has failed. The

system explains the failure and deduces that the plan will not work in
cases where the gear is made of plastic because it will be deformed by
being brought into contact with the heated rod. The system subsequently
modifies the plan to reflect this limitation. The trace for this example follows.

Running: (EXECUTE–EXAMPLE FAIL–EX)
Start state is state 0
Initial State is:
(AT R1 BENCH2)
(AT G1 BENCH3)
(AT BASE BENCH4)
(COMPOSITION R1 METAL)
(STATE R1 SOLID)
(SHAPE G1 GEAR)
(SHAPE BASE SHEET)
(COMPOSITION G1 PLASTIC)
(STATE G1 SOLID)
(STATE BASE SOLID)
Using plan WIDGET776 to achieve goal (WIDGET G1 BASE R1 HOLE3
BENCH3 ?S124752)
Operator 1 is (MOVE R1 OVEN)
Operator 2 is (HEAT R1)
Operator 3 is (MOVE R1 ROLLING–STATION)
Operator 4 is (ROLL R1 15.0CM)
Operator 5 is (MOVE R1 BENCH3)
Operator 6 is (MOVE G1 DRILLING–STATION)
Operator 7 is (DRILL G1 HOLE787 15.0CM)
Operator 8 is (MOVE G1 BENCH3)
Operator 9 is (MOVE BASE DRILLING–STATION)
Operator 10 is (DRILL BASE HOLE788 15.1CM)
Operator 11 is (MOVE BASE BENCH3)
Operator 12 is (INSERT R1 G1 HOLE787)
Operator 13 is (INSERT R1 BASE HOLE788)
Plan WIDGET776 completed.
Verifying achievement of functionality.
Goal does not verify. Backtracing supports.
Verifying (AT BASE BENCH3) in situation 13
(AT BASE BENCH3) in situation 13 Verified in real world
Verifying (SHAPE G1 GEAR) in situation 13
(SHAPE G1 DEFORMED) is not expected value, will investigate.

Verifying (SHAPE BASE SHEET) in situation 13
(SHAPE BASE SHEET) in situation 13 Verified in real world
Verifying (THROUGH R1 BASE HOLE788) in situation 13
(THROUGH R1 BASE HOLE788) in situation 13 Verified in real world
Verifying (DIAMETER R1 15.0CM) in situation 13
(DIAMETER R1 15.0CM) in situation 13 Verified in real world
Verifying (HOLE HOLE788 BASE 15.1CM) in situation 13
(HOLE HOLE788 BASE 15.1CM) in situation 13 Verified in real world
Verifying (THROUGH R1 G1 HOLE787) in situation 13
(THROUGH R1 G1 HOLE787) in situation 13 Verified in real world
Verifying (DIAMETER R1 15.0CM) in situation 13
(DIAMETER R1 15.0CM) in situation 13 Verified in real world
Verifying (HOLE HOLE787 G1 15.0CM) in situation 13
(HOLE HOLE787 G1 15.0CM) in situation 13 Verified in real world
Attempting to explain (SHAPE G1 DEFORMED) in situation 13
Added censor SHAPE31232.
NIL

Now the system does not have any plans for constructing widgets with plastic gears. When confronted with a problem–solving situation of this type, it cannot achieve the goal. A trace of this scenario follows.

Running: (EXECUTE–EXAMPLE NO–SOLVE)
Start state is state 0
Initial State is:
(AT ROD1 BENCH2)
(AT GEAR1 BENCH2)
(AT BASE BENCH4)
COMPOSITION ROD1 METAL)
(STATE ROD1 SOLID)
(SHAPE GEAR1 GEAR)
(STATE GEAR1 SOLID)
(SHAPE BASE SHEET)
(COMPOSITION GEAR1 PLASTIC)
(STATE BASE SOLID)
Could not find a plan to achieve (WIDGET GEAR1 BASE ROD1 HOLE3
BENCH3 ?GOAL–TIME1106).
NIL

Next, the system is shown the original learning example with a plastic gear. Because the plan includes a cooling step, it succeeds. In this case, the system understands that the actions observed are those in its

representation of the original plan, with the addition of a cooling step.
The system also understands that the plan succeeded, in a case where the
melted–gear failure applied. The system then attempts to explain why
the melted–gear failure did not occur. It explains that the failure was
blocked by the cooling step, and hence understands the purpose of the
cooling step. A new plan is now learned with an appropriately constrained cooling step. The trace for this example follows.

Running: (RUN–EXAMPLE *W3*)
Initial State Consists of:
(AT R21 BENCH2)
(AT R2 BENCH1)
(AT G312 BENCH3)
(AT G2 BENCH1)
(AT P1 BENCH1)
(COMPOSITION R21 METAL)
(STATE R21 SOLID)
(STATE BASE16 SOLID)
(COMPOSITION G312 PLASTIC)
(SHAPE G312 GEAR)
(AT BASE16 BENCH1)
(SHAPE BASE16 SHEET)
Start state is state 0
Operator 1 is (MOVE R21 OVEN)
Operator 2 is (HEAT R21)
Operator 3 is (MOVE R21 ROLLING–STATION)
Operator 4 is (ROLL R21 10.0CM)
Operator 5 is (COOL R21)
Operator 6 is (MOVE R21 BENCH1)
Operator 7 is (MOVE G312 DRILLING–STATION)
Operator 8 is (DRILL G312 HOLE1 10.0CM)
Operator 9 is (MOVE G312 BENCH1)
Operator 10 is (MOVE BASE16 DRILLING–STATION)
Operator 11 is (DRILL BASE16 HOLE2 10.1CM)
Operator 12 is (MOVE BASE16 BENCH1)
Operator 13 is (INSERT R21 G312 HOLE1)
Operator 14 is (INSERT R21 BASE16 HOLE2)
Learning plan to achieve (WIDGET ?GEAR401320 ?PLANE371317
?ROD411321 ?HOLE421322 ?LOC381318 ?S1391319).
Generalizing...
Packaging and Indexing...

Ordering Actions...
Comparing to previously learned plans.
Checking previously learned censors.
Investigating fix to failure...
Detected prevention...
Marking assumption intervals...
Learned new plan WIDGET1451
NIL

     With the system's current problem–solving knowledge, the system
will apply the original plan without the cooling step, in cases where the
gear is not plastic. This is because although both plans are applicable,
the plan without the cooling step is easier to execute, having one less step.
A trace of a widget with a metal gear being constructed follows.

Running: (EXECUTE–EXAMPLE EX–EASY)
Start state is state 0
Initial State is:
(AT ROD101 BENCH3)
(AT GEAR12 BENCH2)
(AT BASE BENCH4)
(COMPOSITION ROD101 METAL)
(STATE ROD101 SOLID)
(SHAPE GEAR12 GEAR)
(STATE GEAR12 SOLID)
(SHAPE BASE SHEET)
(COMPOSITION GEAR12 METAL)
(STATE BASE SOLID)
Using plan WIDGET776 to achieve goal (WIDGET GEAR12 BASE
ROD101 HOLE3 BENCH3 ?S124752)
Operator 1 is (MOVE ROD101 OVEN)
Operator 2 is (HEAT ROD101)
Operator 3 is (MOVE ROD101 ROLLING–STATION)
Operator 4 is (ROLL ROD101 12.0CM)
Operator 5 is (MOVE ROD101 BENCH3)
Operator 6 is (MOVE GEAR12 DRILLING–STATION)
Operator 7 is (DRILL GEAR12 HOLE1459 12.0CM)
Operator 8 is (MOVE GEAR12 BENCH3)
Operator 9 is (MOVE BASE DRILLING–STATION)
Operator 10 is (DRILL BASE HOLE1460 12.1CM)
Operator 11 is (MOVE BASE BENCH3)

Operator 12 is (INSERT ROD101 GEAR12 HOLE1459)
Operator 13 is (INSERT ROD101 BASE HOLE1460)
Plan WIDGET776 completed.
Verifying achievement of functionality.
Goal achievement successfully verified.
NIL

However, in cases where the gear is plastic, only the cooling plan will be applicable. Consequently, the system will use that plan, as shown in the following trace.

Running: (EXECUTE–EXAMPLE EX–HARD)
Start state is state 0
Initial State is:
(AT ROD10 BENCH2)
(AT GEAR1 BENCH2)
(AT BASE BENCH4)
(COMPOSITION ROD10 METAL)
(STATE ROD10 SOLID)
(SHAPE GEAR1 GEAR)
(SHAPE BASE SHEET)
(COMPOSITION GEAR1 PLASTIC)
(STATE GEAR1 SOLID)
(STATE BASE SOLID)
Using plan WIDGET1451 to achieve goal (WIDGET GEAR1 BASE ROD10 HOLE3 BENCH3 ?S1241427)
Operator 1 is (MOVE ROD10 OVEN)
Operator 2 is (HEAT ROD10)
Operator 3 is (MOVE ROD10 ROLLING–STATION)
Operator 4 is (ROLL ROD10 12.0CM)
Operator 5 is (COOL ROD10)
Operator 6 is (MOVE ROD10 BENCH3)
Operator 7 is (MOVE GEAR1 DRILLING–STATION)
Operator 8 is (DRILL GEAR1 HOLE1462 12.0CM)
Operator 9 is (MOVE GEAR1 BENCH3)
Operator 10 is (MOVE BASE DRILLING–STATION)
Operator 11 is (DRILL BASE HOLE1463 12.1CM)
Operator 12 is (MOVE BASE BENCH3)
Operator 13 is (INSERT ROD10 GEAR1 HOLE1462)
Operator 14 is (INSERT ROD10 BASE HOLE1463)
Plan WIDGET1451 completed.

Verifying achievement of functionality.
Goal achievement successfully verified.
NIL
T
>

4. Operator and Rule Definitions Used in Melted Gear Example Sequence

Following are the operator and rule definitions used by the system to process the melted gear sequence of examples.

4.1. Operator Definitions

operator:	(heat ?piece)
preconditions:	((at ?piece oven))
effects:	((temperature ?piece hot)
	(at ?piece oven))

operator:	(roll ?piece ?size)
preconditions:	((consistency ?piece malleable)
	(at ?piece rolling–station))
effects:	((shape ?piece cylinder)
	(at ?piece rolling–station)
	(diameter ?piece ?size))

operator:	(drill ?obj ?hole ?size)
preconditions:	((at ?obj drilling–station))
effects:	((hole ?hole ?obj ?size))
create list:	((?hole "HOLE"))

operator:	(insert ?obj ?base ?hole)
preconditions:	((shape ?obj cylinder)
	(diameter ?obj ?size1)
	(hole ?hole ?base ?size2)
	(at ?obj ?loc)
	(at ?base ?loc))
effects:	((through ?obj ?base ?hole))

operator:	(cool ?obj)
preconditions:	((at ?obj ?loc))

effects: ((temperature ?obj cool))

operator: (move ?x ?loc)
preconditions: ((state ?x solid)
                      (at ?x ?old–loc))
effects: ((at ?x ?loc))

4.2. Rule Definitions

rule
antecedent: (and (through ?obj ?base ?hole ?sit–one)
                    (diameter ?obj ?size–one ?sit–one)
                    (hole ?hole ?base ?size–two ?sit–one)
                    (slightly> ?size–two ?size–one))
consequent: (revolve ?obj ?base ?hole ?sit–one)

rule
antecedent: (and (through ?obj ?base ?hole ?s1)
                    (diameter ?obj ?size1 ?s1)
                    (hole ?hole ?base ?size1 ?s1))
consequent: (attached ?obj ?base ?s1)

rule
antecedent: (and (revolve ?obj ?base ?hole ?s1)
                    (attached ?obj ?other ?s1))
consequent: (spins ?other ?base ?obj ?hole ?s1)

rule
antecedent: (and
                    (at ?plane ?loc ?s1)
                    (shape ?gear gear ?s1)
                    (shape ?plane sheet ?s1)
                    (spins ?gear ?plane ?rod ?hole ?s1))
consequent: (widget ?gear ?plane ?rod ?hole ?loc ?s1)

rule
antecedent: (and (temperature ?x hot ?s1)
                    (composition ?x metal ?s1))
consequent: (consistency ?x malleable ?s1)

backrule
antecedent: (and (temperature ?x hot ?s1)
       (heat–path ?x ?y ?s1))
consequent: (temperature ?y hot ?s1)

backrule
antecedent: (and (temperature ?x hot ?s)
       (composition ?x plastic ?s))
consequent: (shape ?x deformed ?s)

backrule
antecedent: (at ?x ?y ?s)
consequent: (touching ?x ?y ?s)

backrule
antecedent: (touching ?x ?y ?s)
consequent: (heat–path ?x ?y ?s)

backrule
antecedent: (and (heat–path ?x ?y ?s1)
       (heat–path ?z ?y ?s1))
consequent: (heat–path ?x ?z ?s1)

5. Conclusions and Future Work

This chapter has described an implementation of *recoverable simplifications*. There are several serious limitations in the current implementation:

(1) The implementation is tied to a situation–calculus representation. For example, the backtracing portion of the failure explanation process is dependent on the situation calculus representation.

(2) Inference by simplification is handled by specialized LISP code; a general inference engine for defeasible inferences would be preferable.

(3) The current implementation is not integrated with a planning component. Ideally, the system should also have the ability to plan to prevent at least some observed failures (presently the system must wait until observing a plan repair).

This chapter has described the implementation of *recoverable simplifications* in greater detail. This implementation has allowed the investigation of this approach to dealing with intractability in explanation-based learning. Based on the lessons learned in constructing this system, a new and improved implementation of recoverable simplifications is currently being constructed.

Chapter 14

Case Study 6 — GRASPER:
Learning to Manipulate an Uncertain World

Scott Bennett

1. Introduction

The GRASPER system described in this chapter is intended as a first–generation EBL system with explicit approximation capability. First, the general architecture for the system will be described. Next, an example involving planning uncertainty tolerant grasping operations in robotics will be described to illustrate how the approach works.

2. System Architecture

Figure 14–1 illustrates how the GRASPER system is organized. The understander portion of the system observes operations being planned and carried out by an external agent. In the case of a robotics system, the understander is monitoring the command the operator gives to the robot through the teach pendant. This is similar to the idea of a "learning apprentice," but emphasis is placed on having the system

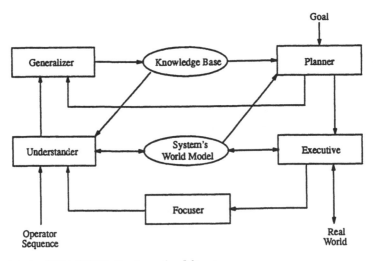

Figure 14–1: GRASPER System Architecture

function in a nonobtrusive way. The system could become a hindrance to the operator if it posed questions about the operator's intent in performing some action. Furthermore, it may be difficult for the operator to explain the intent behind every action. This problem is evident in the design of expert systems where experts can't always explain how they made a decision. The understander continually makes inferences using its knowledge base and world model as to what goals the operator is achieving and how they are being achieved. It is important to point out that where many previous systems assumed rules in the knowledge base to be guaranteed and their model to be correct, this is not necessarily the case with those of GRASPER, which has been designed for handling explicit approximations.

The generalizer receives explanations as to how goals have been achieved from the understander. The explanations are then generalized into efficient rules for accomplishing tasks of that class. These efficient rules are added to the system's knowledge base.

GRASPER can be asked by the operator to achieve goals. The planner will attempt to construct a plan using knowledge the system has. Due to the extreme complexity of real–world domains, the planner, working with finite resources, may not be able to construct plans without the help of the understander and generalizer, which comprise the *learning element* of the system. With them, efficient rules can be used which were already constructed through observation of external problem–solving behavior.

The executive is responsible for carrying out the plans produced by the planner in order to accomplish the desired goal. It uses the system's world model to maintain an expectation of the way the world should behave as execution progresses. Feedback is obtained from the world. For instance, when GRASPER is used in the robotics domain, various sensors are used to give position and force feedback. If the executive senses a conflict between its expectations of the world's behavior and the actual world's behavior as determined through the feedback, it recognizes a failure to have occurred. The system uses the failure to focus on finding possible fixes for it in observed behavior.

In some cases the system has already observed actions which can deal with the failure. The problem is that the system may have used approximations during understanding which obscured uncertainty-tolerant aspects of the external agent's plan. The following are the duties of the focuser:

(1)   Determine plausible candidates from among the approximations.

(2)   Select one or more candidates for tuning.

(3)   Decide how each candidate should be tuned.

(4)   Update the world model in accordance with the tuned approximations.

The focuser is responsible for using information about expectation violations to focus the understander on aspects of the observed sequence that might explain how to avoid the failure. This task is accomplished through the selection and tuning of approximations that led to the failed system behavior.

Figure 14–2 gives a flow diagram for the focuser. First, the failure explainer produces a set of possible approximation failures which explain the expectation violation. This set is filtered based on a domain–specific plausibility heuristic to eliminate possible but extremely unlikely failures. The tuning selector analyzes elements of the remaining set and decides which will be tuned. The important goals in deciding what to tune are really a function of the plan which would result from the tuning. The preferred resulting plan should be judged on its operationality according to the definition proposed in Chapter 2.

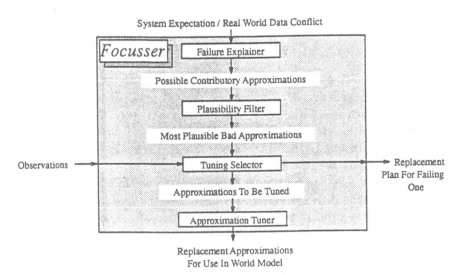

Figure 14–2: The Focuser

The focuser needs a set of observations which are ideally those associated with original construction of the rule which failed. Each candidate plan is constructed by tuning its candidate approximation and using the understander and generalizer on the observations. Once the selector completes its plan analysis, the plan can be entered in the knowledge base while the tuned approximation is included in the world model.

3. Use of GRASPER for Learning in Robotics

To illustrate how this architecture is employed, we introduce an example concerning learning uncertainty tolerant grasping strategies in the robotics domain. The example takes place in a two–dimensional world with a disembodied gripper and a set of polygonal objects. Real-world complexity is introduced through uncertainty in the known positions, orientations, and shapes of the objects. It is assumed that the position, orientation, and shape of the robot are known.

3.1. The Gripper

The two–dimensional gripper is shown in Figure 14–3. The two fingers slide open and closed along the beam, each finger having a motion equal and opposite to the other. The *gripper reference point* is the point at which the gripper's position and orientation are measured.

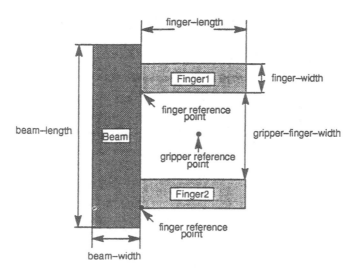

Figure 14–3: The Gripper

3.2. Gripper Primitives

Gripper motion is directed via a set of four primitive actions: *apply–force*, *apply–torque*, *close–fingers*, and *open–fingers*. The format of these actions is illustrated in Figure 14–4. All motion is compliant; the primitives specify forces to be applied. Each operator invocation also specifies expected sensor readings and a termination condition. An operation terminates if any of the sensor expectations is violated, in which case a failure occurs, or if the termination condition is met without a violation of sensor expectations.

3.3. Gripper Sensors

The gripper is equipped with force sensors on its periphery and with position sensors. The sensor expectations consist of a set of position and force specifications with respect to the gripper which must be satisfied at completion of the operation. The termination condition is a partial world state specification which marks completion of the operation. The termination sensor values are a dump of all the sensor values returned at the termination of the operation. Force sensors return information as illustrated in Figure 14–5.

3.4. Object Representation

Objects in the two–dimensional world have their shapes represented by simple polygons. The polygon has a reference point about which the object's orientation and at which its position are measured. Shape, position, and orientation information about each object in the world is contained in the system's world model. This information is treated as precise.

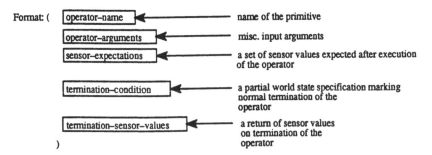

Figure 14–4: Robot Primitive Format

Force representation:

(force ?finger ?contact–x ?contact–y ?magnitude ?x–component ?y–component)

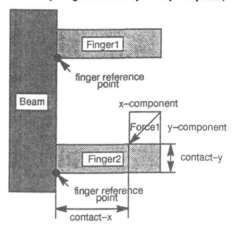

Figure 14–5: Gripper Contact Sensing

3.5. Object Approximations

At plan construction time and in explaining failures, it is necessary to reason about object shape, position, and orientation as approximations

```
(approximation
  :values
      target–type position
      object      square53
      position    (3.5 1.0)
      position–uncertainty   0.5  ←──── explicit uncertainty representation
  :update–function #'position–approx–update
  :deviation–function #'position–deviation)
```

Figure 14–6: A Position Approximation

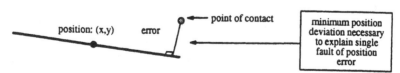

Figure 14–7: Attributing Position Error

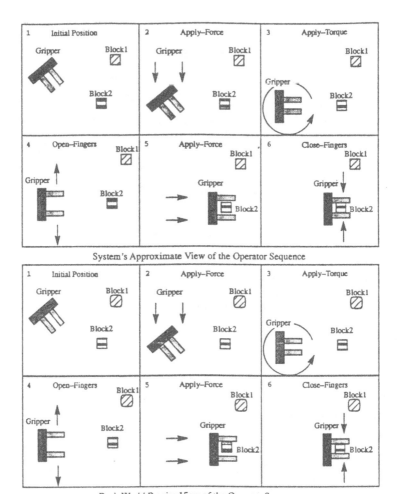

Figure 14–8: System's Initial Observations of a Grasp Being Performed

to their exact values in the real world. These approximations take a form
as shown for the position approximation of Figure 14–6. The approximation has two domain–specific functions associated with it. The first, called
the *deviation function,* in this case measures distance between a specified
position and the position in the approximation. This is used for rating
which of several approximations can be most easily extended to account
for errant positions. The *update function* is used for extending the
approximation to account for such a position. Figure 14–7 demonstrates

the procedure for tuning the approximation to account for an errant position. In this case, one face of a polygon has been assigned an approximate position, but a known contact point has forced modification of the approximation to account for it. The update function extends the value of the position uncertainty to account for it.

4. An Example

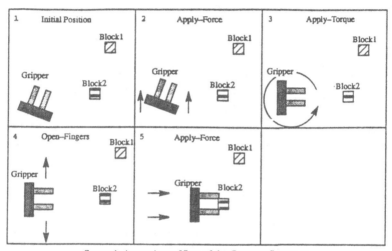

System's Approximate View of the Operator Sequence

Real–World Precise View of the Operator Sequence

Figure 14–9: System's First Attempt at Achieving a Grasp

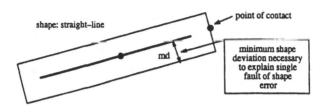

Figure 14–10: Attributing Shape Error

The GRASPER system starts out by observing a *grasp* operation being carried out on *block2* as shown in Figure 14–8. The figure shows the six states involved in the operation both from the approximate view of the system and from an ideal precise view. The system is incapable of getting or processing information in real time as precise as that seen in the latter view. From the initial position (frame 1), an *apply–force* operator leads to a successful translation of the gripper to an approach position (frame 2). An *apply–torque* operator aligns the gripper's fingers toward the object through a successful rotation (frame 3). The *open–fingers* operation is performed to allow the gripper to be opened wide enough to surround the object (frame 4). Another *apply–force* is used to move the gripper to a position around the block (frame 5). Last, a *close–fingers* is used to bring the fingers together enough to achieve a specified gripping force on the object (frame6).

From the initial view of the understander and the approximate view of the world, the extra–wide opening of the fingers for the approach is both inefficient and unnecessary. This view of the observed sequence finds its way into the general rule produced to achieve a grasping goal. Figure 14–9 shows how the system performs with the new rule when asked to apply it to a similar grasping situation. The plan proceeds much as the initially observed plan did up until the *open–fingers* operation. Here, because the system uses only an approximate view of the data, it cannot show the necessity for opening the gripper fingers wider than the block. However, the approximation lends itself to efficient reasoning about and execution of the plan. Unfortunately, in this case, these actions lead to a failure as shown in the precise view of Figure 14–9. Since the block was actually positioned slightly differently, the upper–left edge protruded, making contact with the gripper finger in an unexpected place. The system, only expecting a small contact force on the insides of the fingers, has a violation of expectations.

GRASPER now attempts to explain the failure by explaining the discrepancy between the real sensor readings and the expected ones. The system arrives at four primary single–fault failure explanations in this specific example which are rooted in possible errors in approximations for:

(1)   block1's shape

(2)   block1's position

(3)   block2's shape

(4)   block2's position

In this case, the only approximations not identified as possible causes of the failure are the orientation approximations. This is because no orientation error of either block could explain the encountered contact.

In general, failed approximations receive a likelihood rating in accordance with the degree to which the approximation needs to be changed to account for the failure. In this case, failures receive likelihood ratings inversely proportional to the distance the contact was from their expected positions. This is due to the method for position and shape approximations used for objects, which is illustrated in Figures 14–7 and 14–10, respectively. A threshold is used to avoid consideration of more unlikely causes for the failure. Here, block1's expected position is substantially farther from the point of contact than block2's position. Explanations corresponding to 1 and 2 in the list above are below threshold and are not considered.

GRASPER's focuser suggests methods which the understander can use to focus on possible shape and position discrepancies with block2. Specifically, this is to increase the uncertainty margin considered in the approximate attributes of block2 to allow the understander to recognize fixes for the failures. The amount which the uncertainty margin is increased is a function of the attribution procedure illustrated in Figures 14–7 and 14–10 for position and shape. The approximation for an object is revised as little as necessary through consideration of each individual line segment that makes up its polygonal approximation. Having encountered a failure, the system now has a good reason to invest more resources in trying to understand possible discrepancies in this area.

The understander constructs explanations for a new observed grasp operation from each of the failure perspectives. The generalizer generalizes each of these explanations and analyzes the resulting rules. In attempting to understand a successful grasp operation from each of the failure perspectives, each of the failures actually was determined to be a motive in opening the gripper wider. That is, opening wider and closing actually can take care of small variations in shape and positional uncertainty of the object being grasped. In the postgeneralization analysis, after the system has performed some rule simplification, it is found that one of the rules actually deals with both of the potential failures and is thus more general. Although this may not always be the case, the system is capable of recognizing such occurrences and profiting from them. Naturally, that rule is used in the knowledge base and the system now has a good method for dealing with two types of uncertainty in this type of grasp operation.

INDEX